BIODIVERSITY AND SUSTAINABLE CONSERVATION

BIODIVERSITY AND SUSTAINABLE CONSERVATION

Har Darshan Kumar

Science Publishers, Inc.

Enfield (NH), USA   Plymouth, UK

SCIENCE PUBLISHERS, INC.
Post Office Box 699
Enfield, New Hampshire 03748
United States of America

Internet site: *http://www.scipub.net*

sales@scipub.net (marketing department)
editor@scipub.net (editorial department)
info@scipub.net (for all other inquiries)

© 1999, Copyright reserved

ISBN 1-57808-076-2

Library of Congress Cataloging-in-Publication Data

Kumar, H.D., 1934-
    Biodiversity and sustainable conservation / Har Darshan
    Kumar.
        p. cm.
    Includes bibliographical references (p.).
    ISBN 1-57808-076-2
    1. Biological diversity. 2. Biological diversity
conservation. I. Title.

QH541.15.B56 K86 1999
333.95'16-dc21

                                                        99-049854
                                                            CIP

Published by Science Publishers, Inc., USA
Printed in India

Preface

The Earth's most valuable resource today is the diversity of its biological capital. In a sense, biodiversity is everything because it includes all hereditary variation at all levels of organization from the genes within a species to the diverse species that make up a community, and to the different communities that make up the various ecosystems of the world.

Without doubt, the three most serious and strongly interlinked global problems today are overpopulation, the continuing human-induced destruction of the environment and the projected rapid loss of biological diversity. The rising world population is expected to peak sometime around 2050. Although humanity has improved per capita production, health and longevity, this has been done at the cost of using up the planet's non-renewable natural resources. The world is fast approaching the limit of its food and water supply. A billion people remain in absolute poverty, unable to obtain two square meals a day, and no medical care. Unlike any other species, *Homo sapiens* is also changing the Earth's atmosphere and climate, lowering and polluting water tables, shrinking forests and spreading deserts. It is causing the extinction of many microbial, plant and animal species. Species losses are irreplaceable. Future generations are sure to view these losses as catastrophic.

Since the Earth summit meeting held in Rio de Janeiro in 1992, loss of the world's biodiversity has been considered to be the single most important human problem and has moved to centre stage as a serious issue of scientific and political concern worldwide. However, despite serious concerns about the reckless modification and destruction of the environments resulting from human activities, species of plants, animals and microbes continue to vanish rapidly, taking with them their genetic capital and potential benefits. Indeed, many species disappear before they can even be collected, identified or described. This has highlighted the urgency to conserve rare and threatened species and their natural habitats, and has created strong interest in the dynamic and rapidly developing discipline of conservation biology, with sustainable and adaptive ecosystem management as its central focus. Effective conservation of the germplasm of various species both in their natural habitats and in gardens, parks, zoos, museums and culture collections, all involving a broad-scale, holistic approach towards a healthy human-land relationship, may well be our best hope for a planet in which we and our children can live in harmony with nature.

We must look at ourselves closely as a biological as well as cultural species, whose success is eroding the environment to which the long evolutionary history elegantly adapted us. We must aim for an effective integration not just of the natural sciences, but also of the social sciences and humanities, in order to cope with issues of urgency and complexity that may otherwise be too complex or difficult to tackle.

Indeed, biocomplexity, defined as the interaction of biological, chemical, social, and economic systems is intimately related to, and unifies, biodiversity and sustainability. Biocomplexity builds on the concept of LEE (Life and Earth Environments) to give us a better understanding of the interrelationships between cells and organisms, and between an organism and its environment. Biodiversity is an integral part of biocomplexity, especially with the genomic sequencing, which enables us to learn much more about diversity without the need to culture cells. Biocomplexity also overarches the important themes of conservation and sustainability.

I have attempted to cover the above aspects concisely in the light of our current scientific and sociobiological understanding of the biodiversity of plants, animals, microbes, aquatic and terrestrial ecosystems, giving appropriate examples and illustrations. While the monograph covers global biodiversity, one chapter briefly introduces the rich biodiversity wealth in selected Indian ecosystems. Sustainable conservation of species, habitats and germplasm is discussed with special reference to crop plants, forests and marine resources. The value of *in-situ* and *ex-situ* conservation as complementary strategies is highlighted in this context.

The writing of this book was greatly facilitated by the timely provision of recent literature on ecology, environment, general biology, sociology, geography, agriculture, forestry and marine biology, for which I am greatly obliged to Prof. Dorothy L. Parker (Oshkosh, USA, now at LaJolla, California), Prof. Masayuki Ohmori (Tokyo) and the Indian National Science Academy, New Delhi. I am particularly indebted to the Council of Scientific and Industrial Research (New Delhi) and the Department of Science and Technology (New Delhi) for financial support from 1994 to 1999.

I also thank my coworkers and associates Ashok Kumar, J.B. Singh and L.C. Rai for their help from time to time. Several drafts of the manuscript were ably and patiently composed by Mangala Prasad Dubey and a few of the line drawings were drawn by Subhajeet Saha.

June, 1999 **HDK**

Contents

Chapter 1
GENERAL INTRODUCTION
Definition, Perspective and Overview

Biodiversity is a popular way of describing the diversity of life on earth: it includes all life–forms and the ecosystems of which they are a part. It forms the foundation for sustainable development, constitutes the basis for the environmental health of our planet, and is the source of economic and ecological security for future generations. In the developing world, biodiversity provides the assurance of food, many raw materials such as fibre for clothing, materials for shelter, fertilizer, fuel and medicines, as well as a source of work energy in the form of animal traction. The rural poor depend upon biological resources for an estimated 90% of their needs. In the industrialized world, access to diverse biological resources is necessary to support a vast variety of industrial products. In the continuing drive to develop efficient and sustainable agriculture for many different conditions, these resources provide raw material for plant and animal breeding as well as the new biotechnologies. In addition, biodiversity maintains the ecological balance necessary for planetary and human survival.

At the United Nations Conference on Environment and Development held in Rio de Janeiro in 1992, biological diversity was defined as: The variability among living organisms from all sources including, *inter alia*, terrestrial, marine and other aquatic ecosystems and the ecological complexes of which they are a part; this includes diversity within species and of ecosystems.

Estimates of the total number of plant, animal and other species found on the planet Earth vary widely, from 3 million to 30 million or more. But in the absence of any central archives, no one even knows how many species have already been named and recorded. Whereas birds and mammals have been well recorded, the total diversity of organisms such as insects, spiders, fungi, nematodes and bacteria is poorly known.

This is particularly unfortunate in view of the alarming rate at which wild habitats are being destroyed. A knowledge of the total number and distribution of species is essential for developing a sound strategy to conserve as much as possible of the remaining biological diversity.

1

Biodiversity is a function of both time and space. Genetic diversity can refer to the degree of heterozygosity of a single individual over its lifetime, or it may be applied to the number of alleles of a population over its geographical range at a particular time, or it may be used for the number of alleles of a species over its range and lifespan.

In many temperate and alpine areas where richness of terrestrial species is comparatively low, there are acceptable floristic and faunistic lists of the vascular plants and vertebrate animals. There are also reasonable estimates of invertebrate animals and non–vascular plants, including fungi. Less well known are soil organisms, bacteria and viruses. In many tropical regions having much higher species diversity, there are no reliable lists of vascular plants and vertebrate animals, and there are only very rough estimates of the kinds of invertebrate animals, cryptogams and fungi. Most insects, soil organisms, bacteria and fungi in these regions have yet to be collected and described (Table 1–1).

All cells, organisms, populations, species and possibly even communities originate, grow, reproduce and die. Consequently, the number and abundance of entities is in constant flux. A distinction is usually made between processes that generate diversity, those that maintain diversity and those that reduce diversity. All heritable diversity originates ultimately at the molecular level in the phenomenon of mutation. Genetic recombination also affects individual and population diversity. Diversity is reduced by certain processes (called selection) that eliminate variation (however, balanced polymorphisms and disruptive selection can increase genetic diversity). Though the existence of diversity does not necessarily imply a process of selection, most theories regarding the existence of biological diversity relate it to some process of selection or optimization. Darwinian selection at the organismic level is the oldest and best known of these theories. Less well understood is what maintains diversity in a system (Solbrig, 1991).

New diversity is constantly injected into biological systems through mutation and recombination (Fig. 1–1). On the other hand, it is being eliminated by selection. The fate of every variation, from gene mutations to communities, is to disappear eventually. This can be a very fast process or the variant may survive for a very long time. The rapidity with which new mutations arise in relation to the speed with which they are eliminated determines the actual diversity of a system.

It seems that a certain degree of diversity is needed for biological systems to function properly. There may be system feedbacks that affect the rates of mutation and selection.

2

Table 1–1. Approximate numbers of known species of micro–organisms and probable world species totals (after Solbrig, 1991)

Group	Known species	World species
Algae	40,000	60,000
Bacteria (incl. Cyanobacteria)	3,000	30,000
Fungi (incl. lichen–forming and yeasts)	64,200	800,000
Viruses (incl. plasmids and phages)	5,000	130,000
Protoctists (incl. protozoa, excl. algae and fungal protoctists)	30,000	100,000
Totals	**142,000**	**1,120,000**

Also there may exist diversity thresholds below which the system collapses. Diversity appears to be actively maintained in a system (May, 1984). The nature of the actual processes that actively maintain diversity (Hoffman, 1989; Signor, 1990) is not known.

Reid and Miller (1989) defined biodiversity as follows: the variety of the world's organisms, including their genetic diversity and the assemblages they form. It is the blanket term for natural biological wealth that undergirds human life and well–being. The breadth of the concept reflects the interrelatedness of genes, species and ecosystems. Because genes are the components of species, and species are the components of ecosystems, altering the make–up of any level of this hierarchy can change the others... species are central to the concept of biodiversity.

In recent years it has been increasingly felt that a serious loss of species and a reduction in the genetic diversity of crops and wild species is taking place (Ehrlich and Ehrlich, 1981; Wilson and Peter, 1988). This feeling has arisen because of the greatly accelerated transformation of natural landscapes occurring around the world and particularly in the tropics (Wilcox and Murphy, 1985). An extensive reduction in species diversity may lead to loss of ecosystem stability and function. The danger to crop productivity from a reduction in the genetic variation needed to breed new varieties is also recognized.

Diversity occurs at all levels of biological organization, from molecules to entire biotas. Greater attention is usually given to the biological and ecological significance of biodiversity and its biogeorgaphical implications (Solbrig, 1991). According to Diamond (1988), the great diversity in biological systems is a prerequisite for the proper functioning of the biosphere. Diversity seems to permit biological systems to cope with environmental stress and to recover from disturbance events.

Yet, it is not sufficiently clear what the exact role of biodiversity is. All living systems are variable. Diversity is a universal characteristic of living systems. How may the working of living systems be influenced by being diverse?

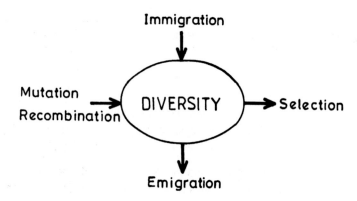

Fig. 1–1. A generalized diversity model.

Human-induced change reduces biodiversity but increases the complexity of human societies. People affect biodiversity both directly and indirectly. Use of renewable natural resources, especially in extractive industries such as forestry or fisheries, usually involves decreases in species diversity as stocks are depleted and unwanted species are destroyed. Agriculture and animal husbandry damage biological diversity by destroying or modifying the native biota. Since pre-agricultural times, the world's forests have declined from 5 to 4 billion hectares. Temperate forests have lost

4

the highest percentage of their area (32–35%), followed by subtropical woody savannas and deciduous forests (24–25%), and old–growth tropical forests (15–20%). Indirect changes come from land–use, use of fossil and biomass energy, and from altering hydrological patterns. Introduction of exotic organisms, both intentional and accidental, has tended to reduce between-region biodiversity. The simplification of landscapes by the removal of hedges and forest fringes has reduced habitat diversity and has resulted in lowered biodiversity. A potent threat to biodiversity is the production and release of novel toxic chemical compounds into the environment.

Although diversity occurs at all levels of the biological hierarchy, it is the issue of species loss that has generated the greatest apprehension (Ehrlich and Ehrlich, 1981; Wilson, 1988). Crop scientists have been more apprehensive about reduction in the number of genes and genotypes (Plucknett, 1987). Conservation biologists concerned with endangered species are also concerned about diminished genetic diversity, with concomitant loss of adaptive potentials and increased breeding defects (Solbrig, 1991). Much less attention has been paid to diversity at the molecular level, even though it is here that biological diversity originates.

Biological diversity varies greatly according to the available habitat or living space. Over a wider range, diversity patterns can be established fairly easily, but this is not possible for a smaller range. There is no single process or theory that can help explain the complexity of the diversity phenomenon. With a view to understanding its occurrence, a knowledge of the ecological, evolutionary, and geological processes and also their interactions, is essential. Only by considering the various aspects of this highly delicate ecosystem can it be possible to preserve the genetic storehouse for future generations. In order to ensure effective protection, one must recognize the global value of our ecosystems ranging from natural reserves (where the legitimate interests of the indigenous population have to be preserved) to the planning of specific reafforestation efforts and appropriate systems of utilization.

Considering that most people had not heard of the term biodiversity even a decade ago, the current common usage of the term is phenomenal. This may be because the word connotes something very good. Genetic variation, individuals, species, ecosystems and landscapes are all good things, with obvious human and non–human benefits (Grizzle, 1994; Callicott, 1995). When it comes to actual management, however, conservation principles are usually ignored because they lack economic value (Wagner, 1996).

Biological diversity is one of the most fascinating aspects of biology. Evolution by natural selection has produced, and is still producing, different species. Organisms generally have a tendency to multiply exponentially *ad infinitum* without intrinsic constraints. What does biological diversity mean for the evolutionary development of life? As genetic variation is pervasive and individual variation is the source of evolution by natural selection, the diversity at the species level has created a vast evolutionary potential (Wuketits, 1997). At least half a billion species have existed on our planet, probably many more. While the number of known extant species is approximately 1.5 million, and earlier estimations of the total number ranged between 5 and 10 million, the results of modern studies concerning biodiversity go far beyond these figures. Some estimates point to 20–80 million species now living on earth, many of them, however, already threatened by extinction (Price, 1996; Wilson, 1992). Wilson estimated an extinction rate of three species per hour. This evolutionary drama is being enacted particularly in the tropical forests which probably have the highest species density.

Each single species has a value in itself, and therefore we humans have no right to destroy the natural order; on the contrary, we must take care to save the other species. Indeed, humans are emotionally attracted by many species and find peace and satisfaction in observing them. According to Wilson (1984), 'to explore and affiliate with life is a deep and complicated process in mental development'. However, one trouble with this argument is that it can hardly be extended to all kinds of organisms. For instance, we do have positive feelings towards flowering plants, songbirds, dogs, elephants, the giant panda, and many other organisms but what are our emotions towards tapeworms, mosquitoes, rats and snakes?

Without doubt, the diversity of species is one of our most precious resources. Yet, we are far from knowing — or guessing — the economic value of many species since our agricultural policies are such that we depend on only a small number of species. A considerable number of now extinct plant and animal species could certainly have been utilized by humans for food.

We are losing biological diversity at an unprecedented rate. The disappearance of species in past eras has occurred through natural processes within the context of evolutionary timescales. But today, human activities are contributing more to the loss of biodiversity than any other factor. Biological resources are renewable resources, but they are being exploited at rates that exceed their sustainable yield. Human destruction of habitats, whether exploited for commercial or subsistence reasons, poses the greatest threat. The clearing of land for agriculture, overgrazing of grasslands, cutting and

6

burning of forests, unsustainable logging and fuelwood collection, indiscriminate use of fertilizers and pesticides, overexploitation of fisheries, draining and filling of wetlands, poor water management, and urbanization and pollution of air and water are prominent factors in the degradation of our biological resources. About seven million hectares of cultivated land are destroyed every year.

Genetic erosion—the reduction of diversity within and the main cause of extinction of a species—is a global threat to agriculture. The greatest loss of crop genetic resources results from the introduction of modern, uniform plant varieties in place of a mix of traditional ones. The Green Revolution introduced high-yielding varieties of wheat and rice in the developing world, but displaced traditional varieties and their wild relatives on a massive scale. In India, agronomists predict that just ten rice varieties will soon cover three–quarters of the total rice area where once over 30,000 different varieties were grown.

According to Wilson (1984), one in about ten plant species contains compounds with an anticancer effect. This underscores the tremendous relevance of biodiversity preservation. But this does not mean that a species should be evaluated only with regard to its utility. The ecological interdependence among all living beings, regardless of whether they may or may not be of some use in agriculture, pharmacy, or medicine, needs to be emphasized.

Each single species needs to be viewed as something unique that interacts with other species. Biodiversity research can go a long way in understanding what holds the biosphere together, and so demonstrates the social implications of biology.

The same is true of animal genetic resources. The introduction of a very few modern breeds that are better suited for the high input-output of industrial agriculture is displacing the diversity of indigenous livestock breeds. In Europe, half of all the breeds of domestic animals that existed at the beginning of the century have become extinct. A third of the remaining 770 breeds are in danger of disappearing within the coming two decades.

Loss of biodiversity is commonly regarded as an environmental problem, but the underlying causes are essentially social, economic and political. The excessive and unsustainable consumption of resources by a small but rich minority of the world's population, combined with the destructive impacts of the world's poor and hungry in a desperate bid for survival, have destroyed or overexploited habitats worldwide (FAO, 1993).

7

Fair and equitable sharing of the benefits accruing from the use of genetic resources is a principal objective of the *Convention on Biological Diversity* (CBD). Use of biodiversity has to be sustainable in order to meet the letter and spirit of the Convention. Lesser (1998) focused on economic incentives for sustainable use of genetic resources. According to him the sharing of benefits might be best ensured by contractual arrangements.

A good knowledge of the fluctuations in numbers of natural populations and the application of this understanding to the conservation of species must be based firmly on an understanding of the factors influencing spatial and temporal variability in population demography. All populations occur in heterogeneous landscapes, with different individuals experiencing different conditions depending on their location.

Population viability depends on the quality of local habitat patches (Fig. 1–2) and on the number and location of patches and the extent of movement between them. The dispersal mode of a population is a crucial factor in determining its viability.

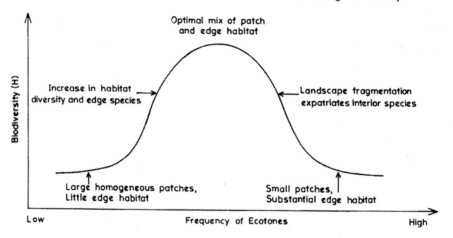

Fig. 1–2. Relationship between ecotones and biodiversity.

Environmental indicators reflect the condition of the environment at any given time. They reveal the pressures and stresses that humans place on the environment, and provide measures of the effectiveness of the responses to any problems. An indicator can be a microbe, plant or animal that is particularly sensitive to an environmental change; it can be a chemical or pollutant in water, soil or air; it can be a quantity measure of a natural resource; or it can even be a change in social or economic activities brought about by some environmental condition. Indicators can provide us with reliable, acceptable and understandable information about the health of the environment.

Without doubt, the best way to save biodiversity is to value it, whether as a resource for direct use on a sustainable basis, or for its indirect functions, such as maintaining freshwater supplies or providing a sink for greenhouse gases. Indeed, biodiversity is an index of how well we are doing in sustainable development. So long as we continue to lose it, our development will not be ecologically sustainable.

As in other Asian countries, in Indonesia also the Green Revolution led to the introduction of certain new high-yielding but genetically uniform varieties of rice that were highly vulnerable to attack by pathogens. Over two decades ago, a mysterious viral disease began to attack crops of the new rice varieties, and within a few years, over a million hectares of the crop were threatened, affecting millions of people throughout South East Asia. The International Rice Research Institute (IRRI), Manila, rapidly screened thousands of varieties in its collections for resistance to the virus and found that only one possessed it. This was a low–yielding, spindly species, collected from the wild in South India but believed to have no commercial value. The resultant new variety, IR36, has since been planted over millions of hectares in Asia.

Climate change is likely to radically alter the patterns of agriculture throughout the world. The question is : where will the genetic material come from to produce the new crop varieties? Gene banks may contain an odd variety that may sometimes turn out to be useful, but the greatest gene bank of all is nature — which is being destroyed at an alarming rate by humankind.

Today, the Earth's biological resources are under serious threat. Biodiversity is nothing but the myriad of genes, species and ecosystems that collectively make up Nature. Biodiversity may have taken a few billion years to evolve, but it may be largely destroyed in only a few human generations. Rates of species extinction are estimated to be 50 to 100 times the natural background rate: this could increase to 1000 to 10,000 times with the forest loss projected for the next 25 years. We must take direct action immediately to protect biodiversity, otherwise we will lose forever the opportunity of reaping its full potential benefit.

Tropical Biodiversity

Tropical forests have for long been regarded as the habitat of some of the richest variety of species on earth. This view has led to the idea that there is a virtually inexhaustible store of exploitable resources in these forests. This fallacy, coupled with man's unsatiable greed for profit, has been a chief reason for the widespread global destruction of these valuable ecosystems. Besides, the increasing overexploitation of resources by the ever–growing human population also contributes to this destruction.

The tropics appear to be at an ecological disadvantage because the tropical soils have only a limited yield capacity due to their low nutrient content. This nutrient paucity influences the process of natural selection and seems to have a significant role in ensuring a wide variety of species. Thus, the wide biodiversity of the Amazonian lowland forests is quite in keeping with the soils in these ecosystems being notoriously low in nutrients. The tropical African rainforests also harbour a wide variety of species but, compared with the Amazonian forests, their biodiversity is lower, possibly due to a greater availability of nutrients. Interestingly, the conditions in SE Asia are totally different: here, despite the high nutrient content of the volcanic ash soils and fertile alluvial lands, an extremely high species diversity occurs, accompanied by a remarkably high density of some.

The availability of nutrients is only one of the parameters affecting species; the other mechanisms and regulatory factors involved in generating biological diversity are poorly known, if at all.

Many tropical areas have for sometime been homogenized, and everyone, forever, is likely to be the poorer for it. This has happened because the tropics have been over–run by alien plants. We tend to think of the tropics in terms of high diversity and yet a striking fact that impresses many travellers in the tropics is that all tropical gardens look exactly the same: *Bougainvillea, Hibiscus, Pyrostegia, Hedychium, Strelitzia* and not much else. A similar situation prevails with many tropical seminatural habitats: they have been infested by a motley assortment of escaped garden plants such as *Lantana camara* and *Rubus alceifolius*, and pernicious vines such as *Cryptostegia grandiflora* and *Passiflora mollissima*. These plants, and others like them, pose an enormous threat to the conservation of biodiversity in natural tropical habitats. Their impact can be devastating: *Miconia calvescens* dominates whole hillsides in Tahiti, travellers palm (*Ravenala madagascarensis*) towers above what was once a species–rich moist forest

10

in Mauritius, or the vine *Hiptage benghalensis* literally buries vast areas of lowland dry forest in Reunion.

Whereas total eradication is seldom achieved, satisfactory management of alien species is achievable. Doubtless, it is far easier to nip problems of alien invasion in the bud, but it is also not wise to give up (as hopeless) cases involving fully naturalized aliens. Unfortunately, however, many of the tropical countries that suffer the greatest problems from alien invasions have neither the resources nor the management structures with which to solve them.

Biodiversity and Community Structure

Community structure includes the various ways in which organisms and populations relate to and interact with one another. An important question is whether communities have both structure and properties not possessed by their component populations, referred to as 'emergent properties'. Possible examples include trophic structure, stability, guild structure, and successional stages (Solbrig, 1991).

Species diversity may be essential for the proper functioning of communities and for the emergence of new properties at the community level. Though species diversity is undoubtedly necessary for community structure, is any amount of diversity sufficient, or are there specific mixes of species that are necessary for the proper functioning of communities and ecosystems? There are two views on this issue. One maintains that a community is formed by those species that happened to arrive there (Gleason, 1926). Under this view the community would not possess any emergent properties. The other view is that of Elton (1933): 'In any fairly limited area only a fraction of the forms that could theoretically do so actually form a community at any one time... the community really is an organized community in that it has "limited membership"'.

Every species in a community occupies a singular niche, defined as 'a region in a factor space whose axes represent the critical resources or environmental variables to which species in the community respond differentially' (Colwell, 1984). The axes of this hypervolume are the types and amounts of resources and the distribution of their use by species in space and time.

According to Diamond (1988), the following four sets of factors determine the diversity of niches in a community: (1) quantity of resources; (2) quality of resources; (3) species interactions; and (4) community dynamics. These factors interact intimately as shown in Fig. 1–3.

11

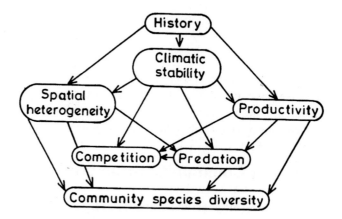

Fig. 1–3. Graphic representation of the interactions between various factors contributing to community diversity (after Pianka, 1970).

Fig. 1–4 shows the interactions of several factors involved in production of high biodiversity in a moist tropical forest.

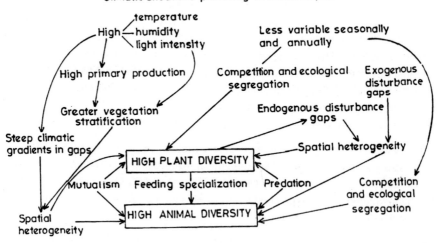

Fig. 1–4. Interaction of several factors in production of high biodiversity in a moist tropical forest. Arrows show 'opportunities' for increased diversity, not proven relationships.

12

The inverse relationship of species richness with latitude has long been well known. High community and regional diversity in the tropics has been linked to available energy, species-specific predation, and delayed competitive exclusion (see Holm-Nielsen *et al.*, 1989; Phillips *et al.*, 1994).

Tree diversity is usually related to disturbance at varying spatial and temporal scales. Frequency- or density-dependent mortality may enhance diversity and local disturbance can counteract the effects of pairwise competitive displacement. Phillips *et al.* made a worldwide analysis of humid tropical forest dynamics and tree species richness. They found that mean annual tree mortality and recruitment (turnover) is the most predictive factor of species richness, implying that small-scale disturbance regulates tropical forest diversity. Turnover rates are also closely related to the amount of basal area turnover in mature tropical forests. Therefore the contribution of small-scale disturbance to maintaining tropical forest diversity may ultimately be driven by ecosystem productivity (Phillips *et al.*, 1994).

In some cases, direct interaction between previously isolated ecological communities occurs when geographical barriers break down, either through natural geological events or through man-made modifications of the landscape. Following the disappearance of a barrier, one community may swamp a second community, causing most or all of its species to become extinct.

Occasionally, two previously isolated communities may merge, following the removal of a barrier. This process is quite rare. Gilpin (1994) showed that two 'naive' competition communities mix randomly following the removal of a barrier. However, if the two communities have been 'assembled', or self-organized, through a history of competitive exclusion, the communities are likely to battle as co-ordinated armies, with one or the other side ultimately claiming the entire landscape.

Genetic Resources and Biodiversity

In the 1970s and 80s, much public interest in the crucial importance of genetic resources for agricultural development and food security generated debates among social scientists and NGOs on control over genetic resources. These discussions had a strong North versus South dimension: plant genetic resources of agricultural interest are mostly concentrated in the tropical and subtropical developing countries (South), whereas the users and conserving institutions are mainly Northern.

13

The genetic resources issue dominated public discussion on genetic resources from the beginning of the 1980s. The conservationist/environmental context gradually became part of the public concern as well and focused principally on the value of genetic resources for preserving the earth's biological diversity. The biodiversity angle differed from the genetic resources issue in that (at least initially) biodiversity aspects did not focus on the agricultural–economic value and use of genetic resources. It was only in the 1990s with the rise of initiatives such as biodiversity prospecting, that biodiversity issues became part of the North–South dichotomy (Pistorius, 1997).

Mooney (1979) conceptualized the economic value of genetic resources for the Northern agroindustry by postulating that:

1. genetic resources are instrumental in capital accumulation;

2. corporate actors have an interest in protecting genetic resources through the industrial patent system; and

3. control over genetic resources both in the public and private sector, and in terms of conservation and use, is not transparent and hence is detrimental to developing countries (Mooney, 1979; Pistorius, 1997).

In 1983, Mooney further stressed the issue of the loss of and access to plant genetic resources—again with emphasis on the socioeconomic impact of breeding and new biotechnologies.

Genetic Resources Issue and Its Critique

During the past several years, many controversies and debates relating to defining and assessing the pros and cons of genetic resources have created some confusion. Pistorius (1997) has attempted to rectify this by listing the criticism/counter-criticism as follows ('a' is a criticism, 'b' a counter-criticism):

1a. The Northern countries are 'gene poor' while those in the South are 'gene rich'. The North is 'technology rich' while the South is 'technology poor'. The Green Revolution and current (biotechnology) research has widened this gap.

1b. To limit the negative consequences of this dichotomy, the North has created the global network of IARCs, including those of CGIAR. The Green Revolution crops which came out of the research of these networks have saved millions of people.

2a. The importation of advanced breeding lines from the North into the South replaces traditional landraces and contributes to a greater yield in the short run,

14

if supplied with enough inputs, but causes unstable and/or lower yield in the long run.

2b. The importation of advanced breeding lines from the North into the South replaced traditional landraces but also contributed to long–term higher yields. Agricultural development has to result in the replacement of diverse ancestral crop varieties by improved varieties.

3a. The value of genetic resources in agricultural improvement in developing countries is misunderstood and underrated. Farmers have identified and classified valuable genetic material in landraces (often according to indigenous taxonomic systems), selected them, bred them and named them.

3b. Genetic resources used in the agroindustry in the North come from agricultural systems that are underdeveloped, agriculturally marginal and poorly controlled by farmers. The landraces have no direct value for crop improvement in agro–industry and, in most cases, are not consciously selected, bred or named.

4a. Farmers in developing countries are not rewarded fo. their contribution to the North's agricultural production since landraces are believed to be freely available. The patent system in the North leaves no room for reward for landraces.

4b. Crop improvement work will be seriously affected if the principle of free availability of genetic resources worldwide is abandoned. It is virtually impossible to trace what the specific contribution of landraces or related wild species has been to an advanced breeding line.

5a. The North controls not only the use of genetic resources, but also their collection and exchange. It favours centralized gene bank systems which limits the South's access to them.

5b. Genetic resources in the IARC, CGIAR Centres and most Western gene banks are freely available, while the South benefits from the know–how and technical assistance offered gratis through these institutions. When genetic resources are collected, duplicates are always left behind in the country of origin.

6a. The agroindustry is mostly dominated by the North and protects its products through property rights even though the basic material for these products usually originates from the South.

6b. The North's investments in research on genetic resources can only continue when intellectual property is recognized worldwide. Unimproved material from the South has no real value for agroindustry, but is freely available to the South.

Notwithstanding the above controversies, however, a core assumption may be defined: genetic resources are indispensable to the improvement of generally all agricultural systems and must be secured to determine their usefulness.

The genetic resources issue is quite distinct from the biodiversity issue. While the term 'genetic resources' refers to the genetic information contained in the genes, the term 'biological diversity'/'biodiversity' encompasses all species of plants, animals and micro-organisms (and the ecosystems and ecological processes of which they are parts). And while the genetic resources issue deals with 'use' and 'valorization' aspects, the biodiversity issue also covers non–use and non–value (such as ethical) aspects.

The genetic resources issue basically relates to power relationships among countries with different abilities to have access to and use of genetic resources. This explains why the conservation strategies (especially the location of genetic resources in gene banks) by industrialized countries attracted much debate and discussion. This point is best exemplified by the IBPGR, since on the one hand it represented 'free access', while on the other hand developing countries suspected that its strong ties with western donors would not guarantee this principle.

Biodiversity as a Renewable Resource

The biological diversity of our planet once seemed inexhaustible but today it is more like a finite, yet renewable, resource. If properly managed, it can support the world's population into the foreseeable future. The future of human civilization might well depend on man's ability to protect, conserve and make sustainable use of biological diversity.

It is biodiversity that nurtures people, contributing to long-term food security for all. Biodiversity forms the foundation for sustainable development. It is the basis for the environmental health of our planet and the source of economic and ecological security for future generations.

Since time immemorial, humans have been influencing the environment; even those ecosystems that appear most 'natural' have been altered directly or indirectly during the course of time. Starting some 12,000 years ago, our forebearers, as farmers, fishermen, hunters and foresters, have created a rich diversity of productive ecosystems. This heritage has spanned numerous generations but is now threatened by the recent rapid pace of change, undesirable side-effects of industrialization and increasing expansion of the world's population.

One notable weakness of the international economic system has been its inability to assign a value of exchange to biodiversity. Ascertaining how to incorporate the cost of conservation into that of production is a daunting task that must be met if we are to fulfill our obligations to future generations and halt the continuing impoverishment and misuse of biodiversity. It needs to be realized that the cost of conserving biodiversity is much less than the penalty of allowing its degradation. Once lost, this heritage cannot be recovered or restored at any cost.

There are some ways in which biodiversity may be exploited as a resource, without leading to its destruction. Loss of biological diversity through land clearance and pollution damage may also mean the loss of biological resources in the form of undiscovered useful plants and animals, as well as losing wild types which could refresh the gene pool of our cultivated varieties. But any exploitation of these resources should also conserve the biological diversity from which they originate: in other words, they should be sustainable over time.

The explanation of biodiversity as a sustainable resource involves the complex problem of how to use multispecies assemblages in a sustainable fashion. It requires that individual populations not be overharvested. It requires that sufficiently large areas of natural and seminatural ecosystems remain to sustain viable populations and ecosystems. Sustainable use also requires that we understand enough about the problems of community assembly, food–web dynamics, and systems of mutualism such that exploitation of part of the assemblage does not threaten the whole. Biodiversity cannot be a renewable resource if the world's human population continues to rise, and per capita consumption of resources continues to increase.

Contacts Between Biodiversity and Biotechnology

Biotechnology is likely to become a driving economic force in the 21st century, and will help provide practical solutions to global problems of food supply, health care, energy, waste treatment and industrial regeneration. It can also become a powerful agent for environmental change.

The practice of traditional (classical) biotechnology began some 10,000 years ago, with the first domestications of plants and animals, and the origin of agriculture. Six thousand years ago the Egyptians were using yeast to produce leavened bread. The plant and animal-breeding programmes throughout history and prehistory also constitute old forms of biotechnology. Modern biotechnology is largely associated with the frontiers of science, with medical biotechnology enjoying a particularly high public profile. Genetic engineering is a subdiscipline of biotechnology that allows gene components to be manipulated and transferred across species.

Biotechnological techniques are being used to introduce desirable traits in existing species more rapidly and more precisely than has so far been possible. In some cases, these advances cannot be achieved using other techniques. They are potent tools which are likely to be increasingly used to develop and produce novel medicines, agricultural products, foods, and other goods for everyday consumption and industrial use.

Biodiversity and biotechnology are mutually dependent on one another. Since biotechnology utilizes the capabilities of living organisms, it relies on biodiversity. The vast, but rapidly diminishing array of Earth's biota contains genetic resources that fuel biotechnology, and so provide opportunities for the future. This is necessary for the security of future generations, a major goal of sustainable development.

Biodiversity is undoubtedly the foundation from which biotechnology develops and upon which the industry is strongly anchored. Likewise biotechnology has much to offer to the conservation and sustainable use of biodiversity. Biotechnology is potentially important in helping us to maintain biodiversity for the survival of species, in restoring or enhancing the resilience of ecosystems, and in reclaiming degraded lands.

The biological resources of each and every country are important, but not all are equally endowed. In general, a small number of countries lying within the tropics and subtropics account for a very high percentage of the world's biodiversity. Tropical forests, for example, cover only 7% of the earth's land surface, but they probably harbour at least 50% of all species. A 13.7 km^2 area of La Selva forest in Costa Rica contains almost 1500 plant species — more than all those found in the United Kingdom's 243,500 km^2. Panama contains more species than all of North America. In the USA, 25% of all prescriptions dispensed by pharmacies are substances extracted from plants. Another 13% come from micro–organisms, and 3% from animals.

The most important food crops, however, appear to have originated in areas that have pronounced seasons, not in the tropical forests. This tends to coincide with arid and semiarid zones, which include famine–prone countries such as Ethiopia. It makes sense, therefore, to look for sources of certain food crop diversity in such areas. A single Ethiopian barley plant, for example, has yielded a gene that now protects California's annual barley crop from yellow dwarf virus.

The fact that the richest nations are home to the smallest pockets of biodiversity while the poorest are stewards of the richest reservoirs underlines the interdependency of all nations, and the urgency of formulating common strategies for sustaining biodiversity that share both responsibility and benefits. On the eve of the 21st century, the challenge for the global community is not to save biodiversity for its own sake, but to ensure that biodiversity is used sustainably and equitably for human development.

One interesting aspect currently attracting attention is the extent to which there may exist redundancy in species functions in various ecosystems. Several species may perform similar roles but further studies may help distinguish them (Steinberg and Geller, 1993).

Cultural Diversity

During the course of evolution, biological diversity has increased because it arises mostly through adaptations to environmental heterogeneity, which itself has continually increased via the activities of living organisms. Part of the adaptation of organisms is behavioural, with behaviour becoming increasingly flexible in higher animals. Thus birds and mammals take to new food sources by imitating other members of their social group (see Gadgil, 1991). Biologists define culture as acquisition of behavioural traits from conspecifics through social learning; and man's close relatives, such as chimpanzees, have progressed further by introducing deliberate teaching. The capacity for tool use and symbolic communication has, however, made it possible for the human species to outcompete all others in the complexity of its culturally transmitted behaviour. This has generated a great variety of cultural behaviours in the different human populations across the world.

Human cultural behaviour includes many traits. Here, we are concerned only with patterns of behaviour relating to other living species. Any given human group may possess a wealth of culturally transmitted behaviour in this context; and just as we talk of alpha species diversity or ecological species packing, such within-group diversity of elements of cultural behaviour patterns may be termed alpha cultural diversity. These cultural patterns also differ from one human group to another, and this may be termed beta cultural diversity in analogy with beta species diversity or ecological species turnover (Gadgil, 1992) (see Fig. 1–5).

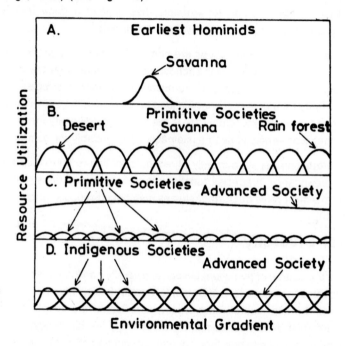

Fig. 1–5. Historical changes in patterns of resource utilization by human societies. (a) The earliest hominids were genetically and culturally adapted to utilize the biological resources of tropical savannas. (b) Cultural adaptation then enabled hunter–gatherer societies to occupy a wide range of environments, with each local society fine–tuned to utilize the biological resources of its own environment. (c) Technological advances enabled a few societies to usurp the bulk of resources from the more primitive and culturally more diversified societies. Technologically advanced societies initially maintained rather high levels of resource utilization, while the availability of resources to more primitive societies was markedly depressed. (d) With diffusion of technologies and depletion

20

of the resource base, the advantage enjoyed by the technologically advanced societies is reduced, so that the less advanced indigenous societies can begin to reassert some control over resources (after Gadgil, 1992).

The variety of biological resources may have been foraged at rates that would maximize immediate energy or nutrient returns, and this might have caused extinction of some biological populations, at least locally.

However, certain patterns of human utilization of biological resources do not form part of an optimal foraging strategy. For instance many biological communities receive total protection (e.g. sacred groves or ponds) and function as refugia. Keystone species such as *Ficus* trees often receive total protection over a wide area and support a wide range of insects, birds, primates and other organisms. These practices suggest that human populations may indeed have developed traditions that specifically serve to conserve a diversity of biological resources of value to them.

Being a *K*-selected species with a long generation time, humans cannot quickly convert resources into increased population size. The well-being of a human group therefore requires the availability of resources, and possibly a wide diversity of resources, at a minimal level over periods of several years.

According to Gadgil (1991, 1992), cultural traditions of conservation would confer no advantage on human groups under the following conditions:

(a) When the resource level fluctuates independently of the extent to which the resources are harvested, for instance with populations of migratory prey species.

(b) When a conquering human group can move into new areas, displacing the former occupants.

(c) When humans have developed the technological abilities to deploy newer and newer resources to meet their various requirements, they may find little advantage to conservative use of any particular resource.

(d) When a human group cannot ensure the co–operative behaviour of its individuals.

Usually technological innovations favour non-conservative use of biological resources. Whenever a technologically superior group moves into a region occupied by groups at more primitive levels of technology, the dominant group has the option of moving on to fresh pastures as resources of any locality are exhausted, and thus would derive no advantage from traditions of sustainable, conservative use. Such a pattern of resource use has been termed sequential exploitation. This process would tend to deplete biological diversity. It also diminishes cultural diversity, for two reasons. First, a significant component of cultural diversity relating to fine–tuning of cultural behaviour to the local biological environment would lose its functionality. Secondly, subordinated groups may imitate the culture of a dominant group, thereby losing part of their cultural diversity.

With groups tuning into the use of local resources, cultural diversity relating to biological diversity can partially reappear.

Creation of genetically engineered organisms has the potential to revolutionize the world's biological diversity. The new, engineered organisms could also convert all lands and waters, however unproductive they may appear today, into highly profitable bases of resource production. This would tremendously increase the pressure for converting all habitats into sites for man-made production—perhaps, in the end, wiping out most natural biological communities and thereby a great deal of biological diversity. As the technological advances provide a competitive edge to technologically sophisticated societies, there is likely to be further erosion of cultural diversity also (see Gadgil, 1992).

Nelson and Serafin (1992) opined that biodiversity will not receive due care and attention unless the multitude of human activities, values and institutional arrangements that influence it are taken more thoroughly into account in conservation efforts. Most definitions of biodiversity do not reflect the importance of understanding how humans have affected it in the past, both positively and negatively, as well as how they might affect it in future. Human activities and impacts are typically treated as interventions into biophysical systems as opposed to being long-standing interactive elements or processes in such systems and as such directly responsible for much of the diversity of species, habitats and ecosystems around the world (Moran, 1990; Nelson and Serafin, 1992).

Biological and cultural diversity are often linked. This is best seen in tropical areas of the world, where the greatest concentrations of species are found, and where people have the greatest cultural and linguistic diversity. Whereas geographical isolation by mountains and river systems favours biological speciation, it also favours diversification of human cultures. The cultural diversity found in Central Africa, Amazonia, and SE

Asia, for instance, is one of the most valuable resources of human civilization, providing unique insights into philosophy, religion, music, art and resource management. Protection of these traditional cultures can contribute much to achieving the dual goals of protecting biological diversity and preserving cultural diversity.

Cultural diversity is also intimately connected with the genetic diversity of crop plants. In montane areas the inaccessible terrain leads to the evolution of various tribes that develop local plant varieties called landraces. These landraces are not only well adapted to the local climate, soils, and pests, but also satisfy the tastes of the local people. The genetic variation found in these landraces is highly valuable to modern plant breeding for the improvement of crop species.

Ecotourism

Tourism is one of the world's largest industries. It is potentially a powerful way to make biodiversity pay. In some countries (e.g. Kenya and Nepal) it is the major earner of foreign currency. In Kenya, land in some National Parks raises $40 per hectare each year, as opposed to the $0.80 it would raise if used for agricultural purposes. Coarse calculations suggest that each lion in the park raises about $20,000 per year and that the elephant herds raise about $610,000.

Most of the financial benefits of ecotourism accrue to the tour companies which are usually not based in the country the tourists have chosen to visit. Some criteria that have to be met before ecotourism can be regarded as sustainable or capable of further development are the following:

(1)   Tourism should provide funds for purchase and maintenance of reserves.

(2)   It should create opportunities for local people.

(3)   It should also help to justify conservation to local governments. In Nepal, a project to build a dam near the Chitwan nature reserve was cancelled when an economic analysis showed that the Park raised more dollars than would the hydroelectric scheme.

Ecotourism is a large, rapidly growing enterprise that is currently estimated to be a $2 billion industry across the world (Herliczek, 1996). An explosive increase in travel (see Fig. 1–6) is occurring internationally, especially in the tropics. In 1988, some 15 million tourists visited South and Central America, many of them going there to see the flora and fauna of natural areas. Thousands of tourists go to Argentina to view a huge colony of 200,000 Magellanic penguins. Visitors to Nepal had increased from 10,000 in 1965 to 250,000 by 1990. Ecotourism is the fastest-growing component of tourism worldwide (Herliczek, 1996). It can be a strong motivation to conserve natural sites. It has a tremendous economic potential for local sustainable development.

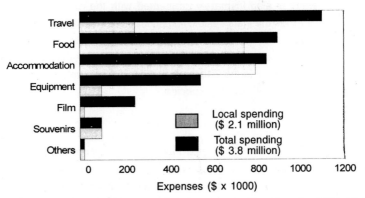

Fig. 1–6. Money spent on ecotourism in Canada. In 1987, bird-watchers at Point Pelee National Park, Ontario, spent $ 3.8 million from May 1 through May 24, the peak of the bird-watching season. Except for travel costs, most of that money was spent locally (from Hvengaard *et al.*, 1989).

Though less destructive than many other uses, ecotourism also involves some unavoidable costs, and a balance has to be struck between preservation and development. Even non-consumptive visitation, if done by large numbers of tourists, can subtly affect ecosystems. Animal behaviours may be altered, breeding grounds may be disturbed, and potential prey may be frightened away. Human intrusions can lead to changes in animal behaviour that may hamper, though not threaten, wildlife (Knight and Gutzweiler, 1995) and some other intrusions may seriously affect populations by inhibiting reproduction.

Ecotourism often results in littering. Although tourists are encouraged to pack out what they bring in, certain objects may be left behind along tourist trails. Ecotourism can also lead to site degradation. Ecotourism reserves must be large enough to support the populations of animals and plants people want to see. Questions such as minimal numbers of breeding pairs and insufficient territory sizes become very critical in small reserves.

Initial development focused on unique natural sites supporting high–profile species such as lemurs, elephants, or grizzly bears, or ecosystems with obvious public appeal such as tropical rain–forests and marine coral reefs as being suitable. In general, rare places having some special attractions have been successfully developed for ecotourism. It appears that ecotourism is likely to result in isolated, specialized reserves scattered the world over, rather than vast protected tracts. Consequently, it will act as a large–scale, sustainable development strategy only in concert with other protective measures. Scattered, specialized ecotourism reserves would be successful in protecting some of the larger and more charismatic vertebrates from extinction, but they would not be big enough to protect the broader diversity of plants and animals.

Ecotourism has the potential to contribute to sustainable development around the world, especially in developing tropical regions. If the earnings from this activity are spent on conservation, it can greatly aid conservation and sustainability. If practised carefully and managed with the interests of the local site and local people in mind, it can be a sustainable source of income conducive to promoting the conservation of many unique habitats throughout the world. However, its potential to protect natural areas is quite low and it can also lead to some habitat degradation (Meffe *et al.*, 1997); it must be so conducted as to minimize threats of degradation from tourist activities.

Role of Traditional Societies in Biological Conservation

A clear separation between lands in developing countries used by the natives to obtain natural resources and strictly protected national parks is often impossible. Local people sometimes live in protected areas and use their resources. In some cases, people are allowed to enter protected areas periodically to collect natural products. In Biosphere Reserves, natives are allowed to use resources from designated buffer zones. The protection of biological diversity, the customs of traditional societies, the genetic variation of traditional crops, and economic development can be meaningfully integrated through what are called Integrated Conservation–Development Projects (Caldecott, 1996; Maser, 1997), which are some of the best conservation strategies known today.

One of the objectives of UNESCO's Man and the Biosphere Program (MAB) is the maintenance of samples of varied and harmonious landscapes resulting from long–established land–use patterns (Batisse, 1997). Under this programme 327 Biosphere

Reserves in 85 countries now cover over 200 million ha (Fig. 1–7). The MAB Program hopes to find ways in which native people may sustainably use natural resources without degrading the environment.

Fig. 1–7. Locations of Biosphere Reserves (dots) in the world. Note the paucity of reserves in some parts, e.g. India, New Guinea and S. Africa.

In-situ Agricultural Conservation. In many areas farmers cultivating locally adapted crop varieties can preserve genetic variability in these species because local varieties often have unique genes for dealing with disease, nutrient deficiencies, pest resistance, drought tolerance and other environmental variations (see Fig. 1–8). These local varieties continue to evolve new genetic combinations, some of which may well be effective in dealing with looming global environmental threats. Unfortunately, however, farmers in many places are abandoning their traditional farming practices with local landraces and going in for new high-yielding varieties using capital-intensive methods, including fertilizers, pesticides and machinery. In some countries such as Indonesia, Sri Lanka and the Philippines, over three-fourths of the farmers have already adopted modern varieties which give them increased yields and income quickly. But this can have adverse effects in the long term in so far as the preservation of the genetic variability in local varieties is concerned. Therefore, some villages are now being identified as *in-situ* landrace custodians. In these the farmers would be encouraged to grow their traditional crops in the old, traditional way: the governments will adequately subsidize/compensate them for the reduction in yields and incomes generally associated with this practice.

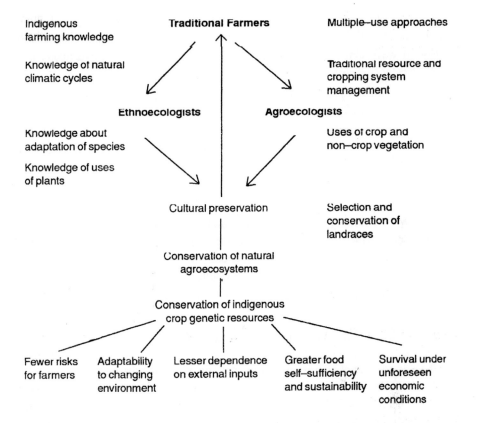

Indigenous
farming knowledge

Knowledge of natural
climatic cycles

Traditional Farmers

Multiple–use approaches

Traditional resource and
cropping system
management

Ethnoecologists

Agroecologists

Knowledge about
adaptation of species

Knowledge of uses
of plants

Uses of crop and
non–crop vegetation

Cultural preservation

Selection and
conservation of
landraces

Conservation of natural
agroecosystems

Conservation of indigenous
crop genetic resources

| Fewer risks for farmers | Adaptability to changing environment | Lesser dependence on external inputs | Greater food self–sufficiency and sustainability | Survival under unforeseen economic conditions |

Fig. 1–8. Conservation of environment, culture, and genetic variation
found in traditional agroecosystems (modified from Altieri and Anderson,
1992).

Creative Conservation

The crisis of species extinctions is one of the greatest challenges facing mankind
and calls for earnest, ingenious and creative means of tackling it.

Society is now struggling with unbearable pressures on land, water and their
biota. Lengthening lists of endangered species show that biological diversity
conservation can be best dealt with at the ecosystem and landscape level rather than

at the species level, and that some form of ecosystem management approach is preferable. Innovative approaches are needed to manage landscapes with some degree of ecological cohesion in ways that provide flexibility, multiple options for human aspirations and opportunities for creative solutions (Lovejoy, 1997).

The best index of whether an ecosystem is being managed sustainably is whether it maintains its characteristic biodiversity and ecosystem processes. In other words, whether the native species list for some particular ecosystem a century hence should essentially be that which it has today, and that functions such as watershed protection, nutrient cycling, or pollination are well maintained. Achieving these goals will require considering every factor intrinsic to the ecosystem, as well as every factor extrinsic to the ecosystem. And it can work only if there is active involvement of local people.

Rather than viewing nature as a fenced-off patch in the middle of a human-dominated landscape where people go on doing what they like, people should learn to live and pursue their activities and aspirations within nature. The two important operational measures of sustainable ecosystem management, viz. characteristic biodiversity and ecosystem processes, should be well appreciated and respected by everybody.

Biodiversity Planning

The current rate of species extinction is some 100 times the natural background rate (Lawton and May, 1995; Stuart and Lawton, 1998). This rate is likely to increase in the coming decades. Only about 5% of the earth's land surface has protected reserves. When humankind destroys or modifies the remaining 95% of the land, only half the world's species will survive in the protected 5%, the other half will be lost forever.

The most vulnerable species are those with the smallest geographical ranges; these are not distributed randomly. There are some natural hot spots where these rare, endemic species are concentrated. Unfortunately, deforestation rates are highest in the richest hot spots (Balmford and Long, 1994). If the reserves are judiciously spread over these special places, there is a slight chance that a greater fraction of species might be saved. It is paradoxical that, globally, the larger reserves (high mountains, tundra, and the driest deserts) are areas not particularly species–rich. Hot spots such as Madagascar and the Philippines protect less than 2% of their land. The need is for setting up reserves in such a way as to protect the maximum number of species at the lowest possible cost.

28

Biodiversity and Development

Human beings as a species are rapidly altering the world in various ways. Unprecedented population growth and non–sustainable development are not only degrading the land, water and atmosphere, but also decimating a wide variety of the Earth's organisms and their habitats.

We humans consume well over a third of the total terrestrial photosynthetic productivity. Human activities threaten, over the next few decades, to eliminate about one-fourth of the world's species. Some of these species we may not use directly but our survival can depend on them in various other ways.

Although population growth is not the only cause of environmental degradation, it is an important exacerbating factor. It can undermine the capacity of many developing countries to conserve resources and meet basic human needs. Increasing population pressures on land and other natural resources can aggravate the intensity of natural disasters such as flood and drought.

Depletion of the Earth's biological diversity has much more profound consequences than some other environmental threats. As the loss of biodiversity is irreversible, the potential impact on the Earth's living systems is enormous. The human species has evolved biologically and culturally in a highly diverse world.

One common myth about biodiversity is that its conservation in protected areas necessarily means totally prohibiting resource use. In keeping with this conventional misconception, land managements were proposed to exclude human use (sustainable or otherwise). Local people were sometimes displaced to make room for the protected area. Consequently, social conflicts arose and the area was threatened by surrounding land–use pressures. The fact is that local support for biodiversity conservation is critical and desirable. What is needed is to provide new options for a limited or sustainable use of biodiversity by actively involving local people in managing protected areas. In integrated conservation, a management unit integrates core natural areas and surrounding land-uses, and managers solicit the support and participation of the local population, in part through research contributing to their social and economic development (UNESCO, 1994).

Local support for effective conservation may be ensured in the following ways:

1. Recognize that it is fundamental to the long-term conservation and sustainable use of biodiversity.

2. Ensure that local populations participate as true partners in designing and managing conservation programmes.

3. Allow local populations to identify their own socioeconomic needs.

4. Ensure that people who bear the costs of conservation projects (e.g. restrictions on fishing) also receive a high proportion of the benefits (e.g. tourist revenues).

5. Identify options for sustainable use of biodiversity.

6. Use indigenous knowledge to manage protected areas as far as practicable.

7. Local populations should have maximum stewardship over local resources.

8. Offer income-earning activities and/or service (e.g. improved access to markets, low-interest credit, controlled access to resources) to local populations as a *quid pro quo* for respecting protected area regulations (Brown and Wyckof–Baird, 1992).

Some conservation programmes focus only on augmenting protected area networks but this is generally not sufficient. Regional planning schemes are needed for conserving biodiversity outside natural areas (e.g. biodiversity in seminatural areas and in cultivated or domesticated species) and for minimizing the impact of human activities on natural areas. In fact, most biodiversity is found outside protected natural areas. No doubt, some protected areas are sites of high biodiversity, but many other areas are located in biologically poor mountains or barren places. Only some 5% of the land area of the Earth lies within protected areas, and no marine protected areas have been established so far. However, even if all remaining wild areas were protected, much biodiversity would remain unprotected. Much of the Earth's biodiversity actually occurs in seminatural and rural areas, consisting of fields, forests, hedges, edges of fields and abandoned areas at various stages of succession. Also much economically valuable biodiversity consists of cultivated plants and domesticated animals rather than the wild species of natural areas (UNESCO, 1994).

Some laymen believe that protected natural areas meet most conservation needs. This is not true because protected areas are not completely isolated; they are affected by activities in surrounding areas. Most protected areas are not large enough to function in a self-regulating manner. They have boundaries set by administrative limits and do not conserve the integrity of ecological processes.

Mining and agriculture upstream of a protected area can affect water quality inside. Industrial activities, even from long distances, affect the air quality of a protected area downwind.

Protected areas surrounded by development effectively become islands vulnerable to environmental change (e.g. global climate change). Species in these areas do not have escape pathways for migrating to new areas when environmental conditions change.

Integration of conservation and development planning can maintain the integrity of ecological processes providing key services (e.g. water quality). Conservation and development planning need to be linked through legislation, regulations and institutional mechanisms. Habitat protection is the single most effective means of protecting biodiversity at all levels of organization (genetic, species, ecosystem).

Chapter 2
ASSESSMENT AND PROSPECTING
OF BIODIVERSITY

Introduction

Biological diversity refers to the variety and assemblages of life-forms and their genetic diversity. Whereas species diversity normally refers to the diversity among different species, genetic diversity refers to the diversity *within* species. All biological systems are functionally complex, their complexity associated with the diversity of their component species. Biological diversity directly benefits humanity in various ways. We depend on animal, plant, fungal, and microbial species for food, fuel, fibre, medicines, drugs and raw materials for many manufacturing technologies. The productivity of agricultural systems depends on interactions of diverse organisms within agroecosystems. Genetic engineering in the pharmaceutical and food–processing industries uses natural genetic diversity for sources worldwide.

According to Noss and Cooperrider (1994) biodiversity is the variety of life and its processes. It includes the variety of living organisms, the genetic differences among them, the communities and ecosystems in which they occur, and the ecological and evolutionary processes that keep them functioning, yet ever changing and adapting. In this definition, the four levels of organization are genetic, population/species, community/ ecosystem, and landscape or regional. Each of these levels may be further divided into compositional, structural, and functional components of a nested hierarchy. Composition includes the genetic constitution of populations, the identity and relative abundances of species in a natural community, and the kinds of habitats and communities distributed across the landscape. Structure denotes, for example, the down logs and snags in a forest, the dispersion and vertical layering of plants, and the horizontal patchiness of vegetation at several spatial scales. Function relates to the climatic, geological, hydrological, ecological, and evolutionary processes that generate and maintain biodiversity.

Conserving biodiversity should involve much more than merely saving species from extinction. Biotic impoverishment can take many forms and occur at several levels of biological organization. So, steps must be taken at several levels to counteract impoverishment.

Although currently available quantitative summaries of the taxonomic diversification of vascular plants are not in numerical agreement, they do permit similar broad evolutionary interpretations of the history of land plants. There can be statistically significant quantitative changes as well as qualitative differences in the patterns of diversity change over geological time (Niklas and Tiffney, 1994).

All published estimates of the world's number of species are based upon assumptions about variables for which data are open to question. Even the number of species already recorded is uncertain. Despite computer technology, records are on file cards and scattered among institutions. Estimates range from 1.4 to 1.8 million (Stork, 1993). Only a very small proportion of these species has been studied in detail and there is no information about variation within most species. In most cases, we have only the name of the species (often inaccurate), a description of its appearance (often incomplete), and the approximate location where it was found. Further taxonomic work is urgently needed.

Knowledge about how species interact to form ecosystems is also limited. A full list of the world's ecosystems is badly needed and a general classification system for ecological units — except at the broadest level of the 'biome'—has not been adopted.

While mammals and birds are relatively well known, smaller organisms, such as insects, fungi, micro–organisms, mites, nematodes, bacteria and viruses are not. Micro-organisms have a crucial role in many ecosystems. They have been responsible for advances in food production and are likely to contain the bulk of the world's genetic diversity. Our knowledge of microbes is particularly limited.

The marine environment holds a vast diversity. Its biodiversity is essentially unknown. The area of the sea floor below 1000 metres is roughly twice the land area of the globe. Estimates of numbers of animal species in the deep sea, in particular, may be low by several orders of magnitude. While diversity tends to increase from the poles to the tropics in terrestrial ecosystems, we do not know whether the same pattern is true for the marine world.

Modern molecular techniques have revealed that previously unknown major bacterial and related groups are common in the sea. This knowledge, combined with the discovery of the widespread existence and abundance of marine viruses, has fundamentally altered concepts of marine microbial diversity and the central role of microbes in global biogeochemical cycles.

About 1.5 million living and 300,000 fossil species have been described and given scientific names (Table 2–1). Current estimates of the total number of living species range from 10 million to as high as 50 million or more. This means that we do not really know the number of living species. Thus, a large fraction of the species likely to be exterminated during the next century will disappear before they have been named.

Although symbolic, biodiversity just cannot be measured by the number of bird species in a forest, wild flowers in a meadow, or algae in a pond. Simplicity is certainly not one of the virtues of biodiversity. Ecosystems are highly complex. Even space shuttles with all their earth–stationed computers are mere toys compared to an old–growth forest, its numerous known and unknown species, and their intricate genetic codes and ecological interactions. Merely identifying and counting species is a difficult enough task, not to mention the virtually infinite complexity of nature which defies man's best efforts to classify or categorize.

One fairly common misconception about biodiversity is that it is equivalent to species diversity—the larger the number of species in an area, the greater its biodiversity. But biodiversity is not just a numbers game. On a global scale, maintaining maximal species richness is a legitimate goal and requires keeping global extinction rates low enough that they remain balanced or even surpassed by speciation. However, when species richness is considered at any scale smaller than the biosphere, quality becomes far more important than quantity: it is not so much the number of species that is interesting, but rather their identity. Fragmenting an old-growth forest with clearcuts, for example, tends to increase species richness locally but would not increase species richness at a broader scale if sensitive species were lost from the landscape (Noss and Cooperrider, 1994).

Quite often, diversification can become homogenization, whose greatest cause worldwide is the introduction of non–native plants and animals (exotics). These are species that have invaded new areas due to either accidental or deliberate transport by humans. No doubt, species do naturally disperse and colonize new areas, but human transport and habitat disturbance have increased the rate and scale of invasions many times the natural rate so that today several regions have about as many exotic as native species. Introductions of exotics sometimes increase species richness locally or even regionally but they do not increase biodiversity. Rather, they disturb the regional floras and faunas and often alter fundamental ecological processes, such as fire frequency and intensity, and nutrient cycles. Even whole ecosystems are changed. Different places tend to look alike; the result is global impoverishment.

Table 2–1. Numbers of species living today (approximate)

Kingdom	Phylum (Division)	Number of described species	Estimated number of species	Per cent described
Monera	Viruses and bacteria[a]			
Protista		100,000	250,000	40.0
Fungi	Eumycota	80,000	1,500,000	5.3
Plantae	Bryophyta	14,000	30,000	46.7
	Tracheophyta	250,000	500,000	50.0
Animalia	Porifera	5,000		
	Cnidaria	10,000		
	Ctenophora	100		
	Platyhelminthes	25,000	–	
	Nemertea	900		
	Gastrotricha	500		
	Kinorhyncha	100		
	Priapulida	16		
	Entoprocta	150		
	Nematoda	20,000	1,000,000	2.0
	Rotifera	1,800		
	Annelida	75,000		
	Arthropoda	1,250,000	20,000,000	5.0
	Mollusca	100,000	200,000	50.0
	Sipunculida	250		
	Echiurida	150		
	Pogonophora	145		
	Ectoprocta	5,000		
	Phornida	70		
	Brachiopoda	350[b]		
	Hemichordata	100		
	Chaetognatha	100		
	Echinodermata	7,000		
	Urochordata	1,200		
	Chordata	40,000	50,000	80.0

Data from World Conservation Monitoring Centre (1992).

[a] Numbers for viruses and bacteria are omitted because species limits are poorly defined and essentialy not known in these groups.

[b] 26,000 fossil species described

For mammals, birds and other large animals, the popular belief has been that there are roughly twice as many tropical as temperate species. Should the same ratio be true for other organisms, then with about 1.5 million species described and two–thirds of these being temperate, the world total would amount to about three million. Gaston (1994) showed that most species described in the late 1980s are from non–tropical regions and from 'non–megadiverse' countries (Tables 2–2; 2–3); the distribution of most described species is largely not known.

Two of the most diverse natural communities on Earth — coral reefs and rain forests — occur in the tropics. Coral reefs resemble rain forests in their biologically generated physical complexity, high species diversity and coevolved associations and interactions among species (Reaka-Kudla, 1997). Although coral reefs undoubtedly represent one of the pinnacles of global biodiversity, precise quantitative data on their total species diversity is lacking. Although coral reefs generally inhabit nutrient–poor waters, they are one of the most productive ecosystems on Earth. Their fishes and invertebrates are important providers of protein for the world's tropical coastal countries.

Table 2–4 shows that there are some 1,450,000 currently described species of terrestrial organisms, about 100,00 symbiotic organisms, and about 318,000 aquatic organisms. Of the latter, about 274,000 species are estimated to be marine (incl. 180,000 macroscopic marine invertebrates; 36,000 micro- and macroscopic marine algae; and 58,000 spp. of other marine groups). This means that approx. 15% of the global described species are marine (May, 1994; Reaka-Kudla, 1997). Over 90% of all marine species are benthic rather than pelagic. Reaka-Kudla estimated that there are about 93,000 described species of coral reef taxa and 68,000 described species of coral reef macrobiota.

Rain forests may account perhaps for over 70% of the described global biota (Table 2–4). Rain forests may possibly harbour about 1,305,000 described species (plus many undescribed ones; see Reaka-Kudla, 1997).

Areas with high α–richness contain many rare species. A tropical wet forest in South America or SE Asia, for instance, may harbour 300 to 400 tree species per square kilometre, whereas a temperate forest harbours an order of magnitude fewer. However, the number of individual trees per square km is about equal in tropical and temperate forests, suggesting that most of the tree species in the tropical forest must be present at very low densities. Many of those species are probably more abundant elsewhere, but some species occur only at low densities throughout their ranges.

Table 2.2. Number of endemic species in some 'Hot spot' areas

Region	Area (km²), (x 1000)	Vascular plants (x 10)	Mammals	Reptiles	Amphibians
Cape region (South Africa)	134	600	16	43	23
Upland western Amazonia	100	500	–	–	70
Atlantic coastal Brazil	1000	500	40	92	168
Madagascar	62	490	86	234	142
Philippines	250	370	98	120	41
Northern Borneo	190	350	42	69	47
Eastern Himalayas	340	350	–	20	25
Southwestern Australia	113	283	10	25	22
Western Ecuador	27	250	9	–	–
Colombian Chocó	100	250	8	137	111
Peninsular Malaysia	120	240	4	25	7
California Floristic Province	324	214	15	25	7
Western Ghats (India)	50	160	7	91	84
Central Chile	140	145	–	–	–
New Caledonia	15	140	2	21	0

Data from Myers (1988); World Conservation and Monitoring Centre (1992).
Note: Original area of rain forest is given only for the tropical regions.

Table 2–3. Geographical distribution of the 24,000 newly described species of Coleoptera (49% of species), Diptera (25%) and Hymenoptera (26%) referenced in the volumes of the *Zoological Record* for 1985–1989 (after Gaston, 1994)

Proportion of species descriptions from the 10 countries from which the most species were described in each case		Proportion of the sum of species descriptions from the 'megadiversity' countries		Proportion of the total number of species described over the 5–year Period from various faunal regions	
Country	%	Country	%	Region	%
CIS (USSR)	8.7	China	6.2	Neartic[a]	8.3
China	6.2	Australia	5.8	Neotropical[b]	12.5
Australia	5.8	India	5.3	Palearctic[c]	19.2
India	5.3	Madagascar	3.6	Ethiopian[d]	12.1
United States	5.1	Brazil	2.8	Madagascar	3.7
Japan	4.6	Malaysia	2.0	Indian subcontinent	9.8
Papua New Guinea	4.1	Mexico	2.0	China, Japan, and Taiwan	13.7
Madagascar	3.6	Indonesia	1.7	Thailand to New Caledonia	12.7
South Africa	3.4	Peru	1.0	Australia	5.8
Brazil	2.8	Zaire	1.0	New Zealand	0.8
		Ecuador	0.7	Oceanic Islands	1.3
		Colombia	0.7		

[a]Includes the Arctic and temperate areas of North America and Greenland.
[b]Includes South America, the West Indies, Central America and tropical Mexico.
[c]Includes Europe, Arabia and Asia north of the Himalayas, but not China, Japan and Taiwan.
[d]Includes the African subcontinent.

Table 2–4. Calculated and expected species diversity on global coral reefs for all taxa and macrobiota (after Reaka–Kudla, 1997)

Organisms	Number of described species (to nearest 1000)	% of total described species (1.87 million)
Total Described Marine Species	274,000	14.7
Macroscopic Described Marine Species	200,000	10.7
Animals	193,000	10.3
Algae	4,000–8,000	0.2–0.4
Total Described Coastal Species (assuming 80% of all marine species are coastal)	219,000	11.7
Macroscopic Described Coastal Species (if 80% of macroscopic marine animals and most marine macroalgae are coastal)	160,000	8.6
Animals	154,000	8.2
Algae	4,000–8,000	0.2–0.4
Total Described Tropical Coastal Species (if communities in tropical coastal zone are as well studied and twice as diverse as those at higher latitudes; tropical coastal zone = 24% of global coastal zone)	195,000	10.4
Macroscopic Described Tropical Coastal Species (same assumptions)	143,000	7.6
Animals	138,000	7.4
Algae	3,000–7,000	0.2–0.4
Total Described Coral Reef Species (if reef communities are as well studied and twice as diverse as those on non–reef level bottoms; coral reefs = 6% of tropical coastal zone)		
Macroscopic Described Coral Reef Species (same assumptions)	68,000	3.6
Animals	66,000	3.5
Algae	2,000–3,000	0.1–0.2

Table 2–4 contd.

Global Rain Forest Species		
(1) if 90% of all currently described terrestrial species live in rain forests	1,305,000	72.5
(2) independent conservative estimate of described and undescribed species in rain forests	2,000,000	–
(3) potential number of described and undescribed species in rain forests	20,000,000	–
Expected Global Coral Reef Species (if coral reefs are as diverse and as well studied as rain forests; global coral reefs = 5% of the area of global rain forests):		
From (1) above	618,000	34.3
From (2) above	948,000	–
From (3) above	9,477,000	–

Sufficient resources could never be available for a complete inventory of biological diversity. We simply decide how little representative information we can get away with. Birds are a good indicator group in the study of biodiversity as they inhabit all ecosystems, they are high up the food chain and they have been better documented than any other group. To be able to conserve the planet's species wealth and their variations, good–quality data on their distributions are needed. Since these do not exist for all life-forms, representative groups of species must serve as indicators of where diversity has evolved and is richest. Birds are very suitable in this context and are accessible to convenient analysis. Certain groups of mammals, reptiles, fish, invertebrates and plants are also pertinent, although often only at the continental or regional level rather than the global. By using distribution patterns to identify centres and pockets of endemism in these groups, it is possible to construct a set of data that shows the major concentrations of unique biodiversity and therefore to map the areas of the planet vital to the maintenance of the global complement of life–forms (Anonymous, 1991).

Despite the many gaps in knowledge, enough is known about biological diversity, and where it is threatened, to focus action for many years to come. Countries such as Brazil, Indonesia, the Philippines, or the Solomon Islands head the list of priorities.

However, loss of biodiversity has a social and economic dimension in addition to a scientific aspect and what happens in practice may differ from what scientists would wish.

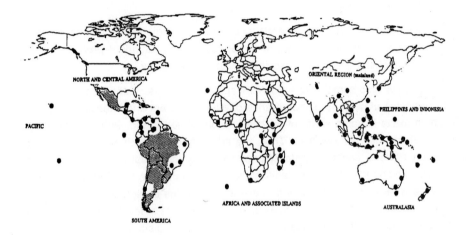

Fig. 2–1. World map of avian endemism, showing areas supporting five or more restricted species (from the International Council for Bird Preservation Biodiversity Project, April 1991). Area of Endemism. Shading indicates that the region is not fully analyzed.

The biggest problem facing biological diversity is population growth. If the planet cannot sustain the current 5.5 billion people without significant loss of biodiversity, how on Earth can it sustain the projected 10 billion?

General Patterns

The basic data of diversity are the numbers of species found in different places. There are relationships between these data and latitude, climate, biological productivity, heterogeneity, and complexity of habitat disturbance, and the sizes and distances of islands. Some of these relationships point to mechanisms that might regulate diversity; hence, a general and comprehensive theory of diversity must account for all of them.

41

Within most groups of organisms, the average number of species in a sampling area of a given size usually reaches maximum in tropical latitudes and decreases toward the poles. The latitudinal gradient in diversity is often very steep. Tropical forests, for example, may support ten times as many species of trees as forests with similar biomass in temperate regions (Ricklefs and Schluter, 1993). In a few cases, however, this general trend in diversity is reversed. Examples are parasitoid wasps and freshwater zooplankton, of which more species occur at high and moderate latitudes than in the tropics.

Species richness is related generally to climate and particularly to conditions that favour biological production, e.g. warm temperatures and abundant precipitation in terrestrial ecosystems are often associated with high diversity.

Disturbance also sometimes influences species richness. Landscapes typically include a mosaic of patches of disturbance of different extent and intensity such that each patch exists in some stage of succession, out of equilibrium with the prevailing climate in its species composition. Thus, the entire mosaic, which is part of a larger regional equilibrium, contains more species than any individual patch. It was this observation which led to the so-called 'intermediate disturbance hypothesis', in which disturbance is regarded as a stress that precludes species at high levels and fails to prevent competitive exclusion by a few superior competitors at low levels, resulting in the greatest species diversity at an intermediate level of disturbance (Ricklefs and Schluter, 1993).

The question of what constitutes the smallest sampling unit of morphological diversity (i.e., the taxonomic level that yields statistically independent observations) has not been resolved for vascular plants. According to Niklas and Tiffney (1994), nested analysis of the per cent distribution of variance for three plant morphological variables (height, tracheid diameter and xylem cross–sectional area) indicates that the taxonomic level at which major evolutionary innovations become apparent shifted from the species–genus level to higher taxonomic levels during the early radiation of pteridophytes. Such shifts may also have occurred during the taxonomic radiation of other broadly defined plant groups (gymnosperms and angiosperms), and thus may have altered the taxonomic level on which selection pressures have operated. This can affect our interpretation of the mechanisms of diversity response to environmental variation (Niklas and Tiffney, 1994).

There usually exists a remarkable connection between diversity and habitat complexity. Salt marshes are extremely productive but have few species of plants and animals; deserts occupy the other end of the productivity gradient but may support a diverse flora and fauna.

Regional or landscape complexity also seems to be involved in patterns of diversity. There is the greater diversity of montane regions compared with flatlands, probably because of the increased numbers of species distributed allopatrically on isolated mountains or in isolated valleys, the greater variety of habitats included within sampling areas of virtually any size, and the increased numbers of species coexisting within habitats (Ricklefs and Schluter, 1993).

Some generalized characteristics of successful invaders include the following: high reproductive rate, pioneer species, short generation time; long-lived; high dispersal rates; single-parent reproduction; vegetative or clonal reproduction; high genetic variability; phenotypically plastic; broad native range; habitat generalist; broad diet (polyphagous); and human commensal. Some characteristics of invadable communities are: climatically matched with original habitat of invader; early successional; low diversity of native species; absence of predators on invading species; absence of native species morphologically or ecologically similar to invader; absence of predators or grazers in evolutionary history ('naive' prey); absence of fire in evolutionary history; low–connectance food web; and anthropogenically disturbed (Lodge, 1993). Characteristics of communities likely to exhibit a large invasion effect include simple communities and anthropogenically disturbed communities.

A regional landscape usually consists of many different plant communities with associated animals; these communities often shift location on the landscape over time. Systematic replacement of biotic communities is termed succession and is well known to all foresters, range managers, and wildlife experts. Succession involves some element of chance, especially with respect to which species reaches a disturbed site first.

Disturbed sites usually depend upon surrounding areas for recovery. When some grassland patch is denuded, adjacent areas with early successional species provide the seed sources that allow colonization by new plants. Later, adjacent mature tall grass communities provide the supply of seeds and animals to revert the area to a tall grass stand.

Community diversity within a regional ecosystem is a function of topographic or landform diversity and natural disturbance cycles which may be generated by the activities of animals or by such climatic or geological events as fire, flooding, landslides, or volcanic activity.

Several approaches are required for proper study of biodiversity. Inputs from disciplines such as palaeontology, ecology, genetics, biogeography, evolution, geology and mathematics are needed for a clear idea of the factors affecting biodiversity. A synthesis of these disciplines allows better study of the factors promoting and limiting diversity, incorporates a range of spatial and temporal scales, and includes aspects of speciation, extinction, historical biogeography and current ecology (Cook, 1998).

According to Robert Ricklefs (University of Missouri), for sister taxa of plants the net diversification has been significantly higher in Asia than in North America (for plant genera shared between the two continents). This undermines the local–determination hypothesis of species diversity (Ricklefs and Schluter, 1993; Rosenzweig, 1995), which predicts similar species diversity in similar habitats. Ricklefs feels that phylogenies could eventually be used to estimate speciation and extinction rates for biogeographical regions and continents, although this would require comprehensive phylogenies of families down to species level (Cook, 1998).

Island Biogeography

Islands are habitats quite likely to spawn new species but equally places likely to see those species become extinct. We should be greatly concerned about the future diversity of life on a planet that is increasingly being fragmented into 'island' habitats.

Alfred Russel Wallace (19th century) knew islands well, and was probably the first man to explore the Amazon rain forest and later the islands of the Malay Archipelago, both as a collector of specimens and as a scientist in search of order in the natural world. Wallace succeeded in establishing the relationship between island size and species diversity (MacArthur and Wilson, 1967; Quammen, 1997). It was later realized that the islands envisaged by MacArthur and Wilson are not islands in just the physical sense, but might be 'islands' of mountain tops or forest fragments scattered and isolated from one another on an otherwise contiguous mainland. The SLOSS controversy (single large or several small) refers to the rather hotly contested debate between ecologists Jared Diamond and Daniel Simberloff as to whether conservation districts should be designed as single, large areas or as several smaller units. Diamond argued for preserves to be as large and as contiguous as possible, for only in large areas could at-risk species find enough habitat to survive. Simberloff argued that other factors besides just sheer area often are more important in sustaining specific species. According to him, relying

44

on only large packets of land for preservation might be a politically difficult thing to do, and consequently species which might otherwise be saved might be lost forever.

Ecologists have asked not only what the 'minimal viable population' of a species might be, but also whether it differs from one species to another. Considering not only demographic but the genetic aspects of uncertainty, Ian Franklin and Michael Soulé showed how genetic variation can be lost in small populations to the detriment of both their short–term and long–term survival. Known as 'the 50/500 rule,' they predicted the minimal population size for short-term avoidance of inbreeding depression to be 50 individuals, while a population of 500 individuals is needed to maintain long–term adaptability in the species. It was this idea of determining species' minimal population sizes that was at least partly responsible for the emergence of conservation biology, and the book *The Theory of Island Biogeography* undoubtedly provided the theoretical basis for this new science (see Quammen, 1997).

The flora and fauna of many islands differ greatly from the continental areas with which they are associated. The species-area relationship, first noted for islands, is an important empirical generalization of biogeography. As the area of any habitat declines, so does the number of species. The species–area effect has been clearly demonstrated, *inter alia,* for oceanic islands, caves, isolated wetlands, alpine grasslands and forest fragments. Typically, a tenfold decrease in habitat area cuts the number of species by one-half, probably because of habitat diversity: as area increases, so does the diversity of physical habitats and resources, which in turn support a larger number of species. In general, larger populations are less likely to become extinct than smaller ones.

According to the island biogeography concept, predicted species richness on an island can be represented as a balance between rate of colonization (immigration to the island) and rate of extinction, see Fig. 2–2. Here, colonization is affected mainly by island distance from the mainland and extinction is affected by island size. Species richness corresponds to the intersection of the colonization and extinction curves. The largest number of species is predicted to occur on islands that are near and large (S_{NL}).

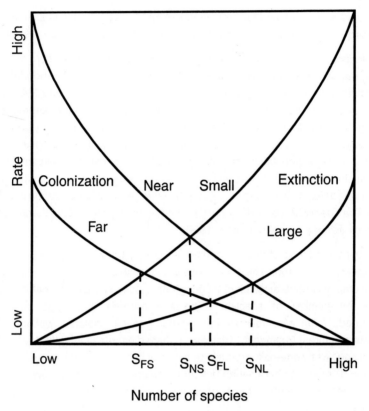

Fig. 2–2. Representation of predicted species richness on an island (after Wilcox, 1980).

Species Vulnerability Patterns

The following three categories of species are strongly vulnerable to extinction.

Rare. In most biotas studied, many or even most of species are, to some degree, rare. A few species tend to be very common and dominate the biota, some species are intermediate in range of abundance, and many species are rare. In general, rarity makes a species more vulnerable to both natural and human-induced extinction. But rarity is not a simple concept. A species may be rare in several different ways, based on different distributional patterns. It may be rare because of a highly restricted geographic range, because of high habitat specificity, because of small local population size, or because of various combinations of these characteristics (Table 2–5). Thus, for example, a species can be distributed across an entire continent and be a habitat generalist, and yet be rare because it occurs at extremely low densities wherever it is found. Alternatively, a species may be locally superabundant, but be rare because it occurs in very specialized, geographically restricted habitats.

Different types of rarity make species vulnerable to different extinction processes. A locally abundant species found at only one location is extremely vulnerable to local stochastic events or intentional habitat destruction. A broadly distributed species that exists at low population sizes may tolerate such events fairly well, but be more vulnerable to loss of genetic diversity and inbreeding. Human–caused rarity is quite often more devastating than natural rarity if the species is not adapted to low numbers. Humans have also driven very abundant species to or near extinction: examples are the Passenger Pigeon, Carolina Parakeet, and bison of North America.

Genetic Level

Species differ from one another and individuals within species vary largely because they contain unique combinations of genes. Gene frequencies and genotypes within a population change over time e.g. by mutations that create new genes or sequences of genes, and loss of genes by chance in small populations (e.g. genetic drift). Genetic diversity is basic to the variety of life. It constitutes the raw material for evolution of new species. Conservation goals at the genetic level include maintaining genetic variation within and among populations of species.

Much is being written about saving the earth's genetic resources. In reality, except for agricultural crops, commercial tree species, rare animals in zoos, and some wild populations, very little is known about genetic diversity.

Species Level

Species diversity is the best known aspect of biodiversity, but unfortunately the vast majority of species in the world are still not known.

A population means local occurrence of a species. Conservation goals at the population/species level relate to maintaining viable populations of all native species in natural patterns of abundance and distribution. These goals grade into community–level goals of maintaining native species richness and composition. Some rare species require individual attention. Certain kinds of species (e.g. keystone species) warrant management emphasis because their protection will conserve more than themselves.

Table 2–5.

Table 2–5.   Seven forms of species rarity, based on three distributional traits

Geographic Range

		Large		Small	
		Large		**Small**	
Population size / **Somewhere large**	Common	Locally abun–dant over a large range in a specific habitat	Locally abun–dant in several geographically restricted habitats	Locally abun–dant in a spe–cific but geographically restricted habitat	
Everywhere small	Constantly sparse over a large range, in several habitats	Constantly sparse in a specific habit–at but over a large range	Constantly sparse and geographically restricted in several habitats	Constantly sparse and geographically restricted in a specific habitat	
	Broad	**Restricted**	**Broad**	**Restricted**	

Habitat Specificity

These play pivotal roles in their ecosystems and a large part of the community depends upon them. The importance of a keystone species is usually disproportionate to its abundance. The beaver, for instance, creates habitats used by many species and also regulates hydrology and other ecosystem functions. Significant declines of keystone species are believed to be far more important ecologically than the loss of the last few individuals of rare species that play minor roles in their communities. Nevertheless, it should be recognized that the term *keystone species* is not well defined, and communities may be better characterized by a wide range of interactions of variable strengths. Because so little is known about the ecological roles of species, each species needs to be considered important (Noss and Cooperrider, 1994).

Plants

Most estimates suggest that there may be about 250,000 species of vascular plants in the world, with about two–thirds of these being found in the tropics, e.g. in Peru, Colombia and Costa Rica.

The ability of plants, algae, photosynthetic bacteria and the recently discovered sulphur–reducing chemosynthetic bacteria associated with some deep-sea thermal vents to convert radiant energy into chemical energy through photosynthesis, places them at the base of all food chains. Because many species depend on specific plants for food and other habitat requirements, the destruction of plant diversity threatens much of the diversity of life in general (NAP, 1992). About one–half of the total species diversity of the Earth is found in the tropical forests and is threatened by their destruction or degradation. Apart from the diverse well–known human uses of plants, new uses are being discovered regularly.

The developing tropical countries probably contain many as yet undiscovered plant species that could be beneficial to society. Legumes are particularly extremely important economically. They have considerable potential as genetic raw material for agricultural biotechnology. Most of those currently used in agroecosystems were discovered quite by chance. There may well be many more among the large number of as yet poorly known or undiscovered legume species.

Fungi

Fungi play an important role in human affairs. Some cause serious crop damage, others are beneficial, for example in the production of foods and antibiotics, maintenance of fertile soils and decomposition of biomass. Mycorrhizal fungi form symbiotic relationships with plant roots and enhance mineral nutrient uptake by their host plants. These fungi have significant impacts on sustainable crop production, forest management and environmental restoration efforts (Cook, 1991). These fungi have been studied much less compared to those few associated with economically important plants.

Unlike many taxonomic groups, fungi may reach their highest levels of diversity outside the tropics, in Temperate Zone forests (Norse, 1990).

The important role of fungi in the degradation of organic material in marine and hypersaline ecosystems has been underestimated. According to Jones (1988), in marine ecosystems, fungi are much more active biodegraders than believed hitherto. To date, about 800 species of obligate marine fungi have been described, including species of Basidiomycota, Ascomycota, lichen–forming fungi, Deuteromycota and yeasts (Kohlmeyer and Kohlmeyer 1979; Hawksworth et al., 1995). A number of salt–tolerant fungi have been isolated from saline lakes, salted fish, sea-water and desert soils.

The Dead Sea, located in the Syrian–African rift valley, on the border between Israel and Jordan, is one of the most saline lakes on earth (salinity about 340 gl^{-1}). The lake differs from other hypersaline lakes in the unique ionic composition of its waters, with concentrations of divalent cations (Mg, 40.7 gl^{-1}; Ca, 17 gl^{-1}) exceeding those of monovalent cations (Na, 39.2 gl^{-1}; K, 7 gl^{-1}). The major anions are Cl (212 gl^{-1}) and Br (5 gl^{-1}). The Dead Sea is known to be inhabited by several types of micro-organisms, e.g. archaeal and eubacterial prokaryotes, unicellular green algae (*Dunaliella parva*), and even some protozoa. Indeed, this lake is a dynamic ecosystem: dense blooms of algae (*D. parva*) and red halophilic Archaea are triggered by dilution of the upper water layers by freshwater floods during rainy winters (Buchalo *et al.*, 1998). These blooms alternate with periods of absence of life-forms (Oren, 1993). Buchalo *et al.* (1998) have now described filamentous fungi isolated from water of the Dead Sea. These include *Gymnascella marismortui* (Ascomycota), *Ulocladium chalmydosporum* and *Penicillium westlingii* (Deuteromycota). *G. marismortui* and *U. chlamydosporum* can grow on media containing up to 50% Dead Sea water. *G. marismortui* is an obligate halophile growing optimally in the presence of 0.5–2 M NaCl or 10–30% (by volume) of Dead Sea water. These fungi seem to be adapted to life in the extremely stressful hypersaline Dead Sea (Buchalo *et al.*, 1998).

Micro-organisms

Since micro–organisms play a crucial role in nutrient cycling, they act as bridges between trophic levels, between abiotic and biotic factors, and between the biogeosphere and the atmosphere. Microflora and microfauna help in maintaining soil fertility and tilth through their ability to catabolize organic matter and produce organic compounds. Some micro-organisms cause disease in plants and animals. Human–induced changes in ecosystems leading to alteration in host species abundances can have unforeseen and undesirable effects on the epidemiology of those diseases. Some microbes have been immensely beneficial to humans. Actinomycetes alone have given us some 3000 antibiotics.

Invertebrates

Similar to micro–organisms, we know very little about invertebrate species diversity, especially in soil and marine environments and tropical forests. Only about 10% of the invertebrate species have actually been described, even though some two–thirds of the 1.4 million known species are invertebrates. Ants alone may make up between 5 and 15% of the biomass of the entire fauna of most terrestrial ecosystems.

Invertebrates play roles in pollination, decomposition, disease transmission and regulation of other populations. The interactions of soil mesofauna (e.g. nematodes, collembolans and mites) and soil micro-organisms are involved in maintaining the plant–soil system. Nematodes both feed on and act as dispersal agents for soil bacteria.

50

Except for pollination, the other aforesaid functions also apply to marine invertebrates. Invertebrates such as corals and some molluscs modify the physical structure of the marine environment by building reefs. Marine molluscs and echinoderms reduce the structural complexity of the marine environment by removing seaweeds and angiosperms. Suspension–feeding molluscs can control particle concentrations in enclosed bodies of water, thereby affecting water turbidity and the column concentrations of nutrients and other compounds.

Terrestrial invertebrates are highly prone to extinction. Many species are highly specialized with respect to food, habitat, or other environmental requirements and so can become extinct as a result of fairly small–scale environmental degradation. This is particularly true for tropical forest insects whose ranges are limited.

The 330,000-odd species of beetles (order Coleoptera) far exceed the number in any other plant or animal group, possibly because of the beetles' fondness for a leafy diet. It appears that the appearance of flowering plants some 100 million years ago set leaf–eating beetles on speciation's fast track. The plants were like a new, unoccupied island, and the herbivorous beetles were some of their first colonizers.

The first beetles were probably not vegetarians. Primitive beetles living today eat detritus and fungi. It only took them 50 million years to figure out that they could survive on cycads, ferns and conifers. Many of these earliest herbivores ate bark or stems of such plants, while their larvae munched the nitrogen–rich, pollen–bearing structures inside the cones. Tissue-eating behaviour could have prepared certain beetle species for the appearance of the juicy flowering plants (the angiosperms).

There is a tight link between plants and beetle diversity. While cycad and conifer-feeding beetles formed the family tree's trunk, angiosperm-eaters dangled from the top branches. Two related superfamilies, Chrysomeloidea (such as the Colorado potato beetle) and Curculionoidea (which includes weevils) may have benefited particularly from the blossoming of a leafy, green world. Together, their known 135,000 species comprise some 80% of all herbivorous beetles and almost half of all herbivorous insects (Morell, 1998). Also, their population boom coincided with the rise of angiosperms.

Vertebrates

Vertebrates have been much better studied than most other biota. Approximately 41,000 species have been described, but many have yet to be discovered (NAP, 1992). About one-half of the known vertebrates are fish. Most of the hitherto undescribed vertebrates are likely to be fish, primarily because of their relatively inaccessible habitats. As many as 40% of the freshwater fish of South America have not yet been classified scientifically. The fish of tropical Asia are also very poorly known. By the analogy of tropical rain forests, there may well be many fish species some of which may turn out to be the sources of useful products. Fish communities may include members whose nutritional modes, defence mechanisms, behaviour, or growth characteristics could find application in the production of proteins, medicines, or fertilizers, and in the management of aquatic habitats.

Unlike other taxonomic groups, a substantial proportion of the species of reptiles, birds and mammals have already been described.

Because the highest trophic levels in many ecosystems are generally occupied by reptiles, birds and mammals, efforts to preserve diversity among these groups will have beneficial impacts on other organisms that share their habitat (NAP, 1992).

Community or Ecosystem Level

Biodiversity may also be considered from the ecosystem level (Begon *et al.*, 1986). Many factors control species and community diversity, and diversity may be a necessary condition for the function of species, populations and communities.

A fundamental difference between molecules, cells and organs on the one hand, and populations, species and communities on the other, is that the former form a nested hierarchy whereas the latter do not (Solbrig, 1991). Molecules are contained in a cell; all cells are of a certain type in a tissue but this is not so with species populations. A population of species X may be part of community A, while another population of the same species X may be part of community B. This difference raises difficulties in applying to higher hierarchical levels concepts such as birth, death, mutation and natural selection that present no problems at the organismic and infraorganismic level (Solbrig, 1991).

Conservation is usually best when it is focused directly on the community or ecosystem. Terrestrial communities are usually defined by their dominant plants but functional or taxonomic groups of animals (for example bird communities, herbivore communities) are also recognized. Functional groups of organisms (species, using resources in similar ways, such as bark-gleaning birds) are termed *guilds*. Similarly, aquatic communities can be taxonomically or functionally defined, e.g. fish communities or littoral (shoreline) vegetation.

An ecosystem is a biotic community plus its abiotic environment. Ecosystems range in scale from microcosms, such as a vernal pool, to the whole biosphere. Some define natural communities by their most striking characteristics, whether biotic or abiotic. The variable spatial scale of ecosystems can be confusing. Although many scientists regard ecosystems as relatively discrete and existing at the same spatial scale as natural communities, conservation ecologists often use the term ecosystem to encompass many different communities. Noss and Cooperrider (1994) view conservation at the community or ecosystem level to complement, rather than replace, species–level management.

Biologists have usually not been able to study species diversity issues using a community focus. Instead, they formulate hypotheses for particular taxonomic groups of organisms in particular geographic areas and then extrapolate to other groups and ecosystems. Generalizations based on particular taxa are flawed because we do not know how representative a particular group of organisms might be of the entire biota. As most theories on species diversity were developed by zoologists, they may not necessarily be applicable to plants.

Landscape and Regional Levels

Since biodiversity occurs at several levels of organization, it should be protected at all levels. A landscape can be defined as some heterogeneous land area containing a group of interacting ecosystems that is repeated in similar form throughout, or as a mosaic of heterogeneous land types, vegetation types and land–uses. Landscapes have a *pattern* which consists of repeated habitat components that occur in different shapes, sizes and spatial interrelationships.

The term *region, bioregion,* or *ecoregion* refers to large landscapes distinguishable from other regions on the basis of climate, physiography, soils, species composition patterns (biogeography) and other variables. Landscape or regional diversity is pattern diversity–the pattern of habitats and species assemblages across a land area of thousands of hectares. Human activities often change landscape pattern and produce impacts on biodiversity that transcend through several levels of organization, affecting species composition and abundances, gene flow and ecosystem processes. A primary conservation goal at the landscape or regional level is to maintain complete, unfragmented environmental gradients. Species richness and composition vary along environmental gradients, such as elevation. Conservation programmes should attempt to maintain natural ecosystems and biodiversity across all the environmental gradients.

Practising conservation, whether at the community or ecosystem level, demands attention to ecological processes, which are valuable for their own sake as part of the diversity of life. The processes most crucial for ecological health can vary from ecosystem to ecosystem. In terrestrial communities, the more important processes are fire, hydrological and nutrient cycles, plant-herbivore interactions, predation, mycorrhizal interactions between plant roots and fungi, and soil-building processes. All processes affect biodiversity at several levels and need to be maintained normally if native biodiversity is to persist. Since clear-cutting and other intensive forest management disrupt nutrient retention, they often fail to conserve biodiversity. Livestock grazing interferes with basic ecological processes and hence fails to conserve native biodiversity in grasslands (see Whittaker, 1972; Alpert, 1995).

Alpha, Beta, and Gamma Diversity

The sum total of species within some relatively homogeneous habitat is called *alpha* diversity or *within-habitat* diversity. On a larger scale, there is greater variation in the underlying physical environment (environmental gradients). As one moves along a gradient, say from one soil type to another, one comes across new species adapted to these different conditions. This turnover in species along an environmental gradient is called *beta* diversity or *between-habitat* diversity.

At a still broader scale, there are many more environmental gradients, so geographic replacements of species occur as range boundaries are crossed. Diversity at this regional scale is termed *gamma* diversity. The three types of diversity allow a comparison of biodiversity in different regions or in the same region under different management patterns. Two regions of about equal gamma diversity may differ greatly in alpha and beta diversity.

We do not always understand the causes of alpha-diversity. Unless we understand the principles, we have no chance of predicting patterns among other species groups and in other areas where the rate of environmental change may preclude even our describing the species, let alone mapping their ranges. We know far too little about beta-diversity to predict its current or future patterns, when remanent natural areas are surrounded by highly modified habitats. Part of the problem is familiar: larger remanents increase alpha-diversity, more remanents increase beta-diversity (Pimm and Gittleman, 1992). 'The optimal allocation of remanents involves knowing both diversities. Even less clear is whether species will survive outside these protected remanants other than human commensals that, like the starling, have followed us worldwide. And to what extent will these commensals penetrate the natural areas? We clearly know too little about where the diversity is, why it is there, and what it will become' (Pimm and Gittleman, 1992).

Tropical Aquatic Systems

Tropical rivers, lakes and wetlands are among the richest but least studied habitats in the developing world. Watershed development projects inevitably change rivers and their biota, usually before scientific investigations of unmodified watersheds and basins are undertaken.

The composition, abundance and functioning of the plankton of large rivers remain essentially unstudied. The high diversity of invertebrates of tropical rivers has not been investigated though knowledge of the fish and other vertebrates is somewhat better.

Lakes are more common in the temperate zones than in the tropics. Nonetheless, the interesting physical features, high productivity and vulnerability of tropical lakes make study of their biological diversity particularly important. Several tropical lakes are rich in endemic fish species and merit study because of their susceptibility to the effects of exotic fish introductions.

Tropical wetlands are some of the most productive freshwater systems known. They are highly vulnerable to destruction by drainage, conversion to intensive rice production and alteration of associated river systems. Many of the most important wetlands show distinctive species compositions, adaptations, energy-flow patterns and population dynamics. Studies of the biological diversity of these systems can greatly advance the understanding of how they function, and how human alteration and use of tropical wetlands may affect their diversity and productivity.

Marine Biota

The vastness of the marine environment, the variety of marine ecosystems and the problem of exploring and studying the life of the sea have hampered efforts to investigate marine biodiversity comprehensively.

Marine systems have a high degree of diversity at all taxonomic levels. Until recently it was estimated that of the total number of species on the planet, about 90% are terrestrial. Recent research, however, revealed that previously unexplored marine habitats such as the deep sea and the ocean–floor may well contain millions of additional species and even rival the species richness of the tropical forests. Also, if we consider diversity in the broader taxonomic categories, then the greatest variety of life on Earth is undoubtedly to be found within the seas (Thorne-Miller and Cantena, 1991). One can even come across representatives of over a dozen basic classes or divisions in the same small space—a breadth of diversity that has no match on land (NAP, 1992).

The phylum Loricifera was first described in 1983 (Kristensen, 1983). An entirely new habitat has become known following the discovery of ocean vent systems. The bottom of the ocean is still virtually unexplored.

Above and beyond their tremendous commodity values, marine organisms are critical determinants of the structure and function of the global environment. Marine phytoplankton are the foundation of marine food chains. The interactions among marine biota, the Earth's geochemical cycles, and global climate change are just becoming known. The study of marine biodiversity is critical to understanding environmental dynamics on the global, regional, and local scales.

Use and abuse of species

Ecologists have mainly focused on 'species' diversity. However, the ecological use of 'species' has certain drawbacks; five aspects of within–species variation that reduce the reliability and usefulness of species as ecological units of diversity in studies of plant communities: genetic variability, phenotypic plasticity, ontogenetic diversity, gender diversity and environmental maternal effects. The species diversity of a region can be partly a function of the taxonomic flora used.

Simple numbers or lists of species, or indices based on the algorithmic manipulation of species relative abundances can underestimate the complexity of systems, and signify very different ecological circumstances, depending on the species within a particular system, their population sizes, life stages and environments (Wayne and Bazzaz, 1991). Some species–rich communities may be less ecologically diverse with respect to certain features than species–poor communities, yet this point is often overlooked by ecologists and conservationists. In studying the ecological and evolutionary processes regulating communities, such as disturbance, competition and mutualisms, it is desirable to explore and employ alternative classes of diversity.

Doubled Genes and Fish Diversity

A dive to the rainbow–hued denizens of a coral reef will reveal that the ray-finned fishes—which include everything from goldfish to sea horses—are the most diverse group of vertebrates. A recent study of the genome of the zebrafish may explain how the 25,000 or so ray–finned species came to evolve such diverse forms (Vogel, 1998).

In an early ancestor of the zebrafish—a common aquarium dweller and research model—the entire genome has doubled. The ray-finned fish seem to put their extra copies of genes to diverse uses and so have evolved a variety of different body shapes, for example, using an extra fin-bud gene to make the stinging fins of the lionfish 'mane'. The genome duplication also has implications for the zebrafish's role as a model research organism, perhaps allowing researchers to spot dual functions of genes that would be hard to discern in species that have only one copy.

The developmental genes called *Hox* genes control some of the earliest patterns in a developing embryo. Most vertebrates, including mammals, have four *Hox* clusters, suggesting that two genome duplications occurred since these lineages split from the invertebrates, which typically have only one *Hox* cluster. But after sequencing and mapping all the *Hox* genes to be found in zebrafish, it was found that the fish have seven *Hox* clusters on seven different chromosomes. Two clusters closely resemble the mammalian *Hoxa*, two resemble *Hoxb*, and two resemble *Hoxc*. Both mammals and fish have only a single copy of the *Hoxd* genes. Although zebrafish have two copies of the *Hoxd* chromosome, one is missing the *Hox* gene segment. It seems that the extra genes are not simply due to occasional gene duplications but stem from an event in which the entire genome was duplicated, with some genes then lost (Vogel, 1998).

Relationship Between Local and Regional Diversity

Caley and Schluter (1997) discussed the relationship between local and regional diversity (see Fig. 2–3) and concluded that local assemblages were not saturated with species. But their analysis of saturation was not accepted by Westoby (1998). He felt that this conclusion should not be generally adopted. Westoby (1998) criticized several aspects of the analysis of saturation made by Caley and Schluter: (1) the sizes of their local assemblages were too large to detect saturation; (2) they inappropriately combined different groups of organisms in their tests; and (3) an alternative method for detecting saturation based on species–area regressions is superior to their method, which used regressions of local on regional diversity. These criticisms were subsequently rebutted by Caley and Schluter.

According to Caley and Schluter (1998), there seems to exist an appropriate locality size for each taxon at which saturation occurs and where this saturation becomes blurred when surveys are conducted using smaller or larger localities. However, an increasing number of local–regional comparisons at a range of scales along the locality-size spectrum from a single oak tree to 25000 km^2 areas on a map suggests that local saturation can be elusive. Many processes can result in the number of species coexisting within any locality of arbitrary size being determined to a considerable extent by inputs from the surrounding region, and hence are determined partly by the diversity of that region. Absence of saturation does not imply that local processes have no impact on the local species assemblages—only that such processes place no hard limits on the number of species that may coexist locally. It appears that regional effects can be strong. Understanding the diversity of local assemblages requires that regional processes be considered (Caley and Schluter, 1998).

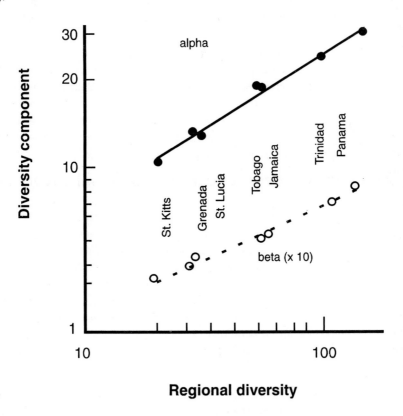

Fig. 2–3. Relationship of alpha diversity (average number of species per habitat) and beta diversity (1/average number of habitats per species) to regional (island) diversity in birds of the Caribbean area (after Schluter and Ricklefs, 1993).

Biodiversity and Body Size

Although biological diversity, population size and body size are interdependent, very little is known about the nature or causes of these relations. Siemann *et al.* (1996) analyzed a grassland insect community sample containing about 90,000 individuals of over 1000 species. Each taxonomic order had a distinct body size at which both species richness and number of individuals were highest, but these peak sizes varied more than 100–fold among five major orders. These results suggest that there may be fewer undiscovered small insect species than previously thought. They also found a strong and simple relation between species richness (S) and the number of individuals (I) within size classes, $S = I^{0.5}$. Because this held across numerous body types and a 100,000–fold body–size range, there may be a general rule that is independent of body size for the relations among interspecific resource division, abundance and diversity (Siemann *et al.*, 1996).

It is well known that local diversity results from the balance between immigration of new species and local extinction. Immigration rate depends on the number of species already present and dispersal ability, which usually depends on body size. Extinction rate depends on population abundances and their distribution, with rare species being more likely to become extinct as a result of population fluctuations. Because of this, S would be expected to depend on the I within a group of interacting species, here assumed to be species of similar body size, especially within taxonomic orders. The number of rare species also depends on the abundance distribution (for example, log–normal), as will the precise relation between S and I.

Global biodiversity based on currently described species is a unimodal function of body size. Some authors have proposed that actual global diversity may be highest at the smallest sizes, with small species greatly undersampled, representing many millions of undescribed species. The data obtained by Siemann *et al.* (1996) suggest that undescribed species may be of intermediate sizes within any taxonomic group, and this is supported by some studies of tropical forest canopy beetles. This seems to suggest that global biodiversity may be closer to the lower end of the estimate of 10–50 million species. However, if $S = I^{0.5}$ holds for nematodes, bacteria and viruses, it would suggest that these phenomenally abundant small–bodied taxa might constitute most of the Earth's diversity.

A few species can have great value for conservation, especially those called 'umbrellas' or 'flagships'. Consider a carnivore (e.g. wolf) that requires millions of acres of land to maintain a viable population. If sufficient wild habitat is secured for this large predator, many other less–demanding species flourish under the umbrella of protection. Often charismatic, umbrella species also function as flagships or symbols for major conservation efforts.

Animals and plants that are highly vulnerable to human activity usually have to be managed individually. Otherwise, biodiversity will continue to diminish with each extinction. Although the egalitarian notion is that all species are ultimately equal, at any given place and time some species thrive on human activity whereas others suffer. Declines in species numbers signal the fact that the environment is not healthy and vulnerable species are in need of intensive care beyond the immediate protection of their habitat.

Considerable global chemical biodiversity exists in the form of say, numerous secondary metabolites of various plants. Some species produce toxic compounds to limit the predation of predators. Other species detoxify or destroy the toxin which means that the species can live in a certain given area. The great chemical diversity of the living world is instrumental in restoring the availability of habitat for the functioning of diverse species of plants, animals and microbes.

Terrestrial ecosystems are greatly dependent on a high diversity of organisms for efficient functioning. In the aquatic world biodiversity is vital in maintaining the purity of water for multiple uses. It has been known for some decades now that a large number of species with fairly small populations characterize natural streams not significantly affected by pollution. These species represent several different groups of organisms. Patrick (1997) has shown that not only are the numbers of species typical of natural ecosystems fairly similar in streams that are quite different physically and chemically, but even the percentage of the total number of species in each stream that perform each of various functions (e.g. primary producers, detritivores, etc.) tend to be quite similar. Further, high diversity helps maintain the proper and balanced functioning of the ecosystem, which typically consists of four levels of nutrient and energy transfer (Fig. 2–4). Undoubtedly, biodiversity is very important in assuring a continued cycling of nutrients and energy in any ecosystem.

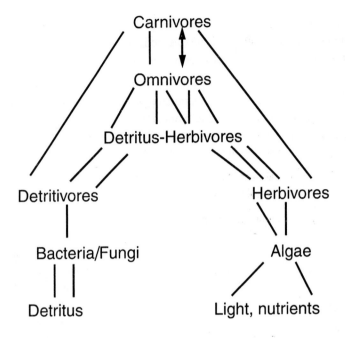

Fig. 2–4. Pathways of nutrient and energy transfer (after Patrick, 1997).

Estimation and Measurement

Biodiversity is the Earth's sum of genes, species and ecosystems. In less than a decade, it has become an important issue.

It is known that a rapid loss of species is under way, but the rate of loss cannot be directly measured. Indeed it is not even known how many species exist. The loss of genetic and habitat diversity cannot be precisely measured and its impact on development prospects are indirect and hard to quantify. Its root causes are complex and diverse: excessive resource consumption, population growth, economic inequities, and international debt. Not surprisingly, no 'magic bullet' solution (like banning ozone-destroying chemicals) exists for the biodiversity crisis (Reid, 1992).

Tropical deforestation is the crucible of today's species extinction crisis. About 17 million hectares of tropical forests are cleared annually. At this rate, at least 5–10% of tropical forest species face extinction in the next 30 years.

Temperate rain forest has shrunk as much as tropical forest has. Even where vast stands of temperate forest remain, much species-rich old-growth forest has been replaced by second-growth forest and plantations. Such other habitats as wetlands and mangrove swamps, tall grass prairles, and Central America's dry forests also have been reduced to mere remanents (Reid, 1992).

Based on the global area they occupy as compared to that of rain forests, coral reefs may well comprise about 600,000–950,000 total species (Reaka-Kudla, 1997).

Although the basic concepts in systematic biology underlying biodiversity studies are well established, the use of different properties to infer evolutionary relationships for different types of organisms leads to a situation wherein above the level of species, equivalence among taxonomic ranks for fungi, other eukaryotic microbes, plants and animals becomes poor. Within the microbial realm, the assignment of taxa to a particular species is generally meaningless. This renders systematic descriptions of biodiversity contentious in several cases. In particular the microbial world has been strongly affected by the impact of molecular approaches on systematics. It is being revealed that previously unknown microbial taxa may constitute significant components of the community biomass (Fuhrman *et al.*, 1993).

Comparisons of ribosomal RNA gene sequences and other molecular studies have revealed three primary lines of descent in evolution, viz. Eukarya, Bacteria and Archaea (Woese *et al.*, 1990; Kumar and Kumar, 1998). Fig. 2–5 shows an evolutionary tree based on similarities in small subunit rRNAs. The earliest diverging lineages in the eukaryotic subtree include diplomonads, microsporidians and trichomonads (Leipe *et al.*, 1993). These organisms are not typical eukaryotes and lack, e.g. mitochondria, typical golgi bodies, or complex cytoskeletons. These early lineages are followed by other independent branches of protists and later by the higher kingdoms of fungi, plants and animals, plus at least two complex evolutionary groups, called the stramenopiles and the alveolates (Sogin and Hinkle, 1997). The stramenopile group (Fig. 2–6) includes diatoms, oomycetes, labyrinthulids, brown algae and many chlorophyll–c containing chromophytes (excluding dinoflagellates, cryptomonads and haptophytes). Most stramenopiles are photosynthetic algae but others are non-pigmented heterotrophs that feed on micro-organisms. The bicocoecids (another class of stramenopiles) are thought

62

to consume as much as 10% of the marine prokaryotic biomass (Sogin and Hinkle, 1997).

The alveolates are equally interesting eukaryotic protists (dinoflagellates, ciliates and apicocomplexans). These three assemblages share some common features in respect of their rRNA and actin genes (Gajadhar et al., 1991). All three classes have alveoli—membranous structures found at the flagellar base.

Although stramenopiles include morphologically and biologically diverse organisms, all members have flagella with tripartite flagellar hairs that are not found in any other eukaryotes (Sogin and Hinkle, 1997).

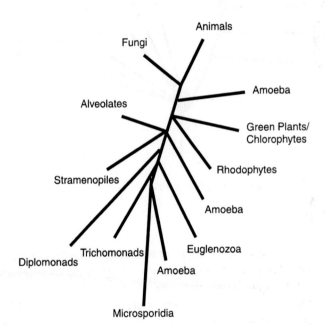

Fig. 2–5. An unrooted molecular phylogeny of eukaryotes, derived by computer–assisted use to align the 16S like rRNA sequences from 600 diverse eukaryotes. The length of segments indicates approx. extent of molecular change (after Sogin and Hinkle, 1997).

63

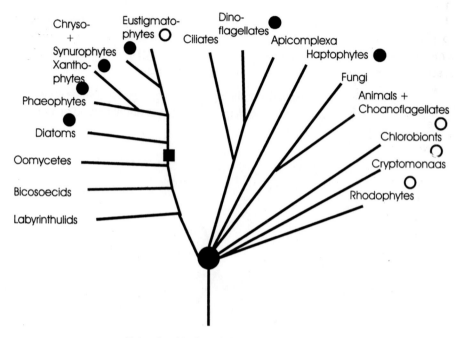

Chryso-
+
Synurophytes
Xantho-
phytes
Eustigmato-
phytes
Ciliates
Dino-
flagellates
Apicomplexa
Haptophytes
Phaeophytes
Fungi
Animals +
Choanoflagellates
Diatoms
Chlorobionts
Oomycetes
Cryptomonaas
Bicosoecids
Rhodophytes
Labyrinthulids

Heterotrophic flagellated ancestor

Fig. 2–6. Speculative sketch of stramenopile evolution, based on the rRNA framework. The last common ancestor to the crown groups was a biflagellated heterotroph with tubular mitochondrial cristae. The occurrence of chloroplasts with chlorophyll a and c is indicated by a shaded circle at the taxon's name. Other autotrophic groups are marked with an open circle. Square denotes some uncertain aspects (after Sogin and Hinkle, 1997).

For over two centuries, taxonomists have been describing species of insects at about 4400 per year and in the last 25 years or so, have described over 8700 ± 360 per year (Erwin, 1997). This published record nevertheless represents only about 3.5% of the species actually living on the planet. Recent estimates of insect species, mostly in tropical forests, point to the existence of at least 30 million species of insects, if not more (Erwin, 1982, 1997). This means terrestrial arthropod class constitutes over 95% of global biodiversity. Thus *Homo sapiens* aside, insects and their relatives (such as spiders, beetles, centipedes etc.) are the most dominant and important group of terrestrial organisms that affect life on Earth. Among the insects, beetles are the most speciose and the most pervasive throughout the world, particularly in tropical forests (Erwin, 1997). Indeed, beetles occur everywhere on Earth except in the deep sea. Over 400,000 species of Coleoptera have been described to date, comprising about 25% of all described species on Earth (see Table 2–6).

Neotropical beetles are second only to ants and flies (the latter in the wet season only) in numbers of free-ranging individuals of arthropods in the canopies and subcanopies of neotropical trees (termites are not usually free-ranging); Psocoptera come a distant third. However, per species, beetles are not abundant. Beetles participate in virtually all aspects of ecosystem processes—as predators, herbivores, folivores, detritivores, scavengers, fungivores, wood–eaters and grazers. They tunnel, mine and chew nearly every substrate. Some are ectoparasites, others are nest parasites, still others are subsocial, with adults participating in the raising of young.

Taxonomists have so far named and described about 1.4 to 1.6 million species (Stork, 1988, 1993; Hammond, 1992) (see Fig. 2–7). The precise number is highly uncertain, one of the reasons being the high level of synonyms in various taxa, e.g. insects (Table 2–7).

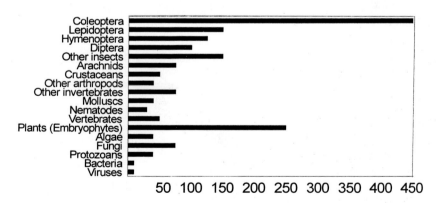

Fig. 2–7. Number of species (X10^3, approx.) described for all organisms (after Hammond, 1992; Stork, 1993).

Table 2–6. Some estimates of species of tropical/ subtropical canopy/subcanopy beetles by using insecticidal fogging techniques in selected countries (after Erwin, 1997)

Country	Approx. vol of foliage (m³)	No. of species	No. of specimens	Families	Density	Species/m³
New Guinea	2150	633	4840	54	2.25	0.29
Australia	4040	68	863	48	4.68	0.02
Panama	1065	1250	8500	60	7.99	1.17
Peru	2283	3429	15869	83	6.95	1.5
Brunei	2690	859	4000	61	0.42	0.32

Table 2–7. Present levels of synonymy in insects (after Gaston and Mound, 1993)

	Names		
	Total species	Currently accepted	Per cent synonymy
Odonata*	7,694	5,667	26
Isoptera	2,000	1,600	20
Thysanoptera	5,479	5,062	22
Homoptera			
Aleyrodidae	1,267	1,156	9
Aphididae	5,900	3,825	35
Siphonaptera	2,692	2,516	7
Diptera			
Simuliidae	1,800	1,460	19
Lepidoptera			
Noctuidae	35,473	28,175	21
Papilionidae and Pieridae*	9,075	1,792	80
Lycaenidae and Riodinidae*	13,108	5,757	56
Hesperiidae*	8,445	3,589	58
Hymenoptera			
Chalcidoidea	22,533	18,601	18

*Subspecific names are treated as synonyms.

66

The list of named species at risk is swelling. Worldwide, more than 700 extinctions of vertebrates, invertebrates and vascular plants have been recorded since 1600 (Reid and Miller, 1989).

Genetic diversity is also diminishing, as unique populations of wild species die out and variations within domesticated plant and animal species dwindle. Worldwide, some 492 genetically distinct populations of tree species are endangered (Fig. 2–8).

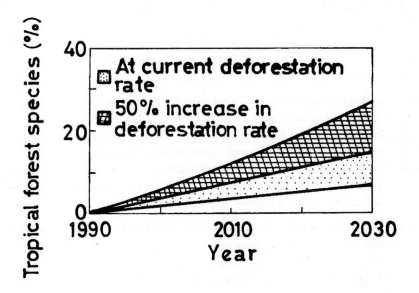

Fig. 2–8. Percentage of tropical forest species likely to become extinct.

The loss of species and ecosystems exacts a high price. There are grave risks in causing the extinction of species whose role in ecosystems we do not yet understand. The loss of wetlands, which provide such critical ecological services as flood control, fish production and pollutant assimilation is a direct economic cost as well as a threat to species survival.

Declining genetic diversity in agriculture can be very costly. In 1991, the genetic similarity of Brazil's orange trees opened the way for the worst outbreak of citrus canker ever recorded in the country. The Irish potato famine in 1846, the Soviet wheat crop loss in 1972, and the citrus canker outbreak in Florida in 1984 all stemmed from reduction in genetic diversity (Reid, 1992).

In many cases, extrapolation can be used to estimate biodiversity. Future biodiversity inventories need to be designed around the use of effective sampling and estimation procedures especially for 'hyperdiverse' groups of terrestrial organisms such as arthropods, nematodes, fungi and micro–organisms (Yoon, 1993; Colwell and Coddington, 1994). As far as terrestrial biodiversity is concerned, a fairly good idea for many groups of vertebrate animals, most plants and a few groups of showy insects can be developed by integrating biogeographic information from faunistic and floristic surveys with the taxon–focused work of systematists (Groombridge, 1992). But we have only a hazy and incomplete taxonomic and biogeographic knowledge for most other groups of terrestrial organisms, especially for 'hyperdiverse' terrestrial groups. Therefore, approximations have to be used to assess the richness, taxonomic diversity and geographic patterning of the hyperdiverse groups.

The task of estimating species–richness patterns from samples may be conveniently divided into estimating local species richness and estimating the distinctness, or complementarity, of species assemblages. These concepts are applicable to a variety of spatial, temporal and functional scales. Local richness is estimated by extrapolating species accumulation curves, fitting parametric distributions of relative abundance, or using non–parametric techniques based on the distribution of individuals among species or of species among samples (Colwell and Coddington, 1994).

Mere numbers of a species found at a site cannot be a quantitative measure of its biodiversity because not all species at a site, within and across systematic groups, contribute equally to its biodiversity (Heywood, 1994). May (1994) posed the question of the extent to which species numbers may measure biological diversity; according to him, both for evolutionary understanding and for practical applications, biodiversity may be better quantified at lower or higher levels, from genes to communities. At the evolutionary level, the intraspecific genetic variability enables a species to cope with old and new pathogens and environmental fluctuations. It is not clearly known how the long–term survival of many species may be influenced by recent and severe reduction in the sizes of their populations.

Some other levels in the context of biodiversity assessment include interpopulation diversity or races within a defined species, and hierarchy of taxonomic levels from genus to kingdom (May, 1994). Quantification of diversity at these distinct taxonomic levels is different from the hierarchy that ascends from species through communities to ecosystems. Thus, whereas taxonomic hierarchies generally emphasize evolutionary origins and relationships, often against long fossil records, species–community–

ecosystem hierarchies tend to emphasize contemporary ecological similarities and differences in various environmental and geographical settings, on much shorter time scales.

Harper and Hawksworth (1994) proposed the use of the adjectives 'genetic', 'organismal' and 'ecological' to describe biodiversity and feel that the terms 'community' or 'ecological' diversity are more accurate and appropriate than 'ecosystem' diversity in view of the fact that the ecosystem also includes the physical environment which does not have a biodiversity.

Now the question arises that if biodiversity is more than the number of species, how may it be measured?

Three possible approaches are described below.

(1) Taxic measures

Can the number of higher taxa (phyla, orders, families) be a more appropriate measure of the biodiversity in a site than the number of species? In marine environments the number of higher taxa is much greater than on land; whereas 13 animal phyla are known only from marine environments, only one is exclusively terrestrial. Less than 15% of all recorded species (various types of organisms) inhabit the marine realm, but the sea becomes more and more represented as we move to higher taxonomic levels, from genus to phylum. Indeed, at the level of phylum diversity is much greater in the sea (Fig. 2–9) (32 of 33 phyla in the sea, versus 12 of 33 on land, by one classification; or, at the level of class, 73 animal classes in the sea, 35 in fresh water and 33 on land) (Nicol, 1971).

Can the number of higher taxa be a convenient, quick estimator of the number of species in an area? In the neotropics only about 6.4% of the species belong to the approximately 40 exclusively or almost exclusively neotropical families (see Harper and Hawksworth, 1994). Greater attention is needed at the species level when assessing biodiversity for conservation planning. Also, complete counts of organisms are not practical and there is need for cheap and quick solutions.

For conserving those plant communities that could provide the richest diversity of pharmaceutical compounds, either family richness or endemic richness might be good candidates but species richness itself could be dangerously misleading (Harper and Hawksworth, 1994).

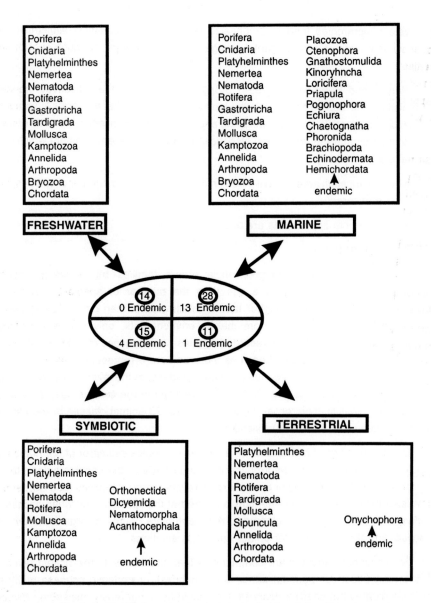

Fig. 2–9. Distribution of animal phyla by habitat (after Grassle *et al.*, 1991).

Some methods for estimating species richness for poorly known taxonomic groups or localities rely on ratios between known values of species richness to permit the estimation of unknown values (Hammond, 1992, 1994). However, one limitation of these methods is that they are based on the assumption that the relevant ratios remain approximately constant among the entities compared—and such as assumption may not always be valid.

Most 'ratio' methods of richness estimation rely on the naming of certain localities as 'reference' sites, at which collection or census methods are calibrated, 'indicator' taxa designated, or taxon ratios established, based on a supposedly known universe of species for one or more taxa. Then, at other sites (called 'comparative' sites), the denominator of some ratio is measured, and its numerator solved for, using a 'calibrated' value of the same ratio established at reference sites. Such an approach has its limitations. For example, the true species richness ratio between a relatively easily censused taxon, such as trees, and a more difficult taxon, say leaf beetles, often varies over an elevational transect, making extrapolations to other sites somewhat unreliable. Within limits, however, the method is certainly of some use as it can give some rough idea about unknown patterns of biodiversity. One may distinguish two types of taxon ratios, viz., hierarchical and non–hierarchical. The leaf beetle: tree ratio exemplifies the latter, as neither taxon contains the other. Non–hierarchical ratios make the most sense when some functional, ecological reason warrants that such a ratio might follow some consistent pattern (Gaston, 1992). Some examples of such ratios might be the ratio of herbivorous arthropods of particular taxa or of plant–associated fungi to their host plants, or the ratio of predator taxa, or the ratios among feeding guilds.

Hierarchical taxon ratios, combined with other ratios, have sometimes been used to estimate the global richness of insects. Such ratios may also be used to estimate local species richness and floral or faunal composition.

(2) Molecular measures

Biodiversity may be measured by using divergences in molecular characters, especially the percentage of either nucleic acid homology or base sequence differences. The DNA and RNA found in all living cells provide a basis for comparing diverse organisms. In a sense, the biodiversity of a community is expressed as the sum of the variety of genetic information coded within the genotypes of the inhabitants. Embley *et al.* (1994) have shown that the application of molecular technology to the study of biodiversity can destroy treasured icons. Some prokaryotic groups have proved so diverse at the molecular level, compared with eukaryotes, that new taxonomic hierarchies above the level of kingdom, e.g. 'domains', have had to be recognized properly to reflect the magnitude of their divergence (Harper and Hawksworth, 1994).

(3) Phylogenetic measures

Cladistics can be a measure of taxonomic distance or 'independent evolutionary history' (May, 1994; Faith, 1994). The approach is of special value for the conservation of target groups and in selecting areas appropriate for their conservation (Pressey et al., 1993). However, generating phylogenetic data for many taxa is a formidable task.

The concept of a species is not always identical in various groups of organisms. Although the 'biological species' is often considered a comparable entity across groups as diverse as insects and fungi (Claridge and Boddy, 1994), comparison does not stand when the different species are examined by molecular or phylogenetic methods. Further, how can a biological species concept be applied in groups that do not reproduce sexually?

Especially in bacteria, the species concept is highly conservative at the molecular level compared with most other groups of organisms. Different strains placed within the single bacterial species *Legionella pneumophila* have DNA hybridization homologies as different as those characteristic of the genetic distance between mammals and fishes (May, 1994).

The biological diversity of an area is usually much greater than the number of species present. Some other aspects of biodiversity are the number of trophic levels present, the number of guilds, the variety of life cycles and the diversity of biological resources. Certain keystone species make a greater contribution to overall species richness because they provide specialist resources for numerous other species (nesting sites, gall wasps, lepidoptera, mycorrhizal fungi, bark– and leaf–inhabiting fungi, pests and pathogens, microalgae, bryophytes and lichens). Trees usually contribute a wider range of biological resources to a site than do annual or herbaceous plants. The role of less obvious 'keystone' species, such as pollinating insects, mutualistic symbionts and population-regulating pathogens can also have effects on the biodiversity of a site (LaSalle and Gould, 1993).

Comprehensive biological inventories of selected sites are needed if full quantitative measures of biodiversity are to be used in making conservation decisions. There is need to find simple, objective ways of predicting where high biodiversity might occur.

72

The most challenging problems confront those persons interested in making any measure of biodiversity in the soil. There are sometimes more than 10^9 microbes per gram of soil. In the sea, microalgae may have average densities of 10^6 cells per litre. A 1-cm marine core can have 4×10^{10} bacterial cells (Embley *et al.*, 1994).

Several phylogenetic measures have been proposed to quantify distinctiveness that marks species of high conservation worth. However, distinctiveness of species and their numbers have different implications for conservation policy, depending on whether moral, aesthetic or utilitarian reasons are given weightage in relation to conservation. The utilitarian position values species according to increasing numbers, and as they are more, as opposed to less, distinctive. It is believed that conservation should seek to maximize the preserved information of the planet's biotas, best expressed in terms of genetic information held in genes and not in portions of the genome of uncertain or no function (Crozier, 1997). Gene number is thus an important component in assessing conservation value. Phylogenetic measures are better indicators of conservation worth than species richness, and measures using branch–lengths are better than procedures relying only on topology. Distance measures estimating the differences between genomes are preferable to substitution distances. Higher taxon richness appears to be a promising surrogate for branch–length measures. Complete enumeration of biotas in terms of phylogeny is desirable to avoid uncertainties in the use of indicator groups, and this can already be achieved for bacteria. Phylogenetic measures have proven important for management of sets of populations within species and are applicable for sets of species. Measures incorporating extinction probabilities and decision costs are now being developed. In conjunction with the use of confidence limits on the conservation worth of alternative reserves, these are crucial for conservation decision–making (Crozier, 1997).

Factors Involved in Species Diversity

Understanding the evolution of species diversity is central to any clear understanding of the natural world. However, this is not an easy task because the phenomenon operates over timescales many orders of magnitude greater than our own lifespans. Recently available phylogenetic information through the use of techniques of molecular biology has opened up new possibilities for statistical tests of hypotheses concerning the evolution of species richness in extant taxa (Mooers and Heard, 1997; Purvis, 1996).

It is well known that lineages vary in the number of species they have, either because of differences in the environment experienced by those lineages (Rosenzweig,

1995; Kerr and Packer 1997), or by mere chance variation in probabilities of speciation and extinction (Raup, 1985). Yet another possibility is that lineages may vary in respect of biological characters that affect the net rate of cladogenesis, either through an influence on speciation rate or extinction rate, or the equilibrium number of species a lineage can realize (Barraclough *et al.*, 1998). Thus it has been suggested that strong sexual selection by female choice can promote speciation and ultimately species richness (West-Eberhard, 1983). Species range size may also strongly affect extinction probability (Jablonski, 1987). These ideas can be tested by examining replicate evidence for an association between the trait of interest and species richness. A recent approach has been to compare sister groups differing in their expression of the trait in question. In fact sister-group comparison (see Table 2–8) is currently the best approach for identifying evolutionary correlates of species richness (Zeh *et al.*, 1989; Barraclough *et al.*, 1998).

As tests of sister-group comparison detect a correlation, it is not always possible to determine the direction of causation between species richness and the study variable, nor to entirely rule out the possibility of confounding variables. Secondly, the approach compares the net rate of cladogenesis between sister taxa and hence cannot show whether effects on speciation or extinction are the cause of any observed novel evidence for the role of several biological traits in promoting species richness (Barraclough *et al.*, 1998). Good examples of this point are found in some plant-feeding insects (Farrell *et al.*, 1991), sexual selection by female choice in birds (Lande, 1981; Mitra *et al.*, 1996), and rate of molecular evolution in birds and plants (Orr, 1995; Slatkin, 1996).

A few known examples of sister-group analyses in the context of the factors promoting species richness are summarized in Table 2–8.

There are four general dynamic happenings leading to today's patterns of species richness: (1) New species may arise through splitting of an ancestral species into two or more daughter species. (2) The geographical ranges of species change, either by contraction/expansion or by range movements. (3) Changes occur in the genotype and phenotype of species. (4) There is extinction. Interactions also occur among these four events. Species-level phylogenies can sometime be used by determining the relationship between geography and species splitting (modes of speciation) and studying the interaction between geography and phenotypic evolution (Barraclough *et al.*, 1998).

Table 2–8.   Selected sister–group analyses of correlates of species richness (after Barraclough *et al.*, 1998)

System	Subject area	Result
Insects and insect–plant relations	Phytophagy in insects	Positive
	Novel oviposition sites	Positive
	Resin/latex canals in plants	Positive
	Parasitic carnivory in insects	None
	Leaf–mining in insects	Negative
Sexual selection, breeding systems	Sexual dichromatism in passerines	Positive
	Nectar spurs in plants	Positive
	Promiscuity in birds	Positive
	Colonial breeding in birds	None
Miscellaneous	Rate of molecular evolution in plants	Positive
	Body size in carnivores/ primates	Negative/ None
	Dispersal ability and island endemism	Trade–off

Current Issues

Several temporal and spatial dimensions influence species diversity. A few of the processes that contribute to patterns of diversity are delinated below.

1. Competition and predation usually reduce diversity through the elimination of taxa (local extinction).

2. The movement of individuals between identical (habitat) patches points to the

importance of regional (external) processes and the transient nature of local populations, and hence the dynamic nature of the local community.

3. The dispersal of individuals between habitats (source–sink dynamics), is an indication of the mosaic nature of the ecological landscape and the interdependence of local and regional diversity due to migration between habitats. Species here flourish in habitats that are unproductive by immigration from more productive ones. Local diversity can reflect the variety and size of habitat patches within the larger region.

4. The spread of taxa within regions according to their habitat of origin and their subsequent ecological diversification is sometimes partly responsible for prevalent relationships between habitat and diversity. Taxa originate and diversify in some habitat types and through evolutionary change expand into other habitats.

5. Allopatric production of species within regions depends on the particular geographic habitats, which differ in influence according to the dispersal abilities and other properties of taxa.

6. The exchange of taxa between regions commonly depends on unique events and geographical patterns, e.g. those operating when barriers between major land masses or ocean basins break down or when habitats are displaced by global climate changes and glaciation.

7. Various kinds of unique events sometimes lead to extinctions that reduce diversity for periods long enough to require cladogenesis and biotic exchange for their recovery.

Hierarchical Indicators for Monitoring Changes in Biodiversity

Because biodiversity is highly complex and ever changing, it becomes very difficult for a conservation biologist or land manager to deal with this mess. However, the issue of complexity can be addressed by dissecting the biodiversity concept into meaningful components and yet retain some idea of how they all fit together. Any comprehensive approach to biodiversity conservation must consider it at multiple levels of organization and many different spatial and temporal scales. Biodiversity is hierarchical in structure, having genetic, population–species, community–ecosystem, and landscape levels.

Each of these levels can be further divided into compositional, structural and functional components (Fig. 2–10).

Some kinds of change threaten biodiversity. Climatic changes, changes in disturbance regimes, novel chemicals and species introductions or deletions are all natural changes likely to reduce native biodiversity, but usually occur faster with human activity. To protect biodiversity against the impact of these factors, it is necessary to have early warning of change; hence the need for monitoring (Noss, 1990).

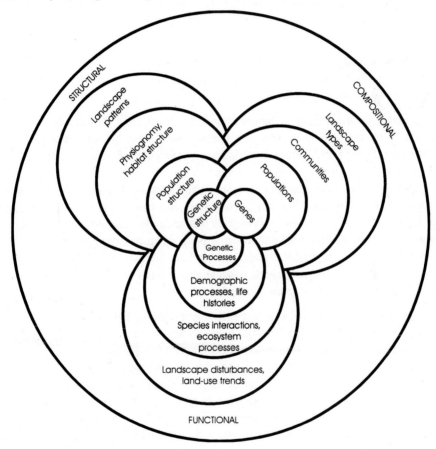

Fig. 2–10. Attributes of biodiversity at four levels of organization (after Noss, 1990).

Bioprospecting

Much recent interest has focused on 'biodiversity prospecting'—the exploration of biodiversity for commercial and biochemical resources—used for·screening biological material in niche-rich habitats for useful or novel compounds with potential for the development of new drugs. Such values can be quite high because of the profitable returns individual drugs can give. In contrast, agricultural values, for genes used in breeding programmes, although potentially enormous (in terms of production) and vital for future development, cannot be so easily appropriated or treated as intellectual property (Pistorius and Van Wijk, 1993).

Funding agencies such as the CGIAR system have a strong preference for *ex-situ* conservation, believing that *in-situ* conservation does not serve breeding efforts better than *ex-situ* (see Chapter 9).

A better understanding of farmer management of crop diversity is linked to sustainable means of disease and pest management. It is generally believed that landrace populations contain diverse resistance genes as inherent safeguards against epidemics. But we know very little about the function of diversity for disease and pest resistance in traditional agricultural systems (Wood and Lenné, 1993). Also, there is virtually no proper research on the identification and description of adaptive gene complexes, or on the way in which diversity is maintained by farmers (IPGRI, 1995). It is often found that *in-situ* conservation demands a much broader approach than the traditional *ex-situ* conservation strategy of landraces and wild relatives. The crucial issue is: How to link conservation and development? This can be possible only through the millions of farmers in various developing countries.

The consequence of the prevailing scientific dichotomy between *in–situ* and *ex–situ* conservation and the lack of linkage between conservation and development has been that most support for *in-situ* projects over the past two decades has come through the efforts made by nature conservation agencies, i.e., the biodiversity issue has taken precedence over the genetic resources issue. Sadly, however, many nature–conservation initiatives tend to neglect the human factor. A situation has developed in which forest preservation projects (whether or not protecting wild relatives) prevent sustainable use by small farmers and negate their historical role in maintaining wild relatives and landraces (for example through slash-and-burn practices) (Pistorius, 1997).

Tropical forests harbour a tremendous variety of living organisms and contain indeterminable amounts of biochemical compounds and biologically active substances. As per the provisions of the *Convention on Biological Diversity* (CBD), all rights concerning genetic and biochemical resources lie in the hands of the country of origin. The biological resources were previously deemed to be a heritage of humankind and freely available to anyone. Developing countries now have larger possibilities to economically exploit their natural potential, particularly among the pharmaceutical industries. It is essential to develop suitable mechanisms for an equitable distribution of the returns on bioprospecting. The biological resources of tropical forests have an enormous use potential because of their huge pool of biochemicals and active substances. New pharmaceutical and biochemical products are constantly being developed with active ingredients either obtained directly from forest plants or synthesized as copies of molecules found in nature. The identification of commercially exploitable substances in the flora and fauna of tropical forests is called bioprospecting and is carried out by random screening, i.e. large–scale and systematic analysis of a large number of samples, or by scientific investigation of selected extracts of species whose traditional uses are already known (Garcia-Brokhausen, 1997).

The vast variety of presently unknown macromolecules in tropical plants, insects, fungi, amphibian and reptile secretions and venoms raise the prospect that active substances may be found for the treatment of such diseases as cancer or AIDS.

The CBD laid stress on the concept of sustainable use of forest products (particularly non-timber forest products), sustainable tourism and bioprospecting. Also, because many traditional and local communities possess long experience in the use of biological resources, their indigenous knowledge should not only be documented, but also protected.

By and large, *in-situ* conservation work relates to areas of highest species diversity, most important for biodiversity conservation. Such a focus on 'climax diversity' can be explained by the growing public awareness to protect nature from man. However, interestingly none of the main food crops are associated with climax vegetation. So far, most *in-situ* management has been concerned with habitat preservation and has focused on ecological rather than genetic considerations. Appropriate conservation strategies and techniques for *in-situ* conservation of useful species are generally lacking.

Happily, this state of affairs is now being rectified and some incentives are becoming available for undertaking *in-situ* conservation projects.

The threatened biological diversity is now being seen in a new light because it has become the input of the new biotechnologies and the object of patent claims. Southern states and indigenous communities are asking compensation for their biological resources whereas Northern states demand intellectual property rights on biotechnologies and their products.

Historically, there has been the continuous leadership of Northern states in the appropriation of genetic and cultural information of Southern people but in recent decades, the structure of the corporations interested in genetic resources has seen some change. Companies having interests in seeds, chemicals and pharmaceuticals have tended to merge into larger and larger transnational corporations which have increasingly spread their operations in global markets. In keeping with the rising power of business, IPRs have been strengthened and sometimes extended to genetic material of plant, animal and human origin.

Never in history has agribusiness been so willing to compensate for the use of genetic resources of the South. Genetic material can be acquired as a normal good in commodity markets within the existing framework of IPP. This principle constitutes the main element of the *Convention of Biological Diversity*. It legitimizes the historical tradition of appropriation by the North of Southern treasures, and virtually completely ignores indigenous people or local communities. There is serious doubt whether farmers or indigenous people will benefit much from any prospecting payments.

The contribution made by many generations of farmers in selecting plants for higher productivity and better quality must be duly considered while reviewing applications for patents. Neither the classical nor the modern methods of plant breeding will prove useful in the absence of this solid foundation laid by traditional farmers following domestication of crop plants. It may even turn out that in the replacement of the concept of common heritage through national sovereignty and the institution of patents for improved plant varieties, hardly any country may really gain but world agriculture may be the loser.

Existing institutional and contractual arrangements fail to address the most contentious issues in the bioprospecting debate: on what legal theories and sources of law are claims to ownership or control of biological diversity justified? For instance, would establishment of commodity values for biological organisms lead to conservation or sustainable development?

Bioprospecting has also attracted criticism because of the negative developments it could trigger. An example: what will be the added costs for societies of developing countries when they sell the right to use their biodiversity? Thus, if the gene responsible for the high protein content in amaranth is introduced into rice, an increasing acreage of rice would mean the disappearance of the valuable crop amaranth. Losses of this kind could never be compensated by the payments received for bioprospecting.

In a nutshell, bioprospecting involves scientific utilization and commercial exploitation of plants and animals. The regulatory framework for bioprospecting includes access, protection and conservation of resources and sustainable use and ensures sharing of benefits among Indigenous Community/Indigenous People whereby traditional uses are allowed and Prior Informed Consent (PIC) is required. It aims to promote development of local capability in science and technology towards technological development and self–reliance.

Potential

As only one of about a thousand analyzed chemical compounds leads to a marketable product following laboratory and clinical investigations, it can take several years to develop a new product successfully. This limits the potential of bioprospecting. But the interest of the pharmaceutical industry in natural resources has increased in recent years because efficient and automated screening technologies now allow samples to be tested quickly.

Reputed drug companies such as *Boehringer Ingelheim, Ciba–Geigy* and *Monsanto* can screen thousands of samples in a year. Moreover, analyzing extracts from those animals and plants which are already being used in indigenous medicine is far more likely to prove rewarding.

Maintenance and Enhancement of Diversity

In view of the enormous number of species that inhabit the Earth it is not possible to maintain biodiversity by taking up one species at a time. One alternative option is using distributional data on large numbers of species to identify areas that would provide refuge for endangered species and also be a haven for the majority of species not yet at risk (Kareiva, 1993). The first results from such an examination made in the UK indicate that there may not be any shortcuts to biodiversity preservation.

All plans for the protection of biodiversity require large tracts of land to be protected from activities that cause species loss. There are limits to the area of land that can be set aside in reserves and selecting the 'best pieces' is crucial to effective conservation. Conservationists have emphasized two criteria for site selection: concentrations of species richness and the presence of rare or endangered species. The process could proceed remarkably well if concentrations of biodiversity for different taxa coincided, and even more so if such concentrations also overlapped regions with large numbers of rare species (Kareiva, 1993). However, the British work has shown that areas species–rich for one group were generally unlikely to coincide with the species–rich areas of other taxa; for example, bird and butterfly presence–or–absence data from over 2500 of the 10–km by 10–km quadrats revealed that less than 12% of the bird and butterfly hot spots coincided. Further, many rare species cannot be found in any diversity hot spots, which means that land acquisition aimed exclusively at maximizing the number of species on protected lands is likely to miss uncommon species which are the ones most likely to be threatened by habitat destruction (Kareiva, 1993).

Very little is really known about complex ecosystems. The focus in conservation biology has until now been mostly on how to save individual threatened species — an approach that ignores the broad diversity of organisms found in an ecosystem, all of which support such threatened animals as the panda or tiger (see Martin, 1995).

A variety of approaches to maintaining or enhancing biodiversity have been proposed since 1987 by various people (see Noss, 1994; Lautenschlager, 1997). The large number of approaches shows that there is no accepted best way. Indeed, according to Harms (1994), little hard data exist to show that these untested approaches really work. Nevertheless, specific direction for biodiversity conservation has been provided. This direction can be a starting point to identify best possible approaches, test them and implement appropriate management practices (Lautenschlager, 1997). What is needed is a clear statement and prioritization.

Lautenschlager (1997) identified some high priority areas for biodiversity conservation in Canada. These are summarized below (all the listed areas have almost equal priority).

1. Defining the productive capabilities of specific landscapes through time, and fixing economic and environmental values on potential alternative management choices.

2. Development of indicators or measures of social concerns enabling quantification of society's biodiversity goals.

3. Quantification of forest composition and structure following natural (e.g. fire, insects) and human-caused (cutting, agriculture, urbanization) disturbances and their suppression.

4. Comparison of impacts of various disturbance types on such ecosystem components as species, populations, communities, or landscapes.

5. Development of good predictive models of effects of disturbance (natural and human-caused) on biodiversity.

6. Identification of what biota should be measured and protected, and to ensure that the data are comparable and assembled into a database that can be integrated into other similar databases.

7. Development of efficient, multiscale techniques to assess biodiversity and threats to diversity (composition, structure and function), not just species.

8. Setting specific targets for landscape diversity that include age, class structure and forest type composition.

9. Determination of how specific management activities affect biodiversity and biota of interest at different scales.

10. Designing appropriate management systems that allow ecosystem-level aspects of biodiversity to be quantified at scales from many metres to many kilometres.

11. Identifying potential indicators of forest ecosystem health and suggesting whether and how the indicators apply at various spatial and temporal scales appropriate to the management unit (Lautenschlager, 1997).

Clearly, managing for biodiversity necessitates trade-offs. If the biologically, economically and socially important components and values are to be protected, importance itself needs to be defined, identified and prioritized objectively (Adams and Hairston, 1996).

Ecological Maintenance of Biodiversity

Over the millennia, biotic communities change dramatically, for instance from prairie to forest and back again. Over shorter periods, measured in decades or centuries, many communities tend to remain markedly stable. Since ecological processes maintain the integrity of communities, ecosystems, and landscapes, their conservation is essential for conserving biodiversity. Six interrelated categories of ecological processes must be understood in order to effectively conserve biodiversity: (1) energy flows, (2) nutrient cycles, (3) hydrologic cycles, (4) disturbance regimes, (5) equilibrium processes, and (6) feedback effects (Noss and Cooperrider, 1994).

Human actions very similar to natural disturbances are less likely to interfere with ecosystem function and threaten biodiversity than human actions that impose novel disturbance regimes on an ecosystem. Whereas several species and communities are fairly well adapted to periodic disturbance, seemingly natural disturbances can still have harmful effects. In particular, they may leave communities vulnerable to invasion by exotic species. Changing the frequency and intensity of disturbance can affect both natural diversity and susceptibility to invasion by exotics (Fig. 2–11; 2–12).

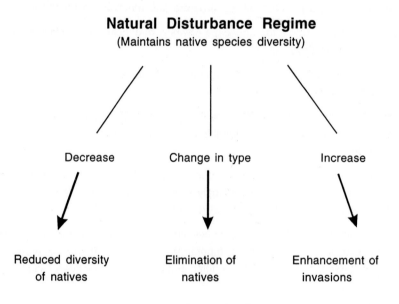

Natural Disturbance Regime
(Maintains native species diversity)

Decrease   Change in type   Increase

Reduced diversity   Elimination of   Enhancement of
of natives   natives   invasions

Fig. 2–11. Effect of change in the historical disturbance regime of an ecosystem on species composition.

84

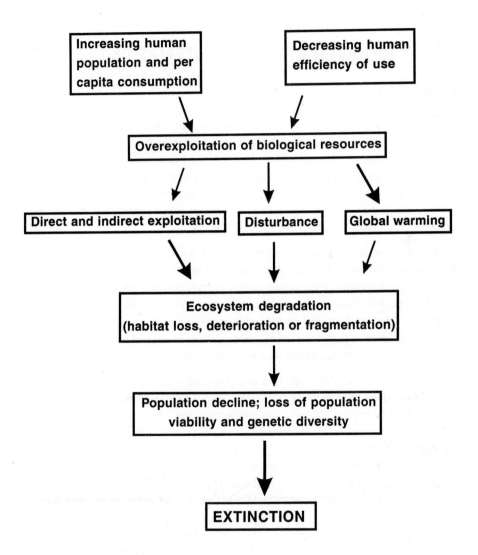

Fig. 2–12. Human influences and resource overexploitation leading to species extinctions.

85

Chapter 3
BIODIVERSITY AND SYSTEMATICS

Introduction

Systematics is undoubtedly central to understanding the extent and significance of the Earth's biological diversity. It is a discipline concerned with identification and description of the variety of species that constitute the building blocks of biodiversity; provision of a system for organising and communicating information about these building blocks; recognition of patterns concerning the distribution and relationships of different elements of this diversity; and construction of hypotheses about evolutionary history and processes in the natural world (Anonymous, 1991).

Some of the most interesting problems of systematics usually concern the nature and interpretation of variation within and between species. All-pervading variation is the characteristic that most obviously separates living organisms from non-living. This variation may be expressed in a combination of morphology, ecology, behaviour and biochemistry. Different biological species often coexist that do not differ obviously in structure or appearance to the human observer. Critical studies of behaviour, ecology and molecular biology are necessary to discriminate these.

Three major radiations of organisms would appear to account for the bulk of the Earth's species—insects, nematodes and fungi; recent estimates of the total numbers of insect species indicate a total of a few million, with the highest diversity in tropical forests; the diversity of free-living nematodes in benthic marine and freshwater habitats is very high, possibly rivalling that of insects in tropical forests (Fig. 3–1). Many ecologically dominant groups of organisms are poorly known even in temperate regions. Priority must be given to funding basic studies on the diversity of such organisms including particularly insects, nematodes, fungi, algae, and other micro-organisms. Until we understand the variety of these organisms, we cannot hope to develop sensible strategies for conservation (Anonymous, 1991). The need for a 'Taxonomic Budget' is genuine and pressing. Evaluation of the biota in critical habitats under different management regimes or under different forms of restoration (e.g. tropical forests) in one geographical region would be a major advance; provision of new systematic data on organisms of ecological and economic importance; development of more effective ways of accessing systematic and environmental information and hence establishment of conservation priorities.

It is indeed paradoxical that most of the taxonomic expertise and the major research institutes and reference collections are found in the temperate world, while biological diversity is much greater in the tropics than in temperate regions. This disparity underpins the need for technology and information transfer between the developed and developing world.

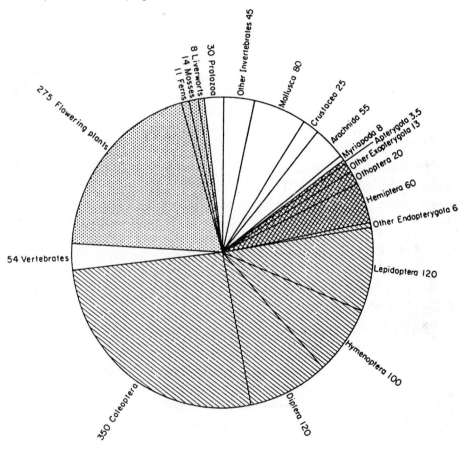

Fig. 3–1. The number of species in different taxa (excluding fungi, algae and microbes). Numbers denote thousands of species. Key to some of the terms (clockwise from Protozoa): Protozoa are single-celled animals. Other invertebrates are animals without a backbone, other than those represented in all the categories round to 'vertebrates'; Mollusca includes snails, mussels and squid; Crustacea includes crayfish, crabs,

barnacles; Arachnida includes spiders and scorpions; Myriapoda includes centipedes and millipedes; Apterygota are wingless insects; Other Exopterygota covers winged insects with incomplete metamorphosis other than Orthoptera and Hemiptera; Orthoptera includes locusts and stick insects; Hemiptera includes aphids and mealy bugs; Other Endopterygota covers insects with complete metamorphosis other than Lepidoptera, Hymenoptera, Diptera and Coleoptera; Lepidoptera are butterflies and moths; Hymenoptera includes ants, wasps and bees; Diptera are flies; Coleoptera are beetles; Vertebrates are animals with backbones, such as fish, amphibians, reptiles, birds and mammals; Liverworts are lower green, non-vascular plants (from The Components of Diversity, T.R.E. Southwood in *Diversity of Insect Faunas* L.A. Mound and N. Waloff (eds.), Blackwell, Oxford, 1978).

For bioprospecting, whether for natural products or genes, the skills of a field taxonomist are indispensable. The most important reason for this relates to the issue of re-collection. If an organism has yielded a natural product with interesting properties, the species must be identified and re-collected. Without an alpha taxonomist present, it is very likely that the wrong species may be re-collected. The skills of the field taxonomist are also valuable in order to collect related species and to avoid accidental re-collection of species of low value. Bioprospecting relies heavily on alpha taxonomy, as taxonomic identification using molecular biology methods is not a feasible option during a field collection tour.

In several fields, there are very few traditional taxonomists left; it appears that soon we may be left with no one capable of identifying species based on morphology.

As the description of species is extremely important in the search for novel pharmaceuticals and genes, there is need to focus on traditional taxonomy, which should complement, and not be replaced by, molecular biology methods. We should strive to achieve a renewal of interest in traditional taxonomy before it is too late.

One of the most unfortunate developments during the last few decades has been the tendency among younger biologists to look down upon taxonomy and systematics as old–fashioned disciplines without much scope in future. Some taxonomists have also developed a kind of inferiority complex and hesitate in letting their expertise be too widely known. The reason, of course, is prejudice against alpha taxonomy. Both at the level of academic research and at the post-graduate level, fewer and fewer courses on taxonomy are available.

Good taxonomy is fundamental to good biology. At the medical level, the routine identification of sub- or sero-types of *Salmonella* and *Listeria* in many laboratories is integral to halting outbreaks of diseases and saving many lives annually. A long–term vector–control program, which has already prevented almost 100,000 cases of river blindness in West Africa, is totally dependent on accurate identification of cytospecies of the vector blackfly (*Simulium damnosum*) and strains of the parasite filarial worm (*Onchocerca volvulus*). Characters routinely used for identification are revealed using chromosome staining, morphometrics, electrophoresis and DNA–blotting techniques (Harvey, 1991).

Natural ecological systems are so highly complex that it is extremely difficult to predict the impact of global environmental changes on ecosystem structure and function. In recent years, functional, rather than phylogenetic, classifications of organisms have been developed to simplify systems and better understand their dynamics. The demand for functional groupings of organisms has further increased since the emergence of global ecology. Ecologists are often asked to reduce biological diversity so as to extrapolate from the local scale to regional and global scales, but there has been no consistency in the application of functional groupings to current ecological studies.

The term 'functional type' is currently being used in two different ways in the literature (Smith *et al.*, 1997). One meaning focuses on species that respond in a similar way to environmental perturbations. The second usage groups together species having similar effects on ecosystem–level processes. Most American researchers often group species with respect to their ecosystem–level effects and many European workers are primarily addressing response groups.

The task of inventorying the Earth's biodiversity has been justfied by a need to catalogue species before they disappear and by the idea that inventories of species will help to conserve biodiversity (see Faith, 1993). However, there is some apprehension that biodiversity inventory may produce data of uneven quality and doubtful utility for conservation purposes, divert attention from more constructive approaches to conservation, and further weaken systematics and other collection–based inquiry as scientific endeavours (Renner and Ricklefs, 1994). There are two important issues here : (1) The contention that biodiversity inventories will make a significant contribution to solving the 'biodiversity crisis'. According to Renner and Ricklefs, lists of species have little intrinsic value and little relevance to the practical problems involved in conservation of natural areas; (2) The idea that museums and systematists are primarily 'service providers' to an outside user community. This attitude ignores the intellectual validity of systematics as a scientific discipline and will ultimately sap the vitality of systematics rather than revive it (Renner and Ricklefs, 1994; Ricklefs and Schluter, 1993).

Reference collections undoubtedly constitute an extremely valuable asset. In studies on diversity, cytology, plant chemistry, agriculture, forestry and medicine, herbaria are the most cost-effective method of encompassing variation. Because much research is dependent on reference collections, it depends even more on the advice of professional taxonomists. They cannot be substituted and the worth of their work is very often under-valued. The very infrastructure of good biology is being lost as an increasing number of research papers are based on inadequate, poor, or even defective taxonomy. The following three reasons underline the importance of taxonomy in the study of biodiversity: the increasingly appreciated importance of cladistics as a basis for biological classification; the emergence of molecular systematics; and the acknowledged importance of taxonomy to good conservation practice (Harvey, 1991).

The coming years are likely to witness more and better molecular phylogenies. In contrast, collecting samples and cataloguing life's diversity is likely to be a lesser enterprise the more it is delayed, simply because there will be less diversity to catalogue. Preserved specimens are often central to that enterprise. Good cataloguing also helps reduce the rate of extinctions. Taxonomic surveys identify geographic areas of high species diversity which can be used to help locate appropriate areas for conservation effort.

Keystone Species

The term 'keystone species' was coined by R. Paine three decades ago. The concept of keystone species has an important bearing in relation to predicting and preventing loss of biodiversity and ecosystem function. Some have attempted to explore whether potential keystone species could be identified before experimental confirmation, or their loss due to local extinction, by any distinguishing traits. According to the original definition, 'keystone' referred to a species that preferentially consumed and held in check another species that would otherwise dominate the system. The latter (target) species could be a competitive dominant, or coupled to a trophic cascade (e.g., sea-urchins suppressed by sea-otters). The interaction should be strong enough to mediate perceptible indirect effects in the community. Traits pointing to a potential keystone role for a consumer were preference for prey of high competitive ability and the ability to control this prey at all sizes so that the prey had no escape in size.

David Tilman (Univ. of Minnesota) defined 'keystone' in terms of the effect of a change in one species on some characteristic of its community or ecosystem, such as species richness, productivity or nutrient availability. The measure should reflect per capita or per unit biomass effects of the species and the total derivative of the change in the community (which reflects indirect as well as direct effects). The change should be measured after all important feedbacks have operated long enough. The term keystone should not be restricted to animals or a particular trophic level; however, consumers at higher trophic levels would be more likely to have larger per capita effects than plants; the latter usually have larger biomass.

Indicator Taxa

An innovative though controversial aspect of biodiversity that has received much attention is the use of indicator taxa (Landres et al., 1988). Critical studies on a small, representative part of the habitat can reveal patterns quickly and clearly (Pearson, 1994). Commonly, indicator taxa tend to be selected largely on non–scientific grounds. Rare and endangered taxa have become indicators because of legal compulsions, regardless of their scientific appropriateness. The general public focuses attention on the taxon itself rather than on what it might be indicating: habitat degradation, ecosystem decline or species distribution patterns (Pearson, 1994). Secondly, some taxa come to be termed indicators solely on the basis of familiarity with them through scientific research in other or related areas of interest, the choice being one of expedience only.

No single taxon can adequately represent or indicate patterns for all other species and taxa. However, the following biological criteria may prove desirable to maximize the generality of indicator organisms (Noss, 1990; Pearson and Cassola, 1992): (1) is taxonomically well known and stable so that populations can be reliably defined; (2) its biology and life history are well understood; limiting resources, enemies, physical tolerance, and all stages of the life cycle are known; (3) populations are readily surveyed and manipulated; (4) at the levels of species and subspecies, specialization of each population within a narrow habitat may make them sensitive to habitat change; and (5) there should be some indication that the patterns observed in the indicator taxon are also reflected in other related as well as unrelated taxa.

There are two broad approaches to fix the relative priorities of the above criteria. *Monitoring studies* evaluate changes in habitats or ecosystems over time, such as habitat degeneration (Kremen, 1992). High priority for potential indicators is placed on sensitivity to environmental changes. *Inventory studies* record the distributional patterns of taxa or ecological units over geographical space, usually for establishing conservation areas. Here high priority for potential indicators is placed on such aspects as endemism, co–occurrence, and centres of evolution (Erwin, 1991).

Among animals, vertebrates have usually been selected as indicator taxa or species of high public interest, but the current trend prefers arthropod species, especially insects and tiger beetles (Samways, 1990).

Pearson (1994) suggested the following criteria for selecting good indicator taxa:

1. Taxonomically well-known and stable.
2. Biology and general life history well understood.
3. Populations readily surveyed and manipulated.
4. Higher taxa occupy a breadth of habitats and a broad geographical range.
5. Specialization of each population within a narrow habitat.
6. Patterns observed in the indicator taxon reflected in other related and unrelated taxa.

He also proposed the introduction of an index. For the seven criteria listed below each potential indicator taxon may be tested and then given an index rating calculated from the number of criteria which could not be rejected. Criteria should be weighted on the basis of differential importance. For establishing a simple index, Pearson ranked the seven criteria with the least important criteria first and the most important last, for each of the two biodiversity research categories:

Monitoring

1. Economic potential
2. Occurs over a broad geographic range
3. Patterns of response reflected in other taxa
4. Biology and natural history well known
5. Easily observed and manipulated
6. Well–known and stable taxonomy
7. Specialization to habitat

Inventory

1. Economic potential

2.   Specialization to habitat

3.   Biology and natural history well known

4.   Occurs over a broad geographic range

5.   Patterns reflected in other taxa

6.   Easily observed and manipulated

7.   Well-known and stable taxonomy.

He also suggested a simple procedure of making a standard but flexible index. The rank numbers are added for all criteria tested and not rejected. In this case the seven criteria would have a potential maximum number of twenty–eight. The percentage of this maximum for the taxon being tested as an indicator would then be used to place it into one of four classes. For example, greater than 90% = class A; 75–89% = class B; 55–74% = class C; and less than 55% = class D. These seven criteria can also be supplemented with other criteria and ranked as special circumstances dictate.

Systematics, Biodiversity and Agriculture

The fabric of agriculture is woven and held together by the threads of systematics and biodiversity. Biodiversity itself is the grist for the agricultural mill — it provides the germplasm. Systematics is the explorer and describer of biological diversity. Agriculture is essentially the first user of the products of the interactions between systematics and biodiversity. The history of agriculture before (and since) the advent of the Green Revolution bears testimony to the above statement: agriculture strongly relied on an understanding of the biology of crops and other agricultural organisms because control strategies for insect pests, for instance, depended on knowledge of life histories — knowledge used to circumvent pest population increases.

Sadly, the most important organisms in agricultural systems are the ones that are the most poorly understood in the context of biodiversity and systematics, including fungi, nematodes, other microbes, helminths, insects and mites. Even for important pest species, superficial understanding of the group is a principal impediment to solving important problems in agriculture (Miller and Rossman, 1997).

Indeed, the agricultural community is now faced with a dilemma: it does advocate environmentally sound approaches such as biological control, sustainable agriculture, and pest management, but lacks a good knowledge of even the most common organisms that form the foundation for these approaches. Continuing destruction of natural ecosystems for new agricultural lands destroys the organisms upon which agriculture must depend for its future, for it is the seemingly less known or non–obvious ('less cuddly') organisms that may be the most important for the future of human existence.

Biological control is going to be more and more important in future pest control strategies. Bioengineering makes it possible to alter a pest organism so that it becomes beneficial rather than harmful (Freeman and Rodriguez, 1993). Development of pesticide–resistant natural enemies is another approach to biological control. Such strategies can prove more effective if they can make use of the genes of some of the countless natural enemies that currently exist in the pool of biological diversity, but are not known to science.

Sustainable Agriculture

Sustainable agriculture relies on comprehensive systematic knowledge of the organisms that occur in agroecosystems. Its aim is to maximize the use of exotic organisms and inorganic chemicals.

Many advances in our knowledge of plant germplasm of species of crops and the world's vascular plants have occurred but this knowledge is still quite incomplete. Plant taxonomists have discovered important but nondescript species of tomatoes and corn. These discoveries attest to the tremendous potential that plants hold for the future of agricultural crops. Much money has been invested in the tomato industry through increased levels of soluble solids derived from an inconspicuous species of Andean tomato, and disease resistance has been added to the genome of cultivated corn from a nearly extinct species discovered in Mexico (Iltis, 1988). With recent developments in genetic engineering, nearly any species of plant may potentially contribute genes of importance in enhancing agricultural crops.

Systematics as the Predictor of Biodiversity

Classification systems serve as a form of database from which certain predictions about organisms may be made. Quite often this predictability is viewed as an innate capacity of the human mind, but in reality it is part of the classification process. One example relates to recent research on the *Trichoderma*–like fungi used in biological control. A species previously placed in *Gliocladium* (*G. virens*) shares many characters with the genus *Trichoderma* and should be placed in the latter genus. The importance of this point stems from the fact that several species of *Trichoderma* contain mycotoxins

94

useful for the biological control of plant–pathogenic ascomycetes, but not basidiomycetes, as is the case for true species of *Gliocladium* (Rehner and Samuels, 1994). The sexual state of *T. virens* is *Hypocrea gelatinosa* or a closely related species, and it has been predicted that other closely related sexual states of *Hypocrea* will prove to be valuable agents of biological control similar to *T. virens*. In fact, quite high levels of mycotoxins have already been detected in some strains of *Hypocrea* (Miller and Rossman, 1997).

Another notable example is that of an anticancer compound detected in extracts of the Kenyan plant *Maytenus buchananii*. Because the species would be eliminated if further collections were made, a systematist was requested to provide information on related species. Based on the classification system of the genus, it could be predicted that *M. rothiana* in India would most likely have the desired compound. This prediction proved correct (Shands and Kirkbride, 1989).

Experts in biological control depend on the advice of systematists about where to look for natural enemies and about species most closely related to the pest concerned. For example, the sugar beet leafhopper, *Circulifer tenellus,* was originally placed in the South American genus *Eutettix*. Exploration for natural enemies in South America was unsuccessful. A systematist examined the species and placed it in *Circulifer,* which is of Old World origin. Natural enemies subsequently could be successfully located in the Mediterranean area (Rosen, 1977).

Being conspicuous and appealing, birds have attracted disproportionately high human notice and attention and so have played a prominent role in our knowledge of how species become rare, endangered and finally extinct.

Because species richness of birds is very high in tropical forests, the most prolific cause of endangerment and extinction in birds (and many other groups of organisms) is the destruction of tropical forests (Remsen, 1995). No doubt extinction occurs naturally also but human impact has increased its rate many times over background rates and therefore is the only significant cause of our current biodiversity crisis (Steadman, 1997).

Bibby *et al.* (1992) identified 2609 species of birds (27% of all living species) with breeding ranges of less than 50,000 km^2, designating these as 'restricted–range species' (RRS). Sets of these species tend to occur together on islands or in well–defined areas of a particular habitat, such as tropical or montane forests. An 'endemic bird area' (EBA) is any place where two or more RRS are sympatric. The 221 EBAs each contain 2–67 RRS. Many of the EBAs correspond with centres of endemism in other organisms; vascular EBAs and RRS are about evenly divided between islands and continents. The tropics have 76% of all EBAs and more than 90% of all RRS (Steadman, 1997). Indonesia boasts the most RRS (Tables 3–1, 3–2) because most islands there are unprotected. The EBA with the most RRS is the Solomon Islands, where none of the land is officially protected (Tables 3–1, 3–2). Of the 10 EBAs with the most RRS, only one has more than 15% of its land under protection. We are rapidly approaching the point of no return for numerous species (Steadman, 1997).

Humans cause the extinction of birds in four major ways: (1) direct predation; (2) introduction of non-native species; (3) spread of disease; and (4) habitat degradation or loss.

Animal Biodiversity

Although there is global concern over dwindling biological diversity, the diversity crucial for agriculture receives little attention. What little is given to agriculture, is mostly directed to food crops, and that too mainly to the 'starchy staples': cereals, roots and tubers. Animals, which help sustain local people and their integrated farming systems, are grossly neglected. Compared to crops, very little is known about the status of animal genetic diversity important to people's livelihoods, but it is definitely disappearing fast.

Pigs, cattle and poultry formed a world population of some 13 billion heads in 1990. This amounts to more than double the human population of the planet! Animals account for about 19% of the world's food basket directly, but they also provide draught power and fertilizer for crop production, especially in developing countries, raising their contribution to global agriculture to 25%. While there exist more than 40,000 species of vertebrates, less than 20 make a significant contribution to the world food supply, and of these 20, just a small number dominate global production. Much of the world's meat production comes from pigs, cattle and poultry, while the world's milk supply is almost entirely provided by cows. These data omit 'minor' species such as camel, rabbit and deer, as well as fish and game, which are vital at the local level. They also mask regional differences. In India, buffaloes contribute more milk than cows. And in China, 80% of the meat production is pork.

While some 70% of all cattle and 60% of all pigs and poultry occur in developing countries, only 30% of all milk and 40% of all meat is producd there. This is because in the developed countries, livestock production is highly intensive, concentrated, and based on a small number of superbreeds. Whereas in India only about 2–5% of all grain consumed is consumed by animals, in the USA this figure is as high as 70% (Anonymous, 1994).

96

Table 3–1. Ten countries with the most restricted–range species (RRS) of birds (after Bibby *et al.*, 1992)

Country	RRS			Endemic bird area
	Occurring	Confined	Threatened	
Indonesia	411	339	95	24
Peru	216	106	51	18
Brazil	201	112	67	19
Colombia	189	61	51	14
Papua New Guinea	172	82	18	12
Ecuador	159	32	38	11
Venezuela	120	40	17	8
Philippines	111	106	36	9
Mexico	102	59	23	14
Solomon Islands	96	43	16	4

Table 3–2. Ten endemic bird areas (EBA) with the most restricted–range species (RRS) of birds (after Bibby *et al.*, 1992)

EBA (some tropical forest)	RRS			Land Area (10^3 km^2)	% Land Area Protected
	Occurring	Confined	Threatened		
Pacific Islands, Indonesia	41–67	23–42	2–10	180	Up to
Central America (Costa Rican and Panamanian highlands)	54	51	2	27	10–15
South America	41–51	35–44	up to 23	170	Up to 70

97

Rather than being simply milk and meat machines, farm animals also provide other important services such as traction, fertilizer, soil management, pest control, fuel, and clothing. On many farms, animals make a major contribution to crop production and energy supplies in the form of manure. Dung and urine enhance the fertility of soil and contribute to plant nutrition; dung is also used as fuel. Not only can animals plough the fields, they can also transport water and fuel to the home, goods to and from markets, fertilizer to the fields and crops to the granary. While some animals such as rats and goats, can be veritable pests themselves, destroying crops with voracious appetites, chickens and ducks can be excellent assistants in pest control strategies. Deployed in the field, they feed on weeds, insects, snails, larvae and other threats to crop production (Anonymous, 1994).

People depend on wild animals for many of the same purposes. Wild animals which can be hunted or trapped provide food, skins, bone and a source of income. Most of the aquatic foods in developing countries (fish, shrimp, crabs, frogs and snails) are wild or semiwild, whether they are farmed or caught.

The domestication of animals started over 11,000 years ago. Goats and sheep were probably the first animals to be tamed, followed by pigs and cattle, in today's Near East. As in the case of plants, most of domesticated animals have originated in developing countries. Chickens come from SE Asia, turkeys from Latin America, and buffaloes from India. Several 'minor' species such as guinea pigs, yaks, musk oxen, as well as miscellaneous fowl and small ruminants also originated in the developing countries.

Despite our overall dependency on a limited number of animal species for global production, farmers have developed much diversity among them, so we have different breeds of animals. For example, Chinese farmers have bred the rare 'Taihu' pig, which can use a very high portion of forage foods in its diet, reaches sexual maturity in 9 weeks, and produces an average litter of 16 piglets! Asians have so far developed more than 140 different breeds of pigs!

In most developing countries, pedigree breeding for uniformity has never been used hence a genetically diverse population of many millions of cattle in northern India goes by the general name of 'Haryana', while the difference between a Holstein cow and Red Holstein cow in northern Europe is traceable to one single recessive gene. Thus when one talks about the diversity of European livestock, one refers to the number of visually different beeds developed, not necessarily to the extent of genetic diversity they contain.

No doubt, the intensive livestock breeding in the North has helped to develop numerous different breeds, but it has also sowed the seeds of diversity's destruction worldwide. Certain 'superior' breeds have been favoured or selected over lesser ones, mainly in respect of higher yields or productivities. The industrialization of farming practices and new technologies for breeding are causing much impoverishment of animal genetic diversity. About one-half of the breeds that existed at the beginning of the century in Europe have become extinct. One-third of the remaining 770 breeds are in danger of disappearing over the next two decades. The Friesian breed now constitutes 60% of the dairy cattle community in the European Union, having gradually replaced other breeds over the past few decades. Agricultural practices promote intensified livestock production systems, wherein animals are reared inside special buildings and forced to produce higher yields through a combination of genetics and management practices. Compared with a few decades ago, the average dairy cow in the United States produces over twice as much milk. Industrial turkeys have been bred for such a wide breast that they cannot mate naturally any more. Artificial insemination and the use of frozen embryos means that one elite bull can fertilize many cows without ever seeing even one of them. Superovulation makes it possible to raise numerous offspring from a single cow.

Intensification of animal production and the new reproductive technologies undoubtedly pose a serious threat to indigenous livestock breeds worldwide. The high productivity from superstocks has prompted developing countries to import exotic temperate breeds. These strains are crossed with indigenous breeds. Frozen sperm and embryos are being flown from Europe and the USA to all corners of the South in the name of improving stocks. Unless regulated, the new biotechnologies that allow massive shipments of embryos can prove disastrous for indigenous breeds everywhere. The replacement of indigenous breeds by such embryos means the loss of important genetic adaptations to unique local conditions.

The loss of traditional breeds not only threatens agriculture but also people's security. With increasing environmental degradation and the need to develop sustainable and integrated agriculture, the role of traditional herds becomes vital for the future. Currently, too few suitable programmes are underway to inventory, assess, conserve and develop animal genetic diversity, which is so important for local people's livelihoods. Unlike crop genetic resources, national programmes in the animal sector are very few indeed. The FAO has recently launched a programme for the global conservation of animal genetic resources with the objective of producing an inventory of those resources, to identify breeds at risk of extinction, and to promote conservation and breeding programmes in the Third World. Like plants, animal genetic diversity can also be protected in the form of live populations (*in-situ*) or stored genetic material (*ex–situ*). NGOs tend to champion the first approach, while most governments focus on sperm banks and frozen embryos. Despite the fact that all our livestock were domesticated by rural folk in the South, FAO estimates that a full 85% of all foetal populations of livestock breeds being stored under *ex-situ* conditions today are housed in or controlled by the industrialized North.

There is more to it than just saving breeds or genes. Conservation must be linked to sustainable utilization. There is a need for decentralized and integrated farmer–based conservation and breeding programmes.

Continuing advances in biotechnology and the application of intellectual property rights to animals will exacerbate the threats to diversity on the farm, in the pond and in the forest. There is need for international policy-makers to give more attention to the animal sector and better support to local initiatives for conservation and use of indigenous breeds.

Birds contribute significantly to the diversity of terrestrial vertebrates. They have a special role in conservation as they help identify suitable areas worth saving. As with other groups of organisms, the chief problem in conserving avian fauna is the paucity of habitats as these are under constant pressure from increasing human populations. Several habitats have totally disappeared whereas some others have become fragmented or patchy, especially in the tropical world. But the various patches are interacting elements in the large matrix of the terrestrial landscape and hence can be of help in conservation efforts.

The Western Ghats area in India has complex, patchy landscapes ranging from wet montane grasslands through a variety of forests to dry rocky scrub, all being interspersed with wetlands and streams forming a mosaic of corridors and patches (Daniels, 1994). These Ghats have over 500 species of birds, some of them quite rare and facing extinction. The Uttar Kannada District in Karnataka has small populations of such rare birds as the Ceylon frogmouth, Wynaad laughing thrush, the great India hornbill, the rufous-bellied hawk-eagle and the Nilgiri wood pigeon (Daniels, 1994).

As a class, birds have acquired a high degree of feeding adaptations for diverse food niches. *Columba* and *Streptopelia* are ground feeders and mainly grain eaters. *Treron* and *Ducula* are almost exclusively fruit eaters. While *Columba* and *Streptopelia*

Table 3–3.   Bird damage to some crops and fruits in India (after Dhindsa and Saini, 1994)

Crop/fruit	Birds	Approx. damage (%)
Crop		
Groundnut	Crows	24
Maize	Parakeets, crows, doves, babblers	20
Mustard	Parakeets	63
Pearl millet	Sparrows, parakeets, weaverbirds	10–100
Peas	Pigeons	54
Pulses	Doves, pigeons, parakeets, sparrows	66
Rice	Weaverbirds, sparrows, munias, parakeets, sarus cranes	26–41
Sunflower	Crows, parakeets	22–65
Wheat	Crows	17–20
Fruits		
Guava	Parakeets	20
Peach	Parakeets, crows	32
Grapes	Munias	12

have jaws adapted for ground-pecking, *Treron* and *Ducula* have a wide gape and stronger grasp of their bill for plucking, grasping and swallowing large fruits. Agroecosystems provide three kinds of food for birds: (1) grain, seeds and fruits, (2) green vegetation of crop plants and grasses; and (3) insects, rodents and other small animals found in the soil, crops and other plants. Many bird species benefit agriculture by controlling insect and rodent pests.   But some granivorous species harm crops (Table 3–3). Bird management involves both the conservation of useful species and control of pests.   Of some 1200 species of birds found in India, only 25 are known to damage crops and fruits (Dhindsa and Saini, 1994). Subramanya (1994) found that weaverbirds and munias preferred rice fields having greater vegetation complexity, not based on the resource status. Within a given area, the concentration of feeding birds was greater nearest the vegetal cover and declined non-linearly with increasing distance. Certain morphological and inflorescence characters of the rice plant predisposed particular varieties for intense grain predation by birds. In the parakeet–sunflower system, the extent of damage among plants within a field was closely related to the parakeet foraging pattern. Selective feeding on sunflower plants appeared to be governed by the predator vigilance pattern: parakeets preferred to feed on plants that offered better field of view. Subramanya concluded that the pattern of bird pest foraging observed by him in agroecosystems is non–random and depends on factors conducive to predator avoidance behaviour and not on resource utilization.

Trade in Wildlife

The world market for wildlife is worth at least US $5 billion and includes orchids, primates, ivory from African elephants; wild birds; reptile skins; furbearers; tropical fish and other items as diverse as kangaroo leather and tortoise shell trinkets (see Table 3–4).

Products from wildlife are usually sold as luxury goods, such as fur coats and reptile–skin accessories or as pets. The glandular scent from the Himalayan musk deer is worth four times its weight in gold. Extremely rare giant pitcher plants from Borneo are sold for US $1000 each. Rare Peruvian butterflies may retail for US $3000 a piece and horn from endangered Asian rhinoceros costs over US $25,000 per kilogram in Taiwan.

Some 40% of all vertebrates that now face extinction do so largely because they are hunted by human beings for trade. Already, the list of species that have disappeared as a result of human exploitation includes *inter alia* Steller's sea-cow, the West Indian monk seal, the Great Auk, the sea–mink and the passenger pigeon. Many other species, such as rhinoceros, sea-turtles, macaws and certain cacti are threatened by unsustainable exploitation for international markets. At least two of the three chimpanzee sub species in Africa are threatened by dwindling habitats; losses to trade may tip the balance towards extinction. Similarly, black market demands in some parts of the world encourage hunters to kill tigers, jaguars, grizzly and black bears, saltwater crocodiles and other species that are already subjected to other pressures from human activities. Commercial hunters and collectors frequently kill or remove these and other species with little regard for how many individuals can be replaced through natural reproduction.

Uncontrolled wildlife trade can have serious ecological consequences. Once a

Table 3–4.   Reported trade in wildlife and wildlife products

		Africa	Asia	Europe	Americas	World
Mammals (in thousands)						
Live	I		7	15	17	42
Primates	E	7.8	22	3	8.8	43
Cat	I	6.7	7	116	44	175
Skins	E	7.7	60	15	90.4	179
Raw	I	14.2	505	133	27	679
Ivory (kg)	E	303.7	280	134	2	720
Birds (in thousands)						
Live	I	13.2	67	196	328	606
Parrots	E	160.3	89	55	301	607
Reptiles (in thousands)						
Reptile	I	3.4	2480	3908	2516	8910
Skins	E	359.7	4198	1539	2830	8953

I = Imports., E = Exports., Source : World Resources Institute.

species is eliminated, natural food chains and delicate predator–prey relationships may be upset. For example, in Bangladesh and Indonesia, malaria infestation has been partly attributed to annual harvests of some 250 million bullfrogs–natural insect predators— for the frog–leg trade.

Biodiversity of Micro–organisms

The tremendous richness of microbial diversity — much of it unexplored —.stems from the genetic constitution of these organisms, the environment in which they are found, and ecological interactions with other components of the biosphere.

Micro–organisms inhabit virtually every ecological niche in the biosphere. In view of their small size, direct observations of species diversity of micro-organisms in natural environments are very difficult except in cases of an unusual abundance of a single species, producing a characteristic texture of growth (e.g., that found in geothermal springs). But new biotechnological methods are revealing a vast, hitherto unknown world of microbial life that has tremendous ecological and medical importance.

Bacteria show much diversity in size and morphology. Some have coccoid, spherical or short, rod–shaped cells. Many species of bacteria have unusual shapes and forms (e.g., helical, coiled, triangulate etc.). Others show unusual biochemical and biomechanical properties, such as the magnetotactic bacteria, which possess intracellular magnetic particles allowing the cells to orient to the Earth's magnetic poles. Only a few bacterial species can be grown easily in culture, the vast majority are not easily cultured. This means that we have no idea of the true morphological and functional diversity of all micro–organisms found on earth (Hawksworth and Colwell, 1992).

Viruses are intracellular parasites containing only one type of nucleic acid, either RNA or DNA, and usually a protein coat. They rely on their host cell to provide part or all of the materials for replication and expression of the viral genetic information. Unlike host cell genetic elements, however, some viruses also can exist functionally as extracellular particles (as seen in the viruses that attack bacteria). Although these viruses are capable of surviving for long periods of time in the external environment, their ecology and reproduction is dependent on their host. Viruses are much more common and ecologically important than believed hitherto. Recent researches indicate that there are more viruses than bacteria in the open ocean. Many of these viruses attack and control bacteria, and some control algal abundance as well.

Surprisingly, only some 3000–4000 species of bacteria have been described so far but it has been estimated that there may be as many as 300,000 species or even 3,000,000. The number of species of viruses has been estimated to be approximately 5000 but only about 500 have been described (Colwell, 1997).

About 17% of known species of fungi have been cultured, but less than 1% of these cultures are available in the world's culture collections; described species represent only 1–3% of the total estimated species of fungi (Colwell, 1997; Hawksworth and Colwell, 1992).

Microbial biodiversity represents the foundation of a sustainable biosphere and is fundamental to sustainable agriculture. The activities of micro-organisms, in the aggregate, and the diversity of species, most of which still remain undescribed, provide a rich source of genetic variation for application to biotechnology (Colwell, 1997). Micro–organisms act as sanitary inspectors of the planet and are useful in restoring habitats to a functional ecological state because they can degrade pollutant compounds, purifying water and soil in the process. Genetically engineering micro-organisms to degrade toxic compounds more effectively holds great promise for bioremediation and biorestoration in future.

Microbial diversity has contributed greatly to biotechnology. But the full potential is not realized in the absence of a full understanding of microbial diversity and microbial interactions. Microbial diversity is a significant component of overall biological diversity and has a major role in maintaining human health and sustaining a healthy environment. In any prospective search for compounds of medical or agricultural value, the microbiological resources that remain to be discovered are going to enrich the lives of the human race, and will reveal the intricate interlocking mechanisms of biodiversity that underlie the well–being of humans and the balance of our biosphere (Colwell, 1997).

Many museums have collected data on numerous species but rather neglected micro–organisms. To date, fewer than 1% of the world's micro–organisms have been identified and described (Hawksworth and Kalin–Arroyo, 1995). To ensure a comprehensive collection of data on biological diversity the taxonomy of micro–organisms must be given greater attention.

In any survey of biodiversity, the smaller micro–organisms can be easily overlooked. A striking example of this is illustrated by the recent discovery of abundance of archaebacteria (Archaea) in oceanic picoplankton not only in the cold surface waters of the Antarctica, but also in deeper waters elsewhere (DeLong et al., 1994). This is surprising as the Archaea were thought until recently to occur only in hostile environments, such as acidic hot springs and saturated brines.

Micro–organisms play an integral and often unique role in the functioning of ecosystems and in maintaining a sustainable biosphere. Indeed, micro–organisms play a very critical role in the continued existence of life–sustaining transformations of matter in both terrestrial and aquatic environments. Virtually all biological processes in the environment either directly or indirectly involve micro-organisms but the potential benefits of regulating, optimizing and exploiting microbial activity have not been well explored.

Genetic diversity in micro-organisms is much broader than that of higher organisms and it is not practical to catalogue and preserve, ex-situ, significant proportions of the diversity except from the simplest of natural habitats.

The extent of microbial diversity has not been adequately characterized and there is a broad mismatch between knowledge of that diversity and its importance in both ecosystem processes and economic development (Zedan, 1993). Microbial ecologists working on natural communities face unique challenges posed by, for instance: (i) the extremely large number of individuals per sample; (ii) differentiating between different populations and the very high diversity at a relatively small scale (Klug and Tiedje, 1994); and (iii) the difficulty of defining and delimiting a bacterial, cyanobacterial or fungal (Claridge and Boddy, 1994) species as the species concepts in microbes are often at variance from those in larger organisms (O'Donnell *et al.*, 1994).

Traditionally, bacterial species have been distinguished by some simple observable features or their phenotypic signatures. In practice, taxonomists working on different groups of organisms use different criteria for delineating taxa. Good recent examples are the treatments of the families Bacillaceae and Enterobacteriaceae; the organisms in the first group are markedly underspeciated (Rainey *et al.*, 1994) whereas in the latter, different generic designations are preserved for bacteria related at the species level.

For cyanobacteria also, some taxonomists have tended to be 'lumpers' and others to be 'splitters'.

The genetic concept of species has contributed nothing towards a better definition of bacterial species. Most examples of horizontal gene transfer come from members of three genera which have a special capacity for the uptake and chromosomal incorporation of DNA. Naturally transformable bacteria are exemplified by *Bacillus, Streptococcus* and *Haemophilus.* Even bacteria which differ in DNA sequence by as much as 20% often exchange chromosomal DNA (Maynard Smith *et al.*, 1991). Whereas certain phages and plasmids have a broad host range, others only mediate transfer between closely related strains or are even species specific (Harwood, 1993). Other plasmids are highly promiscuous in their conjugal transfer.

For fungi also the concept of species is quite unsatisfactory. As with bacteria, approaches have not been consistent across different groups of fungi. Whereas carbohydrate assimilation tests and abilities to grow on particular media are used and accepted in yeasts, host range is of paramount importance in rust fungi (even in the absence of inoculation experiments), and secondary metabolites are given more importance in some lichen-forming fungi. In *Aspergilli,* spore ornamentation at the scanning electron microscopy level has been emphasized.

A currently fashionable approach is to define a species in terms of its 16S rRNA sequences (Li *et al.*, 1994). The application of this technique has great potential in increasing our understanding of the relationships amongst micro-organisms above the genus level but is not without problems in defining species (Kurtzman and Robnett, 1994).

In assessing biodiversity for inventorying purposes, the main challenge is how to quantify the microbial diversity of a given habitat or host. In the case of soil, the highly complex relationships between the environmental niches present and their micro-organisms result in grave problems in defining habitat limits, as soil is in fact a matrix of solid, liquid and gaseous components interacting with the soil biota to provide a fluctuating and dynamic system. Microbial populations of soils vary spatially and temporally according to factors such as the nature of the soil parent material; the availability of carbon sources; seasonal and diurnal variations in temperature, porosity and water–holding capacity; and changes in electrolyte concentration, pH, redox and oxygen availability (Lee, 1991). In the face of such complexity, the reliability of diversity estimates based on species concepts derived from taxonomic analyses of laboratory–grown cultures is patently questionable.

Use has recently been made of the polymerase chain reaction (PCR) technology to amplify 16S rRNA genes so that with amplification, primers of different specificity, different levels in the taxonomic hierarchy, from kingdom to genus or species, may be targeted. The PCR and cloning techniques have potential use in the quantification of not only 'species richness' but also 'taxonomic diversity', and they offer a promising and potent approach to the quantification of diversity in natural habitats.

Molecular methods based on 16S–rRNA are being used to analyze micro-organisms that grow in hot spring habitats but resist cultivation in laboratories. These methods may help reveal the high diversity of these micro-organisms in nature.

Prominent cyanobacterial mats are found in some alkaline siliceous hot springs. Analyses of 16S–rRNA sequences from such habitats has revealed that the diversity of uncultivated prokaryotes within such microbial communities is truly remarkable. This means that the estimates of diversity among the cyanobacteria must be moved upwards.

A decade ago, when researchers observed a single morphotype microscopically and could cultivate only a single genotype by standard methods, they reported that a single *Synechococcus* species made up these mats. But now at least 10 distinct cyanobacterial 16S rRNA sequences can be detected in a single mat, and their genetic diversity rivals that found among all cyanobacteria (Ward, 1998).

Culture and molecular methods give such different ideas of community composition largely because readily cultivated bacteria are 'lab weeds,'; hence it is necessary to find how to exclude them in order to cultivate predominant species which are more difficult to grow.

Patterns of distribution of specific 16S rRNA sequences along environmental gradients highlight the relationship between 16S rRNA sequence diversity and organismic diversity, and suggest that bacteria obey ecological and evolutionary rules applicable to all species. For example, both cyanobacteria and green non–sulphur bacteria inhabiting the mat appear to have undergone evolutionary radiations, much like Darwin's Galapagos finches, with species adapted differently to temperature and light. It appears that even diversity measurements based on 16S rRNA sequences also underestimate microbial species diversity.

According to M. Kuhl of Bremen (Germany), species diversity is important in stabilizing guild activities within the community, and that cyanobacteria that coexist in the mat are adapted to different temperatures. These cyanobacteria reduce the sensitivity of oxygenic photosynthesis, the guild activity to which they contribute and to temperature fluctuation (Ward, 1998).

Termites as Sources of Novel Organisms

So far, relatively few micro–organisms have been isolated from termite guts but this situation is likely to change soon in view of the immense potential of biodiversity represented by over 2000 termite species, with their large spectrum of feeding habits and intestinal diversification (Mackie and White, 1997; Brune, 1998). The termite–gut microbiota makes available depolymerizing enzymes for the principal classes of polymeric carbohydrates encountered within lignocelluloses.

The subfamily Macrotermitinae has developed a unique symbiosis with certain fungi (*Termitomyces* spp.), which are cultivated on prechewed lignocellulosic matter in so–called 'fungal gardens', providing the termites with a significant upgraded food source. It now appears likely that all termites (including those containing cellulolytic hindgut protozoa) have endogenous cellulases that are secreted by the salivary glands and perhaps also by the midgut epithelium. In view of the tremendous species richness of soil–feeding termites and the extreme dynamics of the physicochemical conditions within their guts, they are promising sources of microbial strains having novel metabolic activities.

Chapter 4
VALUE OF BIODIVERSITY

Introduction

Biodiversity is the vast repertoire of non-human organisms of our planet. It is to be valued for four reasons. First, as the dominant species on Earth, *Homo sapiens* has an ethical leadership responsibility towards humanity's only known living companions in the universe. Second, activities as diverse as gardening, making nature films and ecotourism, attest to the aesthetic values of biodiversity. Third, humanity has derived many direct economic values from biodiversity, including all of its food and many of its medicines and industrial products. There is tremendous potential in nature's genetic library for providing more of these benefits. Fourth, and most important from an anthropocentric perspective, plants, animals, and micro-organisms help to supply human beings with an array of free ecosystem services, without which civilization could not persist. These include such things as controlling the gaseous mix of the atmosphere, generating and maintaining soils, controlling pests and running biogeochemical cycles (Ehrlich and Ehrlich, 1992).

A major problem facing us today is how to measure the value of environmental goods whose destruction generates vast externalities. A good example of these goods is biodiversity—the variety of genetically distinct populations and species of plants, animals and micro–organisms with which *Homo sapiens* shares the Earth, and the variety of ecosystems of which they are functioning parts (Ehrlich and Ehrlich, 1992). It is generally agreed that biodiversity has value to humanity, but whether or not it has value independent of human needs is not clear. The value of biodiversity to humanity has both use and non-use components. Biodiversity supplies us with food (fishing and hunting), direct enjoyment (scenic values, bird–watching), or ecosystem services (recycling of nutrients). Its non-use values are, for example, the pleasure a non-African who will never travel to Africa may derive from knowing that free–living black rhinos exist there. Interface ecosystems such as estuaries are rich in biological diversity and serve as important life-support systems also for human beings. The economic values of biodiversity can be divided into four categories: ethical, aesthetic, direct economic and indirect economic (Ehrlich and Ehrlich, 1992).

Natural ecosystems provide civilization with a variety of essential services *gratis* and on a large scale. The strongest anthropocentric reason for the preservation of Earth's life–forms is their intimate involvement in the delivery of these services. One very essential ecosystem service is maintenance of the gaseous composition of the atmosphere. Ecosystems prevent changes in the mix of gases and particulate matter from being too rapid. They act as a sort of buffer.

Sea–birds regulate fish populations and transport nutrients and organic materials from the sea to the land. They are important nodes in the structuring of both aquatic and terrestrial ecosystems, and therefore contribute to the generation of indispensable environmentally produced goods and services.

Value of Species

Although the value or usefulness of many species of plants, animals and microbes is very well known, there are countless other species to which no known use or value can be assigned. So what, if any, may be the justification or reason for preserving these species? Organisms have direct value as resources for humanity, both now and in the future. Also, species provide goods and services indirectly as important components of the web of life. Some workers question economic arguments for protecting species. Ehrenfeld (1988) stated that the value of biodiversity does not depend on the uses to which particular species are put, or their role, if any, in global ecosystems.

Why should conservation biologists care about saving any threatened species that have no known economic value? They should care because each species is important in its own right. The extinction of any species represents an aesthetic and moral loss— like the destruction of a work of art. *Homo sapiens* cannot arrogate to itself the right to exploit any other species to a point where it becomes prone to extinction (see Dworkin, 1994).

Some conservationists believe that even if the *in–situ* protection of an endangered species cannot be justified by its potential as a source of pharmaceutical, agricultural, or other raw materials, the species nevertheless plays some role in supporting the ecosystem services and processes on which all life depends. But this belief is not shared by others (e.g. Lawton and Brown, 1993) who feel that the functional redundancy of species is so great that ecological processes would function quite well even if all the creatures now threatened and a great many more besides become extinct (Lawton and Brown, 1993) because the functions of the lost species would be taken over by some other living species. The Global Biodiversity Assessment (Perrings, 1995) makes this point, as does Holling (1992): 'Although any ecosystem contains hundreds to thousands of species interacting among themselves and their physical environment, the system seems to be driven by a small number of biotic and abiotic variables on whose interactions the balance of species is carried along' (Holling, 1992; Perrings, 1995).

As the real reasons for protecting species in their habitats are not economic or utilitarian but moral and cultural, there is need to emphasize moral, cultural and spiritual reasons rather than to highlight economic arguments about benefits and costs.

Just what is a species worth? It is very difficult to evaluate biodiversity because it is concerned with unpriced goods and services, and because it cannot be assigned a value in terms of production and sustainability.

Even though both diversity and the ecosystem have long been central concepts in ecology, the merger of the two concepts is quite recent. Research on food webs and energy flow (Hairston *et al.*, 1960; deAngelis, 1992) conceptually linked the concerns for declining biodiversity and for ecosystem function. Tilman *et al.* (1996) showed that ecosystem productivity may be affected by diversity but many workers feel that this issue is highly complex (Bengtsson *et al.*, 1997).

Work in Finland has cast doubts on the importance of species diversity; experimental data from mini-ecosystems suggest that while no doubt the number of functional groups of soil animals is important, soil animal species diversity does not affect primary production. In this case an enchytraeid worm had a marked effect on ecosystem productivity, whereas mites and springtails did not.

The complexity of ecosystem responses to diversity has been further borne out by a Swedish study on aquatic systems where zooplankton grazer diversity did affect primary productivity, and phosphorus levels, size- and species-related effects were more important for plant biomass and nitrogen levels. It was also observed that different ecosystem processes can respond in different ways to variation in diversity. It appears that ecosystem processes often respond to variation in diversity in a system-specific, species-specific and process-specific manner, and that diversity may sometimes not have much effect at all.

Diversity at the Landscape Level

Several current definitions of biodiversity have lacked the ecosystem and landscape perspectives. According to Gaston (1996), greater consideration has been given to the species–diversity component of the individual landscapes, in most cases, even when landscapes themselves were purported to be the level of study. What role do landscape – scale processes play in our understanding of diversity? What is the 'minimum diversity' necessary for riparian habitats to provide important ecosystem services such as nutrient retention in agricultural landscapes? There is need to intensify work on how to use biodiversity to manage landscapes sustainably and restore habitats.

Many ecologists dislike the idea of judging biodiversity and the processes that species perform in ecosystems in economic terms. The value–criterion of welfare economics is that human preferences should count and constitute all values; the words 'ecosystem services' contributing to the satisfaction of human preferences have an economic value. Economic values of ecosystems can be use–motivated (e.g. production of food and recreation) as well as non–use–motivated.

Costanza *et al.* (1997) estimated the short–term economic benefits of ecosystem services globally at roughly US $33 trillion annually, which is almost twice the global gross national product (GNP).

But what is the role of biodiversity in providing ecosystem services? Biodiversity may be needed to maintain ecosystem functions at current levels and also, even if biodiversity is not important today it may be vital as an insurance for rare events or environmental changes that may impair ecosystem functions (Folke *et al.*, 1996).

In the first case, biodiversity can be directly important for managing ecosystems, in habitat restoration and in landscape planning. It will then have an instrumental value that might possibly be evaluated from existing market prices. Table 4–1 is a tentative list of ecosystem services that may be needed for managed landscapes to function and provide values for humans, and ascertaining for whether present knowledge can assign some importance to biodiversity for these services. A diversity of primary producers is important, for example, for food production, production of materials and energy, environmental protection, recreation and culture. Decomposer diversity is needed for many functions.

Although many ecologists do not think that species are redundant or substitutable, species redundancy may in fact be a highly valuable factor that increases the reliability of ecosystem function. Thus, both functionally unique and functionally redundant species may have high economic and conservation value.

Table 4-1. Some selected ecological functional groups for a landscape to provide ecosystem services for humans, and the possible importance of biodiversity for these functions (modified from Bengtsson et al., 1997)

Ecosystem service/ landscape function	Primary producers	Herbivores	Predators	Decomposers	Pollinators	Bioturbators
Plant production (cereals, vegetables, fruit)	++	-	-	++	+++	-
Meat production	++	+	+	++	+	+
Fuel (bioenergy)	+	-	-	++	-	+
Building materials	++	-	-	++	-	+
Fibre production	++	-	-	+	+	+
Erosion control/flood regulation	+	-	-	+	-	-
CO_2 fixation	+	-	-	+	-	-
Drinking water	+	+	+	+	-	+
Waste treatment	+	-	-	++	-	+
Landscape heterogeneity	++	++	++	++	-	++
Recreation and natural history	++	++	++	++	++	(- to ++)
Urban environment (aesthetics)	++	-	-	+	+	+

Key : ++, biodiversity is important; +, some biodiversity is needed; -, no obvious relation to biodiversity, or no information available.

Note : Some biodiversity is needed for functioning of dispersers for landscape heterogeneity and for urban cultural values.

Economics and Agriculture

Biological resources, especially wild species, contribute significantly to economic activity and, if well managed, also to sustainable development. For instance, Brazil nuts and wild rubber in Brazil and the *Babassu* palm forests of Amazonia are potentially promising as extractive reserves. In South East Asia, the various wild species of the climbing palms known as rattans are of great economic vaue.

Another way in which biodiversity contributes to economic development is via nature tourism (Boo, 1990). In Kenya and Costa Rica, nature-oriented tourism is the most important foreign exchange earner.

Agricultural uses of biodiversity for economic activity include the use of genetic traits from wild relatives of domestic crop species. The international centres for such crops as rice and wheat look for wild relatives for disease and pest resistance. Biodiversity also contributes to economic activity in the area of integrated pest management. Thus, the fungi *Metarhizium flavoviride* and *Beauveria bassiana* are effective in field testing against migratory locusts and agriculturally problematical grasshoppers (Lovejoy, 1994). In Australia the spread of two species of *Opuntia* (cactus) has been effectively controlled by the introduction of the moth *Cactoblastis cactorum*.

Certain choking mats of the Brazilian waterweed *Salvia molesta* which once suffocated the natural productivity and value for fish production of certain freshwater ecosystems could be controlled by introducing Brazilian *Cyrtobagous* weevils. Another weevil, *Euhrychiopsis lecontei*, once a pest of an indigenous aquatic plant, mutated to a form which effectively attacks Eurasian water milfoil, *Myriophyllum spicatum* which has become a serious problem species in the United States (Sheldon, 1993; Lovejoy, 1994). The Indian neem tree *Azadirachta indica* is a source of the commercial insecticide azadirachtin.

Two kinds of ecosystems are crucial to the functioning of human society today. (1) Agricultural, which are simplified versions of natural ecosystems, artificially maintained by humanity to increase the production of commodities people need and desire and (2) Natural ecosystems, whose importance is less widely appreciated, but society depends upon them as much as it depends upon agricultural ecosystems. That is because agricultural ecosystems are embedded in natural ones and depend on the natural components for their sustained productivity (Ehrlich and Ehrlich, 1992). Natural ecosystems directly provide us with food and materials of all sorts. A crucial portion of the protein in our diets comes straight from nature in the form of fishes and other animals harvested from the seas. This service is provided by the oceans in conjunction with coastal wetland habitats, which are nurseries for marine life that is either harvested directly or serves as a food supply for the sea–life that we eat. Forests also provide timber and other wood products. Rubber, oils and organic chemicals, spices and herbs, and game are provided by natural ecosystems. The active ingredients in at least a third of the prescription drugs used by civilization come directly from or were derived from chemical compounds found in wild plants, fungi, or other organisms, especially in tropical forests; digitalis, morphine, quinine, and antibiotics are familiar examples.

Biodiversity has a strong relationship with sustainable development, including direct harvest, nature tourism, wild genes improving domestic crops, wild species contributing to crop productivity, pest management, sources of medicine and bioremediation (Lovejoy, 1994). Biodiversity relates through services, individual species indicating environmental change or stress, and through wealth generation. Sustainable development relates to the quantification of biodiversity through organizing information to enable the above activities. It also relates in hitherto little-explored ways to ecosystem function, stability and resilience. Biodiversity is already a proven indicator of environmental change in freshwater systems (Lovejoy, 1994).

A major weakness of the international economic system has been its inability to assign a value of exchange to biodiversity and other environmental components. Determination of how to incorporate the cost of conservation into that of production is a challenge we must meet with a view to fulfilling our obligations to future generations by halting the continuing impoverishment and misuse of biodiversity.

Natural ecosystems maintain a vast genetic library. Wheat, rice, and corn used to be scruffy wild grasses before they were developed by selective breeding into the productive crops for man's use. Wild relatives of those and dozens of other crops still represent important reservoirs of genes that are essential for improving the crops of developing new strains to keep them from being overwhelmed by stresses such as changing climate or the evolution of new pests or diseases. All crops and all domestic animals, of course, originated from that library (Ehrlich and Ehrlich, 1992).

Genetic diversity in agriculture enables crops and animals to adapt to different environments and growing conditions. The ability of a particular variety to withstand drought or flooding, or resist insect pests or diseases, give higher protein yields or produce a better–tasting food, are traits passed on naturally by its genes. This genetic

116

material constitutes the raw material that plant and animal breeders and biotechnologists use to produce new varieties and breeds. Without this diversity we would lose the ability to adapt to ever-changing needs and conditions. Sustainable agriculture could not then be achieved in many of the world's different food production environments. The rural poor depend upon biological resources for an estimated 90% of their needs.

Diversity among individual plants and animals, species and ecosystems provides the raw material that enables human communities to adapt to change. Deprived of biodiversity, the ability of humankind to meet environmental challenges would be severely limited. The diversity found within the small number of plant and animal species which form the basis of world agriculture and food production remains a small but vital part of the earth's biodiversity. Through modern biotechnologies, wild diversity can also be incorporated into crops and contribute to world agricultural development.

Pest Control and Pollination

Natural ecosystems help control an estimated 99% of pests and diseases that can potentially attack crops or domestic animals. Most of the potential pests are herbivorous insects, which are controlled primarily by predacious insects that consume them. This service has been disrupted by the misuse of artificial insecticides, because insect pests are generally less susceptible to pesticides than are their predators. Populations of pests tend to be large and so have a better chance of evolving resistance to pesticides. Herbivorous insects also have long been engaged in a coevolutionary race with plants. Plants have evolved many deadly compounds in attempts to poison their attackers, compounds familiar as the active ingredients of certain spices, drugs, and medicines. In turn, the insects have evolved resistance to these poisons; this ability to evolve resistance preadapts them for dealing with the insecticides developed to poison them.

Repeated heavy application of insecticides kills off predacious insects much more effectively than the pests. Pests quickly become resistant to the pesticides and often thrive unless dosages are continuously escalated or different insecticides substituted. Meanwhile, other herbivorous insects, previously not counted as pests because their populations were small, may be relieved of pressure from their predators, and their populations may explode, thus becoming pests. Insecticide resistance is considered one of the serious threats to both agriculture and public health, the latter because of resistance in malarial mosquitoes and other disease carriers (vectors).

Natural ecosystems provide crop plants with stable climates, water, soils and nutrients, and protect them from pests.

Pharmaceuticals

Ever since Hippocrates prescribed infusions of willow bark (the precursor of aspirin) as an analgesic, wild species (mostly of plants) have yielded valuable medicines for humans.

More recently, taxol has been isolated from the Pacific yew tree (*Taxus brevifolia*) and is being used in the treatment of cancer. The vine *Ancistrocladus korupensis*, collected from Cameroon, has yielded the compound michellamine B, which protects human cells from the HIV virus *in vitro*; it is the first natural compound to move to animal testing for AIDS research (Stix, 1993). Squalamine is an aminosterol from the dogfish (*Squalus acanthias*) that shows antiparasitic, antifungal, antiprotozoan and antibacterial activity (Moore *et al.*, 1993). The Ecuadorian arrow poison frog *(Epipedobates tricolor)* secretes a substance which blocks pain far more effectively than morphine but is not an opioid (Spande *et al.*, 1992).

Certain constituents of marine organisms have been examined for various uses: discodermolide from a Bahamian sponge *(Discodermia* sp.) appears to be useful in suppressing organ rejection after transplant operations; macrolectins from the Bahamas sea-floor mud bacteria hold promise in inhibiting growth of melanoma and colon cancer cells as well as the herpes simplex virus and HIV (Fenical, 1993).

The potential for biodiversity to supply new foods and medicines alone is enormous (Ehrlich and Ehrlich, 1981; Myers, 1979). Mankind depends for its very existence on other organisms in all their extraordinary variety. We are completely dependent on the totality of life–support systems to maintain the habitability of this planet. The basic dependence of mankind on other organisms is through the process of photosynthesis.

Ethical and Aesthetic Values

These are based on the religious or quasi–religious feelings of many people in many cultures that other life-forms have intrinsic value and deserve to be protected from destruction by humanity. Buddha preached that man has no right to kill other animals at all.

The notion of *rights* now applies to animals also. Today, both domestic and non–

domestic animals are being legally protected against abuse as is suggested by increasing opposition to hunting, laws to protect birds, the movement to protect whales and dolphins, and the general revulsion at the slaughter of baby seals.

As the dominant species on the planet, *Homo sapiens* carries an ethical responsibility to preserve biodiversity. This means opposing intentional exterminations of other species and supporting conservation efforts.

The beauty of birds, tropical fishes, butterflies and flowering plants is widely enjoyed and supports extensive economic activity, including bird-watching and feeding, scuba diving, butterfly collecting, photography and the making of nature films. Some tiny wasps and flies, when seen under the microscope, appear to be made out of solid gold. Diatoms have silica shells that are as exquisite and varied as snowflakes. Most organisms at least exhibit the beauty of design. Even the tiniest beetles have complete external skeletons, nervous and digestive systems, and complex musculature. Such insects show a degree of sophisticated miniaturization beyond the reach of human engineers. Many insects show the type of beauty, intricacy and diversity that captivates gun collectors, philatelists, computer hackers, bibliophiles and others.

Indigenous Knowledge

Human cultures have adapted to many diverse habitats and have used, changed and nurtured biological resources to meet innumerable needs. As a result of plant and animal domestication, and resource harvesting, a strong interdependence has evolved between 'natural' and 'human-induced' biodiversity. Rural people have managed genetic resources for as long as they have cultivated crops. For over 10 centuries they have selected varieties of crops and livestock breeds to meet environmental conditions and diverse nutritional and social needs. The immense genetic diversity of traditional farming systems is the product of human innovation and experimentation.

For many developing countries, self–reliance in food production will depend on improving low-input agriculture in difficult environmental conditions. The raw materials for these improvements are the biological resources sustained in forests, rangelands, fields and farms. The accumulated knowledge of farmers, coupled with access to modern technologies, provides vital clues to developing sustainable agricultural systems.

In many parts of the world, wild species and natural habitats still help support household food security—access by all people at all times to the food they need for a healthy life. In Nepal, for example, 135 tree species are used as fodder. In Ghana, most people depend on wildlife for their requirement of animal protein. There is now increasing recognition of the value of indigenous knowledge to address global agricultural, health and environmental problems. Conservation and use of biodiversity must be concerned not only with genes, genotypes, species and ecosystems, but also with the traditional knowledge that has helped to produce and maintain this diversity (FAO, 1993).

Traditional Medicines

An estimated three–quarters of prescription drugs derived from plants were discovered because of their prior use in indigenous medicine. Forest-dwelling indigenous people employ at least 1300 plant species for medicines and related purposes.

Traditional Food Plants

Subsistence farmers have been producing or gathering plants from the wild or semi–wild that have long been accepted as desirable sources of food. Millions of people use such traditional plants to satisfy their food needs. They are essential to the diets of rural subsistence households throughout the developing world, providing sources of energy, vitamins and minerals. In recent times, however, many countries have seen a shift away from traditional foods, resulting in a narrowing of the food base. Failure to appreciate their benefits, together with a growing demand for imported foods, is reducing availability and consumption of these foods.

The International Centre for Living Aquatic Resource Management (ICLARM) in the Philippines has been using traditional knowledge to conserve and utilize fish genetic resources. It is compiling a comprehensive database on all of the 24,000 species of cartilaginous and bony fishes in the world. Besides scientific and technical information, the database incorporates indigenous knowledge such as common names, traditional management practices and uses of each species (FAO, 1993).

In Nagaland, an agricultural system has evolved that centres on the alder tree (*Alnus nepalensis*) which is a source of fuelwood, timber and mulch. It is a nitrogen-fixing nodulated tree that enriches the soil nitrogen status. In the fields, alongside the alder trees, farmers grow main crops of maize, millet, potato, barley and wheat and secondary crops of chilli, pumpkin and taro.

The alder tree cycle starts when the tree is pollarded. In pollarding, the main trunk of a 6-10 year-old tree is cut off at a height of about two metres from the ground. It then sprouts 50 to 150 shoots or coppices, most of which are cut when they are one year old. When these trimmings are burnt together with crop waste, fertilizing wood ash becomes added to the soil and a second crop can be grown in the fertilized field. The field is then left fallow for 2–4 years. This allows the trees to grow. Later, when the remaining coppices are about six metres long and 15 centimetres in diameter, the tree is pollarded again. These larger coppices are used for fuelwood and poles. About 120 ha of alder plantation can provide all the fuelwood needed by 100 Naga families (FAO, 1993).

Endod (*Phytolacca dodecandra*), commonly known as the African soap berry, is a perennial plant that has been cultivated for centuries in many parts of Africa where its fruits are used as a laundry soap and shampoo. In 1964, the Ethiopian biologist Aklilu Lemma observed that downstream from where people were washing clothes with endod berries, dead snails were found floating in the water. Further research revealed that sundried and crushed endod berries are lethal to all major species of snails, but do not harm animals or people, and are completely biodegradable.

For Africa, where one of the most serious diseases, schistosomiasis, is transmitted by freshwater snails, discovery of a low–cost and biodegradable lumicide is a major breakthrough (FAO, 1993).

Indian farmers have been using seeds from the neem tree (*Azadirachta indica*) as a natural insecticide to protect crops and stored grain. Scientists have isolated compounds that are extremely effective against insects, even in minute quantities. They control more than 200 species of insects, mites and nematodes, including major pests such as locusts, rice and maize borers, pulse beetles and rice weevils. Yet neem extracts do not harm birds, mammals and beneficial insects such as bees. Unlike most synthetic pesticides, insects apparently do not develop resistance to neem extracts because they contain several biologically active ingredients (FAO, 1993). In 1993, the world's first commercial-scale facility designed and built for neem–based natural biopesticide production opened in India, capable of processing 20 tons of neem seed per day.

Human Health

Growing human populations and their plundering and blatant exploitation of natural resources deplete or destroy many natural habitats and not only create a less healthy environment, but become exposed to a variety of new pathogens. This has been occurring at a time when global climate change may lead to expansions in the range of several infectious diseases and when resistance can evolve to the antibiotics used to cure many common diseases. There are potential interactions between human health, the destruction of tropical forests, the emergence of new pathogens and the loss of natural products with therapeutic potential that could be used to treat new and existing ailments. The potential dangers to human health of the continued assault on the environment, particularly the destruction of tropical forests, should be realized.

The potential for tropical (and temperate) forests to supply agents with medicinal value that might be used to treat infectious and congenital diseases has been known for some time. So far, one of every 125 plant species studied has produced a major drug. If we lose one tree species a day, then we lose three to four potentially valuable new drugs every year. If we contrast this with the synthesis of new drugs from chemicals, the potential for finding major new drugs is in the order of one in 10,000 for each compound tested. The difference in the success rate between screening programmes and searching for natural products from plants is patentability. Pharmaceutical companies face a much greater difficulty in patenting natural products than ones they have synthesized. Their potential profits are thus diminished when they market natural compounds over which they have only a limited monopoly. This is partly because of the litigation associated with the potential misuse of drugs, but it is also because of the trade barriers and tariffs that the pharmaceutical industry has canvassed for to prevent the import of drugs based upon plant products (Dobson, 1995). The American reluctance to sign the Rio biodiversity treaty was based on pressure from pharmaceutical companies that felt their competitiveness might be threatened by a treaty that acknolwedged the potential use of tropical plant-based drugs.

Despite significant trade and legislative barriers, the overwhelming majority of prescription drugs used at present in the US are based on natural products. In the USA, 118 of the top 150 prescription drugs (74%) are based on plants, 18% on fungi, 5% on bacteria and 3% on vertebrates (indeed, all of the latter are from one species of snake, *Bothrops asper*). If we consider the top ten prescription drugs in the US, nine of the ten are based on natural plant products. And the USA is conservative in terms of its pharmaceutical diversity! According to the World Health Organization, more than 80% of the world's population relies upon traditional plant medicine for primary health care.

In Europe, compounds distilled from leaves of the *Ginkgo* tree increase rates of cerebral blood flow and help prevent senile dementia. Other compounds widely available in Europe, but not available in the US, include (1) an extract of mistletoe, which increases the survival time of women suffering from breast cancer, (2) Theokal, a hawthorn extract, widely used as an antiarrhythmic that is safer to use than digitalis, having fewer side effects on people with heart problems, and (3) Thisilyn, a derivative of milk thistles, that all European hospitals stock and which is used for liver damage from alcoholism— also relieves sufferers from hepatitis. Garlic–based compounds are being used all over the world. Garlic reduces cholesterol through its action as an antioxidant.

Only about 1100 of the world's 365,000 known species of plants have been examined for their medicinal properties thus far. Indigenous cultivators are the *in-situ* protectors of 90% of the world's remaining diversity. Their knowledge of medicinal plants and their uses is of great value to human health. Currently, one indigenous cultivation goes extinct in the Amazon basin every year. Every time an old man of these tribes dies, knowledge of some tropical plants and their medicinal properties is lost. If tropical rain forest's products are used to put a value on preserving biodiversity, then intellectual property rights agreements must ensure that some proportion of the financial benefit goes back into protecting the concerned habitat and the indigenous tribes.

We need these new drugs for four main reasons (Chivian *et al.*, 1994; Rosenthal and Grifo, 1995): (1) increasing large-scale development of resistance to many antibiotic and anthelminthic compounds currently in use, (2) emergence of new human diseases, particularly HIV/AIDS; (3) the resurgence of diseases such as TB, and (4) changes in the geographical distribution of older diseases owing to increased human movement and global climate change. Conservation biologists are desperately searching for examples of human benefits that might come from conserving biodiversity. Pharmaceutical products from rain forest plants can be a good justification for rain forest protection in a world where we are beginning to lose our battle with infectious diseases. Nothing may convince people more of the value of biodiversity than if it can be demonstrated to provide cures and treatments for many of the diseases that constrain human health and economic development in areas rich in tropical biodiversity (Dobson, 1995).

New pathogens continue to emerge. The larger the number of humans sampling the environment, the greater the chance that some of them may pick up a new pathogen and transport it to a sufficiently populous area to cause an epidemic outbreak. However, parasites and pathogens that have been with us for a long time still pose the greatest threat to the welfare of human populations, particularly in a world where a changing climate allows pathogens to establish either in areas where they have previously been eradicated, or in areas that have become noticeably warmer and damper. Resistance has already evolved to many of the manufactured compounds used to control these pests and their vectors; hence the search for new compounds will intensify. Drugs derived from natural products are likely to have novel properties to which the pathogens are unlikely to show much resistance. Furthermore, as many natural products contain not one but several active compounds, this would be like using more than one drug to treat an outbreak and could considerably reduce the rate at which resistance evolves.

Plant–derived Drugs

Over 110 pure chemical substances extracted from higher plants are used in medicine throughout the world (see Table 4–2). Discovery of the drugs mostly emanates from knowledge that their extracts can be used to treat one or more diseases in humans.

A large majority of the people in developing countries depend on traditional medicine for their primary health care needs, and most of traditional medicine involves the use of plant extracts.

Aloe

Extracts from the *Aloe vera* plant (related to the onion and garlic plants) are now extensively used for softening the skin and warding off wrinkles. It is used as an ingredient in many skin creams and other cosmetics. The enormous medicinal importance of aloe has earned it such names as the Burn plant, Medicine plant, First Aid plant, Miracle plant, Wand of Heaven, and Plant of Life. *Aloe vera* has been claimed to kill *Mycobacterium tuberculosis* which causes TB as well as the herpes virus responsible for herpes genitalis. It inhibits growth of many common organisms, such as yeasts, fungi and the bacteria associated with wound infections. The genus *Aloe* has over 300 species, of which the following *four* have been proven to have medicinal properties: *Aloe barbadensis*, *Aloe perryi*, *Aloe ferox* and *Aloe arborescens* (Atherton, 1998). It is quite possible, however, that some other species may prove medically important.

Most aloe plants are non–toxic but a few are poisonous. *Aloe barbadensis* may be the most potent medicinally. The resinous mucilage from the cut leaves of aloe is used as a wound healer to treat cuts, stings, abrasions, incised wounds and ulcers. The plant contains the following ingredients:

Vitamins—including the important antioxidant vitamins A,C,E,B (thiamine), B_3 (riboflavin), as well as choline, folic acid and vitamin B_{12}.

124

Table 4–2. Source and uses of some secondary plant constituents used as drugs (after Farnsworth, 1988)

Name	Therapeutic category	Plant source	Plant use in traditional medicine	Correlation between two uses
Acetyldigitoxin	Cardiotonic	*Digitalis lanata*	–	Indirect
Adoniside	Cardiotonic	*Adonis vernalis*	Heart conditions	+
Aescin	Anti–inflammatory	*Aesculus hippocastanum*	Inflammations	+
Aesculetin	Antidysentery	*Fraxinus rhynchophylla*	Dysentery	+
Ajmalicine	Circulatory stimulant	*Rauvolfia serpentina*	Tranquilizer	Indirect
Anabasine	Skeletal muscle relaxant	*Anabasis aphylla*	–	–
Andrographolide	Antibacterial	*Andrographis paniculata*	Dysentery	+
Arecoline	Anthelminthic	*Areca catechu*	Anthelminthic	+
Asiaticoside	Vulnerary	*Centella asiatica*	Vulnerary	+
Atropine	Anticholinergic	*Atropa belladonna*	Dilation of eye pupil	+
Caffeine	Central nervous system stimulant	*Camellia sinensis*	Stimulant	+
Chymopapain	Proteolytic; mucolytic	*Carica papaya*	Digestant	+
Codeine	Analgesic; antitussive	*Papaver somniferum*	Analgesic; sedative	+
Colchicine amide	Antitumour agent	*Colchicum autumnale*	Gout	–
Curcumin	Choleretic	*Curcuma longa*	Choleretic	+
Danthron	Laxative	*Cassia* species	Laxative	+
Digitalin, Digitoxin	Cardiotonic	*Digitalis purpurea*	Cardiotonic	+

Table 4–2 contd.

Digoxin	Cardiotonic	*Digitalis lanata*	–	Indirect
L–Dopa	Antiparkinsonism	*Mucuna deeringiana*	–	–
Emetine	Amoebicide*;* emetic	*Cephaelis ipecacuanha*	Amoebicide; emetic	+
Ephedrine	Sympathomimetic	*Ephedra sinica*	Chronic bronchitis	+
Glycyrrhizin	Sweetener	*Glycyrrhiza glabra*	Sweetener	+
Gossypol	Male contraceptive	*Gossypium* species	Decreased fertility	+
Hyoscyamine	Anticholinergic	*Hyoscyamus niger*	Sedative	+
Kainic acid	Ascaricide	*Digenea simplex*	Anthelminthic	+
Khellin	Bronchodilator	*Ammi visnaga* (L.) Lamk. (toothpick plant)	Asthma	+
Lobeline	Respiratory stimulant	*Lobelia inflata*	Expectorant	+
Menthol	Rubefacient	*Mentha species*	Carminative	–
Monocrotaline	Antitumour agent (topical)	*Crotalaria spectabilis*	Skin cancer	+
Morphine	Analgesic	*Papaver somniferum*	Analgesic; sedative	+
Nicotine	Insecticide	*Nicotiana tabacum*	Narcotic	–
Noscapine (narcotine)	Antitussive	*Papaver somniferum*	Analgesic; sedative	+
Papain	Proteolytic; mucolytic	*Carica papaya*	Digestant	+
Protoveratrines	Antihypertensive	*Veratrum album*	Hypertension	+
Pseudoephedrine	Bronchodilator	*Ephedra sinica*	Chronic bronchitis	+
Quinidine	Antiarrhythmic	*Cinchona ledgeriana*	Malaria	–
Quinine	Antimalarial; antipyretic	*Cinchona ledgeriana* Moens ex Trimen (yellow cinchona)	Malaria	+

Table 4–2 contd.

Quisqualic acid	Anthelminthic	Quisqualis indica L.	Anthelminthic	+
Scopolamine	Sedative	Datura metel	Sedative	+
Silymarin	Antihepatotoxic	Silybum marianum (L.) Gaertn.	Liver disorders	+
Strychnine	Central nervous system	Strychnos nux–vomica	Toxic stimulant	+
Theobromine	Diuretic; vasodilator	Theobroma cacao	Diuretic	+
Theophylline	Diuertic; bronchodilator	Camellia sinensis	Diuretic stimulant	+
Trichosanthin	Abortifacient	Trichosanthes kirilowii	Abortifacient	+
Vincamine	Cerebral stimulant	Vinca minor	Cardiovascular disorders	+
Vinblastine, Vincristine	Antitumor agent	Catharanthus roseus	–	–
Yohimbine	Adrenergic blocker; aphrodisiac	Pausinystalia johimbe	Aphrodisiac	+

Note : + means yes, – means no; a few of the compounds are currently being synthesized commercially.

Enzymes—several different types incl. amylases, lipases and carboxypeptidase which has an anti–inflammatory effect.

Minerals—sodium, potassium, calcium, magnesium, manganese, copper, chromium and iron. Magnesium lactate inhibits histamine decarboxylase, preventer of formation of histamine from the amino acid histidine. Mg lactate has powerful anti–itching effect.

Sugars—the most important are the long–chain polysaccharides, e.g. glucose and mannose. If taken orally, some of these polysaccharides bind to receptor sites lining the gut and help prevent 'leaky gut syndrome'. Unlike the other sugars which are broken down before absorption, the aloe polysaccharides are fully absorbed and appear in the bloodstream unchanged where they act as immunomodulators, both enhancing and retarding the immune response.

Anthraquinones—these phenolic compounds found in the 'bitter aloes' exert a powerful purgative effect.

Lignin—facilitates penetration of other active ingredients deep into the skin.

Saponins—These soapy substances form 3% of the gel and are general cleansers with antiseptic properties.

Sterols—three important anti–inflammatory plant steroids present (cholesterol, campesterol, β–sitosterol.

Salicylic acid—An aspirin–like compound with anti–inflammatory and antibacterial properties.

Amino acids—*Aloe vera* gel provides most of the essential amino acids.

Aloe vera gel is particularly effective on burns, soothing, relieving pain, reducing inflammation and promoting healing with minimal scar formation. Its anti–inflammatory action probably depends on its ability to inhibit the blood–clotting agent thromboxane and prostaglandin production, causing increased blood flow to the area and reduced platelet aggregation (Atherton, 1998).

Chapter 5

BIODIVERSITY, ECOSYSTEMS AND ENVIRONMENT

Introduction

The concept of 'diversity' and its relationship to other aspects of community organization and dynamics is of great significance in the development of plant ecology, but a precise meaning of diversity is lacking. The term 'diversity' usually conveys some sense of the number of interacting species in a system. Two individuals are not diverse if they are of different sexes; they are diverse only if they are of different species. Similarly, subspecies do not count as diverse, nor are larvae from adults. There has been little critical evaluation of whether species are the most appropriate units of currency of diversity for understanding ecological phenomena. Cousins (1991) discussed the limitations of treating all species equally, and suggested that ranking or weighting species with respect to function or size or systematic relationships provides a better and more relevant measure of diversity.

According to Harper (1977), the stable conservative characters that define plant species may not be appropriate for describing many aspects of diversity in ecological communities: 'If generalizations are to be made about the relationship between community diversity and, for example, its stability or productivity, there is no special reason to pick the species as the relevant element in diversity' (Harper, 1977).

Notwithstanding these problems, however, species diversity is attracting increasing interest. Two active areas in community ecology concern the relationship between species diversity and both disturbance and non–competitive biotic interactions such as mycorrhizal infections (Wayne and Bazzaz, 1991). The rapid loss of natural areas and high rates of extinction of species and subspecies in the tropics has led to a resurgence of interest in cataloging species in unexplored areas and trying to understand the factors generating and maintaining this 'bio'–diversity (Wilson, 1988).

The ecologist's definition of a diverse community implies that it is biotically and/or abiotically heterogeneous in space or time. More often it is the biotic components of communities that are described with measures of diversity. It is not clear, however, why ecologists have mostly tended to describe biotic diversity using species classes.

In reality, the term 'diversity' biologically denotes little on its own; it requires an adjective such as 'species', 'genetic' or 'chemical' to be meaningful. The potential number of abiotic and biotic classes of diversity in natural ecosystems can be quite high. The adjective most appropriate to describe ecological phenomena will depend on the patterns and processes one hopes to study. For systematic inventory, species or generic diversity is the most appropriate unit of study. To understand the influence of vegetation on the diversity of bird communities, one could study canopy structural diversity or fruit size diversity. For pollination biology, floral–colour diversity is the appropriate parameter.

Use and abuse of species

Ecologists have mainly focused on 'species' diversity. However, the ecological use of 'species' has certain drawbacks. Wayne and Bazzaz (1991) discussed five aspects of within–species variation that reduce the reliability and usefulness of species as ecological units of diversity in studies of plant communities: genetic variability, phenotypic plasticity, ontogenetic diversity, gender diversity and environmental maternal effects. The species diversity of a region can be partly a function of the taxonomic flora one uses.

Simple numbers or lists of species, or indices based on the algorithmic manipulation of species relative abundances can underestimate the complexity of systems, and signify very different ecological circumstances, depending on the species within a particular system, their population sizes, life stages and environments (Wayne and Bazzaz 1991). Some species–rich communities may be less ecologically diverse with respect to certain features than species–poor communities, yet this point is often overlooked by ecologists and conservationists. According to Wayne and Bazzaz, in studying the ecological and evolutionary processes regulating communities, such as disturbance, competition and mutualisms, it is desirable to explore and employ alternative classes of diversity.

The ecosystem is the 'life–support system' for the community and has a strong relationship to biodiversity.

Species Interactions

All species in a community do not contribute equally to community structure and processes. Some special (called 'drivers') species interactions are quite critical because they affect many other species and process materials out of proportion to their numbers or biomass, or show particularly strong linkage to other species. In contrast, the loss of some species (called 'passengers') from a community has little or no effect on its structure or function. For conservation the focus should be more on the drivers rather than the passengers (Holling, 1992, 1995).

Mutualisms

Mutualisms are relationships in which two or more species benefit from a specific and often highly coevolved interaction. They can be very important in conservation. Good examples are seen in flowering plants, some of which have evolved elegant mechanisms to attract the services of their pollinator, while others have evolved similar mechanisms to attract the animals that disperse their seeds. Legumes and their nitrogen–fixing Rhizobia in root nodules also exemplify mutualism.

Some animals also form mutualistic relationships with other animals. Parasite pickers remove parasites from other species. Some birds clean parasites from rhinoceroses or other large mammals. Some small marine fishes establish 'cleaning stations' where large, often predacious fishes come for removal of their parasites (Feder, 1966).

Since they affect more than one species, and often incorporate a critical function with far–reaching community effects, mutualisms need to be identified and maintained. Loss of a specialist pollinator can lead to local extinction of its host flowering annual, which in turn may lead to loss of other insects associated with that annual. Tropical *Ficus* trees are keystone species; if their specialized wasp pollinators were to decline, the fig resource would be in jeopardy.

Indirect Effects and Diffuse Interactions

The indirect interactions of keystone predators with non–prey species can be very strong and their presence in a community often has far–reaching effects, even on other species not consumed. These indirect effects can be critical to community structure and hence are of conservation relevance. Good examples are known from some birds, e.g. the peregrine falcon (*Falco peregrinus*) and fishes (e.g. *Campostoma anomalum*).

Table 5–1 summarizes some critical keystone and mutualistic interactions, and the potential effects of their losses.

Keystone Species

Some species, because of their trophic position, their production of food resources, or other interactions, have a disproportionately great role in community structure. These species are called keystone species. One good example is the sea otter (*Enhydra lutris*)

131

Table 5–1.   **Possible keystone species, mutualisms and the potential results of their losses (from : Soule and Kohm, 1989)**

Class of keystone species	Effect of losses
Top carnivores	Increases in abundance of prey species and smaller predators; overgrazing
Large herbivores and termites	Habitat succession, reduction in habitat diversity
Habitat modifiers	Disappearance of habitat features
Pollinators and other mutualists	Reproductive failure of certain plants
Seed dispersers	Recruitment failure of certain plants
Plants providing essential resources during scarcity	Local extinction of dependent animals
Parasites and pathogenic microbes	Population explosions of host species
Mutualists with nutritional and defensive roles for their hosts	Increased predation, disease and dieback of plants

which preys heavily on sea–urchins (*Strongylocentrotus droebachiensis*). When sea–otter populations declined in the 20th century due to fur trapping and removal by fishermen, sea–urchin populations increased greatly and grazed heavily on seaweed, occasionally destroying entire kelp forests, which in turn lowered the diversity of the other plants and animals in that habitat (Estes and Palmisano, 1974). The situation could be successfully reversed by reintroducing sea–otters.

Another type of keystone parameter is a keystone food resource. Best examples in tropical forests include figs, nectar and certain fruits, representing less than 1% of plant species diversity; these resources sustain nearly the entire frugivore community at times when other food sources are scarce.

A habitat modifier (an ecosystem engineer) (Jones *et al.*, 1994) exemplifies yet another type of keystone species, e.g. the Canadian beaver and the African elephant (*Loxodanta africana*). The African elephant (like the bison) is herbivorous, browsing on a variety of woody plants and grasses. When feeding on shrubs or small to large trees, the elephants strip bark and branches, and occasionally uproot entire trees. Dense woodlands are often transformed by elephant–feeding into woodland–grasslands or even open grasslands. These areas support more grazing ungulates but are more susceptible to fire, which further favours grasses over woody plants. This animal can therefore change whole landscapes.

Several microbes (bacteria, algae, fungi, protozoa) are found in soils; they break down and decompose dead matter that would otherwise accumulate in a form that is unavailable to living species. Natural cycles would shut down were it not for these inconspicuous but keystone species.

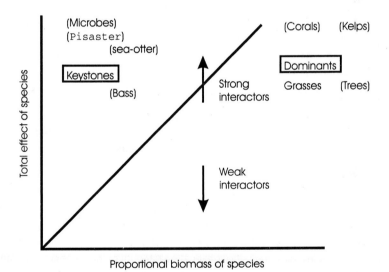

Fig. 5–1. The concept of keystone species. The diagonal line represents species whose total impacts are proportional to their abundances. Some keystones include freshwater bass, the sea–star *Pisaster*, and sea–otters. Species such as reef–building corals, giant kelp, prairie grasses and trees dominate community biomass, but not disproportionately and are merely community dominants rather than keystones (after Meffe *et al.*, 1997).

133

A good working definition of a keystone species is a species whose impact on its community or ecosystem is large, and disproportionately large relative to its abundance (Power and Mills, 1995). An abundant species is not a keystone species simply due to its abundance (unless its effects are out of proportion to that abundance), but rather is a community dominant (Fig. 5–1). A true keystone species is less abundant in a community but has a marked influence on other species and on community structure. Removal, addition, or local changes in population size of keystone species have wide–ranging effects on other species, on processes and interactions, and even on landforms.

Ecosystem Processes

Although a substantial fraction of the Earth's species are likely to become extinct as a result of human activities before we even document their existence, we cannot predict the consequences of this loss. Nonetheless, certain patterns of biodiversity are emerging. There has been a general increase in species diversity throughout the fossil record, despite periods of mass extinction. In contrast to the wealth of geographic diversity of plant and animal species, most of the world's major taxonomic groups of micro–organisms can be found in a small sample of garden soil.

The concept of functional groups involves the grouping of species that have 'similar' effects on ecosystem processes. Functional groups are a practical necessity because it cannot be determined how each species affects ecosystem processes. Such groups are generally useful in organizing our ecological understanding of diversity.

The functional–group concept implies that species within a functional group are equivalent or 'redundant' in their impact on ecosystem processes and that ecosystems could function equally well with fewer species. There are two extreme viewpoints on redundancy: (1) Each species in an ecosystem plays a fundamental role, such that removal of each species incrementally weakens the integrity of the system. Alternatively, (2) a community is composed of a few functional groups, each with several ecologically equivalent species, such that species can be lost from the community with little effect on ecosystem processes, as long as each functional group is represented (Chapin et al., 1992). The truth may lie between these extremes.

A keystone species is a functional group without redundancy. Addition or removal of a keystone species causes massive changes in community structure and ecosystem processes. To predict which species in a community are keystone species or could

134

become so under reasonable scenarios of environmental change is a daunting task.

Manipulation of plant diversity can alter the stability of plant communities. This occurs partly because the high phenological and physiological diversity associated with high species diversity enables a community to capture resources and grow over a wide range of unpredictable and constantly changing conditions. In several ecosystems, long–term population stability — which is often a product of community diversity—may be at least as important as ecosystem measures as an index for the long–term maintenance of communities (see Chapin *et al.*, 1992).

Without human intervention, one to ten species may be lost per year. Conservative estimates are that 100 species are becoming extinct *each day*. The tragedy is that the numerous potential benefits are lost not just to people of this generation, but to future generations as well.

Despite the predicted increase in world economic activity, the reality in many developing countries is bleaker than ever. The economic growth experienced on a global level during the 1980s was accompanied by greatly increased world poverty in most developing countries (Abramovitz, 1991). A major factor in the global economic crisis is that during the 1980s the net flow of financial resources was reversed: the countries of the South began exporting more money in the form of debt service than they received in development assistance and private investments (Schmidt, 1990). When falling commodity prices, rising debt and inflation combine with such misleading economic indicators as Gross National Product—which does not accurately reflect either women's labour contribution to the economy or the depletion or degradation of natural resources—the results are often austerity measures and policies that may hinder or preclude measures that would improve natural resource management (WRI, 1990) and slow population growth.

Ecosystem Productivity

Many ecologists once believed that diverse, complex ecological communities are the most stable but during the last three decades the universality of this theory came to be questioned when it was observed that the nature of species interactions, rather than species number alone, determines the stability of ecological systems. Recently, expanding concern over loss of biodiversity has led to a reappraisal of the idea that species diversity enhances the productivity and stability of ecosystems (Baskin, 1995).

According to the diversity-stability hypothesis (see Kumar, 1995), increasing the

135

number of trophically interacting species in an ecological community should increase the collective ability of member populations to maintain their abundances after disturbance. Energy is transferred from one trophic level to another as a quintessential ecosystem function. MacArthur's idea that species diversity is crucial for maintaining ecosystem functions received support from the results of a microcosm experiment in a controlled laboratory facility called the Ecotron, and from plant community responses in field experiments conducted in herb–dominated systems in seasonal environments (Tilman and Downing, 1994; Johnson *et al.*, 1996).

Table 5–2 summarizes a few selected experimental approaches and the results of some classical studies on the influence of species diversity on the productivity and stability of terrestrial ecosystems.

Generally, species diversity increases and biomass production decreases with successional time. In some cases it was found that primary productivity increased with plant species diversity (see Johnson *et al.*, 1996).

The quintessential issue of how important species diversity is to ecosystem function boils down to the way the species in that system interact (Walker, 1992). The inherent properties of an ecosystem affect the feedback interactions among its resident species.

Besides disturbance, some other environmental factors also can influence the functional redundancy of various species.

In the context of the role of species diversity in maintaining ecosystem function, the critical point is whether or not species designations best distinguish functional groupings. Where in taxonomic hierarchy do functionally distinct phenotypes exist? Phenotypes have a strong genetic determinant, and it is the phenotype that translates into functional role. Taxonomy itself has continually evolved to embrace new technology and conventions in classifying biotas. With recent advances in protein, chromosome and DNA isolation, genetics has become increasingly important in species determination. However, explicit functional distinction has not yet become an important taxonomic criterion for species identification. As some species designations are controversial and dynamic, species names seem unreliable as a basis for differentiating functional groups (Johnson *et al.*, 1996). In some cases, either genetic or functional differences are prominent between taxonomic levels other than species. Populations of the tropical legume *Pterocarpus macrocarpus* have been found to differ from one another in resistance to drought stress. The results from some recent studies have supported the

Table 5–2. Summary of a few selected diversity/ecosystem function studies (after Johnson *et al.*, 1996)

Ecosystem	Disturbance type	Diversity measure	Productivity measure	Stability measure	Diversity/ productivity relationship	Diversity/ stability relationship
California annual grassland	Annual variation	S	SC (aboveground)	SC(NPP)$^{-1}$	plant (−)	plants (0)
Yellowstone grasslands	Drought; grazing	H'	SC (aboveground)	D relative abundances	NA	plants (+)
British grasslands	Fertilization; mowing;	S	SC (aboveground)	D vegetations; composition	plants (−)	plants (−), (+)
Costa Rican tropical forest	Annual variation	S	soil fertility	D soil fertility	NA	plants (+)
Ecotron	S	S	NPP	NA	plants (+)	NA

S, species richness; SC, standing crop; NPP, net primary productivity; D, change in parameter; H', Shannon index; NA, not assessed; +, positive association; −, negative association; 0, no relationship.

137

hypothesis that species diversity enhances productivity in some ecosystems but not in others (Johnson *et al.*, 1996).

Environmental Services of Biodiversity

Environmental or ecosystem services are defined as any functional attribute of natural ecosystems which is beneficial to humankind. They comprise the main indirect values of biodiversity, as opposed to direct values in the form of material goods such as timber, fish, plant–based pharmaceuticals and germplasm infusions for major crops. They include generating and maintaining soils, converting solar energy into plant tissue, sustaining hydrological cycles, storing and cycling essential nutrients, notably through nitrogen fixation, supplying clean air and water, absorbing and detoxifying pollutants, decomposing wastes, pollinating crops and other plants, controlling pests, running biogeochemical cycles of vital elements, controlling the gaseous mixture of the atmosphere and regulating weather and climate (Myers, 1996, 1997). They basically include three forms of processing, namely, of minerals, energy and water (Perrings, 1987; Perrings *et al.*, 1992; 1995).

The services supplied by one form of biodiversity in one locality may not necessarily be supplied by a similar form of biodiversity in another locality. Services are often site–specific.

Regulation of climate and biogeochemical cycles, hydrological functions, soil protection, crop pollination, pest control, recreation and ecotourism are some of the environmental services of biotas and ecosystems. The services are indeed significant, both in an ecological and economic sense. Ecosystem resilience underpins many of the services. It should not be inferred however, that environmental services stem necessarily and exclusively from biodiversity. While biodiversity often plays a key role, the services can also come from biomass and other attributes to biotas.

Conservation biologists emphasize the numerous contributions of biodiversity to the human cause. These contributions fall into two classes: material goods and environmental services. The first is widely documented (Schulze and Mooney, 1994; Myers, 1996) in the form of new and improved foods, medicines and drugs, raw materials for industry and sources of bioenergy. The second is less well known even though it may be even more valuable than the first. Whereas the benefits of material goods tend to accrue to individuals, often as producers or consumers in the marketplace, the values of environmental services generally pertain to society and therefore they mostly remain unmarketed (Brown *et al.*, 1993; Barbier, 1994).

Interest in below–ground phenomena has increased greatly in recent years, largely due to the fact that, globally, the majority of primary production goes below ground. In the global carbon cycle, below–ground processes play important roles. A popular current view of below–ground parts of ecosystems is based on the realization that organisms exist as functional groups. According to this idea, below-ground biotas can largely be treated as biomass and their taxonomic composition may be ignored because our understanding of their taxonomy is very poor (Ritz *et al.*, 1994). This view tends to ignore biodiversity in soil (Groombridge, 1992). Surely a large proportion of all bacteria, fungi, nematodes and other micro–organisms are found in the soil. What is their significance in ecology? Does this amazing diversity mean that only an approach based on functional groups can help us understand the control of critical ecological processes operating in soil? Of course, any attempt to deal with individual species may be doomed in a welter of detailed and uninterpretable studies.

Below–ground and above–ground ecology has diverged. The properties of communities such as resilience, stability and persistence are not being seriously tackled in below-ground ecology probably because soil ecologists have become distracted by the great complexity of the system and the various kinds of technical difficulties it poses (Fitter, 1995).

Climate Change

Thousands of species are believed to become extinct each year due to habitat destruction (Peters and Myers, 1992). Now, an even more dangerous and literally invisible threat looms—global climate change caused by the build-up of greenhouse gases in the atmosphere. Greenhouse warming is likely to trigger a massive disruption of natural environments and may set off a wave of mass extinctions. According to Peters and Myers, most scientific reports downplay the dramatic changes global warming could wreak on the world's biotas.

If global warming occurs, the ensuing ecological reorganization might well be as great as the one at the end of the last ice age, a time of mass extinction of species and reshuffling of biological communities. Many scientists have speculated about the shape of things to come in the future: they describe a world filled with biological refugees, species forced to move as local climates become too hot or dry, and one in which more frequent storms and fires will accelerate the disappearance of several ecosystems. Vegetation belts will move hundreds of kilometres towards the poles and hundreds of metres up mountains. Rising seas will inundate coastal marshes and melting polar ice will disrupt the Arctic food chain. Coral reefs will die, migratory birds will find it difficult to locate their food sources or breed, and fish restricted to streams and rivers in drying regions will perish. The future world may turn out to be one in which large areas are biologically impoverished, inhabited primarily by weedy plants and species such as raccoons and deer that reproduce rapidly, colonize well, and do not need mature biological communities to thrive. Of course, the picture isn't uniformly bleak. New coral reefs would grow in some areas and migrating trees would form new colonies. But overall, the speed and magnitude of change would cause the majority of species to decrease in abundance and distribution, and many will be lost entirely (Peters and Myers, 1992).

Massive changes in vegetation would dramatically affect the lives of many people. Deciduous forests will decline (Peters, 1990), damaging economies, particularly those dependent on the recreation and lumber industries. The disturbances would also reduce other benefits of natural ecosystems that are critical for the quality of human life yet difficult to quantify economically and thus often undervalued by economists when they assess climate change impacts (Peters and Myers, 1992).

Since climate-caused disruption is likely to be a severe ecological disaster, action must begin now to ward off some of the consequences. Efforts currently underway at slowing global warming may not be sufficient to preserve biodiversity.

Any efforts to conserve biodiversity should not only ultimately reach beyond the species level, but also include communities and ecosystems. Understanding a community's critical components and strong interactions, such as keystone species and mutualisms, can aid and guide conservation efforts. A species may be a keystone component because of some aspect of its trophic ecology (e.g. being an important predator), changing habitat structure through its foraging efforts, or providing a critical food resource. Mutualisms create critical links among species that perform a function such as pollination or seed dispersal, that are sometimes crucial for continued community composition.

Though a variety of changes occur in communities over ecological time, natural disturbance regimes and introductions of exotic species are particularly important in relation to conservation. Most or all natural communities suffer some normal disturbance regime, such as fire, flooding, drought and herbivory. Understanding the scale, frequency and intensity of natural disturbances is critical to conservation at the community level. Continuance of normal disturbance regimes at appropriate scales needs to be encouraged and new artificial disturbances may be avoided. New disturbance through invasion by exotic species can be highly damaging. But not all species introductions to and losses from communities are equal with respect to their community effects — some are benign whereas others are devastating.

Many available scenarios depict human–induced environmental changes, including those impending from a change in global climate. Woodwell (1990) reviewed the impacts of such changes on the loss of species and overall biotic impoverishment. 'The current tragedy ... is not simply the loss of species, but the transformation of a highly productive, self–sustaining landscape of great versatility and considerable resilience into a barren landscape of limited potential for support of life, including people. The tragedy is compounded by the widespread assumption that human interests are advanced by the transformation'.

Evidence of biotic impoverishment has been gathered from tundra, forest, grassland, wetland, and freshwater and marine ecosystems. Biotic impoverishment appears to be a multifactorial intrigue. Air pollution alone may not kill the ecosystems but multiple and chronic effects can. Until recently most ecologists used to study ecosystems to satiate scientific curiosity. Only recently have they begun to relate ecosystem processes to applied issues. 'To arrest the trend of biotic impoverishment by legislation, the following vital attributes need to be considered: economic prosperity and environmental richness, realistic and workable policies, and the political and social will to overcome degradation' (Wali, 1992).

Global environmental change demands detailed understanding of how biological diversity works but we do not yet have that understanding. It is not enough to know which plant and animal species are present, locally or globally. We also need to understand how individual populations and communities of interacting populations are affected by habitat fragmentation, and by other changes in their physical environment, such as long–term changes in temperature or soil moisture, resulting from global climate change. Policy choices require a better knowledge of the degree to which particular ecosystems continue to function as constituent species become extinct or substituted, in other words, the relation between diversity and community stability. We need to know much more about the mutual influence of physical and ecological systems on each other,

141

For instance, to what extent do tropical forests generate cloud cover or buffer carbon dioxide inputs? It should be remembered that our oxygen-rich atmosphere was produced by living organisms. We need to know how, ultimately, biological diversity may influence climate.

Irreversibility

As against many uncertainties relating to biodiversity, there is one certainty—once lost, species cannot be brought back from extinction. Changes which are irreversible assume a special status in environmental policy. They prompt us to look very carefully at the need to be precautionary. If by reversibility we mean the complete reconstruction of a species lost from the gene pool altogether, then the loss of a species is indeed totally irreversible within the bounds of our present knowledge.

Of course some species losses have been occurring naturally during the course of evolution. Darwin's theory of natural selection was based on the idea that species become extinct if they are unable to adapt to a change in conditions. But, the rate of species lost through man-made effects is much greater than those lost through the evolutionary process of 'natural wastage'.

Tropical Forests

Tropical forests cover about 7% of the earth's land area, but they contain more than half the world's known plant and animal species. Human population increase dictates that the forests provide revenue or resources for people living in rain–forest areas. In the absence of sustainable means of economic use, destructive exploitation for timber and mineral resources can eventually lead to the disappearance of rain forests from most parts of the world (Connell, 1975; 1978).

Forestry, fisheries, mineral resources and pharmaceutical and tourist opportunities are the ways by which tropical rain forests have been used on a global scale.

The economies of most rain-forest countries need strengthening. However, there is a difference between a stable economy that allows a low-density human population to maintain itself and a developing economy that allows a country to compete internationally. 'Sustained' implies equilibrium, while 'development' implies non-equilibrium. Many economists would argue that the present problems of sustainable development stem from inaccuracies in pricing mechanisms. Most ecologists woud argue that attempts to value any individual resource usually ignore the ecological interactions between the resource and other species in the community. This highlights the marked differences between sustained economic use and sustained ecological use.

Unfortunately, most exploited systems are susceptible to capitalization—the tendency towards overexploitation that occurs when the growth rate of the managed resource is less than that of capital invested in alternative ventures.

Forests provide local communities with food, shelter, medicinal plants, firewood, lumber, and other goods and services including employment opportunities, income, and soil and water system protection.

During the last few decades concern about the fate of tropical forests and, more recently, about all types of forests has grown. Strong arguments have been raised about protecting tropical and non-tropical forests from exploitation and misuse; saving old-growth forests and reducing consumption of firewood by local populations.

The overall situation is alarming not only in the developing countries but also in the industrialized world. Fires and acid deposition ravage forest ecosystems in the Mediterranean countries and the temperate and boreal forests of Asia, Europe, and North America. By the year 2010 Europe could be losing more than US $25 billion a year in forest revenues because of atmospheric depositions on forests.

The forces changing the extent, distribution and quality of forests in the past are largely still at work today, although not always in the same area (Zentilli, 1992). The needs for energy, for agricultural land, and for urban settlements and infrastructures have been the basic factors of deforestation, which now happens much faster and dramatically affects the livelihood of rural and urban people.

In most of the developing countries the higher rates of deforestation started soon after the arrival of European settlers, who, in many cases, expanded needs for agricultural lands.

Forests are traditionally considered as wastelands or hunting grounds rather than a comprehensive system of physical and biological components that benefit society by producing goods and services and moderating climate and water cycles (see Ewel, 1977).

The world forests are subject to natural and anthropogenic pressures: climate changes; air, water and soil pollution; pests and fires; recreational needs; needs for more farmlands to produce food, fodder, or raw materials; and needs for timber, fuel, or other goods. Indirect pressures derive from the burden of the foreign debt on developing countries, the deleterious effects of some foreign loans and investments, and conditions of aid and trade that promote unsustainable exploitation of natural renewable resources. All these pressures have resulted in substantial forest loss.

Probably the only new factors are air pollution, the effect of population increase, and the much shorter time frame in which the process is developing.

For many years approaches to forests have centred around the timber produced and the effects of the logging industry. Existing methodologies to assess the value of forests are based mainly on the value of the wood produced; little is known of the value of the other goods and services produced by the forest. The recent interest in conserving biodiversity and in better understanding the role of forests in climate change is changing this pattern.

Precise and reliable data on the total area of world forests are lacking; the figures used are an aggregation of figures from different sources based on various definitions of trees, forests, forestland and forest cover.

Forest inventory plots provide a good approach to documentation and monitoring of plant diversity. They are a means for obtaining long–term data on the growth, mortality, regeneration and dynamics of forest trees. Many forest plots have been set up over the last few decades in some couintries. In recent years, modern computer–based technologies have created novel possibilities for surveying and establishing forest plots, for inventories and monitoring of plants growing in those plots, and for using the inventoried plots in resource management efforts.

The permanent plot methodology is used to document species diversity and tree composition in protected forest areas. The plot is designed as a zone encompassing 25 hectares divided into 25 plots of 1 ha. Each 1 hectare plot is in turn subdivided into 25 quadrats 20 x 20 m in size, with the quadrats permanently marked. Each tree greater than about 10 cm dbh (diameter at breast height) is mapped in relation to two adjacent corner stakes, tagged and identified. The data generated from each plot are entered, stored and analyzed in computers. Tree co–ordinates and preliminary species information are entered in the field on laptop computers for later transference to desktop computers (Dallmeier, 1992).

To conserve tropical forest diversity and promote sustainable use of forest resources, it is necessary to understand how forests change. The permanent plot inventory system provides a baseline distribution of tree species and describes habitats within a particular site. Monitoring any changes in these plots over time enables an understanding of the impact of natural and man–made disturbances on the composition of species and communities. Data produced through monitoring may be used to predict future changes. Small plots up to two ha in size and containing 1200 to 1400 trees within a protected area can reveal much about species diversity and allow good characterization of the larger forest (Dallmeier, 1992).

Long–term forest inventories provide important information needed to establish conservation priorities. They are also used in integrating management of protected areas with compatible development on surrounding lands and timber lands, information that is critical in planning for sustainable logging. Similar information is needed to ensure that logging in tropical forests proceeds in a sustainable fashion (Dallmeier, 1992).

Medicinal Plants

An important reason to save the world's tropical rain forests is the potential medicinal value of their plants. The World Health Organization estimates that 80% of the world's population relies on traditional plant–based medicines. Products of rain–forest plants have been used to treat many devastating diseases including childhood leukemia, Hodgkins disease, glaucoma and heart disease. Unfortunately, however, a mere 1100 of about 365,000 known species of plants have been examined for medicinal properties (Dobson and Absher, 1991).

Three different strategies to speed up the rate of identification of species having medicinal properties are possible: random search, screening species from families with known biotic action; and interviews with ethnobotanical healers. The last of these has proved the most efficient. Species collected at random are much less likely to show activity against an HIV–screen than species classified as 'very powerful plants' by a traditional herbalist. However, increasing destruction of rain forests makes it harder for traditional healers to locate the plants they need.

In general, there seems to be greater success with plants that are used to treat pathogens that only require small populations to sustain them, such as fungal infections. Nevertheless, the potential for drugs to assist with the world's biggest problem (i.e., birth control) may lurk in the rain forest; a number of rain–forest tribes in different parts of the world have discovered plants that may be used for this purpose.

Developing local supply and extraction methods is important and it may be wiser to concentrate on weedy species. The chances of success seem to be greater if searches are directed not to miracle cures for AIDS or cancer, but to drugs effective against fungal infections, cold sores and herpes; these are common both in temperate and tropical countries and there is a large market for drugs used to treat them.

Aquatic Biodiversity

There are at least 20,000 species of fish in a variety of marine aquatic ecosystems worldwide, and in freshwater environments many new fish species continue to be discovered by science. Yet, 40% of the world's fish catch comprises only 20 species. This attests to the potential of other types of fish in providing food for humankind but masks the fact that complex, far–reaching interdependencies occur between fish species and their environment that are essential to sustaining global fisheries production.

Over 90% of the marine fish catch comes from the 9.9% of the ocean that lies over the continental shelf, especially in key habitats in the nearshore waters, in the intertidal zone and in the land areas immediately adjacent to the coast, e.g. coastal rivers, bays, wetlands, estuaries, mangroves, salt-marshes, mudflats, sea–grass and seaweed beds, and coral reefs. About two–thirds of all commercially valuable fish species spend the first — and most vulnerable — stages of their life in these waters (Weber, 1994). About 90% of the remaining open oceans yield relatively few fish but are essential for providing resources needed to maintain fish populations in the productive 10% of the seas. Fisheries ultimately depend on the quality and integrity of the whole ecosystem and the biodiversity within it. Any severe loss or degradation of biodiversity in an aquatic ecosystem causes irreversible changes in that system. Therefore, it is essential to conserve habitats and within–habitat diversity, providing varied environmental niches to which particular species are genetically suited. These not only afford shelter from predators, but also provide a variety of feeding, spawning and nursery grounds for a wide range of potentially competing species. This diversity of habitats allows otherwise incompatible, but often interdependent species to coexist (MacLean and Jones, 1995).

Aquatic biodiversity is also an important indicator of sustainability. A high level of aquatic diversity results in diversity and security in people's livelihoods, and indicates the use of sustainable fishing practices.

All the world's 17 main fishing grounds are now being fished at or above their sustainable limits. Because of habitat destruction through trawling, many fishing communities in India no longer catch 150 species that used to be commonly caught two decades ago. In Africa, up to 75% of endemic species have been lost in Lake

Victoria, replaced by introduced Nile perch which makes up 80% of the catch. In other African lakes introduced species now constitute 60–90% of the total catch.

The following are four principal and interrelated causes of the loss of aquatic biodiversity:

1. **Habitat destruction:** reduces the number of species of all aquatic organisms.

2. **Overfishing:** affects whole ecosystems because of disruptions to the food web caused by the loss of the targeted species that is overfished.

3. **Wasting of fish:** the losses of untargeted species caught unintentionally and simply thrown away.

4. **Introduction of exotic species:** deliberate or accidental introduction disturbs the ecological balance between aquatic species.

Capture Versus Nurture Fisheries

Capture fishery strategies consider fishing a hunting activity, targeting selected species for mass markets, where the range is open access and the fish stocks are common property. Responsibility for managing fisheries is ill defined leading to the so-called 'tragedy of the commons' where what is left by one user is taken by another. So, all the world's main fishing grounds are being fished at or above their sustainable limits. Some 70% of global fish stocks are now regarded as fully exploited, overexploited, depleted or recovering (Garcia, 1994).

In contrast, nurture fishery strategies give due importance to the time needed for stocks to replenish themselves and the need to conserve species diversity. The nurture fishery strategies of coastal fishing communities throughout the world have evolved several practices to regulate their fisheries. Some govern who may fish in which season and where; others stipulate the sort of fish that may be caught; others relate to the kind of fishing gear that may be used; and still others govern onshore activities such as processing, net-making, and marketing (Fairlie *et al*, 1995). Sustainable nurture fisheries techniques developed and used by artisanal fisherfolk, especially in tropical waters, are now having to compete with the industrial fishing fleet (Mulvany, 1996).

Tropical Rivers and Their Fisheries

Tropical rivers contain some of the world's most complex fisheries. Fish species diversity in the Amazon exceeds the total number of known mammal species. Each year, 80,000 tons of fish are removed from the Amazon River. On any day there may be 50 different species for sale in the local markets. Many of the fish species are frugivores or detritivores; they eat the products of the forest that humans don't. Unfortunately, the fisheries of many rivers are being perturbed in various ways, e.g. hydroelectric projects which may affect both fish survival and migration patterns through their effects on temperature and turbidity. Siltation due to deforestation and mineral extraction is sure to cause the collapse of some populations. Changes in the habitat are compounded by changes in fishing technology: most fish are now caught either by gill nets or seine nets; both of these have only been introduced in the last few decades (Dobson and Absher, 1991). For the Amazon fishery a serious threat is the mercury poisoning which occurs as a by-product of gold mining. Large amounts of mercury are accumulating in the Amazonian food chains, not only disrupting animal and plant communities, but also causing widespread human debilitation (Dobson and Absher, 1991).

Anthropogenic eutrophication (the human addition of nutrients above natural values) is a major environmental problem in many water bodies. Good understanding of the mechanisms of nutrient dynamics in lakes can help design management strategies for tackling such eutrophication issues as nuisance algae.

In temperate lakes planktivorous fish play a fairly minor role. It is commonly assumed that phosphorus (P) is the primary limiting nutrient of primary production. A link exists among P loading rate, hydraulic loading rate, and P retention in the lake with total P concentration. Purely physical principles can help one to estimate total P; but biotic interactions create interesting deviations from this value. The biotas are aggregated into a few key functional components: algae biomass, algal P and zooplankton. The key biological processes of nutrient uptake, algal growth and zooplankton consumption affect algal biomass and P retention (DeAngelis, 1997). In temperate lakes where there is little influence by planktivorous fish, we may assume that large zooplankton such as daphnids constitute the herbivore component. The zooplankton growth is affected by the variable P content of the phytoplankton as well as its biomass density. When phytoplankton biomass is high, P concentration in phytoplankton is low. Both a stable equilibrium point and a 'saddle cycle' type limit cycle are possible in this system; when the P loading exceeds a bifurcation level, the stable focus becomes a stable limit cycle. Andersen (1997) suggested that the existence of this saddle cycle may partly explain the 'spring clear–water phase' observed in some field studies. Below the bifurcation level, where a stable focus exists, algal biomass is controlled by grazers; above it, energy transfer to zooplankton is less effective and no control is possible.

Andersen (1997) categorized the algae into functional types, including differences in their exploitation by zooplankton. Species replacement can occur along a P loading rate gradient. If one species is edible and the other inedible, a resident edible species must possess both higher capacity for growth and nutrient uptake than an inedible species, to prevent invasion by the latter. But what happens when the loading rate is high enough to produce a limit cycle? In this case, three species can coexist on the single limiting nutrient (DeAngelis, 1997; Andersen, 1997).

What happens when one includes a second limiting nutrient, nitrogen? Here the implication is that the inclusion of differential nutrient recycling would make stable two-species coexistence more difficult for two limiting nutrients.

Riparian zones have been found to have an unusually high diversity of species and environmental processes. The ecological diversity is related to variable flood regimes, geographically unique channel processes, altitudinal climate shifts and upland influences on the fluvial corridor. The resultant dynamic environment supports a variety of life-history strategies, biogeochemical cycles and rates, and organisms adapted to disturbance regimes over broad spatial and temporal scales. Innovations in riparian zone management have been effective in ameliorating many ecological issues related to land–use and environmental quality. Riparian zones play essential roles in water and landscape planning, in restoration of aquatic systems, and in catalyzing institutional and societal co-operation for these efforts (Naiman and Decamps, 1997).

Biodiversity and Small Islands

Many small islands are rich reservoirs of flora and fauna. Almost 900 bird species—10% of the world's total—are endemic to one or other of the world's islands. About 2470 of New Caledonia's 3250 plant species are endemic. So are 50% of Cuba's 6–7,000 plant species. A single volcanic island in the Philippines, Mount Makiliang, has more types of woody plants than the entire USA (Cropper, 1994).

About 75% of all the animals and birds known to have become extinct in recent history used to live on islands. The dodo, the most famous of all extinct species, lived on Mauritius until the last bird was killed in 1662. About one-half of the island's endemic bird, mammal and reptile species have now followed it to extinction. About 60% of its endemic plant species are rare, threatened or extinct. Of the bird species, 108 are known to have become extinct over the last four centuries; 97 of them were island dwellers. Of the birds listed in the Red Data Books, 60% are island birds. Of the endemic plant species of Lord Howe Island 97%, those of St. Helena, Rodrigues and Norfolk Islands, 96% of those on Ascension Island 91% and of those of Juan Fernandez 81% are rare, threatened or extinct. So are 81% of those in the whole of the Seychelles, 67% of those in the Canaries and 66% of those of the Galapagos.

The Cafe Marron tree on the island of Rodrigues is the rarest in the world—just one tree survives today (Cropper, 1994).

Marine Biodiversity

In recent years, the conditions of the ocean environment, its resources, biodiversity and the livelihood of coastal people and economies of maritime developing states have been declining at an unprecedented rate, and there are no signs of reversal in these negative trends. Added to this, there will be impacts to the ocean ecosystem from global warming and ozone depletion. The very survival of some coastal communities which include some of the poorest people in the world who greatly depend on coastal resources for their food and livelihood, is at stake. In the majority of cases the ocean is the only source of protein and income. Over 90% of the fish production comes from ocean waters over continental shelves and from major ocean currents.

According to the United Nations Food and Agricultural Organization (FAO), the maximum production from world marine fisheries is about 82 million tons. Therefore, the current annual fish production of about 84 Mt means that we are harvesting the full potential of wild captured fisheries. Further, some 27 Mt, consisting of low value and juvenile fish as well as by-catch and incidentals (sea-birds, sea-turtles, marine mammals and other ocean life), are discarded annually, raising the average annual production to 110 million metric tons. Also, fish pirating is a major factor in fisheries management, especially in developing countries. In 1993, the top five captured fishes were anchoveta, Alaskan pollock, Chilean jack mackerel, silver carp and Japanese pilchard, accounting for 20% of the total catch. China, Peru, Japan, Chile, and the United States landed most of the fish (Ngoile, 1997).

Overfishing is the main problem plaguing our oceans. Fish have never been in greater demand as seafood, nor more threatened as marine wildlife. Fishing is the last major industry exploiting wild animals for food. Yet, the worldwide marine fish catch has been declining since 1989, following a 500% increase since the end of the Second World War. Excessive fishing in some areas has driven staple species such as Atlantic cod to commercial extinction.

Fishing activities significantly affect the productivity and biodiversity of the oceans. Fishing gear such as bottom trawlers, longlines and driftnets damage ocean ecosystems, reducing the oceanic biodiversity. Shipping adds hydrocarbons which pollute waters, harming biotas. Ships also introduce several alien species when emptying their ballast waters.

Since Rio, some intergovernmental agreements have been concluded. Integrated Coastal Management (ICM) has been identified as the key process for conservation and sustainable development, but the chief constraint has been in implementing these agreements and programmes.

There are not enough Marine Protected Areas — as yet 0.25% of the ocean surface — to realize the benefits of these in maintaining marine biodiversity (Ngoile, 1997).

Marine biodiversity is higher in benthic rather than pelagic systems, and in coasts rather than the open ocean since there is a greater range of habitats near the coast. The highest species diversity occurs in the Indonesian archipelago and decreases radially from there (Gray, 1997). The terrestrial pattern of increasing diversity from poles to tropics occurs from the Arctic to the tropics but does not apppear to occur in the Southern Hemisphere where diversity is high at high latitudes. Highest losses of marine diversity occur in coastal areas largely as a result of conflicting uses of coastal habitats. The best way to conserve marine diversity is to conserve habitat and landscape diversity in coastal areas. Marine protected areas form only a part of the conservation strategy needed. A suitable framework for coastal conservation is integrated coastal area management where one of the primary goals is sustainable use of coastal biodiversity (Gray, 1997).

Angel (1993) reviewed some possible causes for the observed patterns of the pelagic biodiversity in the ocean. Temperate systems are some of the most productive and diverse systems known. Coral reefs, with their associated flora and fauna, although highly diverse are still relatively poorly described and their functioning is not well understood (Sebens, 1994).

There are genetic differences both among individuals and among populations. Populations with higher genetic diversity are more likely to have some individuals that can withstand environmental change and thereby pass on their genes to the next generation. On an evolutionary timescale, genetic diversity is higher in species found in unstable, stressed environments compared with counterparts from more stable environments. In contrast, on an ecological timescale (only a few generations), stress reduces genetic diversity; long–term exposure to contaminants can decrease genetic diversity, the remaining population becoming more vulnerable to extinction. Commercial fishing, which concentrates on specific size ranges, has significantly altered the genetic composition of populations (Elliott and Ward, 1992). In general, marine species have higher genetic diversity than freshwater and terrestrial species.

Most marine species diversity is benthic rather than pelagic (Angel, 1993), probably because the marine fauna originated in benthic sediments. The pelagic realm has an enormous volume compared with the inhabitable part of the benthic realm. Yet there are only 3500–4500 species of phytoplankton (Sournia and Chretiennot–Dinet, 1991) compared to the 250,000 species of flowering plants on land. There are probably only 1200 oceanic fish species against 13,000 coastal species (Angel, 1993). In the pelagic realm, diversity is higher in coastal rather than oceanic areas and, therefore, conservation efforts should be concentrated in coastal areas.

In the Red Sea, 90% of some groups of fishes are endemic. Of the 482 coral species recorded in the Indian Ocean, 27% occur only at one site (Gray, 1997). High endemism poses serious problems for development of conservation strategies. Two important questions are : (1) Are all species equally important for conservation purposes? (2) Do some endemic species play more significant roles than others in the structuring or functioning of the habitat concerned?

According to Gray (1997), in the marine domain there are more animal phyla than on land. Thirty-five phyla are marine and of these 14 are endemic, whereas only 14 occur in fresh water, where none are endemic. Eleven are terrestrial with one phylum being endemic and 15 phyla symbiotic with 4 endemic (Briggs, 1994). This figure includes the newly described phylum Cycliophora found in the gills of the Norway lobster (Funch and Kristensen, 1995). Thus phyletic diversity is also highest in the sea. Of the 35 marine phyla, only 11 are represented in the pelagic realm; most phyla occur in the benthos which is the archetypal habitat.

Functional diversity is the range of functions that are performed by organisms in a system. The species within a habitat or community can be divided into different functional types such as feeding guilds or plant growth forms or into functionally similar taxa such as suspension feeders or deposit feeders. Functionally similar species may come from very different taxonomic entities.

The concept of functional redundancy suggested that there are more species present in communities than are needed for efficient biogeochemical and trophic functions, but recent researches have shown that this is not the case — the higher the number of species in a community, the greater the efficiency of biogeochemical processes (Naeem *et al.*, 1994; Tilman and Downing, 1994). Unfortunately, however, no such work has been done in the marine environment.

It is now generally agreed that species are distributed along environmental gradients in approximately log–normal abundance patterns. However, various biotic interactions between species lead to there being co–occurring groups of species under given environmental conditions. Thus communities are convenient groupings of species which merge gradually into other groupings unless there are sharp boundaries in the environment. The term 'assemblage' is a more neutral term that does not imply the tight interspecies organization implied in the term 'community' with its anthropocentric overtones.

The most frequently used quantitative measure of biodiversity is for a given area rather than for a given biological community. In ecological terms, physical areas and the biotic components they contain are termed habitats. Habitat diversity is a more useful term than 'ecosystem diversity' since habitats are easy to envisage (e.g. a mangrove forest, a coral reef, an estuary). Furthermore, habitats often have clear boundaries. Indeed habitats have been termed 'templets' for ecology (Southwood, 1977). Within coastal areas, a wide variety of habitats are known to have high species diversity. Examples are sea–grass beds and coastal sedimentary habitats.

Patterns

Whereas in terrestrial systems, species diversity of genera and families commonly increases from poles to tropics, in the marine domain there is an apparent increase in species diversity of hard substratum epifauna from the Arctic to the tropics. Whereas the Arctic is dominated by many commercial fish species, the Antarctic is characterized by invertebrates (krill and squid) which support birds and mammals but only a small fishery (Gray, 1997).

Bivalve molluscs (at species, genus and family levels) tend to have increased diversity towards the tropics in the Indo–Pacific. Seaweed (macroalgal) diversity is usually higher in temperate latitudes than in the tropics and lowest at the poles (Silva, 1992).

The best known marine diversity pattern is that of corals which show highest values in the Indonesian archipelago and falling values radiating westwards across the Pacific Ocean (Stehli and Wells, 1971). The Indonesian archipelago may well be the 'epicentre' for evolution of marine tropical biodiversity (Veron, 1995).

Another notable pattern is that soft sediments harbour increasing diversity from shallow areas to the deep sea. There may possibly be a general pattern of low species diversity in shallow coastal areas.

Threats

Two important human activities that pose major threats to open ocean biodiversity are ocean dumping and UV–B radiation. Long–transported materials enter the open ocean and concerns have arisen about effects of organochlorine compounds on marine planktonic and benthic systems. It seems unlikely that contaminants will lead to measurable effects on oceanic diversity, such as local or regional extinctions. The serious threats to biodiversity are in the coastal zone and are a direct result of human population and demographic trends.

Some important threats to coastal systems are: habitat loss; global climate change; overexploitation of fishing; pollution, eutrophication, algal toxins; radionuclides); species introductions/invasions; watershed alteration and physical alterations of coasts; tourism, marine litter; and the fact that humans have very little perception of the oceans and their marine life (Norse, 1993; Sebens, 1994). All these are frequently interlinked. The most critical threat is undoubtedly habitat loss.

Another grave problem is that habitats become divided into small fragments. The resultant small habitat islands experience higher rates of species extinctions and lower immigration rates than larger 'habitat islands'. Fragmentation of habitats increases losses of species diversity.

The warming of the coastal ocean produces strong effects on corals. As a consequence of ozone depletion in the stratosphere, UV–B radiation flux on the earth is increasing. Consequently, productivity of phytoplankton in surface waters is being reduced (Häder et al., 1995). Effects on the symbiotic zoozanthellae in corals are likely. There are also concerns about impacts on diatoms on sand and mud flats. Dunlap and Yamamoto (1995) showed that several marine organisms contain mycosporine–glycine which functions as a biological antioxidant, thereby protecting the marine

154

organisms from the adverse effects of UV–B radiation. More research is needed before reliable predictions can be made of effects on marine biodiversity.

In summary, there are few threats to the open ocean: they are concentrated in coastal areas. Habitat destruction is particularly severe in tropical areas where mangroves, coral reefs and wetlands are being destroyed at alarming rates. In temperate areas there are severe threats to wetland areas and estuaries; also conflicts between industrial and tourism development and conservation are universal (Gray, 1997).

Marine Protected Areas

In 1995, Kelleher *et al.* reported over 1300 marine protected areas (MPAs) throughout the world, covering more than 80 million hectares of coastal seas. Many of these suffer from the lack of good management. According to Agardy (1997), many of these subtidal protected areas are really paper parks, with no sound management plan.

The concept of an MPA is simple — a marine area with defined boundaries within which there is some planned protection of species, systems, and/or processes. They range in size from a couple of hectares to the Great Barrier Reef Marine Park, which extends over 35,000 km^2 of Australia's continental shelf. For conservationists, MPAs represent tangible steps to protect natural systems from our overuse; for managers they provide a better alternative to control human use of coastal seas.

Some have claimed (see Sale, 1997) that an MPA will sustain or even enhance fishery yield from neighbouring localities. There is no evidence that the enhancement will surpass the total yield if fishers have not been excluded from the MPA, or that it is long term. Even the enhanced biomass that develops inside an MPA can be fished down within days when protection is removed (Agardy, 1997).

Sustainable use requires basic knowledge about the underpinnings of the system. From a fisheries management perspective, an important consideration in the identification of refugia is where the recruits come from. In this context, Agardy (1997) suggested the following to identify ecologically important areas : high species diversity, high endemism, significant productivity, concentration of important ecological processes, habitat for keystone or commercially important species, and high habitat diversity (beta diversity). The multistep process is a complex one and ecologists, managers and conservationists need to develop the science to guide these decisions (Sale, 1997).

Deep–sea Biodiversity

There has been a common misconception that organisms living at the bottom of deep seas are immune from large–scale shifts in climate. Recent studies have demolished this myth: there are links between benthic biodiversity, glaciation and the Earth's obliquity (Rex, 1997). It used to be assumed that the sea–floor is spatially and temporally uniform, and therefore deep–sea biodiversity is buffered from climatic change at the surface by the overlying water column. That changed with the finding of surprisingly high species diversity in the deep sea. It is now known that deep–sea biodiversity also varies on geological timescales of 10^3–10^4 years. These long–term fluctuations in diversity correspond to climatic shifts at the surface associated with glaciation and are linked to changes in solar insolation (Rex, 1997).

Surface–benthic coupling is mediated through the rapidly sinking remains of phytoplankton as well as through those organismic life cycles which include migration between benthic and pelagic habitats.

For certain benthic ostracod species, diversity has been found to decline most during severe glacial episodes.

Recent researchers suggest that some features of nutrient input (rate, spatio–temporal variation, quality) may be involved in shaping patterns of past and present deep–sea biodiversity. In the deep sea, species diversity varies geographically and bathymetrically, and can reach levels that rival tropical communities. The nature of sediments may be important in structuring deep-sea communities because deposit feeders rely on the sediments for nutrition and comprise most of the organisms in the deep sea. The composition of soft sediment communities is influenced by sediment particle size. Shallow–water deposit feeders selectively ingest particular size fractions of the sediments and there are interspecific differences in particle size preference (Etter and Grassle, 1992). Partitioning of sediments with respect to size may be more likely in the deep sea if there is strong selection for macrophagy as a result of reduced food supply and digestive constraints imposed by feeding on deposits; macrophagy would enable species to ingest selectively the more labile components of the sediments. If deposit feeders in the deep sea partition the sediments with respect to size, species diversity may at least partly be a function of sediment particle size diversity. Also, sediment particle size diversity may reflect habitat complexity because the organisms live on or within the sediments. Etter and Grassle (1992) have shown that species diversity is a significant positive function of sediment particle size diversity. The relationship seems to be scale invariant, accounting for a similar proportion of the variance at interregional, regional and local scales. Bathymetric patterns of species diversity also seem largely attributable to changes in sediment characteristics with depth. Sediment diversity may have an important role in determining the number of species within a community.

In the near future, any sustainable use of marine resources will compel us to change our ways of exploiting marine resources. These changes may range from simply not fishing during the spawning season of a given species, or using biodegradable fishing nets, to banning all development around the few remaining pristine coral reefs. Norse (1993) reviewed the information relevant to the conservation of marine biological diversity. The five major anthropogenic kinds of threat to marine biodiversity are: overexploitation, physical alteration, pollution, introduction of alien species, and global atmospheric change. In the face of the various impediments to marine conservation, there is an intrinsic need to manage marine biological resources (e.g., commercial fisheries) at scales which cross geographical and political boundaries. Yet, many of the effective management schemes so far have been effective because they were local, grass–root type efforts motivated by a strong commitment to protect and sustain resources in one's own backyard. The recommendations for implementing the conservation efforts range from managing particular species to broad mandates for entire organizations, governments and institutions.

Species Introductions in Marine Environments

Rather little is known about the potential effect of species introductions in marine environments. Countries at high risk from marine species introductions are those in which most of the trade is done via international shipping — the prime medium for the spread of marine species worldwide. In the USA, zebra mussels (*Dreissena polymorpha*) introduced from Europe via shipping have been spreading through the Great Lakes and clogging waterways. The costs of controlling the spread of the mussel run in the millions. In Tasmania, a Japanese starfish (*Asterias amurensis*) has assumed plague proportions in the Derwent Estuary, threatening mussel and scallop–farming industries. Understanding the risks and controlling the impacts associated with marine invasions is vital for many maritime countries.

The Asian (Japanese) alga *Undaria pinnatifida* has invaded New Zealand, probably through international shipping. It first appeared in 1987 in Wellington Harbour and has gradually spread throughout New Zealand; it is now found along even the southern coast of North Island and in numerous South Island harbours (Miller *et al.*, 1997).

Undaria generally grows in shallow water, from the low tide level out to depths of about 6 metres. The highest densities in Wellington are on artificial substrata such as wharf pylons, jetties, retaining walls and marine farms. It is also found in natural rocky-reef habitats where it coexists with native macroalgae such as *Carpophyllum* and *Macrocystis pyrifera*.

Undaria can spread either as whole plants or by spores. Its long–distance dispersal occurs on the hulls of commercial and recreational boats. Its spores are transported via shipping, for instance in the ballast water of freighters, or attached (as gametophytes) to artificial structures such as aquaculture floats, mooring lines, barges and boat hulls. The spores and gametophytes are hardy and can survive a wide range of conditions including darkness (i.e., in ballast tanks) and desiccation, and still be capable of germination (Miller *et al.*, 1997).

Chapter 6
BIODIVERSITY IN THE TROPICS

Introduction

The diversity of life is not evenly distributed on the surface of the earth. Some regions are much richer than others. The lower latitudes by and large have much greater variety of life than the higher ones. Hill tracts with their greater range of environments also harbour greater diversity than an equal area of plains at similar latitudes. Finally, regions colonized by organisms from different evolutionary lineages have greater diversity than those colonized by a single or fewer lineages.

It is only within the last decade that the scientific community and the public at large began to become aware of declining biodiversity, particularly in the tropics—and the sadly coincidental decline in the number of biologists in tropical countries that could analyze the diversity of their flora and fauna. In most tropical and subtropical countries, the number of trained specialists (e.g. taxonomists) is now woefully low whereas the task of understanding the biodiversity in these countries is vast and urgent.

The decline in the number of taxonomists throughout the world (particularly in the tropical developing countries) has occurred since the advent of the more fashionable areas of modern biology such as molecular biology and biotechnology. The newer areas of biology have tended to eclipse the science of biodiversity during the past three decades and it was the publication of *BioDiversity* by Wilson and Peter in 1988 that reawakened interest in biodiversity. Growing awareness in this area in recent years has highlighted the urgent need for a new exploration of the biosphere, and a strong co-ordinated effort analogous to the Human Genome Project has become the need of the hour to explore and describe the biotas of the planet with special emphasis on the tropics.

Today, the scale and scope of human activities have grown to rival the natural processes that built the biosphere and that maintain it as a place where life can thrive. Somewhere between 20 and 40 per cent of the earth's primary productivity, from plant photosynthesis on land and in the sea, is being appropriated for human use. The global amounts of biologically available nitrogen and phosphorus associated with fertilizers and other chemicals used in agriculture rival the amounts mobilized by natural processes. Vast holes in the ozone layer have been made by chlorofluorocarbons. Carbon dioxide from the burning of fossil fuels and tropical forests, along with other greenhouse gases,

159

is changing the composition of the earth's atmosphere in a manner that may cause profound global environmental changes. It is likely that today's living species may be swept away by a wave of extinction more rapid and extensive than any in the fossil record.

Five major cataclysms have diminished global diversity over the past 600 million years, each requiring 10 to 100 million years of evolutionary repair. Recently some understanding has emerged of the factors that structure communities of plants and animals and that govern the numbers and biogeographic distribution of species among real or virtual archipelagoes of islands and certain innovative approaches have been suggested (see Wilson, 1992) for evaluating the economic value of biological diversity, as the potential capital stock for pharmaceutical and agricultural industries and as the gene store that will provide the raw stuff for the biotechnological revolution.

Wilson (1992) prescribed a five-point plan for action: survey the world's fauna and flora; create wealth out of biological products (medicines, foods and other materials); promote sustainable development; save what remains of biological diversity; and restore wildlands in regions that have been exhausted and abandoned.

We can make crude estimates of species extinctions by combining knowledge about habitat destruction with established 'species area' relations (which roughly says that if one reduces the area to one-tenth, one halves the eventual number of species in it). Wilson (1992) gave a good survey of specific and detailed studies: for instance, only about 1% of the world's 9000 bird species have been certified extinct since the 17th century, and the current *Red Data Book* of the International Union for the Conservation of Nature (IUCN) in Switzerland lists only about 11% as threatened with extinction. But J. Diamond believes that many tropical birds in poorly studied regions are extinct or severely threatened but have not made it into the *Red Data Book*; Diamond estimates that a 'Green Book' of unthreatened bird species would include less than half. Wilson surveyed other studies pointing in this direction, including a three-year search for 266 species of freshwater fishes that had been recorded in rivers in Malaysia in Victorian times; only 122 were found.

Odd patterns emerge if we go through the fraction of species in different taxonomic groups that are listed as 'endangered' or vulnerable in the IUCN lists. Thus, it has been noted that the percentages listed as threatened in the following animal groups are: mammals, 11; birds, 11; reptiles, 3; and insects, 0.07. For trees, we have 32% of the 70 species of gymnosperms but only 9% of the roughly quarter of a million species of angiosperms (8.5% of monocots and 9.3% of dicots). It appears that the data speak mainly to how much attention you get, not how threatened with extinction you are!

160

Wilson (1992) emphasized that extinction threats are by no means confined to the tropics. He cited the alarming numbers of insect and other invertebrate species classified as endangered or vulnerable to extinction in Germany, Austria and England. In the UK, 1% of all insect species have become extinct this century, and 7% aré currently classified as endangered or vulnerable; the 7% figure also applies to invertebrates other than insects. There are some 5700 designated Sites of Special Scientific Interest (SSSI) in the UK. These do not receive absolute statutory protection and are being destroyed at about the same rate as the tropical rain forest is being burned.

Although *ex-situ* methods have their important uses, real hope for the future rests on the preservation of natural ecosystems. And above all the most crucial issue is of human population: unchecked human population can nullify any or all of the five proposals made by Wilson.

Continuing growth of human populations is the engine that drives everything. Patterns of accelerating resource use and their regional variations are important but secondary: problems of wasteful consumption can be solved if population growth is halted, but such solutions are essentially irrelevant if populations continue to proliferate. Every day there is a net increase of about one quarter of a million people in the world.

Species Diversity

There is a great deal of uncertainty and an enormous amount of variation in the estimates of species numbers in the tropics made by different workers from time to time. There are also examples in the tropics that suggest ecosystem resiliency in the conservation of species diversity. This warrants an urgent critical analysis of the loss-of-species issue which arises from the unquantifiable importance of species diversity to life support on a global scale.

Myers (1979) felt that the world was losing one species per day in the 1970s and by the end of this century, we might lose from 20 to 50%. Humans are the prime cause of these losses: the human population is growing much faster in tropical latitudes than elsewhere, resulting in more habitat destruction in the tropics. In fact, the greatest losses of species are reported to occur in the tropics, which contain half of the world's remaining forests. Some have even suggested that present tropical forests would be destroyed by the beginning of the next century and that because these forests are the world's richest in terms of species numbers, their destruction becomes the primary source of a global loss of species (Lugo, 1988).

Estimating the total species richness of the tropical biome appears to be impossible at this time. A total species inventory of even a single tropical ecosystem does not exist. Scientific understanding of total numbers of species is fragmentary. Therefore it may be best to use relative distributions of species in different forest types when making global estimates of species extinctions.

Lanly (1982) discussed the rate of change in tropical forests and attempted to document the rate of increase in the area of secondary forests (by reforestation, afforestation and natural regeneration) as well as the rate of foret loss. He showed that of 11.3 million hectares of mature forest land deforested annually, 5.1 million hectares are converted to secondary forest fallow. According to him, the total area of this forest type is 409 million hectares and almost 1 million hectares of secondary forest is created every year on unforested land through natural regeneration or human intervention. These large forest areas certainly must have a bearing on the conservation of species diversity because they support an extensive biota and because they can support more complex biota than the mature system they replace (Ewel, 1983). Lanly also showed that deforestation rates are higher in closed than in open forests. Within closed forests, a large fraction of the conversion involves logged forests (i.e., those that have previously been modified by human activity).

The Holdridge Life Zone Classification System identified some 120 ecological life zones in the world, of which 68 are tropical or subtropical (Holdridge, 1967). Thirty-two of the tropical and subtropical life zones can support forests. About 19 million square km of mature forests exist in the tropics and are distributed as follows: 42% in the dry forest life zones, 25% in the wet and rain-forest life zones, and 33% in the moist forest life zones. Life zone conditions relate to characteristic numbers of tree species, biomass and rate of primary productivity (Brown and Lugo, 1982), and capacity to resist and recover from disturbance (Ewel, 1983).

The total number of tree species increases linearly with rainfall and correlates negatively with the ratio of potential evapotranspiration to rainfall (Holdridge *et al.*, 1971; Lugo and Brown, 1981). It appears that species richness doubles from dry to moist forests and triples from dry to wet forests. Conceivably, the number of species lost when forests are destroyed depends on the type of life zone environment being destroyed. A proper recognition of the fact that tropical forests are highly diverse in respect of their ecological and species richness is crucial for global estimates of species extinctions. Further, life zones are subjected to different deforestation and regeneration rates. The fact that the intensities and consequent impacts of human activity vary among life zones

162

has important implications for the reliability of species extinction estimates.

To estimate the reduction in number of species in the tropics, Lugo (1988) emphasized the need for considering the effect of forest types on species abundance, the spatially selective (life zone) intensity of human activity, the role of secondary forests as species refugia, and the role of natural disturbances in maintaining regional species richness. Further, at a regional level, the importance of exotic species in the maintenance of species richness, particularly in ecosystems subjected to the impact of human activity, should be duly considered.

There is evidence to show the resiliency of the functional attributes of some types of tropical ecosystems (including their ability to maintain species richness) when they are subjected to intensive human use (Lugo, 1988). Initial human intervention results in the loss of the highly vulnerable species and massive forest destruction removes more widely distributed species. As massive species extinctions are likely if human destruction of forests continues unabated, the evidence for ecosystem resiliency should not be an excuse for continued abuse of tropical environments. Rather, ecosystem resiliency may be an additional tool available to managers if they choose to manage tropical resources prudently. It appears that a good strategy for forest and species conservation in tropical regions ought to focus on the restoration of forest production on former forest lands where food production is not sustainable. This, together with sensible use of secondary forests and tree plantations, should help reduce pressure on forest lands with mature forests or with unique ecological characteristics and set us on a course to meet the needs of the needy while protecting species diversity (Lugo, 1988).

Latitudinal Gradients in Species Diversity

Should increased productivity lead to increased population densities, it may also be expected to lead to increased species diversity because of a decreased probability of random walks to extinction. This is the 'species–energy' concept of diversity (Wright, 1983), a variant on the island biogeographic theory of diversity. The species–energy concept is based on the assumption that the productivity of a habitat determines the number of individuals that can survive per unit area. When multiplied by the area of the habitat, it gives the total number of individuals that can live in the habitat. The probability of extinction probably decreases as the total number of individuals increases, assuming that probability of immigration, or of speciation remains as it is in the island biogeographic theory. The theory can be applied by using a measure of total habitat productivity (productivity per unit area x habitat area), rather than the total number of

163

individuals, in making species–area curves. Use of actual evapotranspiration as an estimate of primary productivity enables generation of diversity patterns on islands of vastly different sizes and latitudes.

This approach may account for latitudinal gradients in species diversity. But the model assumes that the total number of individual organisms in a habitat is directly dependent on total productivity; this is okay for birds, and perhaps for mammals, but is incorrect for terrestrial plants. The $-3/2$ thinning relationship (Yoda *et al.*, 1963) and its application to monospecific stands shows that increases in productivity lead to major decreases in the densities of individual plants. Gorham (1979) found small increases in standing crop of vascular plants could lead to sharp decreases in plant density. In general, tropical habitats are much more productive and have greater standing crops than temperate habitats (see Tilman and Pacala, 1993). Thus, they have many fewer adult plants per unit area. When considered in the light of the species–energy concept this should make the forests of a tropical island less diverse than those of a comparably sized temperate island, but in fact the opposite is true (Wright, 1983).

According to Tilman and Pacala, the underlying logic of the species–energy concept fails to explain latitudinal gradients in plant species diversity. Although it may describe plant diversity relationships, the species–energy approach appears not to explain them because its underlying logic is not supported. Even if total energy provides a better empirical fit than latitude and area, it seems that some explanation other than that underlying the species–energy view needs to be found (Tilman and Pacala, 1993).

A unimodal curve best describes the effect of productivity on diversity and may fit vascular plant diversities. The number of species within a region usually varies unimodally with the rate of ecosystem energy flow and this hump–shaped pattern shows up in many biogeographical provincs. Plant and animal taxa, including vertebrates and invertebrates, follow it. It does fit the diversities of several marine invertebates. It fits the diversities of mammals in tropical and subtropical latitudes, and the diversities of birds along a tropical elevation gradient (Rosenzweig and Abramsky, 1993).

In theory, the average time required for competitive exclusion increases as the competitive abilities of species become more nearly equal. To test the importance of this relationship for understanding diversity patterns, Hubbell (1979) modelled tropical rain–forest dynamics under the assumption of competitive equivalence. In such a system, species tend to disappear slowly by chance fluctuations in their populations, in a process analogous to genetic drift. Eventually, the diversity of this kind of system will decline to a single species if there are no invasions by new species. Since the time course of this process is extremely long, the addition of new species by species production or invasion from adjacent habitats may suffice to maintain an equilibrium diversity at a high level. Furthermore, the equilibrium number of species should be directly related to the rate of production/immigration (Ricklefs and Schluter, 1993).

Empirical data on tropical forest trees and several groups of tropical animals point to much specialization within diverse natural communities. Species are not ecologically equivalent and each must predominate over some part of the total community niche. So, Hubbell's approach cannot fully explain diversity patterns. Of course, some systems, such as the insects of bracken may be non–competitive in the sense that large portions of the potential niche volume for herbivores remain unoccupied. The diversity of these systems may depend largely on access to sources of colonists (Caswell, 1976). In plants and many vertebrates, competition can be demonstrated experimentally and long–term coexistence of potential competitors depends more on competition coefficients being nearly equal than on their being very small (Ricklefs and Schluter, 1993). According to Ricklefs and Schluter, within complex natural environments, large numbers of species can distribute themselves so as to achieve competitive equivalence. With interspecific competition, the niche space occupied by each species may contract until, with an increasing specialization to utilize the most favourable portions of the niche space, the per capita growth rate of its population increases. The more numerous the species, the smaller the portion of niche space that each dominates.

Specialization in respect of habitat may occur within ecological time when populations fail to maintain themselves in a variety of different habitat types (that is, when source populations cannot maintain sink populations). Similar specialization may also conceivably occur when individuals evolve to utilize narrower ranges of resources and conditions that they exploit more efficiently. Such specialization may require individuals to increase the habitat area over which they forage to procure resources, so reducing the density of the population but permitting its continued existence in the face of strong interspecific competition (Ricklefs and Schluter, 1993).

Tropical Vertebrates

Though it may sound strange, nonetheless some work in Australia suggests that higher productivities depress tropical bird and tropical mammal diversities. Australian tropical mammal diversity first rises to a peak from the dry–wet tropics to the wet tropical highlands and then declines substantially in the wet lowlands (Rosenzweig and Abramsky, 1993). Also, it is well known that bird species abound in the lowland tropics. Censuses of birds in a lowland foodplain forest in the Amazon basin of Peru revealed

319 species in a 97–ha study site, and point diversities of over 160 species (Terborgh *et al.*, 1990). Such point diversities greatly exceed the highest of those of any uniform habitat in North America. Yet it is often said that in one sense, compared with the less productive higher elevations, the lowlands are depauperate. It appears that productivity is not the only influence on diversity: the best established influence of all may be area. In any biogeographical province, larger areas usually always harbour many more species. Ecologists should no longer ignore area when comparing the diversities of tropical uplands and lowlands. Elevation probably is a good inverse index of productivity in the tropics.

In the Neotropics, lowland tropical area can far exceed that of any other elevation. But, over similar–sized areas, the more productive lowlands tend to have fewer bird species than subtropical elevations do.

In general, from high elevations down to subtropical elevations, the more the productivity, the higher the bird diversity. But the even greater productivity at low elevations does not add to diversity; rather it decreases diversity. So, many more birds are seen in the lowlands merely because they are so extensive (Rosenzweig and Abramsky, 1993).

It seems that within large regions diversity rises over low productivities and falls over high productivities but it is not known why the rising phase of the pattern most likely emerges because higher productivities can support larger population sizes. Larger population sizes should experience lower extinction rates. Possibly, environmental heterogeneity and intertaxon competition may account for the observed patterns to some extent. The heterogeneity hypothesis states that heterogeneity peaks at intermediate productivities. The other hypothesis of intertaxon competition predicts great variety from taxon to taxon in the place of the peak diversity, and this is often seen.

On a global scale, Terborgh (1973) observed a marked gradient in area from tropical to polar climates. Tropical regions cover far more territory. Terborgh's gradient coupled to allopatric speciation accounts for the latitudinal gradient in diversity (Rosenzweig, 1995). At any diversity, tropical regions should experience higher speciation rates and probably lower extinction rates. Consequently, steady-state tropical diversities exceed those of any other latitude. Only if tropical biotas were significantly younger than biotas of other latitudes could they be less diverse (Rosenzweig and Abramsky, 1993).

Beetles and Butterflies

It has long been known that the greatest proportion of species on Earth are insects

(Gaston, 1991). Erwin (1997) focused on beetles in rain forest canopies and showed how critical studies in local geographic areas can advance our understanding of which and how many species occur in natural tropical communities. Robbins and Opler (1997) have shown that biogeographic patterns of butterfly diversity are quite similar to those of birds, which means that conservation efforts aimed at particular regions can protect both these important groups of organisms.

The aspect of butterfly diversity that has received the greatest attention is the remarkable difference in species richness between tropical and temperate regions. This is best illustrated by the fact that whereas over 600 species can be found within an hour's walk of Belem, a town near the mouth of the Amazon River, the total number found in the British islands does not exceed 70 and the whole of Europe supports no more than about 325! (see Scriber, 1973). As to general patterns for butterflies, however, variation of species richness within temperate or tropical regions, rather than between them, is poorly known. Indeed, comparisons of numbers of species among the Amazon basin, tropical Asia and Africa are still mostly uncertain and conjectural, even for vertebrates (Gentry, 188).

One broad general pattern seems to be that the greatest undocumented diversity is found in organisms of small body size and in tropical regions and that many species in these groups and regions are likely to become extinct before they are even known if immediate conservation steps are not taken.

Snout Moths

Snout moths (Pyraloidea) are primarily tropical in distribution but occur worldwide, including many oceanic islands. Neotropical pyraloids comprise about 20% of the world fauna (Solis, 1997). Pyraloid caterpillars have diverse habits. They eat dried or decaying plant or animal matter, wax in bee and wasp nests, as well as living plant material. Some are found in ant nests, predators of scale insects and aquatic scavengers in flowing water. Snout moths show considerable plant specificity. For example, the Midilinae bore in the family Araceae whereas the genus *Diaphania* feeds only on the Cucurbitaceae. Snout moth caterpillars are intimately associated with their plant hosts and have developed elegant, concealed feeding strategies such as folding, rolling, webbing or tying of leaves; making tunnels or tubes of silk or frass; mining leaves; and boring into stems, buds, roots, and fruits (Solis, 1997).

The hyperdiverse pyraloid moths are major pests of crops and stored grains as well as important agents of biological control for weedy plants. Solis (1997) demonstrated that in order to increase the taxonomic self–sufficiency of tropical countries and to be effective in pest control, taxonomic studies in specific countries ought to be framed in a global context and made readily accessible to ecologists, conservationists, quarantine officers and farmers.

Neotropical Primates

New World primates are called platyrhines because of their flat nose and wide–set nostrils. They appear to have evolved as forest dwellers, never descending to occupy the terrestrial habitats used by Old World primates (Dietz, 1997).

There are 16 extant genera of platyrhines; a few examples: *Ateles, Lagothrix, Callicebus, Saguinus* (tamarins) and *Saimiri* (squirrel monkey).

Hershkovitz (1977) used pelage and cranial descriptions to classify most of the extant species of neotropical primates, contributing greatly to our knowledge of their diversity. The geographic ranges of many species have suffered change by recent anthropogenic habitat modifications, obscuring correlations between geographic distribution and morphological characteristics.

For conservation we need (besides the geographic range) a reliable estimate of how many individuals of a particular species remain in the wild and some idea of their population structure. Censuses have indicated that the numbers of many neotropical primates have been decreasing in recent years. The use of remote sensing technology and geographic information system analysis has advanced our capability to quantify and evaluate primate habitats. Images derived from satellite–borne instruments can go a long way in integrating large sets of data and constructing conservation strategies. Captive breeding and reintroduction provide hope that these endangered primates will survive.

Strangler Figs

Strangler figs (*Ficus* sp.) are semiparasitic trees that grow throughout the tropics. They are often colonies of individual plants that merge into a single entity. This highlights the difficulty of measuring biodiversity, let alone preserving it. There is some concern about the survival of the strangler fig because its life cycle is fragile and its fruit is a dietary staple of tropical mammals and birds (Rennie, 1992).

The figs propagate from seeds in the animal droppings that collect in the crotches of trees. Their roots grow and fuse into a woody lattice around the trunk of the host choking off the tree's access to nutrients. In Panama, very few fig trees were found to be single individuals—most were two or three fused plants. One tree seemed to be fused from eight individuals.

The mosaic nature of the strangler figs may have implications for conservation efforts. Many strangler figs alternate between male and female phases and they reproduce with the assistance of tiny symbiotic wasps. The male wasps live inside a female plant syconium, which houses the developing flowers and fruits; a female wasp leaves to lay eggs in a new syconium only after the male flowers bloom, carrying pollen from one fig to another. A population cannot survive unless it simultaneously contains male and female plants within a distance that wasps can cover within two days.

For conservation, it is not enough to count trees: the blooming schedules of each individual within a tree also need to be considered. If the branches flower at different times, then only a few trees might be needed because they would act like many more. Conversely, if all the fused individuals in a tree bloom simultaneously then more trees would be required to ensure that plants in the right stage of development are always available. Strangler figs would then be much more vulnerable to deforestation (Rennie, 1992). Preliminary studies have shown that branches of strangler fig trees generally do bloom simultaneously, a gloomier outlook for conservation.

Species Flocks

The term 'species flock' refers to an unusually large number of closely related species coexisting within a given region, among which there may be extensive sympatry of ecologically and morphologically similar species (Brooks, 1950). Species flocks offer important opportunities for studying the relationship between species production and diversity. The best studied species flocks are the cichlid fishes of the African rift lakes (Greenwood, 1974, 1981) and the amphipod crustaceans of Lake Baikal (Kozhov, 1963).

The 200 or so species of 'haplochromine' cichlid fish of Lake Victoria appear to be monophyletic, having evolved within the last 200,000 years, judging from mitochondrial DNA divergence (Meyer et al., 1990). If their diversity resulted from serial bifurcation of species into daughter species, speciation events would have to have occurred every 26,000 years on average. Conceivably, allopatric speciation of rock-dwelling species could have occurred on the small scale of rock outcroppings separated by sandy bottom, accentuated by attractions in lake level that joined and separated suitable areas of habitat.

Several authors have favoured the idea that species flocks may form when a taxon enters a depauperate system, such as cichlids found in a newly formed lake (Strauss, 1984). In most cases of species flocks, niche space is packed very densely with species, but the entire flock also shows a greater variety of morphologies and ecological roles than the parental taxon does (Dominey, 1984). Thus, the haplochromines of Lake Victoria exhibit greater ecological diversity than cichlids in general. The study of species flocks, especially in comparison to coexisting clades that have not undergone such high radiation, may reveal much about the processes of species production and the development of ecological communities (Ricklefs and Schluter, 1993).

Mangroves

Mangrove areas constitute a natural feature of the tropical forests which have suffered increasing destruction in the past few decades through the damage caused by the excessive intervention of plant and animal life, human impacts and the irretrievable loss of natural resources. In order to protect the natural environment for future generations worldwide, it is essential to preserve the earth's natural resources and to prevent their waste and overexploitation.

Increasing attention has recently been drawn to mangrove forests, which are being threatened to an even greater extent than other tropical forests or have already been completely destroyed. In contrast to the tropical rain-forests, however, the dramatic devastation of these saline–tolerant tidal forests, which represent an open ecosystem, has not yet been the subject of major discussion. The tropical mangrove forests provide a significant habitat for a wide variety of animals, including many commercially important species. They serve as a nursery for numerous species of fish and crustaceans. They provide natural surf protection, supply wood and are presumably an important carbon dioxide reduction system. The mangroves colonize the strip of land between the lowest and highest water levels determined by the changing tides along the sheltered tropical and subtropical coasts and estuaries. These partially flooded thicket and forest areas are termed tidal forests. Until recently, mangrove areas were generally regarded as useless, hostile territory and therefore used to be destroyed. A good 80% of the previously existing mangrove forests have been devastated or have been subjected to degradation as a result of land deposits, construction of sanitary landfills or simply due to overuse, whether this be through charcoal extraction or the setting up of aquaculture systems. Unlike tropical rain forests, mangrove areas can be reafforested provided the hydrologic system is still intact. The high efficiency of the mangrove forests lies in their exceptional ability to adapt to extreme conditions with fluctuating daily rhythms. This is further accentuated by the viviparity of several plant species.

Mangroves make up extraordinary ecological formations in the coastal lowlands of the tropics. Neither land nor sea, they consist of trees with flying buttresses, and are adapted to brackish waters and unstable, often highly saline soils. This type of vegetation provides fish nurseries, rich fishing grounds and a vast number of both timber and non–timber products. Globally, mangroves suffer from the cumulative effects of natural disasters, clear–cutting, overlogging, fish– and shrimp–farming, industrial and domestic pollution, dredging and industrial and agricultural land reclamation as well as fragmentation — all of which threaten their continued existence.

The world's mangrove ranges differ significantly in respect to numbers and diversity of species. Based on the number of woody plant species which may serve as an indicator of the total number of species occurring in the tidal forests, an eastern range encompassing the coasts and islands of the Indian Ocean and the West Pacific with a large diversity of species is clearly distinguishable from the western mangrove province with a much poorer diversity, which includes the coasts of America and West Africa (see Fig. 6–1). The eastern, Indo–Pacific province divides into three groups, of which the Indo–Malaysian group is the richest in species (Chapman, 1970). This in turn embraces subgroups, and of these the Burma–Indo–Malaysian subgroup is the richest. South East Asia thus has the largest mangrove stands in the world but the mangrove ecosystems with the greatest species diversity suffer some impoverishment eastwards towards the Philippines (Chapman, 1970; Uthoff, 1996).

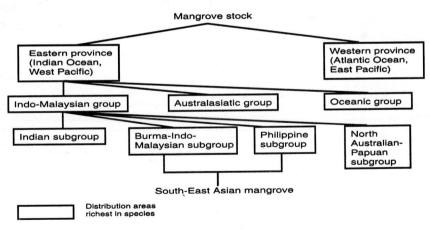

Fig. 6–1. Diversity of mangrove stands in the world (after Aksornkoae, 1987; Chapman, 1970).

171

Table 6–1. List of speices for the mangrove forests in Thailand (after Aksornkoae, 1987)

Organisms		Number of species
FLORA		
Woody plants		74
(trees, shrubs, ferns, palms)		
Epiphytes		18
Algae		44
Total		**136**
FAUNA		
Fishes		72
Shrimps		37
Crustaceans		54
Molluscs		20
Birds		88
Mammals		35
Insects		38
Reptiles		25
snakes	12	
amphibians	6	
turtles	1	
lizards	5	
crocodiles	1	
Total		**369**
Grand Total		**505**

In the mangroves between India and northern Australia, (in other words, in the Indo–Malaysian and Australasiatic group), there occur 193 plant species, 397 fish species, 259 crab species and 256 mollusc species (Rao, 1987). The species estimates made by Aksornkoae (1987) for Thailand are shown in Table 6–1. Other countries of SE Asia also show great diversity (see Uthoff, 1996).

Selective use of the original tidal forests leads to some degradation of the natural mangrove stands accompanied by a loss of species. The conversion of tidal forest into intertidal commercial forests has the same effect. Anthropogenically induced mangrove destruction occurs basically in two ways. What has to be distinghished is degradation as a consequence of selective use, extraction and stand alteration adding to a loss in species diversity and loss of quality, and destruction by deforestation which, by excluding the tidal influence, deprives the mangrove ecosystem irrevocably of its basis of life (Uthoff, 1996). Of course, some mangrove destruction also occurs naturally. Rapid rises in sea level on the one hand, or increasing alluvial deposits on the other, lead to natural stand alterations similar to degradation processes and can reduce species diversity. The same applies to changes in salinity.

For the people living on the edges of the mangrove forests, intact tidal forests furnish fuel, building material for houses, boats and fishing equipment, foodstuffs, such as fish, mussels, crustaceans, poultry, eggs, leafy vegetables, honey, sugar, raw materials for household utensils, clothing, tanning agents and traditional medicinal remedies. The mangrove ecosystem not only allows some subsistence living, but also the chance to extract market products as a source of income (Uthoff, 1996).

The traditional diversity of utilization is based on the horizontal and vertical differentiation of the mangrove forests. The horizontal differentiation is expressed in clear zonation as the result of different durations of water submersion and corresponds to the transition from the marine to the terrestrial habitat, in which more and more marine elements decline and more and more terrestrial elements increase from the sea towards the land. Vertical differentiation is expressed in a clear layered structure, in which the following faunistic habitats are arranged one above the other:

— canopy of the trees as a habitat for birds and insects;

— trunk and branch area, where rain water collects in the branch holes and axils, making a freshwater supply possible above the salt and brackish water, as a suitable habitat for mammals, reptiles and birds;

— subaerial soil surface as a habitat for mammals, reptiles and snails;

— permanently or periodically filled ponds as a habitat for crabs, frogs and shrimps;

— mangrove channels and tidal canals as a habitat for pelagic fishes and reptiles;

— submarine soil surface as a habitat for benthic organisms such as demersal fishes, shrimps, crabs and molluscs; and

— submarine soil as a habitat for mud–burrowing molluscs and worms.

With the changing tides the levels shift periodically. It is the multistorey structure and the zonation that make the high species diversity possible.

The species diversity goes hand in hand with the diversity of utilization, shown in Table 6–2. For wood formation alone there is an enormously wide range of products from traditional and current exploitation (see Table 6–2).

Some mangrove products from woody formations and associated fauna are listed below.

Fuels (firewood for cooking, smoking fish, burning bricks; charcoal for cooking and grilling; lighting oils; and alcohol). Building materials (timber for construction; scaffolding; beams and poles for buildings; rail sleepers; pit props; bridge building, boat building, quay construction, or for water pipes; floorboards; timber for wall filling; woven matting; fence stakes, and chipboard). Material for fishing (poles for fish traps; poles and beams for net cages; timber for rafts and floats; piscicides; tanning material for impregnating nets, lines and ropes). Materials for textile and leather production (fibres for weaving; dyes for textiles; tannins for leather production; hides and furs, synthetic silk). Products for agriculture (fodder; green manure). Paper and paper raw materials (lignocellulose; wood chips; fibres for kraft paper and other papers). Household goods (furniture; mortars and pestles; handles for household items; matches). Food and luxury items (sugar; edible oils; alcohol; vinegar; alcoholic beverages; tea substitute; spices; vegetables from seeds, fruits and leaves; confectionery from seeds; cigar substitutes; cigarette paper; honey; fish; crustaceans; mussels; eggs and meat from birds). Chemist's goods (wax; aromatic substances; skin–care products; hairdressing oil; glue; mosquito repellents). Other products (packing cases and baskets; tar; and pharmaceutics) (see Mercer and Hamilton, 1984; Uthoff, 1996).

The substances contained in the mangrove woods are also used as ethnopharmaceuticals in traditional medicine (see Table 6–2), as remedies for treating

Table 6–2. Selected ethnopharmaceuticals from mangrove forests (after Uthoff, 1996)

Species	Parts	Preparation	Use for/treatment of
Heritiera littoralis	seeds		diarrhoea
Rhizophora mucronata	bark	infusion	diarrhoea, dysentery
Ceriops decandra	bark	infusion	diarrhoea, dysentery
Xylocarpus granatum	seeds		diarrhoea, cholera
Bruguiera parviflora	heartwood	extract	constipation
B. gymnorrhiza	fruits	sap	eye diseases
Rhizophora mucronata	fruit	sap	insect repellent
Xylocarpus moluccensis	seeds	extract	insect bites
Avicennia spp.	bark	extract	skin parasites
Clerodendron inerme	leaves	extract	skin parasites
Acanthus ilicifolius	bark, root	bath	skin diseases, allergies
Thespesia populnea	fruit and leaves	ointment	scabies
Acanthus ilicifolius	bark	extract	smallpox
A. ilicifolius	fruit pulp		snake bites, blood–cleansing
A. ilicifolius	leaves	ointment	rheumatism
Ceriops tagal	bark	extract	wound–cleansing
Excoecaria agallocha	wood	smoke inhalation	leprosy
Rhizophora mucronata	bark	infusion	leprosy
Excoecaria agallocha	leaves		epilepsy
Clerodendron inerme	roots	extract	hepatitis
Hibiscus tiliaceus	blossoms	infusion	infection in ear canals
Avicennia alba	resin		contraceptive

wounds, because of their anti-inflammatory, haemostatic, wound-cleansing and antiseptic properties, and also against chronic illnesses. Seeds (*Xylocarpus granatum*) and leaves (*Excoecaria agallocha*) are taken directly.

Some animal products of mangroves are highly valuable. Among the crustaceans they include the giant tiger prawn (*Penaeus monodon*), the somewhat smaller banana shrimp (*Penaeus merguiensis*) and the mud crab (*Scylla serrata*). Fish use the mangroves as spawning grounds, nurseries, feeding areas, shelter or permanent habitats, depending on species and, accordingly, inhabit the tidal forests temporarily, permanently or in particular phases of their life cycle. Economically important species are the milkfish *Chanos chanos*), mullets (*Mugilidae*) and various tropical perch species (*Epinephelus* spp., *Lates calcarifer*). Among the molluscs the oyster (*Crassostrea commercialis*) is commercially the most valuable.

The nipa palm (*Nypa fructicans*) occurs especially on the landward edge of those mangroves where there is little periodic water covering (i.e., in the tidal forests of South and SE Asia). It is probably the most valuable plant within the mangrove and is often cultivated in plantations (Uthoff, 1996). Its fronds are made into shingles used in rural areas to thatch houses and as outer wall elements. One ha of nipa plantation can yield about 15,000 of these palm-leaf elements annually. Mats, baskets, and hats are also woven from nipa fronds. The leaf shoots serve as a substitute for cigarette paper. Young leaves are used to wrap food, while the ribs are used as fuel. The sap of the young inflorescence is tapped for sugar production, alcohol distillation and vinegar production. One ha of nipa plantation can yield 3000 litres of alcohol per year (Fong, 1980). The soft endosperm of the fruits is edible and is greatly relished in Thailand, Indonesia and the Philippines. The hard shells of the ripe fruits are used for making buttons.

The following are the chief competitors for the existing natural mangrove sites: wood production and wood exploitation; rice, coconut and oil palm growing areas; marine aquaculture of shrimps and other fish; transport facilities such as roads, docks and airfields; settlement area development; development of coastal industrial areas; raw material extraction in the intertidal zone; and areas used for tourism. Together these utilizations have led to the degradation or destruction of about 50% of the mangrove stands of SE Asia.

Tidal forests provide a multilevel, dynamic coast protection in areas under threat by flooding from the sea. The mangrove fringe helps in breaking down the force of tidal storm energy, prevents the mobilization of sediment and reduces the danger of coastal

176

erosion. The root system of the tidal forests helps keep the substratum firm and so contributes to the long term stability of the coast.

Tidal forests provide shelter and feeding area for many species of marine animals. They are the spawning and growing areas for numerous species of marine fauna.

Until recently, species diversity has been the basis for the traditional utilization diversity. Conversely, a diversity of sustainable uses must today be regarded as the basis for maintaining the diversity of species (Uthoff, 1996).

Sustainable Conservation

Sustainable development is the need of the hour to improve the general living standard of tropical and subtropical people and is even more specially needed to conserve biodiversity. The two goals are not independent, but they must be interlinked intimately to achieve effective conservation. Biodiversity is essential for maintaining the life-support system of humankind the world over and as a direct source of products for the use, economy and well-being of human beings. It is necessary to design a truly symbiotic relationship between sustainable development, biodiversity and its conservation in the tropics.

At least some of the current problems of development in the tropics are not new (Kangas, 1997). Although the tropics do present some unique problems (see Kamarck, 1976) several of the ideas for sustainable development are being tested. But without doubt there is a newly appreciated urgency for tropical sustainable development. Happily, this has already catalyzed hybrid approaches such as political ecology (Guimaraes, 1991), conservation biology, and ecological economics. Biologists are learning economics (e.g. how to market rain forest products) and economists have become interested in the importance of species diversity. Let us hope that time to learn these lessons does not run out before tropical biodiversity is seriously lost.

Wildlife and Sustainable Development in Kenya, India and South Asia

Kenya

In Kenya, economy is intimately linked with tourism and wildlife. Tourism ranks second only to agriculture and is largely dependent on the wildlife resources base. Many tourists find recreation and enjoyment in visiting national parks and reserves to see different kinds of game animals. And yet, Kenya is losing wildlife resources quite fast, the losses being associated with extensive ecological degradation as a result of significant changes in socioeconomic activities, coupled with increasing human population.

With a view to strengthening its capability to manage wildlife resources and promote tourism, Kenya has introduced major institutional reforms (Mugabe and Wandera, 1995). National parks and reserves have been created to conserve a representative sample of fauna and flora for educational purposes, and for aesthetic and recreational enjoyment both by Kenyans and overseas visitors. These areas are mainly established to ensure sustainable management of both fauna and flora, through propagation and preservation. Within national reserves, some human economic activities such as pastoralism and agriculture are allowed provided they do not damage wildlife resources. The protection of wildlife resources is contemplated through control of poaching.

In 1963, there were only four national parks and six game reserves in Kenya. By 1992 the country had 26 national parks, 29 national reserves and one local sanctuary. Terrestrial national parks, reserves and sanctuaries cover a total area of about 4.4 million hectares i.e., about 7.5% of the country's land area. Marine reserves have been created to control fishing and destruction of coral reefs in the coastal region. The marine protected areas cover about 114,000 hectares.

Hand in hand with the increase in number of national parks and reserves there has been a substantial increase in the number of tourists. The total number of tourists to the country's national parks and reserves increased from 424,000 in 1976 to 730,000 in 1989. Total revenue generated from tourism increased from 41.1 million Kenya pounds in 1976 to 432 million Kenya pounds in 1989.

The growth of national parks has resulted in displacement of some local communities while the growth of tourism has contributed to ecological degradation in some parks and reserves. Some persons feel that rapid population growth and wildlife management for purposes of tourism has not contributed to the socioeconomic welfare of the majority of the Kenyan population. Indeed economic revenue generated directly from tourism has not gone to meeting the socioeconomic needs of the local communities living near parks and reserves. Some part of foreign currency earned through tourism has gone to the Treasury and been used to import luxury consumables for the rich (Mugabe and Wandera, 1995).

In the process of creating national parks and reserves, some local communities have been displaced from their homes. Some of the communities have been settled in marginal lands not suitable for agricultural activities.

Wildlife management in Kenya has largely focused on conservation of big species of animals (e.g., elephants and rhinos) for tourist recreational purposes. Not much has been done for conservation of small species of animals nor most indigenous plants.

The growth of tourism and increase in the number of national parks and reserves have not always been conducive to effective management of wildlife resources. Rather, the loss of wildlife resources has increased. According to Mugabe and Wandera, by 1986 Kenya had lost approximately 48% of its wildlife habitat. The population of elephants had decreased to 18,000 in 1988 from 165,000 in 1973 and that of black rhino decreased from about 20,000 in 1970 to 350 in 1986. Crowned cranes had declined from 35,000 in 1978 to about 19,000 in 1987. As a matter of policy, wildlife is being managed for sustaining the tourist industry. Happily, focus is now shifting towards integrated wildlife management. Attempts are being made to introduce reforms so as to create an institutional system with flexibility, efficiency and capability to undertake wildlife management; to ensure that wildlife management takes into account the socioecological and economic needs of local communities residing near parks and reserves; to ensure the conservation of both flora and fauna; to ensure that the country's wildlife resources are utilized in a sustainable manner to enhance national economic development; and to ensure that people and property in areas adjacent to national parks and reserves are protected from injury.

India and South Asia

The Indian subcontinent is essentially tropical and has a rich wealth of living organisms. The country supports a tremendous variety of environmental regimes from the warm, humid tracts of Kerala to the cold, dry heights of the Ladakh plateau, and the hot desert of Rajasthan to the swamps of Sundarbans. It is also a country situated at the trijunction of African, European and South East Asian realms and derives characteristic elements from each of them. To these are added elements that developed independently in peninsular India from its history as part of a southern Gondwanaland. This renders India one of the biologically richest tracts in the world. The full diversity of the country's plant and animal life is only partially known. Whereas birds have been well studied and comprise about 1200 described species, groups such as insects have been only partially investigated and another 20 to 50,000 species may easily be added to the 67,000 species already described from India.

India covers about 2% of the earth's land. It has about 45,000 species of wild plants and over 77,000 species of wild animals, an estimated 6.5% of the world's known wildlife (see Kaushik, 1996). At least 10% of India's recorded wild flora and fauna are threatened species, many of them near extinction. During the last few decades India has lost one-half of its forest, polluted over 70% of its water bodies and degraded most of its coasts. The rate at which India is now eroding its biodiversity has not been estimated but may be assumed to be quite high. The causes of this loss lie not only in population explosion, but also in the overexploitation, by pharmaceutical industries and in deforestation, leading to drastic changes in the environmental conditions and original vegetation. The northern districts of the state of Madhya Pradesh supported luxurious vegetation in the past but today mostly have dry deciduous vegetation. Over 1200 angiospermic plant species have been recorded from this area, out of which about 16% species are endemic to India. Family Leguminosae is the largest family followed by Gramineae. Over 480 genera have a single species each. *Cyperus* has the largest number of species in the area. Flora of the area is dominated by herbaceous species (847), 136 species of climbers and 70 aquatic species. Some common herbaceous species are *Alternanthera sessilis, Argemone mexicana, Cassia obtusifolia, Tephrosia hamiltonii, Crotalaria medicaginea, Bothriochloa pertusa, Cynodon dactylon* and *Heteropogon contortus.* Due to human activities, some species show a changing pattern in distribution and some 'ultraneophytes' have been introduced to this area. *Ceratopteris thalictroides, Butea monosperma* var. *lutea, Caesalpinia sappan, Crescentea cujeje* and *Striga* spp. have eroded from the area. *Utricularia aureus, Gymnema sylvestris, Zizyphus glabberima* are threatened. 'Ultraneophyte' *Parthenium hysterophorus* is invading and colonizing all types of habitats and reducing the number (plants/m^2) of other species, such as *Cleome gynandra, Amaranthus spinosus, Argemone mexicana, Tephrosia hamiltonii* and *Cassia obtusifolia.* But species establishing themselves through underground vegetative parts in addition to seeds can coexist with this 'ultraneophyte'. These species are *Bothriochloa pertusa, Boerhavia diffusa, Cynodon dactylon* and *Merremia emarginata* (Kaushik, 1996).

As of today, the number of animal species described from India, apart from the 67,000 insects, includes (approximately) 4000 molluscs, 6500 other invertebrates, 1400 fishes, 140 amphibians, 420 reptiles, 1200 birds and 340 mammals. Thus about 80,000 species of animals have been described from India, compared to the world total of 1.5

million. Of the 240,000 species of higher plants known from the world, some 15,000 have been described from India. Thus around 5 to 6% of the known species of living organisms of the world occur in India with a land surface of only 2.2% (see Gadgil, 1996).

The enormous natural diversity of India extends from mangrove forests of the Sunderbans, rain forests of Western Ghats, coral reefs of Lakshadweep and wetlands of Bharatpur to the great Thar desert in Rajasthan. This great diversity, coupled with its position at the trijunction of African, Eurasian and Oriental biotas places India among the world's 12 megadiversity countries. Over 125,000 species of living organisms have been described from the Indian subcontinent which probably harbours another 400,000 still to be described. India is also one of the global centres of diversity of crops and livestocks (Gadgil, 1996).

Only about one-fifth of the species found in the Indian subcontinent appear to have been scientificially described, and most of these were studied and described by British and other foreign scientists. Their specimens are usually located in the British Museum of Natural History London or Kew Herbarium in London. Of about 82,000 described species of animals, specimens of only 51,000 species are located in the Indian Museum in Calcutta. Of course, specimens of an additional few hundred species of animals are available in Indian universities but unfortunately most of these are not well maintained, cared for or preserved. There may be some 30,000 species whose specimens are available only abroad. We do have in India specimens of all the bird species but, even in this case, there may be 10 times as many specimens abroad as in India. Of aphids, India holds specimens of only about 10% of the described species. Aphids being important crop pests, some foreign agencies holding specimens of Indian aphid species are charging heavy fees for identifying aphid specimens. For plants the situation is just as bad: the rice germplasm collection of the International Rice Research Institute is much richer, even in terms of Indian material, than any of our own collections. We do have a few culture collections of micro–organisms but not one of them can compare with reputed international-class microbial collections in respect of quality and proper maintenance (Gadgil, 1996).

Identification and inventorying of the enormous biological diversity in the Indian subcontinent is a truly formidable task in view of the fact that expertise for identifying plants, animals and micro-organisms is either lacking or extremely inadequate, especially for smaller organisms such as mites, bacteria, protozoa, algae, fungi, lichens and benthic marine worms. There is an urgent need for monitoring the ongoing changes in the populations of living organisms throughout the country; this is necessary to ascertain whether populations of medicinal herbs are on the decline through overharvests, or if wild relatives of cultivated plants are being eroded through habitat transformations, or populations of weeds such as water hyacinth are exploding and choking our wetlands, or new species of insects are becoming pests for our crops, and to keep track of populations of vectors of human diseases such as mosquitoes. According to Gadgil, this work does not require the ability to identify most of our known or unknown species but can be effectively done by developing the capability to reliably identify only a few hundreds of species each of medicinal plants, edible fishes, butterflies, frogs, turtles, birds, mammals, insect pests of crops, bacteria, fungi, intestinal worms and other human and livestock parasites and their vectors. These significant species need to be monitored throughout the Indian terestrial, aquatic, and marine ecosystems. As only a few hundreds out of this set of a few thousands will be present in any given locality, it is not difficult to learn to identify this small subset.

In those areas where biological resources are being depleted to meet the basic needs of local populations, *in situ* conservation has to be reconciled with immediate human needs. Successful conservation depends upon meeting the needs of local people, while ensuring sustainability of the resource. One good example of this is encountered in Uttar Pradesh (Chakranagar) which is home to the Jamunapari breed of goat. These locally adapted goats, a large dairy breed with a good meat carcass, can survive in arid and barren conditions. Recent introductions of new breeds have led to a decline in numbers of the pure-bred Jamunapari goats. The Central Institute for Research on Goats in Makhdoom has established a herd of Jamunapari goats, as well as a village-based conservation and improvement programme. Farmers who maintain herds of Jamunapari goats are involved in all aspects of the conservation, breeding and improvement of the breed.

India has a seed bank for 'crop plants' at the Indian Agricultural Research Institute, New Delhi. A seed bank of flowering plants has been set up at the Regional Plant Resource Centre in Bhubaneshwar (Orissa).

India's flora comprises an estimated 15,000 species of flowering plants, with nearly 5000 endemic to the country. There are several rare and endangered species. About 10% of the country's flowering plants are threatened species which require urgent conservation.

One popular misconception is that the threat to wildlife comes mostly from the local communities in sanctuaries. This is far from true. The Bishnoi tribe in western Rajasthan, for instance, reveres deer and other wild animals. They have prevented hunters from India and abroad from hunting the Great Indian Bustard.

Wildlife conservation in our country faces several obstacles, the chief obstacle being that at least 30–40 lakh people live within or near areas designated as national parks and sanctuaries. Most tribes have practised some form of conservation but the growing pressure of the human population places an increasing burden on flora and fauna. The issue of community rights has not yet been settled in India's over 440 sanctuaries, even after the Wildlife Protection Act (1972) was amended in 1991 to the effect that no area other than a reserved forest could be declared a sanctuary without settling the rights of the local people. Another problem may be the focus on the tiger to the exclusion of other species. Save-the-tiger campaign has already produced positive results and the sale of medicines made from tiger organs has been banned all over the world. But little has been done to prevent the indiscriminate killing of the tiger's prey, e.g. the sambhar, black buck, cheetal and deer. Any hunting or poaching of these animals will make it more difficult to save the tiger. India's famous game reserves such as Dudhwa, Palamu and Corbett contain many deer which are preyed upon relentlessly by humans.

Project Tiger with 17 reserves in the country has saved this animal from extinction. Cultural traditions have so far preserved the trees belonging to the genus *Ficus,* which is an important keystone resource throughout the countryside, but these trees are now being increasingly felled in some parts of the country to bake bricks and to make crates. Monkeys (and cows) are also protected, being considered sacred animals by the Hindus. But in some cases they may be threatened (Rodgers and Panwar, 1988; Gadgil, 1991). Also, some reserves in the network of Project Tiger (e.g. Kanha and Manas) are threatened by discontented tribal people. There is need not only to identify the deficiencies in the coverage of the national network of nature reserves, but also to identify specific elements of biodiversity to be conserved.

Lichens

Lichens are intimate symbiotic associations of algae and fungi. Lichen diversity in the Himalayas stands 5th in terms of lichen genus diversity in the world, and the Himalayas are a hot spot of lichen diversity within India. About 230 genera of lichens commonly found in India, Nepal and Sri Lanka have been recorded (Negi and Gadgil,

1996). In India, many lichen–rich areas are yet to be explored. One such area is the Nanda Devi Biosphere Reserve in the Garhwal Himalaya of Uttar Pradesh, spreading over an area of more than 220 sq km. It has a mosaic of diverse habitats at different altitudinal gradients ranging from 1000 m to 7817 m. Negi and Gadgil (1996) inventoried the lichens, mosses, ants and molluscs in 16 vegetationally classified macrohabitats, dispersed at altitudes ranging from 2100 m to 4500 m. They identified 33 lichen genera whereas the entire biosphere area constitutes just 0.068% of total Indian landmass. Amongst these genera, *Cladonia* had the broadest niche width across 12 microhabitats and 16 altitudinal gradients. *Hypogymnia–Candelaria, Leptogium–Diploschistes* and *Lecanora–Ochrolechia* are extreme habitat specialists with complete niche overlap among themselves (Negi and Gadgil, 1996).

Nanda Devi Biosphere Reserve (NDBR) is one of the seven established biosphere reserves in India, situated in the central high Himalayas of Almora, Pithoragarh and Chamoli districts. Pithoragarh district shares its north–east boundaries with Nepal. On the basis of their field studies and computer analysis of data, Negi and Gadgil concluded: NDBR is rich in lichens but has low generic richness as this depends on the number of microhabitats as well as the type of macrohabitat. There appears to be cent per cent turnover of the genera between two entirely different macrohabitats. Generic turnover may be increased across heterogeneous macrohabitats whereas the same remains uniform along homogeneous macrohabitats. *Cladonia* had the broadest niche across microhabitats and altitudinal gradients. The genera *Nephroma, Mycomicrothelia, Squamarina, Ochrolechia, Diploschistes, Leptogium, Hypogymnia, Evernia, Candelaria, Lecanora, Caloplaca, Verrucaria* and *Xanthoria* were restricted to one particular type of habitat and formed a group of specialist lichens whereas the remaining genera showed a generalistic behaviour (Negi and Gadgil, 1996).

Sacred Groves

Thousands of sacred groves (religiously protected forests) are found in India. In these forests, trees are not allowed to be felled and even dead or windfall trees within the groves are not removed for fear of incurring divine wrath. These groves vary in size from a few square kilometres to over 1 million m^2. They provide a countrywide network of 'protected areas' wherein the inherent diversity of flora and fauna is preserved for present and future human use. While adjoining areas are cleared for agricultural and other land uses, the sacred groves are preserved intact for generations and are the best places for studying endemism. Kerala today has about 760 sacred groves (Induchoodan, 1996), most of which are highly fragmented, at less than 0.5 ha in size. Groves larger than 5 ha constitute only 3% of the total number.

Sacred groves contain a very high floristic richness and diversity. Over 700 species spread over 128 families and 474 genera have been recorded (Induchoodan, 1996). Dicotyledons account for 107 families (19 monocotyledons and 2 gymnosperms). Some of the dominant families in sacred groves together with number of species encountered (in parentheses) are as follows: Fabaceae (51), Rubiaceae (45), Euphorbiaceae (44), Acanthaceae (30), Poaceae (20), Moraceae (19), Verbenaceae (17), Apocynaceae, Lauraceae and Scrophulariaceae (16 each), Asteraceae (15), Rutaceae and Orchidaceae (14 each), Asclepiadaceae (13), and Anacardiaceae, Araceae and Zingiberaceae (11 each). Some important genera with more than 5 species include : *Ficus* (14), *Syzygium* and *Diospyros* (10 each), *Phyllanthus* (8), *Curcuma* (7), *Cinnamomum, Ixora* and *Jasminum* (6 each), and *Albizzia, Clerodendron, Garcinia, Impatiens, Terminalia* and *Litsea* (5 each). Phytogeographical analysis of the vegetation reveals that Asiatic elements are preponderant (32%) and that the groves are anthropogenically greatly disturbed.

Sacred groves may be broadly classified into five main categories : (i) seashore, (ii) forest areas, (iii) hilly areas, (iv) near river banks, tanks or reservoirs, and (v) near villages and towns. In the Saurashtra region, 20 main sacred places have been identified, where more than 50 plant species are reverenced. Of these, some species are confined to the sacred areas only. In many villages, temple trusts and panchayats manage the sacred groves. The ones associated with urban areas are mostly managed by religious trusts. Historically, both Hindu and Muslim rulers have patronized and safeguarded these groves.

In some parts of India, even non-religious considerations have inspired some enlightened people to protect certain animals. For instance, near Jodhpur, villagers have done much to protect and even welcome the Demoiselle cranes which migrate there from Mongolia and Central Asia to pass the winter. These cranes have been flying to a village called Khinchan every year as well as to near-by villages in which there are ponds. Thanks to the protection, feeding and conservation efforts by the villagers, the number of visiting cranes has tended to increase in recent years. Besides Jodhpur, these cranes also come to the wetlands of Kutch and Saurashtra (Gujarat) and, after overwintering there, go back to Mongolia and Central Asia.

Biogeographic Provinces

Typical communities of living organisms differ not only because they are subjected to different environmental regimes, but also because of their different evolutionary histories. Thus the African grasslands and forests have a variety of antelope species, while species of deer play a similar ecological role in many Asian grasslands and forests. The alpine grasslands in the Himalayas support a different species of mountain goat, *Hemitragus jemlahicus,* from grasslands of the Western Ghats which harbour *H. hylocrius.* Biologists classify the world in different biogeographic realms and provinces to account for this variation in composition of their biota due to historical factors. Each biogeographic realm and its province has its own characteristic set of plant and animal species.

The terrestrial world has been divided into eight biogeographic realms. The Indian subcontinent comes under the influence of three of these; viz., Palaearctic, Afrotropical and Indomalayan. Physically, parts of our Thar desert and north–western Himalayas are included in the Palaearctic realm, while the rest of the country is included under the Indomalayan. The desert as well as some other adjoining semiarid tracts show a significant incursion of Afrotropical elements.

The distribution of plant and animal species is therefore best summarized through a joint consideration of the distribution in terms of ecological regimes via biomes and biogeographic provinces. Udvardy (1975) has done so for the terrestrial environments of the world as a whole; the world is divided into 8 biogeographical realms and 14 terrestrial biome types. A total of 227 biogeographic provinces is proposed. In this classification the Indian subcontinent is divided into 2 biogeographic provinces of the Palaearctic realm and 6 biogeographic provinces of the Indomalayan realm.

Vegetation Types

Probably, the best vegetation classification is that developed by Gaussen (1954). It is based on a detailed mapping of the vegetation of the entire country except the Himalayas. This system introduces the notion of a series of vegetations. A series includes the various physiognomic stages ranging from the forest to scattered scrub created through degradative biotic influences (Fig. 6–2). The final stage of the series, expected to be reached if successional processes are permitted to proceed without human interference, is termed plesioclimax, the potential vegetation of a place. A series is named after three or more species of its plesioclimax stage, selected because of their dominance, abundance, fidelity or economic value (Puri *et al.*, 1983).

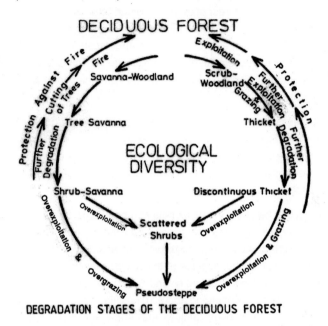

Fig. 6–2. Various degradation stages of a dry deciduous forest constituting the series for this vegetation type (after Gadgil and Meher–Homji, 1986).

On the basis of the distribution patterns of plants and animals, India was divided into 16 biogeographic zones and 43 vegetation types. According to Gadgil and Maher-Homji (1986), the 16 biogeographic provinces of the Indian subcontinent are: (1) Wet evergreen forest of the west coast-Western Ghats, (2) Transition zone between wet evergreen forests and teak forests, (3) Teak zone, (4) Transitional zone between teak and sal, (5) Sal zone, (6) *Hardwickia* zone, (7) *Albizia amara* zone, (8) *Anogeissus pendula* zone, (9) Deccan thorn forest, (10) *Acacia–Capparis* scrub, (11) Indian desert, (12) Western Himalayas, (13) Himalayas, (14) Eastern Himalayas-North-eastern India, (15) Andaman-Nicobar and (16) Mangroves. While certain vegetation types, such as the evergreen forest types of the Western Ghats are reasonably well preserved, others such as the *Acacia–Anogeissus latifolia* thorn forests of the semi-arid Deccan are almost entirely wiped out. This destruction of India's natural vegetation has rendered nearly two-thirds of India not under cultivation or human settlement totally unproductive. Very little is being done to revegetate this land; rather, more and more natural vegetation is being destroyed to raise forest plantations which often fail to support unsustainable marginal cultivation. There is need to devise programmes of rehabilitating these wastelands to generate rural employment on a large scale and to reduce the pressure on our few remaining pockets of natural vegetation. This should be coupled to a conservation programme which would stress the conservation of the country's overall biological diversity.

India possesses a wealth of scattered and partly unorganized information on floristic diversity. This information needs to be collated for ready use in various exercises in biodiversity inventorying and monitoring of the country's floristic wealth. Keeping track of population sizes of threatened and endangered species should be a high priority aspect of biodiversity monitoring.

Some important natural habitats in India are mountains, forests, grasslands, plains, rivers, wetlands, coastal and marshy areas and islands. India is located at a junction of three biogeographic realms — Afro-tropical, Indo-Malayan and Paleo-arctic. India harbours about 9% of the total species of the world. Having only 2.4% of global area, India exhibits 12.51% of floral diversity and 6.67% of faunal diversity. It has about 48,000 species of plants representing about 10% of the world's flora (Hajra and Mudgal, 1997; Venu, 1998). Some plant families that show enormous species diversity are Poaceae, Orchidaceae and Balsaminaceae.

Endemism is a significant factor in diversity assessment and conservation. About 4,900 species of flowering plants (33% of total recorded species) are endemic to the country (141 genera distributed over 47 families). Families such as Poaceae, Acanthaceae, Rubiaceae, Orchidaceae and Fabaceae show a higher representation of endemic taxa (Nayar, 1997). Many endemic taxa of Bryophyta, Pteridophyta and angiosperms are concentrated in floristically-rich areas of the North East India, the Western Ghats and the North West Himalaya. The Western ghats and Eastern Himalayas harbour some 1600 and 3500 endemic species of flowering plants, respectively. Around 220 species of flowering plants are endemic to Andaman and Nicobar Islands.

India is the homeland of 167 important cultivated plant species. Many wild relatives of domesticated crops originated in the Indian Subcontinent (see Venu, 1998).

Ecological Diversity

Similar ecosystems are customarily classified into broad biome types such as tropical rain forests or hill streams. Biomes such as tropical rain forests are zonal, i.e. coincide with broad climatic zones, while others such as hill streams are azonal. For the sake of convenience, broad ecological classifications emphasize zonally distributed biomes. The biomes are identified with the major plant species rather than with the more mobile and less obvious animals and micro-organisms. Ecological diversity of a region is therefore summarized in the form of zonally defined biomes identified with their dominant vegetation type.

Ideally, the entire diversity of life should be explored and studied but this is an extremely difficult task. Therefore some groups of organisms have received greater attention than others. Those attracting greater attention have been non–timber forest species including medicinal plants, endangered and threatened flora and fauna, and wild relatives of cultivated crops. India is particularly rich in wild relatives of minor millets (e.g. ragi), major cereals (e.g. rice), spices (e.g. turmeric, cardamom, pepper) and several pulse crops (e.g. *Cajanus,* horsegram and field bean). Indeed it was the spices of the hills of the Western Ghats that attracted Europeans to India several decades ago. The Indian Western Ghats now rank as one of the eighteen hot spots of diversity in the world.

Several attempts made to develop objective estimates of the various parts of the diversity of various biological communities have usually suffered from their inability to incorporate the biological heterogeneity of the constituent species. Pramod *et al.* (1997) tried to overcome this shortcoming. According to them, species assemblages may be characterized in terms of how widespread their constituent species are and how cohesive the assemblages are. They defined measures of these properties, termed ubiquity and hospitality respectively, with reference to 132 bird assemblages censused in 21 localities covering 9 major types of habitats from across the entire length of the hill chain of the Western Ghats. Here, ubiquity means the extent of cohesion, i.e., rarity of species or their being widespread, and hospitality means the extent of cohesion of species in any particular assemblage. They found that while biological parameters characterizing individual transects correlated positively amongst each other, various measures of ubiquity and hospitality formed a distinct group of parameters correlated positively with each other, and physical parameters such as latitude and rainfall formed a third independent group of positively correlated parameters. Hospitality and ubiquity are therefore independent, biologically useful parameters. For instance, both montane evergreen forests and monoculture plantations were seen to harbour species-poor communities. However, those of montane evergreen forests tend to be cohesive assemblages of restricted geographic distribution, whereas those of monoculture comprised species of widespread occurrence drawn from many different habitat types (Pramod et al., 1997).

Most indices for quantifying the diversity of biological communities assume that biodiversity can be satisfactorily described by the number of species and their relative abundances. These indices treat all species as being equal and ignore taxonomic, morphological, or other biological differences among species of a community. However, two biological communities with similar number and frequencies of species can differ, for instance, in respect of the taxonomic diversity of the constituent species. Ecologists have generally assumed that any measure of biodiversity should incorporate biological differences among species or the heterogeneity of the community as an important component. Ganeshaiah et al. (1997) proposed a new measure of diversity, termed the 'avalanche index' which, besides species numbers and frequencies, takes into account biological and ecological differences among the species of a community. This index aims to integrate, over various possible species combinations, the biological differences among species in proportion to their relative frequencies in the community. They successfully applied this index to estimate the biodiversity of dung beetles.

Designing good strategies of conservation relies heavily on identifying major spatial and temporal patterns of change in biodiversity. Menon and Bawa (1997) and Subash Chandran (1997) attempted to identify these patterns in the Western Ghats using two different approaches. Menon and Bawa used the Geographic Information System approach to trace the major patterns of biodiversity loss over a period of seventy years and identified some likely factors driving these changes. On the other hand, Subash Chandran reconstructed the ecological changes of the Ghats based mostly on the historical and archaeological records as well as social and biological relics.

Lokesha and Vasudeva (1997) analyzed the life history strategies that predispose plant species to become rare, endangered and threatened. They showed that specific features such as habit, pollination and dispersal modes are significant in threatened plants. It is well known that a species can become rare in many ways and the process has several ecological consequences. Human-induced perturbations such as habitat loss are important causes of rarity. But such features as breeding behaviour, dispersal modes and habitat specificity also affect the distribution and survival of species in their

190

natural habitats, thereby making species vulnerable to rarity and endangerment. Among Indian orchids, a larger fraction of terrestrial species are endangered as compared to the epiphytic species, and rare orchid species differ in their flowering phenology compared to the common ones (Lokesha and Vasudeva, 1997). These workers compared a few life history traits of rare/endangered (RE) species of South Indian flora with those of common ones to identify specific life history syndromes, if any, that could predispose a species to become RE. For a set of 487 rare/endangered (including 'rare', 'endangered' and 'vulnerable' groups) angiosperm species of South India, Lokesha and Vasudeva formed a database on their life-form (herb or shrub, or tree or liana) and reproductive features, e.g., dispersal modes (animal or explosive, or wind/water), and dispersal unit (fruit/pod or seed) by consulting published floras, forestry literature, the Red Data Book of IUCN etc. Frequency tables were constructed for the various categories of the three features and were compared with those observed from natural flora. These authors found that more shrubs and fewer herbs than expected from a random distribution among natural flora, fell in the RE group, while the frequency of trees and lianas did not differ from that to be expected naturally. This points to shrubs being at greater risk of becoming endangered than herbs. Data on dispersal modes suggests that many more species dispersing biotically than through abiotic or passive means are likely to become RE. Further, RE species usually have fruit (or pod) as the unit of dispersal rather than seed.

Biodiversity and Its Conservation in the Himalayas

The Himalayan region is the largest mountain system in the world, of paramount importance in the context of biodiversity. The traditional utilization of biologically diverse resources in the Himalayas not only reflects a diverse resource use pattern, but also a respect for preserving biological diversity by the mountain people. Appreciating the indigenous knowledge of mountain people in relation to biodiversity resource management is one of the key issues for sustainable development of the Himalayan region today (Pei, 1996). Many farming systems in the world and all productive systems in the Himalayan region operate under indigenous knowledge systems. They are not only valuable for the native people but also for scientists and planners striving to improve conditions in rural societies (Warren, 1990). The rich biodiversity of the Himalayan region has been greatly impoverished along with the overall degradation of montane environments due to human activities.

191

Biodiversity is actually a product of the interaction of both social and biophysical systems. It can be defined as a fundamental natural resource on which humans have been, and are now, dependent for their livelihood and socioeconomic development from ancient to present times, and will continue to be dependent in future. Utilization and conservation of biodiversity involves intrinsic interactions between species, genetic populations, communities, landscape and natural ecosystems on the one hand, and culture, technology, social, economic, indigenous knowledge and social systems, on the other. Natural and social systems have always been interrelated and interwoven in the evolutionary process of biosystems at different levels in a given area; human activities influence the level of biodiversity, either decreasing or increasing its components in different conditions or settings (Pei, 1996).

Forest management may be defined in terms of protection, utilization and distribution of products, and the relevant organizational arrangements. The scope of forest management covers harvesting, distribution, protection and planting practices.

Forests undoubtedly are the most important biodiversity resource in the Himalayan Mountain Region. In montane agriculture both permanent farming and *swidden* systems are directly or indirectly nurtured by montane forests. Montane forests also provide numerous products and are essential for environmental protection. The villagers utilize various biospecies found in forests. They manage the environmental resources in their habitat as per their subsistence needs. The native mountain people regard themselves as a part of the ecosystem. The forest management practices are based on their perception of the man–forest relationship from which they evolved the concept of the 'Holy Hills', i.e., an area of forested hillside where the gods reside. A respect for the gods promotes peace and well–being of the villagers. Likewise any disrespect, on the other hand, incurs the wrath of the gods.

To reap the benefits of biodiversity, local communities have to make themselves well aware of technological developments, develop market intelligence, and organize themselves for co-operative marketing to resist economic exploitation (see Ramakrishnan *et al.*, 1997). Quite often, conservation concerns are more preached than practised. While diversity of socioeconomic and environmental conditions does help maintain biodiversity, differences can create hurdles in conservation. People living in and around the wilderness or natural areas find themselves pushed to the wall when conservation is thrust upon them. The long-term conservation goals and rural development schemes need to be made compatible rather than conflicting, and development is usually not possible without conservation. it is now emerging that complete or total conservation may be impossible to achieve. For rational use and management, a good health care delivery system and medicinal plants may meet the twin objectives of conservation of genetic diversity and development of the people of hilly areas (see Ramakrishnan *et al.*, 1997).

In Bhutan, anybody who violates the Forest Act is penalized. Cutting of trees, fishing, and killing of stray dogs are all prohibited. The Bhutanese have successfully maintained forest coverage on their land (60% of the total area of the kingdom).

All indigenous health care remedies, whether traditional or modern, have originated directly or indirectly from folklore, and rituals hold the key to the treasures of folk medicinal knowledge and ethnomedic–botany. The Himalayan region is rich in diverse traditional medical knowledge systems due to cultural and environmental diversity. In this vast mountain region, Chinese medicine, *Ayurveda, Rigveda* medicine, Tibetan medicine, and Arab medicine are practised. Even today, at least 70% of the medicinal plants and animals in the region consist of wild species and about 75% of the population in this region depend on traditional medicines for health care (Pei, 1996). In India, about 2500 plant species are used by traditional healers and some 100 species of plants serve as regular sources of medicine (Shah, 1990). In China, there are as many as 2294 traditional Tibetan medicines from plants (1106), animals (448) and natural minerals (840) (Yang, 1988).

'Jhum' and 'taungya' are two very important environmental problems in the Eastern Himalayas. Whereas jhum is an old and traditional agricultural practice prevalent among the native people, taungya is an agroforestry system of recent origin, introduced by foresters. Tawnenga *et al.* (1996, 1997 a,b) suggested that regular cropping for the second year in every jhum cycle could significantly reduce the area of forest land required for swidden. Uma Shankar *et al.* (1998 c) reported how conversion of natural forest into taungya plantations in Darjeeling causes considerable loss of species, greatly alters the landscape and interrupts ecosystem recovery.

Successful *in-situ* conservation of biodiversity depends on a balanced trade-off between the extracted quantities of non-timber forest products (NTFPs) (extracted by sustenance the local tribes for their sustenance and cash income) and the regeneration and renewability of these products. Whereas some NTFPs are not very attractive in this context, *Phyllanthus emblica* (amla) can potentially meet the cash requirements if processed by the local Soliga tribe (Uma Shankar *et al.*, 1996). It has also been observed that declines of natural populations of broomgrass (*Thysanolaena maxima*) due to excessive harvesting often leads to its domestication in Darjeeling Himalaya since the species is fairly adaptable, its market demand exceeds natural production and profitability from cultivation is quite high. Fuelwood is the largest product threatening biodiversity and its assessment in the Himalayas (Uma Shankar *et al.*, 1998 a,b). Uma Shankar (unpublished) has recently found that Mahananda sanctuary (dry forest) probably contains the highest richness and diversity of tree species (recorded so far in any Indian dry forest), with mixed dominance and satisfactory regeneration— a triad of characteristics unique to a deciduous community. However, the rare species that contribute maximally to the tree diversity, are at high risk of local extinction because of unauthorized human interference.

The Himalayan people have protected many biological species in their environment through the rational use of biological resources and ecosystems. Domestication of the tea plant, buckwheat, barley, finger millet, jute, yak, honeybees, lac insect, chinese gallnut, and many other crops and animals, are some examples. The wide variety of medicinal plants, aromatics, natural dyeing materials, and ornamental plants in the Himalayan region have contributed to the world civilization.

Besides material culture (food, medicine and shelter), plants are closely associated with many social customs and religious rituals. Many flowers, fruits, or whole plants and ecosystems have been used and protected as ritual offerings for worship. Some plants are themselves worshipped or believed to be sacred. The holy tree (*Ficus religiosa*) and various temple yard plants; the 'Holy Hills' of the Dai people, the sacred forest of Indus, and the numerous plants offered in worship, have been described (Jain, 1987).

Wild Relatives of Food Grain and Vegetable Crops

Among wild relatives of the food grain crop plants, wild rice plays an important role. Shrestha and Shrestha (1996) collected and identified four different wild rice species from the Nepalese Terai and river basin areas between Churiya and Mahabharat range. Among them, *Oryza nivara* and *O. rufipogon* are natural parents of the present–day cultivated rice (*O. sativa*). Weedy rice *(O. sativa f. spontanea)* was observed in many rice fields of Nepal. Two wild relatives of rice *(Hygroryza aristata* and *Leersia hexandra)* were also collected. Wild rice has high cultural value in Nepalese society and is much more costly than the normal rice.

At least three species of *Agropyron* (wild relatives of the wheat *Triticum aestivum*) could be identified in the north–west high hills of Nepal (Kihara, 1955). Wild fingermillet

(*Eleusine indica*) is widely distributed from the Terai region to the high hills of Jumla. Its cultivated species is *E. coracana*. Two species of wild buckwheat (*Fagopyrum dibotrys* and *F. megacarpum*) were identified in Nepal. Buckwheat is known as 'the poor man's food' in the hills. Wild relatives of the present-day cultivated arhar (*Cajanus cajan*) grow in several parts of Nepal.

Thirty-seven wild species of vegetable crops in 20 different genera of 12 different families were listed by Shrestha and Shrestha (1996) from Nepal. Wild colocasia (*Colocasia antiquorum*) is widely distributed from the Terai to high hills. The natives collect its tender shoots and cook them as feed for their animals. Three wild species of *Amaranthus* grow widely in cultivated fields: *Amaranthus viridis*, *A. spinosus* and *A. blitum*.Young plants of *A. viridis* are consumed as a green vegetable.

Wild spongegourd and wild bittergourd (Cucurbitaceae) are found in the Churiya range. Wild cucumber and wild snakegourd occur in tropical to subtropical Nepal. Several wild varieties of yams, *Mentha, Rumex. Asparagus* and other vegetables have also been reported from Nepal.

Biodiversity in the Western Ghats

In the Western Ghats in peninsular India, seven different vegetation types that are distinctive in species composition have been recognized (see Utkarsh *et al.*, 1998). These seven types include (1) closed canopy evergreen, (2) semiclosed canopy evergreen, (3) stunted evergreen, (4) semievergreen, (5) moist deciduous, (6) dry deciduous forests, and (7) scrub/savanna vegetation. Dry deciduous forests usually have low density and diversity and harbour a rather exclusive set of species. The most diverse tree assemblages are found in the semievergreen forest type, which harbours widespread species extensively shared with other vegetation types. Whereas semiclosed evergreen forests resemble semievergreen forests in several ways, stunted evergreen forests and scrub/savanna have low tree density and diversity, their component species showing weak tendencies to co-occur with each other. The evergreen and moist deciduous forests show moderate to high density and diversity and moderate levels of distinctiveness of species composition. The evergreen forests resemble dry deciduous forests in having species with a strong tendency to co-occur and also have many species with restricted distributions. More moist vegetation types shelter a higher proportion of evergreen and endemic trees and a lower proportion of medicinally useful species.

India is an important centre of wild relatives of cultivated plants which are particularly concentrated in the Western Ghats tract (Arora and Nair, 1984). This tract is really a hot spot—an area of high biological diversity that is under considerable threat.

The Western Ghats alone contain at least 5500 species of flowering plants alone. Worldwide flowering plants are thought to constitute 2.5% of the total number of species of all groups (Heywood, 1995), which extrapolates to an estimated 220,000 species in the Western Ghats.

As forests are the natural climax vegetation over most of the Western Ghats, proper knowledge of the distribution of tree species is important in understanding the largest patterns of distribution of biodiversity. These patterns are determined by rainfall, slope, aspect and soils as well as by biotic interactions such as grazing by herbivores and by a variety of human interventions such as biomass harvests, fire, and planting of economic species. The resultant complex distributions of the 800 or so tree species of the Western Ghats have been captured by Somasundaram (1967), Champion and Seth (1968); Pascal (1988), and Utkarsh *et al.* (1998), in terms of the distribution of assemblages assigned to a few forest types, vegetation types, or vegetation series.

Champion and Seth (1968) suggested a structural–phenological classification framework but ignored the more human–impacted vegetation types. Pascal (1988) identified various human–impacted categories. The system proposed by Utkarsh *et al.* (1998) recognized the following seven types of vegetation:

(1) Evergreen forests comprise 25–30 m tall trees, with erect, closed, dense canopy covering nearly 95% of the ground. Most trees are evergreen. Leaves thick, dark or blackish and shiny. Bark generally smooth. Many trees have large buttresses. Lianas (woody climbers) not uncommon. Undergrowth mostly devoid of herb species. A few thorny species (canes and pandanus) are common.

(2) Semiclosed evergreen forests have 20–25 m tall trees with partially closed (80–95%) canopy. Up to 95% trees belong to evergreen species. A few herbaceous species and several pioneer woody species, including some deciduous ones, grow on the forest floor. Lianas and thorny species are common.

(3) Stunted evergreen forests have dwarf (10–15m) trees with a closed (80–95%) canopy. Over 80% of the trees are evergreen, often branching at the base and with a spreading canopy. Buttressed trees very rare. Lianas very common. The forests are rich in undergrowth of pioneer shrubs such as *Strobilanthes*, which have thin, hairy leaves. Thorny species common but canes and pandanus are rare.

196

Table 6–3. Correspondence of vegetation types of the Western Ghats among three systems of classification (after Utkarsh *et al.*, 1998)

Utkarsh *et al.* (1998)	Pascal (1988)	Mueller–Dombois and Ellenberg (1974)
Evergreen forests	Lowland wet climax evergreen forests	Tropical lowland broad–leaved seasonal evergreen forests
Semiclosed evergreen forests	Disturbed lowland wet evergreen forests	same
Stunted evergreen forests	Stunted submontane evergreen forests	Tropical broad–leaved seasonal evergreen submontane/cloud forests
Semievergreen forests	Secondary semi–evergreen forests	Tropical lowland broad–leaved semideciduous forests
Moist deciduous forests	Secondary/climax moist deciduous forests	Tropical broad–leaved drought deciduous forests
Dry deciduous forests	Secondary/climax dry deciduous forests	same
Scrub/savanna	Scrub woodlands, tree savannas	Tropical broad–leaved drought deciduous, woodlands, scrub, short–grass savanna

Table 6–4. Some characteristic species of the 7 vegetation types of Western Ghats (condensed from Utkarsh *et al.*, 1998)

Family	Species	ceg	sce	ste	seg	ssv	mde	ddc
Euphorbiaceae	*Baccaurea courtallensis*	++	+					
Burseraceae	*Canarium strictum*	++	+		+			
Meliaceae	*Aglaia elaeagnoidea*	+	++		+			
Myristicaceae	*Knema attenuata*	++	+	+	+	+		
Lauraceae	*Beilschmiedia dalzelii*	++	+	+	+			
Lauraceae	*Litsea stocksii*	+		+	++			
Anacardiaceae	*Holigarna grahamii*	+	+	++	+			
Sapindaceae	*Dimocarpus longan*	+	++	+	+	+		
Moraceae	*Artocarpus lakoocha*	+	++		+	+		
Lauraceae	*Persea macrantha*	++	+	+	+	+	+	
Dipterocarpaceae	*Hopea parviflora*	+	++	+	+	+	+	
Lauraceae	*Cinnamomum spp.*	+	++	+	+	+	+	
Melastomaceae	*Memecylon umbellatum*	+	+	++	+	+	+	
Oleaceae	*Olea dioica*	+	+	++	+	+	+	
Sapotaceae	*Xantolis tomentosa*	+		++	+	+	+	
Myrtaceae	*Syzygium cumini*	+	+	++	+	+	+	
Verbenaceae	*Vitex altissima*	+	+		++	+	+	
Dilleniaceae	*Dillenia pentagyna*		+		+	++	+	
Lytheraceae	*Lagerstroemia microcarpa*	+	+	+	+	+	++	+
Combretaceae	*Terminalia paniculata*	+	+		+	++	+	+
Papilionaceae	*Butea monosperma*					+	+	++

N.B. ceg, closed canopy evergreen forests; sce, semiclosed canopy evergreen forests; ste, stunted evergreen forest; seg, semievergreen forests; mdc, moist deciduous forests; ddc, dry deciduous forests; ssv, scrub/savanna. Entries with (++) denote the vegetation type where the species attains peak frequency.

(4)   Semievergreen forests have a mixture of moderately tall evergreen and deciduous trees (15–20 m tall) and closed (60–80%), dense canopy. About 40–80% trees are evergreen. Many trees lack straight, tall boles and have an irregular canopy. Herbaceous species are quite common on the forest floor and climbers grow in profusion. Lianas common. Canes are uncommon and pandanus is rare.

(5)   Moist deciduous forests have moderate (up to 20 m tall) trees and closed but not very dense canopy (40–70%). Up to 40% trees may be evergreen. The deciduous species usually shed leaves around January..Trees have rough thin bark and pale green leaves. Buttressed stems rare. Undergrowth contains many herbaceous species. Occasionally, there is extensive growth of weeds such as *Lantana* or *Eupatorium*. Lianas are very few, but climbers are common. Thorny species are not uncommon. Canes and pandanus are absent.

(6)   Dry deciduous forests have tall (up to 15 m) trees with a rather open (40–60%) canopy. Evergreen and buttressed trees not found. Lianas rare. Thorny species common. Canes and pandanus absent. Herbaceous and grassy undergrowth rich and diverse.

(7)   Scrub/savanna are non-forest formations with shrubby (scrub) or grassy (savanna) undergrowth both with some scattered trees. Trees may be 5 to 15 m tall. Deciduous trees generally more common. Lianas absent. Thorny species and herbs, including weeds, quite common (Utkarsh *et al.*, 1998).

Table 6–3 gives a comparison of vegetation types of the Western Ghats according to the three systems of classification mentioned above.

Of the above 7 vegetation types, the evergreen, moist deciduous and dry deciduous types are distributed throughout the Western Ghats. The tall, semiclosed evergreen forests are largely not present in the northern region where some stunted evergreen forests sometimes appear in disturbed localities.

Table 6–4 lists a few characteristic species of the 7 vegetation types representing a range of distribution patterns, from ones confined to a single type to those inhabiting all the types. Of these 7 vegetation types, the semievergreen and semiclosed evergreen forest types have the least distinctive species composition and are also richest in the α- and β-diversities, as measured by the mean number of species in a given transect, as well as levels of species dissimilarity amongst pairs of transects of the same type. These forest types constitute assemblages of widespread species

199

with little affinity to each other. The two types appear to be derived from the original evergreen type by moderate disturbance from selective harvesting of trees and incursion of more widespread, pioneer species, including deciduous ones in the openings created.

Evergreen forests are the climax vegetation in the high rainfall zone of the Western Ghats. They harbour the highest levels of tree densities with moderate levels of α- and β-diversities as well as distinctiveness. The moist deciduous forests are the climax vegetation in the medium rainfall zone and show much lower tree densities and lower levels of cohesiveness compared with the evergreen type, but resemble the latter in being moderately distinctive with moderate levels of α- and β-diversities and prevalence (Utkarsh *et al.*, 1998). Another natural climax vegetation type is the dry deciduous forest of the lower rainfall tracts. It is the most distinctive in composition, with low tree densities and low levels of α-diversities. The assemblages have the lowest levels of prevalence and highest levels of cohesiveness, with a rather constant composition so that β-diversities are the lowest of all types.

The closed canopy evergreen forests rank the highest in the proportion of trees belonging to endemic species of the Western Ghats. Whereas the dry deciduous forests have poor representation of the endemic species, at least 80% of the tree species here have some medicinal importance. The semiclosed canopy evergreen forests have the lowest proportion of medicinal species. The proportion of trees belonging to wild relatives of cultivated plants remains nearly the same across all the types (i.e., one–fourth) with dry deciduous forests having the lowest values and stunted evergreen forests the highest.

Whereas prevalence and cohesiveness do not depend on the vegetation type, α–diversity is negatively, and prevalence is positively, correlated with latitude and in turn with the length of the dry season. Prevalence also correlates negatively with cohesiveness. Alpha-diversity is negatively correlated with the rank aridity of the vegetation characteristic of the types. Increasing evergreenness of the forest corresponds to increasing endemicity, but is accompanied by a significant reduction in proportion of medicinally important trees (Utkarsh *et al.*, 1998).

Biodiversity and Vegetation in the Indian Thar Desert

The Western Indian (Thar) desert represents a characteristic environment where plants have adapted to arid conditions. Water is scant and erratic. The prevailing high temperature has a marked effect on the vegetation. But several plant species are nevertheless found and thrive quite well despite the inhospitable conditions. Examples are : *Aerva persica, Crotalaria burhia, Calotropis procera, Leptadenia pyrotechnica, Prosopis cineraria,* and *Tecomella undulata* (Sen, 1996). Sand–dunes comprising vast mounds of shifting sand, devoid of plants and human habitation, are very common. In these, animals and plants bravely face and endure the acute scarcity of water, high salinity and scorching heat from March to August. After some rain showers, many plants sprout through the perennated root system, when hardly any shoot remains alive or green. These can be stated as resurrection plants of the desert. *Lasiurus sindicus* has a sheathing root system at Jaisalmer with intact particles adhering in a mucilaginous substance. Some other grasses, such as *Aristida, Oropetium, Melanocenchrus* on rocky areas, *Eleusine, Dactyloctenium, Cenchrus, Cymbopogon* on sandy areas and *Panicum* on sand–dunes, are of common occurrence (Sen, 1996).

A considerable part of the Rajasthan desert contains some salt basins or lakes, characterized by high sodium chloride content and less negative osmotic potentials. These factors adversely affect the nutrition, growth and reproduction of most plants. The high soil salinity allows only a sparse cover of salt–tolerant species such as *Salsola baryosma, Sesuvium sensivoides, Suaeda fruticosa, Haloxylon recurvum, Trianthema triquetra, Tamarix* spp., *Zygophyllum simplex* and grasses such as *Aeluropus lagopoides* and *Sporobolus helvolus.* In the salt basins of Rajasthan, various plant species are used as fodder for domestic animals: examples *A. logopoides, Cyperus* spp., *Dactyloctenium aegyptium, D. sindicum* and *S. helvolus.*

The growing human and animal populations have put heavy stress on the desert vegetation. The trees, shrubs and even their roots are indiscriminately cut by the rural population for fuel, top feed, thorn fencing, and building of thatched huts (see Singh *et al.,* 1994). Air-dried seeds and pods of some trees are used as delicacies. The seeds of *Acacia senegal,* fruits of *Capparis decidua* and pods of *Prosopis cineraria* are harvested for human consumption. The seeds of several grasses are collected during drought years. Unless the intensity of these activities remains low, the species diversity can be adversely affected.

Charan (1978) divided the western Indian desert into 5 major phytogeographical divisions, viz. (i) sand-dunes, (ii) sandy plains, (iii) stony and hilly tracts, (iv) gravel and compact tracts and (v) saline areas. These divisions differ from each other in their floristic composition due to topographical and geological formations. According to Charan and Sen (1985), *Calligonum polygonoides* occurs only within arid regions, thus providing an index for demarcation of arid regions in Rajasthan state. Phytogeographical demarcation of arid and semiarid regions coincides approximately with the demarcation line between the western and eastern elements as indicated by vegetation type (Gaussen *et al.*, 1971).

Many wild plants (weeds) are the ancestors of the cultivated varieties. A variety of wild watermelon found in this desert is smaller than the cultivated one, but the plants can resist the adverse desertic conditions. Valuable germplasm of *Sesamum* also grows in the desert areas, as do some varieties of *Vigna radiata, Phaseolus aureus* and *Cyamopsis tetragonoloba.* Many of these wild legumes have a very hard seed coat which adapts these plants to survive in the desert. These need protection against genetic erosion and loss of biodiversity.

Biodiversity in South Asia

The South Asian countries (Bangladesh, Bhutan, India, Maldives, Nepal, Pakistan and Sri Lanka) occupy 3.15% of the global land and are inhabited by over one–fifth of the world's population. The region has about 11% of the global biodiversity with a number of endemic plants and animals. Due to the high rate of deforestation and overexploitation of resources, biodiversity is under tremendous pressure and conservation measures need to be strictly enforced.

South Asia boasts a variety of ecosystems such as tropical, temperate, alpine, savanna, dense forests, mangroves, desert and marine. It has the highest mountain peak. Great similarities and diversities in socioeconomic, cultural conditions and environment are found here. A comparison of forest and biodiversity indicators in the S. Asian countries is given in Table 6–5.

The Indian subcontinent is one of the twelve centres of genetic diversity. Recent habitat destruction and human activities have accelerated losses of the wild relatives of our food crops; many traditional crop varieties were also dropped from cultivation with the advent of the green revolution, which encouraged use of a limited number of high-yielding varieties. Before the green revolution, Indian farmers cultivated thousands of varieties of rice. By 2000 AD they will probably grow no more than 50 (CSE, 1985). Every single species or variety could be potentially valuable. For instance, in 1963 a single sample of wild rice (*Oryza nivara*) from Gonda in U.P. gave Asian farmers a gene that saved 30 million hectares of paddy from the dreaded grassy stunt virus. A wild melon from India has provided resistance to a form of mildew and has saved the melon crop in California, USA (CSE, 1985). A wild onion from Nepal has given

Table 6–5.   Forest and biodiversity indicators (from Jha, 1996)

Indicators	Bangladesh	Bhutan	India	Maldives	Nepal	Pakistan	Sri Lanka
Good forest land (%)	16	55	22	3	17	4	27
Annual forest loss (%)	0.9	–	0.3	–	1–2.0	0.4	35
Annual reforestation (000 ha)	17	1	138	–	4	7	13
Higher plant species	5000	5446	15,000	260	>6000	5000	2900
Endemic flora (%)	–	10.15	31.3	1.8	4.5	7.5	28
Fern species	–	–	1000	15	450	–	314
Gymnosperms	–	–	–	2	23	21	–
Threatened plant spp.	33	15	1349	0	33	14	220
Threatened plants per 1000 existing taxa	1	1	90	–	3	1	56
Rare and threatened plant taxa per sq km	3	4	206	–	9	2	113
Mammal species	109	109	317	–	167	157	86
Endemic mammal species	0	0	38	0	1	3	12
Rare and threatened mammal species	15	15	39	1	22	15	7
Bird species	354	448	969	24	629	476	221
Endemic bird species	0	0	69	0	1	0	20
Rare and threatened bird species	27	10	72	1	20	25	8
Reptile species	119	198	389	–	80	143	144
Endemic reptile spp.	–	–	156	–	–	22	75
Rare and threatened reptile species	14	1	17	–	9	6	3
Amphibian species	19	24	206	–	36	17	39
Endemic amphibians	0	0	110	–	7	2	19
Threatened amphibians	0	–	3	0	0	0	0
Rare and threatened mammal spp. per 10,000 sq km	6	–	6	–	9	4	6
Rare and threatened bird spp. per 10,000 sq km	11	–	11	–	8	6	4
Threatened fish species	0	–	2	0	0	0	2

resistance to the onion crop in the USA against blight (Jha, 1996).

Two species of mammals (Indian cheetah and lesser Indian rhinoceros) are on the verge of extinction. Three bird species (*Athene blewitti*–forest onlet, *Ophrysia superciliosa*–Himalayan mountain quail and *Rhodonessa caryophyllacea*–pink headed duck) have already become extinct in India (WRI, 1992; WCMC, 1992). Plant species that can no longer be found on the Indian subcontinent are : *Isoetes dixitii, Isoetes sampathkumarini, Ophiorrhiza brunonis, O. caudata, O. radicans, Wendlandia angustifolia, Sterculia khasiana, Carex repanda, Eragrostis rottleri, Hubhardia heptaneuron, Dipcadi concanense, D. reidii, Urginea polyphylla, Calanthe whiteana, Pleione lagenaria, Corypha taliera* and *Hedychium marginatum* (see UNESCO, 1990; SAARC, 1992; Jha, 1996).

The first modern national park in the region (Corbett National Park) was established in India in 1936. India had 'Abhayaranxyas' or forest reserves in the fourth century B.C. when other countries of the world knew nothing about the concept of protected areas. South Asia has about 5.70% of global protected parks by number. An appreciable number of world heritage sites, biosphere reserves, botanical gardens and seed banks are located in the region (Table 6–6).

Adaptive Management of Biodiversity Resources

As per the Convention on Biological Diversity (CBD), genetic resources are the sovereign property of a country. Every country must facilitate access to these resources on the basis of prior informed consent on mutually agreed terms. The terms should favour the country of origin of genetic resources through concessional transfer of technology. Parties to the Convention should respect the role of indigenous communities in conservation and sustainable use of biodiversity resources and share with them the benefits accruing from commercial uses of these resources (see Figs. 6–4, 6–5).

In the light of the CBD provisions, two possible options are available to India: either we could sit tight on our resources and not allow other countries to exploit the same, or we can adopt a positive and progressive approach, and thereby reap full benefits from a sustainable exploitation of our biodiversity resources in collaboration with, or through the expertise of, other countries to take full advantage of our sovereign rights over biodiversity resources. The former negative approach is unworkable because much of our biodiversity resources and information have already been taken away by industrial countries and some others are being shared with neighbouring countries. In any case, we have no effective enforcement machinery and it is quite easy for anybody

Table 6–6. **State of protected areas and conservation efforts in South Asia (from UNESCO, 1990; WCMC, 1992; Jha, 1996)**

Indicators	Bangladesh	Bhutan	India	Maldives	Nepal	Pakistan	Sri Lanka
Land area under protection (%)	0.67	19.7	4.35	0.0	14	4.6	11.94
Protected areas (No.)	15	12	362	0	15	77	43
Natural World Heritage sites	0	–	5	–	2	0	1
Wetlands	12	5	93	–	17	48	41
Major wetlands (%)	–	0	–	–	–	2	–
Botanic gardens	2	0	68	–	1	5	6
Zoos	–	–	17	–	1	2	1
Seed banks	1	–	12	–	1	3	3
Red Data Book list	No	No	Yes	No	Yes	IP*	Yes
National conservation strategy	Yes	–	Yes	No	Yes	Yes	Yes
Biodiversity profiles	–	–	Yes	–	IP	Yes	–

* IP = in preparation

any case, we have no effective enforcement machinery and it is quite easy for anybody to smuggle out our biological specimens without let or hindrance. Therefore we should pursue a positive, promotional approach aimed at developing a sound system of information on these resources, making this information accessible to those interested by charging reasonable fees for information or materials (see Fig. 6–3, 6–4; Table 6–7). This would help promote the growth of biodiversity–based enterprises in India and at the same time help generate additional revenues through taxation which could be used to reward people living close to nature for their contribution to continued conservation and sustainable use of biodiversity resources (see Gadgil, 1985; Gadgil et al., 1995).

As our own resources, infrastructure, and scientific and technological competence are not well developed, multinational corporations will continue to play a significant role in adding value to our indigenous biodiversity resources. The unfortunate reality is that the information on our biodiversity resources is woefully incomplete, fragmented and inaccessible, although in theory it is available virtually free of charge. There is need to build up more reliable, accessible biodiversity information systems as a self–sustaining service industry through a partnership of scientific institutions, private enterprise and government. Such an information industry could attract considerable support from abroad through research and service contracts. In the light of the provisions of CBD, we could negotiate suitable terms with the multinational corporations in such a way that due encouragement and strength are given to our own entrepreneurial and scientific capabilities.

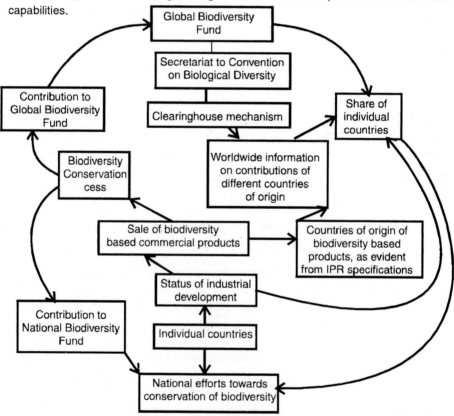

Fig. 6–3. Financial mechanisms to promote worldwide biodiversity conservation efforts.

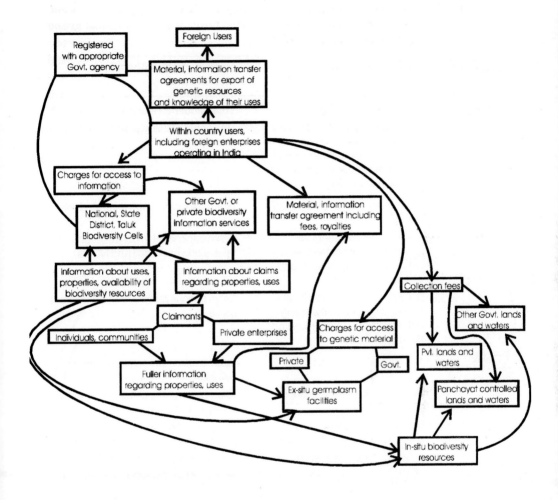

Fig. 6–4. System of access to informational and material resources relating to biodiversity (after Gadgil *et al.*, 1995).

Table 6–7. The hierarchy of tasks and responsibilities for managing biodiversity resources, information and financial flows at different spatial scales (after Gadgil *et al.*, 1995)

Spatial Scale	Tasks Envisaged	Implementation Agencies/ Mechanisms
Village	1. Preparation of CBR	Local students–teachers
	2. Conservation of biodiversity in private lands of residents, common and public lands and waters within the revenue boundaries of village	Residents of the village, hamlet/ settlement
Panchayat	1. Maintenance and validation of CBR	Gram panchayat with local students
	2. Levy collection fees for commercial use of biodiversity resources of public lands and waters	Gram panchayat in consultation with taluk biodiversity cell and NGOs.
	3. Assigning grants to constituent villages and rewarding individuals and user groups on the basis of CBR	Gram panchayat through a transparent process.
Taluk	1. Compilation of CBR	Taluk Biodiversity cell with degree colleges
	2. Rechecking and validation of compiled CBR data	Taluk Biodiversity cell with degree colleges and parataxonomists.
	3. Storage of data–textual, specimens, aids to identification	Taluk Biodiversity cell with degree colleges; computerization of data
	4. Conflict resolution and redressal of grievances	Taluk panchayat in consultation with Taluk Biodiversity cell and NGOs
	5. Value addition to CBR data	Research by Taluk Biodiversity cell and degree colleges
District	1. Methodology to be followed in CBR preparation, including curriculum of high school and college level	Designed by District Biodiversity cell periodically as per its requirements

Table 6–7 contd.

	2. Compilation of taluk level data on CBR comparing with existing scientific knowledge and further validation of CBR	District Biodiversity cell with post-graduate centres and research institutions
	3. Further research on data and material from CBR	R & D institutions, colleges, universities in collaboration with commercial interests and District Biodiversity cell
	4. Devolution of funds to gram panchayats	By zilla parishads on the basis of indicators recorded in CBR
State	1. Norms for MTA, ITA with respect to claims recorded in CBRs	To be evolved in consultation with commercial interests, NGOs, indigenous people
	2. Set priorities of data collection for CBR	State Biodiversity Cell with professional consultation regarding commercial prospects
	3. Devolution of funds to Zilla Parishad	By State government based on data contributed by district biodiversity cell to data bank of State Biodiversity Cell
	4. Fostering close co–ordination with government agencies, Panchayat Raj institutions, commercial interests, scientific and R & D institutions	Mechanisms to be set up by the state government
Nation	1. Norms for MTA, ITA with foreign enterprises	To be evolved in consultation with enterprises, technical experts, NGOs
	2. Levy Biodiversity Conservation Cess	By Central Excise Department as per advice of National Biodiversity Cell
	3. Devolution of funds to State	On the basis of biodiversity stock level and recording of folk level knowledge
	4. Fostering close co–ordination with government agencies Panchayat Raj institutions, commercial interests, scientific and R&D institutions	Mechanisms to be set up by Central Government
	5. Constructive participation in international forums, agreements such as GATT, IPF to further national interests	Such national interests should take into consideration priorities of commercial interests, indigenous people, through a consultative process

Table 6–7 contd.

International	1. IPR protection to biodiversity based enterprises	As per the provisions of GATT, administered by WTO
	2. Mandatory disclosure of origin of genetic material and public knowledge systems	To be proposed by conference of parties to CBD
	3. Assigning countries of origin for genetic resources	Clearinghouse mechanism
	4. Creation of a global biodiversity fund based on national contributions from a cess on sale of biodiversity–based products in each country	To be proposed by Conference of Parties to CBD

Chapter 7
LOSS AND EXTINCTION OF SPECIES

Introduction

All human activity is underpinned by biological resources. We exploit plants and animals for food and raw materials at differing levels of sophistication in different societies. We cannot exist in isolation from the rest of the natural world. Biological resources and biological diversity are two quite different things. Globally, we derive most of our food from less than 20 species of domesticated plants and animals, and exploitation as raw materials accounts for a small proportion of total diversity. Then why should we worry about species loss? There are three reasons for concern. The first is that all species deserve respect regardless of their usefulness to mankind. The second reason is that the living systems constitute our life support and that we do not know the precise role that each species plays within this global system. It is unwise to reduce its diversity, lest we also upset its functions. Thirdly, wild nature is highly important to us economically. It provides food, fibre, timber, fruits and drugs. The wild relatives of crop plants are essential sources of genetic material. As we face climate change, crop breeders will be going back to the wild more and more to select strains that will arm our cultivated organisms against an uncertain future.

The distribution of living species in the world is not uniform. Species richness increases from the poles to the equator. Freshwater insects, for example, are 3 to 6 times more abundant in tropical areas than in temperate zones. Tropical regions also have the highest richness of mammalian species per unit of area, and the diversity of vascular plant species is much richer at lower latitudes. As many as a hundred species of trees can be found on one hectare of tropical rain forest in Latin American forest. A few hectares of rain forest in Borneo can harbour over 650 species of trees, as many as in the whole of North America. A region in lowland Malaysia near Kuala Lumpur has over 600 plant species per hectare. In comparison, all of Denmark possesses no more than 300 species. Global patterns of species diversity in the marine environment resemble those on land. The number of tunicate (sea squirt) species increases from 103 in the Arctic to some 625 in the tropics. These terrestrial and marine patterns of increasing diversity in the tropics reach their peak in tropical forests and coral reefs.

Wetlands are among the most biologically productive ecosystems in the world, yet are often regarded as a nuisance, as wastelands, habitats for pests and threats to public health. In reality, wetlands help to regulate water flows and provide essential services.

The study of life has always been an attempt to understand the biosphere and its history, and biodiversity research is undoubtedly one of the most important enterprises in biology today. One major aim of biodiversity research is the calculation of the genetic information content of the biosphere and the identification of species extinction rates accompanying the loss of information.

Biological diversity is now being reduced, but we do not know at what rates. We do not even know how many species there are on Earth: science has described perhaps 1.5 million and some calculations suggest that there may be 10 or 20 times as many species in total. What we do know is that humanity is transforming the Earth faster and on a larger scale than at any time in history. Part of this change is being caused by the transformation of land from one kind of use to another: from forests to agriculture and rangeland, from wetland to rice paddy, or from coastal mangrove swamp to mariculture. Other changes have been caused by pollution.

There are several scientific uncertainties in the measurement of biological diversity. The layman usually equates biodiversity with the flora and faune of a rain forest and feels that saving the rain forests will prevent the loss of biodiversity. But this gives only an incomplete picture, for biodiversity is by no means confined only to rain forests. It is everywhere, on the land and in the sea. The greater attention given to the species rich tropical forests is not surprising because we believe that perhaps half of all the species on Earth inhabit those forests, and that, as the forests are cleared, this richness of life is at risk. But we must not forget the biological diversity of the seas. Coral reefs have been described as the tropical forests of the oceans. And we must not equate quantity of species with significance; very often even a small number of species that make up the biological diversity of a country can become critical in terms of preserving the fertility and maintaining the biogeochemical cycles of that country. Every area's biological diversity is important to it, and to the world as a whole.

Habitat Fragmentation

Fragmentation which occurs at several different spatial scales can have various short–term and long–term effects. A few species benefit from fragmentation whereas others are exposed to increased risk of extinction. Global biodiversity can be maintained by conserving resources to those species and ecosystems most at risk, and by reversing the processes that place them at risk. In addition, even those species not currently at great risk, should also be saved from the adverse impact of habitat fragmentation. There is a need to develop effective management strategies for landscapes that are already fragmented.

Fragmentation can be countered by maintenance or restoration of large, intact core areas which span large portions of regional landscapes. These core areas harbour source populations of many fragmentation–sensitive species. Truly large reserves may also be established to conserve biodiversity. Entire landscapes need to be managed in ways that minimize destruction and isolation of natural habitats.

Eight categories of species are likely to be especially vulnerable to the effects of fragmentation: rare species, those with large home ranges, those with limited dispersal and low reproductive potential, species with short life cycle, those that depend on unpredictable resources, ground–nesting birds, species of habitat interiors, and species exploited or persecuted by humans.

Some recommendations for maintaining biodiversity in fragmented landscapes are briefly stated below (see Meffe *et al.*, 1997).

1.   Conduct a landscape analysis and look for the pattern of habitats and connections. Relate these to the needs of the native species.

2.   Find out whether the landscape forms part of a critical linkage of ecosystems at a regional scale.

3.   Avoid any further fragmentation or isolation of natural areas. Developments, resource extraction activities, and other land uses should be clustered and minimized so that large blocks of natural habitat remain intact.

4.   Minimize edge effects around remanent natural areas by establishing buffer zones with low-intensity land-uses.

5.   While the larger unfragmented patches of habitat should be duly conserved, the smaller fragments may also be important as the last refuges for many species in highly fragmented regions and can maintain populations of many species for decades. These small fragments contain the sources for recolonization of the surrounding landscape, once destructive activities cease (see Turner, 1996).

6.   Identify and protect traditional wildlife migration routes by diverting human activities away from critical wildlife movement areas.

7. Maintain native vegetation along streams, fence rows, roadsides, and other remanent corridors in transects or belts as wide as possible in order to minimize edge effects and human disturbances.

8. Minimize the area and continuity of artificially disturbed habitats that are dominated by weedy or exotic species so as to reduce the potential for biological invasions of natural areas.

9. Small fragments often suffer from disruption of natural processes, such as fire regimes. Active management is necessary to maintain the native flora and fauna of these fragments.

In the case of fragmented habitats, species richness does not always decline on isolated habitat patches, as predicted by island biogeographic theory. In some cases, richness can even increase for some time as species invade from adjacent disturbed areas. In such a case, species composition often shifts towards weedy, opportunistic species while sensitive species of habitat interiors are lost. The matrix in a fragmented landscape is also constantly changing as crops are planted and harvested, as tree plantations go through their rotations, as farming or silvicultural methods change, and as human settlements flourish or decline. Thus, sometimes the external environment of a habitat patch may not be as constant or predictable as per the island biogeographic theory.

In the early stages of habitat fragmentation, the original landscape is perforated by man-created openings but the matrix remains natural habitat, so the abundance of native species of the original landscape is not much affected although the access created by human trails or roads can reduce or eliminate large carnivores and other species vulnerable to human exploitation or persecution. When human activity increases in the landscape, the gaps in the original matrix expand in size and number until eventually they occupy more than half of the landscape and therefore become the matrix. A highly fragmented landscape may consist of a few remanent patches of natural habitat in a sea of converted land. Many landscapes around the world have suffered this pattern of change.

Of course, fragmentation does not necessarily always lead to extinction. A species might persist in a highly fragmented landscape in three ways: (i) it might survive, even thrive, in the matrix of human land-use, e.g. some weedy plants, insects, fungi, microbes, and house mice; (ii) it might maintain viable populations within individual habitat fragments; e.g. many plants, microbes, and small-bodied animals with modest

214

area requirements; (iii) it might be highly mobile and able to integrate a number of habitat patches, either into individual home ranges or into an interbreeding population. For example, pileated woodpeckers fly among a number of small woodlots to forage in landscapes that were formerly continuous forest. A species that cannot pursue any of the above three options will eventually become extinct in a fragmented landscape.

As a general rule, reducing the size of a habitat by 90% will reduce the number of species which can be supported in the long run by about 50%. The second reason for the loss of species is overexploitation. Commercial harvesting has been a threat to many marine species. Overexploitation has been the cause of extinction of some large terrestrial animals, and well-known species such as the African elephant are under threat today. Pollution is the third reason for the continuing loss of species. Pesticides have affected several species of birds and other organisms. Air pollution and acid rain have been linked to forest diebacks in Europe and North America. Acid rain has resulted in the loss of a number of fish species in European lakes. The fourth reason for the loss of species is the impact of introduced exotic species as they threaten natural flora and fauna by predation, competition or by altering the natural habitat.

Loss of Genes

A species consists of many genes; genetic diversity refers to the variation of genes within species, as expressed, for example, in the thousands of rice varieties in Asia. The genetic variability of many species is diminishing and hence reduces their ability to adapt to pollution, climate change, disease, or other forms of environmental stress. The remaining gene pools in crops such as maize and rice amount to only a fraction of the genetic diversity they harboured only a few decades ago. Many agriculturalists argue that the loss of genetic diversity among domestic plants and animals looms as an even greater threat to human welfare than the loss of wild species, because it is the diversity that will enable crops to adapt to future environmental change.

Wild species and the genetic variation within them make a substantial contribution to the development of agriculture, medicine and industry. Many species help in stabilization of climate, protection of watersheds, soils, nurseries and breeding grounds. It is not possible to estimate the total economic value of the full range of goods and services that biological diversity provides, but a few selected examples are given below:

1.   About 4.5% of the GDP in the United States can be attributed to the harvest of wild species.

2. In Asia, by the mid–1970s genetic improvements had increased wheat production by $2 billion and rice production by $1.5 billion a year by incorporating dwarfism into both crops.

3. A 'useless' wild wheat plant from Turkey has been used to confer disease resistance in commercial wheat varieties worth $50 million annually to the United States alone.

4. One gene from a single Ethiopian barley plant now protects California's $160 million annual barley crop from yellow dwarf virus.

5. An ancient wild relative of corn from Mexico can be crossed with modern corn varieties with potential worldwide savings to farmers estimated at $4.4 billion annually.

6. Worldwide, medicines from wild products are worth some $40 billion a year.

7. In 1960, a child suffering from leukemia had only one chance in five of survival. Now the child has four chances in five, due to treatment with drugs containing active substances discovered in the rosy periwinkle, a tropical forest plant found in Madagascar.

Biotechnology now offers novel possibilities of increasing the production of food, drugs, energy and speciality chemicals and of improving environmental management. This reinforces the need to maintain the richest possible pool of genes. The loss of biodiversity can cripple the genetic base required for the continued improvement and maintenance of currently utilized species and deprive us of the potential use of developments in biotechnology.

Adequate appreciation of the ecological dimension of the problem of genetic erosion emerged only in the 1980s. Before then, concern for the conservation of genetic resources was mainly in relation to agriculture. The growing environmentalism during the 1980s led to the UN Conference on Environment and Development (UNCED) in Rio de Janeiro (1992), whereafter genetic resources began to be dealt with in two arenas, instead of only one. These arenas were:

1) the agricultural arena, as represented by FAO and IBPGR, and

2) the environmental arena, as represented by the United Nations Environment Programme (UNEP), the International Union for the Conservation of Nature and Natural Resources (IUCN) and the World Wide Fund for Nature (WWF).

Threatened and Endangered Species

It is feared that a quarter of the earth's species could be endangered within the next 30 years. There are various ways of countering the threat to genetic resources and biological variation. Rich natural habitats can be preserved in national parks and reserves and the overexploitation of particular species in nature can be banned. Seeds may be stored for *ex situ* conservation in botanic gardens or gene banks. It is also important to try to preserve an undisturbed environment for the species to live in, for example by reducing pollutant emissions to the biosphere.

Conservation of the earth's living resources is important in maintaining essential ecological processes and life–support systems, preserving genetic diversity and ensuring the sustainable utilization of species and ecosystems (Hanneberg, 1992).

Paradoxically, museum curators have been collecting unusual endemic specimens from Madagascar for over a century and yet Madagascar's biodiversity is among the least understood.

There is a woeful paucity of information on the consequences of historical and modern land–use change on the physiography and biodiversity of Madagascar (see Goodman and Patterson, 1997).

Recently, some integrated conservation and development projects have been started to solve the biodiversity crisis at local levels throughout Madagascar. These should stimulate attempts to link development alternatives with natural resource conservation.

Besides indicating the geographical and taxonomic groups containing most threatened species, lists of endangered species often provide other kinds of information (see Tables, 7–1, 7–2). Data from classifications of threatened species using quantitative criteria provide a new method for estimating extinction rates in diverse vertebrate taxa. This analysis has revealed that during the next century the extinction rate might rise to 15–20% in these groups (Mace, 1994). These values are comparable to those based upon extrapolations from species–area curves. However, allocating threatened species categories is only a first step towards developing rational systems for setting conservation priorities. There is also a need to consider a quite different set of variables, including those for incorporating species conservation priorities in area–based planning (Mace, 1994).

217

Table 7-1. Some parameters used in definitions of some globally threatened species categories (condensed from Mace, 1994)

Taxon	In danger of extinction	Will become endangered	Population* size small	Recovered from threat	Probably threatened but no data	Not threatened
Vertebrates	+	+	+	+		
Swallowtail butterflies	+	+	+	+	+	
Dolphins, porpoises and whales	+	+	N		+	
Amphibians and reptiles	+	+	+	+	+	
Invertebrates	+	+	+		+	
Cycads			N			+

*N = numerical guidelines available.

218

Table 7–2. Numbers of plant and animal species to have become extinct since 1600, and presently threatened with extinction (from Smith *et al.*, 1993)

Taxon	No. extinct since 1600	No. presently threatened*
Corals	1	—
Molluscs	191	354
Crustaceans	4	126
Insects	61	873
Fishes	29	452
Amphibians	2	59
Reptiles	23	167
Birds	116	1029
Mammals	59	505
Total (animals)	**486**	**3565**
Ferns and fern allies	16	–
Gymnosperms	2	242
Monocotyledons	120	4421
Monocotyledons: palms	4	925
Dicotyledons	462	17,474
Total (plants)	**604**	**23,062**

* Includes IUCN categories of 'vulnerable,' 'endangered,' and 'probably extinct'.

Threatened species lists are given in a series of several Red Lists and Red Data Books of the IUCN—the World Conservation Union (see, e.g., IUCN, 1989). These provide readily assimilated information to focus attention on the plight of endangered species. The idea of the Red Data Book has been very attractive and there now exist many regional, national and taxonomic lists based upon it (Burton, 1984; Fitter and Fitter, 1987). The lists are also now being used for setting priorities for species conservation.

Recent years have witnessed marked declines among some amphibian populations in many parts of the world, including some species extinctions. These events have generated particular concern because many have occurred in protected areas such as nature reserves and national parks (Halliday, 1998). Amphibian declines are occurring throughout the world. At most affected sites some species are declining whereas others are not. Finally, there is no single cause for these declines. Berger *et al.* (1998) identified a pathogen that links declines among frog populations in two geographically distinct parts of the world, Panama and Queensland, Australia. They studied many dead and dying frogs and identified the cause of population declines as they occurred (rather than after the event) and found that the same pathogen, a chytrid fungus, was the cause of mortality at the two localities. The chytrid invades the skin of adult frogs, and kills them by interfering with their cutaneous respiration and water uptake. It particularly infects the pelvic patch, an important site of water absorption in many frogs (Halliday, 1998). The chytrid is a newly discovered genus. Rather than having a typical branched, filamentous structure, it resembles a protozoan and was originally misidentified as such. Chytrids have been known to attack plants and insects, but the new one is the first to be identified as a vertebrate pathogen. It seems common among captive amphibians in zoos and aquaria. Interestingly the chytrid attacks just adult amphibians, probably because it only attacks skin that contains the protein keratin, which does not occur in amphibians until metamorphosis. This feature differentiates the Berger *et al.* study from previous reports of amphibian population declines, a characteristic of which has been reproductive failure owing to mortality among eggs and larvae (Halliday, 1998).

The significance of the work of Berger *et al.* goes beyond the mystery of amphibian declines—this is the first time that an infectious pandemic disease has been implicated in the decline and possible extinction of animals.

Extinctions

Species extinctions have been occurring in recent years at a rate exceeding that recorded for the past 65 million years. This is one of today's most serious global problems and, unlike other global environmental problems, is completely irreversible.

Homo sapiens first appeared about 500,000 years ago in the Earth's 4.5 billion year history. Our hunter–gatherer ancestors began to exterminate some of the large animals and birds that they killed for food. Agriculture developed independently in eastern Asia, the eastern Mediterranean, Mexico and Peru some 11,000 to 8000 years ago; in those times there were only about 5 million human beings in the whole world.

This number then began to increase quickly and the extensive land clearing and grazing that characterized early agriculture brought in its trail rapidly increasing extinctions (Raven, 1994). The number of people has now increased to an estimated 5.5 billion. Over the last 4 decades, about a fifth of the world's topsoil has been lost, so also about an eighth of our cultivated lands have been lost to desertification, waterlogging and salinization.

Homo sapiens is just one of an estimated 10 million species on earth, but is estimated to be consuming, wasting or diverting some 40% of the net photosynthetic production on land. Man is using about one–third of the planet's available fresh water. And yet our numbers are continuing to grow and the proportion of young people in developing countries is also rising. As a result of our great impact on forests and other biologically rich communities, we are losing species at up to 10,000 times the natural rate that prevailed before our ancestors first appeared on Earth. The background rate of extinction is about four species a year but we are actually losing around 50,000 species a year (Raven, 1994). Indeed it is possible that we may lose two–thirds of all living species over the course of the next century.

It is ethically, aesthetically and economically important to minimize or prevent species losses. We use organisms for food, medicines, chemicals, fibre, clothing, structural materials, energy and many other purposes. Only about 100 kinds of plants provide most of the world's food; their genetic diversity needs to be preserved. There are also thousands of other plants, especially in the tropics, that have some edible parts and might be cultivated for food, if we knew them better. But overconcentration on the 20 or so best known food plants makes us neglect the others.

Plants and other organisms are natural biochemical factories. A large number of the world's people depend directly on plants for their medicines: the Chinese use more than 5000 of the estimated 30,000 species of plants for medicinal purposes. Most of the Western medicines come from the natural products that organisms produce. Very few of the 250,000 kinds of plants of the world have been fully examined, so it seems reasonable to suppose that the remaining species may contain hitherto unknown therapeutically important compounds. It is not possible for any chemist to imagine the complex bioactive molecules produced by nature, but he can often proceed with synthetic modifications to improve on what nature has produced.

Artemesin is the only drug effective against all of the malaria–causing strains of *Plasmodium*. It differs chemically from quinine. Neither its existence, nor its effectiveness against malaria, could have been predicted had a Chinese not traditionally been using an extract of natural wormwood *Artemisia annua*, to treat malaria. Similarly, taxol is the only drug that shows some promise against some cancers; it was initially found in the western yew by a United States Government programme randomly screening plants for anticancer activities. Its molecule has a unique chemical structure and there is no way it could have been visualized had it not been discovered in nature (Raven, 1994).

A novel compound called Michellamine B has been extracted from the African vine *Ancistrocladus korupensis.* It shows some anti–HIV activity. Further studies on its mode of action may facilitate the discovery of other drugs that will be more effective against AIDS.

Yet another reason for being concerned about the loss of biodiversity relates to the variety of essential services provided by natural ecosystems, e.g., the regulation of local climates, the maintenance of atmospheric quality, absorption of pollution, and the restoration and maintenance of soils.

Much of the quality of ecosystem services will be lost if the present episode of species extinction is allowed to run unhindered for much longer.

The first prerequisite of a sustainable world is a stable human population, but this will not in itself mean the attainment of a stable world: for this, the problems of global poverty and social justice will have to be dealt with much more effectively. Over four-fifths of the world's resources are consumed by the people (now less than a quarter of the total) that live in industrialized countries; this overconsumption needs to be checked.

If the problems of population and poverty in the developing world and of overconsumption in the developed world are tackled adequately, several startegies could be used for the management of biodiversity, including the conservation of a reasonable sample of the species living now. One approach is to establish a system of protected areas (biosphere reserves). Another strategy is to preserve the samples of selected organisms outside their natural habitats. For plants, botanical gardens need to be encouraged to form an operational network to conserve plants throughout the world, and a global network of seed banks should also be created. Culture centres should preserve bacteria, algae and fungi.

In the context of extinction, large areas generally hold more species than smaller areas and larger populations persist longer than smaller ones. There is no similar generalization in respect of ecological interactions. If some plant–pollinator mutualisms involving the subtle, complex web of interactions are broken by human actions, this could cause a cascade of extinctions (Janzen, 1987; Gess and Gess, 1991).

Both vertebrate and invertebrate pollinators and dispersers face several threats including poisoning by pesticides, habitat change, invasions of alien animals and plants, and insularization of habitats (Diamond, 1988). These and other forces tend to reduce the diversity of animal mutualists and change the population densities of the survivors. Conceivably, specialists dependent on a few species might be more vulnerable than generalists.

It is possible to assess the risk of plant extinctions by considering the probability of dispersal or pollinator failure, reproductive dependence on mutualism and demographic dependence on seeds. Certain traits can enable us to rank species rapidly according to these three criteria. Plants often compensate for high risk in one of the three categories by low risk in another. For example, self-incompatible plants with rare specialist pollinators often propagate vegetatively. Some systems, e.g. elements of some tropical rain forests, lack compensatory traits and in these the risk of plant extinction from failed mutualism can be fairly high.

Extinction Thresholds

Metapopulations involve a shifting mosaic of presence and absence, with certain patterns of patch occupancy (as opposed to details of within–patch events). A population governed by metapopulation processes is vulnerable to a threshold of habitat availability, below which the metapopulation may be doomed to extinction because colonization is too infrequent to overcome random local extinctions.

The extinction of a metapopulation when too much habitat has been lost is analogous to the collapse of a disease epidemic following the removal of too many susceptible hosts (Kareiva and Wennergren, 1995).

Most research relating to the dynamics of a single species in complex landscapes entails simulations that move individuals around in landscapes drawn from actual maps of habitat. However, while it is easy to map vegetation, it is quite difficult to obtain information on dispersal behaviour or animal movements (Kareiva and Wennergren, 1995).

The metapopulation processes of extinction and colonization that are central to the fate of single species also influence communities. Removal of habitat can alter patterns of coexistence because it favours organisms with high colonization ability over less mobile, but more competitive species. This entails declines in biodiversity when too much habitat has been destroyed because some species may fail to colonize vacant patches fast enough.

Kareiva and Wennergren (1995) proposed the following general principles for the guidance of resource managers:

1. Species that act as metapopulations live with a threshold requirement for habitat, below which they face inevitable extinction (long before all of the habitat has been removed).

2. Destruction of habitat can cause dramatic loss in biodiversity that is long delayed, non–linear and conspicuous only after substantial habitat disappearance with surprisingly negligible obvious effects has occurred. Monitoring programmes and trend analysis can mask the risk of continued habitat loss.

3. A good knowledge of how habitats are arranged and how organisms move between them can mitigate the above risks, and determine whether species persist or become extinct, or whether populations fluctuate wildly or remain stable. Management options that emphasize dispersal rates or the deployment of habitat can help to maximize the benefit of conservation efforts.

Population Extinction and Biodiversity

It is difficult to estimate the vulnerability of a species to extinction from the number and size of its populations, but in some cases reduction in number and size of populations dooms a species to extinction long before it becomes scarce in nature, as was true for the passenger pigeon, *Ectopistes migratorius* (Blockstein and Tordoff, 1985).

Species can usually be distinguished using a criterion of breeding isolation. Subspecies (or 'races') are simply goegraphic units (normally suites of populations) that have evolved sets of differences that a taxonomist subjectively feels deserving of formal recognition with a latinic name.

The two most common definitions of population refer to related kinds of geographic collections of individuals. One is a demographic unit, which is simply an interbreeding group sufficiently isolated from other such interbreeding groups so that changes in its size do not greatly influence the size of near–by groups and vice versa. The other is a *Mendelian population,* in essence a genetically defined entity that can evolve independent of other such units; i.e., its evolutionary future is not primarily determined by flows of genetic information from other populations. These two kinds of populations

224

often exist as parts of continua, just as many species do. Demographic units may be Mendelian populations and vice versa, but the two are not necessarily congruent. The important point is that populations are geographic entities within species that may be defined either ecologically or genetically.

In general, while animal species diversity tends to decline as one moves towards the poles, the geographic range of each species appears to increase. The average range of temperate–zone species is between two and three times larger than that of their tropical counterparts. Thus, there are almost certainly more populations per animal species in temperate, subarctic,and arctic regions than in the tropics. Biodiversity as a whole represents billions of populations.

In many parts of the world the extinction of populations, rather than a species, appears to be the most important aspect of the decay of biological diversity. Consideration only of species extinctions can greatly underestimate the rate of loss of organic diversity as a whole. Extinctions of animal populations appear to be more frequent in proportion to species extinctions in temperate and polar regions than they are in the tropics. The average extratropical species might suffer many more population extinctions before becoming threatened globally than could the average tropical species.

Ecosystem services are provided by populations on global, regional, and local scales—and such services are the most important source of benefits received by humanity (Ehrlich and Ehrlich, 1992). Globally for instance, destruction of the vast majority of tree populations, without wiping out any tree species, might add enough additional carbon dioxide to the atmosphere to make the difference between relatively slow climatic change resulting from global warming and a change that is very rapid and catastrophic for agriculture.

It is not wise to downgrade the importance of the extinction of populations on the assumption that other populations of the same or similar species elsewhere can supply the same services. A crucial question in ecosystem ecology currently is the extent to which species diversity may be required to maintain ecosystem services. The quality of local ecosystem services is strongly tied to exactly what populations are in a given area.

The loss of diversity in an area means a loss of 'ecosystem plasticity'. A diverse mix of species which can change in proportions and distribution in a forested area has a much better chance of maintaining forest cover than a monoculture (Ehrlich and Ehrlich, 1992).

Causes of Extinction

The chief causes of today's global mass extinction spasm are the activities and overpopulation of *Homo sapiens* (See Flessa, 1986). Species–rich biotas are being destroyed at high rates, especially in tropical lowland forests, but also in other environments including coral reefs and freshwater lakes. Consequently, the biological diversity of all types is declining. Although predictions of future losses vary, all point to extinctions of significant percentages of existing life-forms, most of which are unknown today. One easy and efficient way of halting this loss would be protection of 18 identified 'hot spots' of diversity, small areas of the earth that contain exceptionally high concentrations of species found nowhere else.

Not all species are equally vulnerable to extinction. Rare species and long–lived species are especially vulnerable. Keystone species support many other species that are dependent on them. If these keystones are lost, the vulnerability of their many dependent species increases and cascading extinctions can occur.

Not only species losses but also genetic diversity—the basis for evolutionary change and adaptation—and population diversity—the result of local adaptations—are also being lost rapidly. This problem is particularly serious with respect to losses of crop genetic diversity, which forms the basis for agricultural production. Most of the world's major crops and domestic animals have fairly narrow ranges of genetic variation, and the wild ancestors of some of these species have already become extinct. As a result of this impoverishment, the human sustenance base is becoming more and more vulnerable to pests, diseases and changing environments.

Besides outright habitat destruction, fragmentation and degradation of habitats pose grave threats to biodiversity. Creating ever smaller chunks of forest exposes the remaining habitats to edge effects, invasive species and other troubles that hasten extinctions. Species introductions, overharvesting, pollution and toxification, are some other principal types of threats to biodiversity. Global climate change is certain to add to and complicate all the other problems leading to extinctions.

There can be several causes of species declines in a country. Studies in Germany on over 700 species of ferns and flowering plants have revealed the nature and source of threat (Fig. 7–1) which has caused or contributed to their decline. Many of these species have been affected not by single but multiple factors which, in combination, have posed a much stronger threat than posed by any single cause.

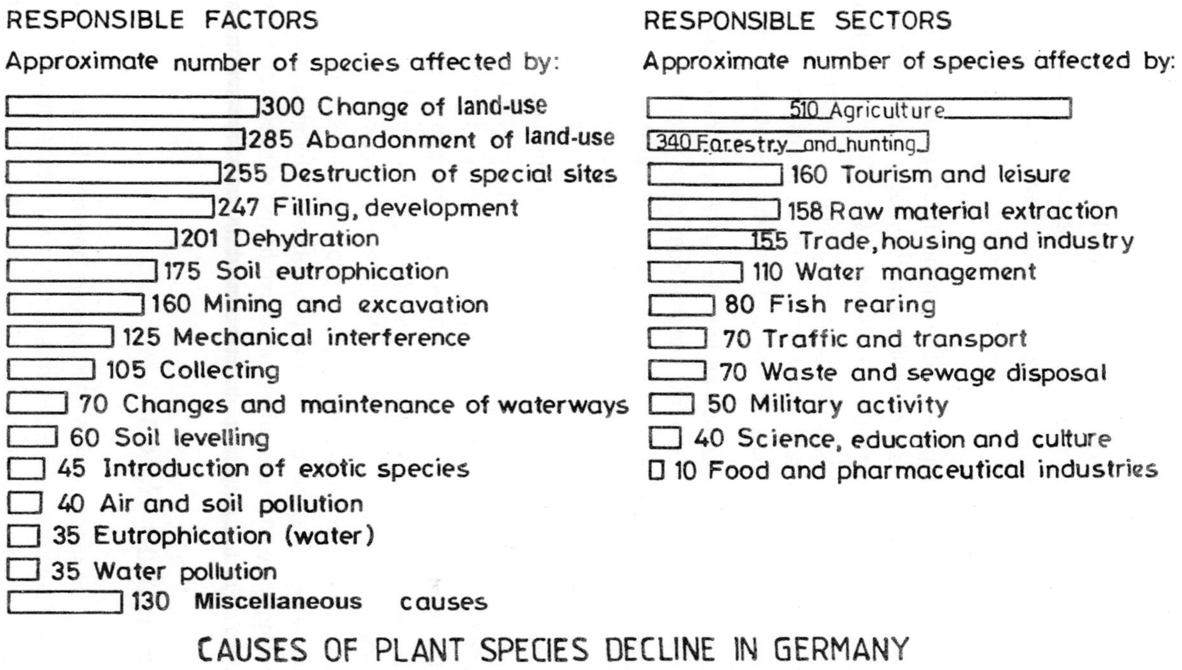

RESPONSIBLE FACTORS

Approximate number of species affected by:

- 300 Change of land-use
- 285 Abandonment of land-use
- 255 Destruction of special sites
- 247 Filling, development
- 201 Dehydration
- 175 Soil eutrophication
- 160 Mining and excavation
- 125 Mechanical interference
- 105 Collecting
- 70 Changes and maintenance of waterways
- 60 Soil levelling
- 45 Introduction of exotic species
- 40 Air and soil pollution
- 35 Eutrophication (water)
- 35 Water pollution
- 130 Miscellaneous causes

RESPONSIBLE SECTORS

Approximate number of species affected by:

- 510 Agriculture
- 340 Forestry and hunting
- 160 Tourism and leisure
- 158 Raw material extraction
- 155 Trade, housing and industry
- 110 Water management
- 80 Fish rearing
- 70 Traffic and transport
- 70 Waste and sewage disposal
- 50 Military activity
- 40 Science, education and culture
- 10 Food and pharmaceutical industries

CAUSES OF PLANT SPECIES DECLINE IN GERMANY

Fig. 7–1. Causes of decline of plant species in Germany.

227

One problem that has attracted some notice is that conservation and protection are not the sole objectives of national parks and certainly not of many provincial and regional parks, nor a wildlife or biosphere reserve area. Indeed, wildlife refuges are sometimes manipulated to enhance habitat for particular species such as ducks which are hunted to the detriment of non-game birds or habitat diversity generally.

The Evil Quartet

According to Woodruff (1992), genetic factors do not figure among the four major causes of extinction (the Evil Quartet): overkill, habitat destruction and fragmentation, impact of introduced species and secondary or cascade effects. Thus, although genetic factors are major determinants of a population's long-term viability, conservationists can do more for a threatened population in the short term by managing its ecology. Ecological management remains the best way of conserving genetic diversity.

There is no doubt that genetics has an important role in modern conservation biology. Genetic variation provides the raw material from which adaptation proceeds and is vital for the march of evolution. This variation occurs at three levels: within individuals, within populations and among populations. Loss of variation can have adverse fitness consequences and can hinder adaptive change in populations. Loss of variation occurs in small populations through founder effects, genetic drift and inbreeding. Management of genetic variation in nature should proceed with immediate (months, years), moderate (decades, centuries) and long-term (millennia) temporal scales in mind. Genetically, conservation units are defined through a hierarchical gene diversity analysis, which divides the total genetic diversity of a species into within-population and among-population components, the latter in a geographic perspective. This biogeographic aspect is an index of natural population genetic structure and probable historical levels of gene flow among populations. Genetics may be best viewed as 'fine-tuning' to be attempted after the 'coarse-tuning' of habitat protection has been accomplished. For the long term, habitat availability must receive the highest priority.

Species Extinction Rates

We are losing at least 27,000 to 50,000 species annually (Raven, 1994; Myers, 1990a, b, 1993). In the future, and in the absence of greatly expanded conservation efforts, independent analyses have proposed (Diamond, 1989; Wilson, 1997) that we face the prospect of losing 20% of all species within 30 years and 50% or more by the end of the next century.

Extinction rates have been estimated in various ways. Usually, estimates of the rate of habitat loss (e.g. deforestation) are combined with those of species numbers to get a general idea of the numbers of species expected to become extinct over a certain time period. These estimates vary greatly because different authors have chosen different baseline estimates of (1) the number of living species in the world (range 3–10 million), (2) the proportion of species found in tropical rain forests (range 25%–75%), (3) the nature of the relationship between habitat loss and extinction, and (4) the rate and extent of habitat loss (range 0.5%–2.0% annual global deforestation). Because of these, extinction estimates suffer from several limitations, e.g. the enormous uncertainty in our estimates of the numbers of species worldwide.

Habitat loss is usually accompanied by habitat degradation, including fragmentation effects. Many studies have shown an increase in local extinctions with fragmentation of tropical forests. Degraded forests may lose species, though perhaps not as rapidly as forests destroyed outright. Usually, losses due to habitat degradation are not included in extinction estimates so there is a tendency to underestimate this component of extinction. Likewise, as cleared areas of forest recover, they will be able to support more species again. Extinction estimates usually ignore recovery processes and thus may overestimate extinction rates.

According to Ehrlich et al. (1995), rates of population and species extinction may be estimated from total consumption of energy (industrial plus traditional) by man. Three assumptions underly this proposition: (1) The rate of extinction is proportional to the rate of habitat destruction because most organisms are adapted to rather limited environments. (2) The rate of habitat destruction is correlated with the scale of human enterprise: the product of the number of people, average consumption and the environmental damage wrought by the technologies used to supply each unit of consumption. (3) Average energy may be used as a surrogate for the above two factors (consumption x technology) (Ehrlich and Ehrlich, 1981). Total energy use is therefore an indicator of trends in extinction rates, and thus could be used to estimate the rates themselves.

Population Extinctions

It is much more difficult to estimate rates of population extinctions than those of species extinctions because populations are more difficult to define than species and no systematic attempt seems to have been made anywhere to keep track of population extinctions in any major taxonomic group.

The impact (I) of humanity on Earth's life–support systems may be considered the product of the size of the human population (P), average affluence (A) (as measured by average consumption), and an index of the environmental damage of the technologies (T) used to supply each unit of consumption (Ehrlich and Ehrlich, 1990). Average energy use (for which numbers are generally available) may be substituted for $A \times T$ in the equation $I = P \times A \times T$ (Ehrlich and Ehrlich, 1990).

Ecological and climatic systems often show non-linearities, prolonged lags and threshold effects that tend to make projections conservative. Neither species nor population extinctions occur independently. Extinction cascades may well become commonplace in the next century. Humans now threaten to alter the climate dramatically and already use or destroy roughly 40% of terrestrial net primary productivity, the food supply of virtually all animals and most micro–organisms that live on land (Vitousek *et al.*, 1986). There is no guarantee that technological changes such as those in forest harvesting techniques will not accelerate the expansion of human enterprise and accelerate the exponential rate of diversity loss. It seems logical to infer that projections based on past and current rates of anthropogenic extinction may well be underestimates.

Pivotal Linkages in Ecosystems

Species known as keystone mutualists are rare species which are likely to suffer differentially high rates of extinction (Terborgh, 1986). The Brazil nut tree is a cash crop in Amazonia. It is pollinated solely by a euglossine bee, which also pollinates orchids and many other plants. These other plants often supply prime sources of food to sundry other insects, which pollinate further plants, and so on. In this crucial sense, the bees serve as a *Mobile link* species, and their plant host, by virtue of supplying food to extensive associations of mobile links, serves as a *keystone mutualist* (Owen–Smith, 1988; Pimm, 1991).

These pivotal linkages within tropical forest ecosystems are manifested by thousands of plants that through their nectar, pollen and fruits supply critical support for multitudes of insects, mammals and birds. If human disturbance eliminates a keystone mutualist, the loss can often spell a loss of many other species as well. Sometimes these additional losses can in turn trigger a chain of linked extinctions. Eventually, entire series of forest food webs can become lost.

In the long run, many species can be eliminated not through destruction of habitats but through the fragmentation of extensive habitats into isolated patches that are too small to maintain their erstwhile species stocks (Shafer, 1991).

Fig. 7–2 shows the general relationship between the rates of species colonization and extinction in large islands. It also indicates the factors that successively dominate the above rates.

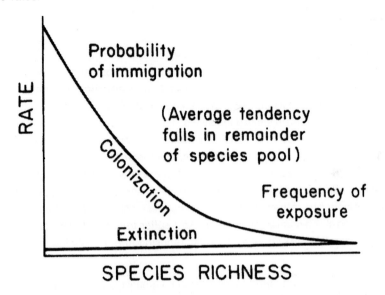

Fig. 7–2. The rates of addition to species richness and extinction against the species richness in large islands (whether geographical or ecological), with a large species pool indicating the factors that successively influence determination of the rate (after Southwood, 1977).

Extinction Epidemic

Biologists often watch the flora and fauna fading away before their very eyes. Coral reefs on which the behavior of fascinating fishes is studied have been destroyed by the sewage from tourist cruise ships. Many habitats of butterflies have been converted to freeways, parking lots or farm fields.

Some biotic diversity is constantly but slowly being generated by natural speciation. But the present–day extinction rates are much higher than the rates at which the natural speciation can compensate for the losses. The extinction outputs greatly exceed the speciation inputs.

To biologists, perhaps the most ominous data pointing to the urgency of dealing with the extinction problem are those relating to the human impact on the planet's total supply of energy produced in photosynthesis—global net primary production.

Extinction Vortices

Smaller populations are particularly vulnerable to demographic and environmental variations and genetic factors that contribute to further population decreases and even doom the population to early extinction. Random environmental variation appears to be usually more important than random demographic variation in increasing the probability of extinction in small populations. This tendency of small populations towards extinction is analogous to a vortex (a whirling mass of gas or liquid which spirals inwards); the closer it gets to the centre, the faster it moves. At the centre of an extinction vortex, the species is lost forever. If the species gets trapped in this vortex, it cannot resist being pulled toward its fate — extinction. This happens when some natural catastrophe, a new disease, or human disturbance reduces a large population to a small size. This small population might suffer from inbreeding depression with a lowered juvenile survival rate, thereby reducing the population size even more (Fig. 7–3).

Smaller populations tend to lose genetic variability just by chance. This process is known as genetic drift and leads to inbreeding depression and a lack of evolutionary flexibility. Experience with captive animals has suggested that isolated populations should have *at least* 50 to 500 or more breeding individuals to maintain genetic variability.

The central factor in the protection of small populations is determination of effective population size based on the number of individuals that are actually producing offspring. Variations in reproductive and mortality rates and environmental variation often cause small populations to fluctuate randomly in size, leading to extinction.

Protection and judicious management of any rare or endangered species need to be based on a firm grasp of its ecology and natural history. One must know the species' environment, distribution, biotic interactions, morphology, physiology, demography, behaviour and genetics. Demographic studies are especially valuable in estimating the long–term stability of populations.

It is feared that some wild species may suffer extinction; these must therefore be saved. This can be done by maintaining them in artificial conditions: this is known as

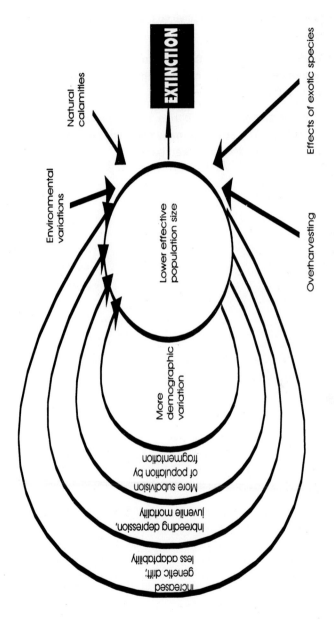

Fig. 7–3. An extinction vortex.

Natural
calamities

Environmental
variations

Effects of exotic species

Overharvesting

EXTINCTION

Lower effective
population size

More
demographic
variation

More subdivision
of population by
fragmentation

Inbreeding depression,
juvenile mortality

Increased
genetic drift;
less adaptability

233

ex-situ or *off-site* preservation. These captive colonies can be used later to re-establish species in the wild.

All over the world, major zoos are attempting to house self-maintaining populations of some rare vertebrates, by using modern animal breeding and biotechnology techniques to increase their reproductive rates.

Similarly, botanical gardens and arboreta are engaged in collecting rare and endangered plant species. The seeds of many plant species can be stored for long periods of time under cold conditions in seed banks.

Chapter 8

BIODIVERSITY CONSERVATION

Introduction

The conservation of biological diversity constitutes an essential aspect of sustainable development worldwide. It is biodiversity that basically determines the structure and function of all ecosystems (see Hawkes, 1991). It is the foundation on which the future well–being of human society rests. It has a powerful role in building sustainable human societies.

Unfortunately, many countries having the largest concentrations of biological diversity are also characterized by persistent poverty and high rates of population growth; both these factors work against conservation as they increase the pressure for inappropriate and harmful land–use, and limit the ability of individuals and governments to halt the loss of diversity.

In most tropical countries, conservation efforts have been largely influenced by foreign agencies. The traditional conservation model followed by industrial countries and adopted by many developing countries emphasizes custodial management, such as parks and reserves, that ban most human activities within their boundaries. Protected areas have been set aside to preserve the so–called charismatic species (e.g., elephants, tigers, or bears), spectacular vistas or geologic formations, and recreational or historic sites. Some areas have also been reserved for protecting watersheds or reserving timber supplies. Until recently, however, few areas were established expressly for conserving biological diversity (Anonymous, 1994).

Many species hybridize sometimes and reproductive isolation is often incomplete. This is true of both animals and plants, even those with elaborate 'reproductive isolating mechanisms'. Occasional hybridization, even leading to gene flow, does not necessarily violate a species' integrity. Arnold (1997) discussed the extent of natural hybridization in animals and plants. This occurs despite many obstacles. According to him, hybridization is not only common but is also a creative force in evolution, with novel genotypes resulting from hybridization providing source material for further evolution and speciation.

There has been much debate concerning whether hybrids might in fact be more fit in their own habitat. Whatever the source of selection, it is clear that some genes can freely permeate hybrid zones, whereas others are restricted to limited introgression by selection (Ritchie, 1998). Recent developments include the role of habitat mosaicism and possible amelioration of hybrid dysfunction. Arnold suggests that 'evolutionary stable lineages' (new species) can evolve if selected hybrid genotypes are more fit than parentals, particularly if they happen to occupy novel habitats.

Plant diversity is certainly the basis of all life, and one of the most troublesome questions today is: what to conserve? Any acceptable answer to this poser is severely limited by the fact that in reality we know nothing about plant diversity in many countries and so it is not possible to select certain areas as the most 'worthy' of conservation. Areas such as the tropical Andes or the Amazon basin are still dark holes of ignorance. For plants, the intensity of collecting effort has perhaps had a greater influence on perceived centres of diversity than does the true nature of that diversity. For example, the heavily collected area around Manaus (on the Amazon near its confluence with the Rio Negro in Brazil) is shown as a centre of endemism in all compendia of plant diversity.

It is okay to protect and conserve areas which already have some degree of protection, but what is undesirable is to pretend that we know these same areas are *the* high points of plant diversity in any complex and poorly understood area. Quantitative methods of the assessment of priorities in biodiversity conservation (Mace *et al.*, 1998) are sure to have a profound impact, if decision–makers can be lured away from the quick and easy answers.

Hot Spots

The term 'hot spot' is generally applied to a geographic area that is particularly high in one or more of the following: species richness, levels of endemism, numbers of rare or threatened species and intensity of threat (Reid, 1998). The term biodiversity hot spot is most commonly used for regions of high species richness. Hot spots are used to identify gaps in the exsiting network of protected areas, by mapping hot spots of species richness, followed by determining which species are already well conserved in existing protected areas and thereafter mapping the pattern of species richness for the remaining species. By using various selection algorithms, the minimum set of grid cells that encompass the unprotected species is chosen. Hot spots of species rarity or endemism—regions rich in species with restricted distribution ranges—can also be used to help fix priorities for bird conservation (Balmford and Long, 1994).

Hot spots can also be defined on the basis of both species richness and endemism.

Megadiversity countries (for example, Brazil and Indonesia) are nations that either have extremely high species richness of plants and vertebrates or are relatively less species rich but with very high levels of endemism (e.g. Madagascar and Australia). Finally, hot spots have been defined as regions with the largest number of threatened species, independent of the overall species richness or endemism of the region.

Two key aspects of the analysis of biodiversity hot spots are valuable for setting conservation priorities. First, because species distribution data for most taxa are either very limited or unavailable, use of the hot spot approach in setting priorities depends on the assumption that patterns of diversity among relatively well-studied 'indicator' groups, such as birds, mammals and plants, are good predictors of patterns of diversity in less-studied groups. Second, research aims to determine the optimal method of analysis for using hot spot information in setting conservation priorities (Reid, 1998).

At both coarse and fine geographic scales, richness of genera and families has proved to be a fairly good predictor of species richness (Balmford *et al.*, 1996a,b). For example, at a continental scale, 99% of the variation in bird species richness in North America can be explained by genus richness, and 91% of variation by family richness. Likewise, at a fine scale, in 35 forest reserves of different sizes in Sri Lanka, 96% of woody-plant species richness can be explained by genus richness and 86% of variation by family richness (Balmford *et al.*, 1996b).

It appears that patterns of higher taxon richness can serve as surrogates for species richness but it is not known whether this same correspondence is true for patterns of endemism as well.

One important lesson that has emerged from studies of diversity hot spots is that the extent of the biodiversity crisis is often highly localized. A substantial fraction of species diversity can be found in very small regions and most threatened species can be found in smaller regions still. Rarity hot spots covering just 5% of the UK represent 98% of the British species of breeding birds. Richness hot spots in the UK covering a similar area encompass 91% of the butterflies, 92% dragonflies, 95% liverworts, 96% aquatic plants and 87% breeding birds (Prendergast *et al.*, 1993; Reid, 1998).

At the national level, biological diversity can be efficiently protected by including all major ecosystem types in a system of protected areas. These types should include those that are unaffected by human activity as well as those managed or disturbed (such as managed rangelands and forests). Another approach is to compare a detailed vegetation map with lands under governmental protection.

In Geographic Information Systems (GIS), computers are used to integrate the natural environment data with known species distributions (Sample, 1994). This enables identification of those critical areas that need to be included within national parks and areas that should be avoided by development projects. The GIS approach involves storing, displaying and manipulating many types of mapped data such as vegetation types, climate, soils, topography, geology, hydrology and species distributions. Satellite imagery is also useful. Images taken at different times reveal patterns of habitat fragmentation and destruction that need to be promptly considered.

Certain hot spots are being identified worldwide to establish priorities in conservation efforts. These are key areas having great biodiversity and high levels of endemism; they are areas facing immediate threat of species extinctions and habitat destruction (Table 8-1). On the basis of these criteria for rain–forest plants, Myers (1988) identified 12 tropical hot spots that together include 14% of the world's plant species on only 0.2% of its total land surface. Later on, 8 non–forest habitats were also added, — four in the tropics and four in Mediterranean–type climates. Also 12 megadiversity countries have been identified that together contain 60%–70% of the world's biological diversity: Mexico, Colombia, Brazil, Peru, Ecuador, Zaire, Madagascar, Indonesia, Malaysia, India, China and Australia (Table 8-2). In these countries, greater conservation attention is warranted. Most workers are agreed on the special need for increased conservation efforts — and the establishment of additional protected areas — in the following regions:

1.　　*Latin America:* The coastal forests of Ecuador; the Atlantic coast forest of Brazil.

2.　　*Africa:* The mountain forests of Tanzania and Kenya; the large lakes throughout the continent; the island of Madagascar.

3.　　*Asia:* South–western Sri Lanka; the eastern Himalayas; Myanmar, Thailand, Kampuchea, Laos, Vietnam and south–eastern China; the Philippines.

4.　　*Oceania:* New Caledonia.

Wilderness Areas

Large blocks of land that have been minimally affected by human activity, that have a low human population density, and are not likely to be developed in the near future, may well be the only places in the world where large mammals can survive in the wild. These wilderness areas serve as controls showing what natural communities can be like with the least human influence.

Table 8–1.   Approx numbers of endemic species in some 'hot spot' areas (from: Myers 1988; World Conservation and Monitoring Centre 1992)

Region	Area (km²) (x 1000)	Vascular plants (x 1000)	Mammals	Reptiles	Amphibians
Upland western Amazonia	100	–	–	–	70
Atlantic coastal Brazil	1000	–	40	92	168
Western Ecuador ·	27	2.5	9	–	–
Colombian Chocó	100	2.5	8	137	111
Philippines	250	3.7	98	120	41
Northern Borneo	190	3.5	42	69	47
Peninsular Malaysia	120	2.4	4	25	7
South–western Australia	113	2.83	10	25	22
Western Ghats (India)	50	1.6	7	91	84
Madagascar	62	4.9	86	234	142
Cape region (South Africa)	134	6.0	16	43	23
California Floristic Province	324	2.14	15	25	7
Central Chile	140	1.45	–	–	–
New Caledonia	15	1.4	2	21	0
Eastern Himalayas	340	3.5	–	20	25

Note: Only the original area of rain forest is given for tropical regions.

Table 8–2. 'Top ten' countries with the largest approx. number of estimated species of selected well–known groups of organisms

Rank	Mammals	Birds	Amphibians	Reptiles	Swallowtail butterflies	Flowering plants (x 10^3)
1	Indonesia 515	Colombia 1721	Brazil 516	Mexico 717	Indonesia 121	Brazil 55
2	Mexico 449	Peru 1701	Colombia 407	Australia 686	China 99–104	Colombia 45
3	Brazil 428	Brazil 1622	Ecuador 358	Indonesia ca. 600	India 77	China 27
4	Zaire 409	Indonesia 1519	Mexico 282	Brazil 467	Brazil 74	Mexico 25
5	China 394	Ecuador 1447	Indonesia 270	India 453	Myanmar 68	Australia 23
6	Peru 361	Venezuela 1275	China 265	Colombia 383	Ecuador 64	S. Africa 21
7	Colombia 359	Bolivia ca. 1250	Peru 251	Ecuador 345	Colombia 59	Indonesia 20
8	India 350	India 1200	Zaire 216	Peru 297	Peru 58	Venezuela 20
9	Uganda 311	Malaysia ca. 1200	USA 205	Malaysia 294	Malaysia 55	Peru 20
10	Tanzania 310	China 1195	Venezuela Australia 197	Thailand Papua New Guinea 282	Mexico 52	USSR (former) 20

Centres of Diversity

There are instances when specific data about whole communities are not available. In these cases, certain organisms can be used as biodiversity indicators. Diversity in birds, for example, can be a good indicator of community diversity in some areas.

Attempts are underway to identify over 200 global centres of plant diversity with large concentrations of species. Also, the International Council for Bird Protection ICBP (1992) has identified over 200 Endemic Bird Areas (EBAs) (Stattersfield et al., 1998). These are localities containing about 245 restricted–range bird species. The localities include islands and isolated mountain ranges that also contain endemic lizards, butterflies and plants, and so represent priorities for conservation : certain EBAs contain no protected areas and require urgent conservation measures.

Protecting habitats is undoubtedly the best method for preserving biological diversity. The human impacts on protected habitats vary greatly and compromises need to be made between protecting biological diversity and satisfying human needs. Protected areas include nature reserves, national parks, wildlife sanctuaries, national monuments, and protected landscapes and seascapes. Considerable biological diversity is often found in unprotected multiple–use management areas. About 6% of the Earth's surface today is included in about 8600 protected areas. And in many countries 10%– 20% of the land is managed for multiple–use resource production. To begin with, well– selected protected areas can protect large numbers of species. But the future fate of some of these species is in doubt due to small population sizes, the inability of the protected area to supply all of the needed requirements of species, the tendency of many species to migrate, and threats from outside the protected area. Effective preservation can be achieved by means of large and well–managed protected areas that include examples of all biological communities.

Some of the issues being debated by conservation biologists are the following:

1. How large must nature reserves be to protect species?

2. Is it better to have a single large reserve or many smaller reserves?

3. How many individuals of an endangered species need to be protected in a reserve to prevent extinction?

4. When several reserves are created, should they be close together or far apart, and should they be isolated from one another or interconnected by corridors?

In general, the following principles may be recommended for designing better reserves: protection of complete ecosystem, larger size, unfragmented, larger number (of reserves), maintenance of corridors that interconnect different reserves, diversity of habitats, more or less rounded (spherical) shape (to prevent edge effects), mixing of reserves of various sizes, and regional, planned management of reserves.

Fig. 8–1 shows the relationship between park size and population size for some large vertebrates.

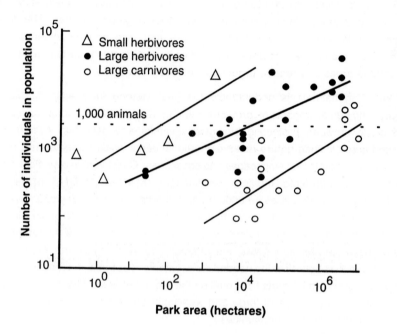

Fig. 8–1. Relationship between park size and population size for large vertebrates. Each symbol represents an animal population in a park. If the viable population size of a species is 1000 (10^3; broken line) individuals, parks of at least 100 (10^2) ha will be needed to protect small herbivores (e.g., rabbits, squirrels); parks larger than 10,000 ha are needed to protect larger herbivores (deer, zebra, giraffes); and parks of at least a million ha to protect lions and wolves (from Schonewald–Cox, 1983).

Landscape Ecology and Park Design

Landscape ecology is the study of patterns of habitat types on a regional scale and their influence on species distribution and ecosystem processes. A landscape is an area where a cluster of interacting communities is repeated in similar form. Fig. 8–2 illustrates four landscape types in which interacting communities form repetitive patterns.

(A) Scattered patch landscapes

Open clearings in a forest	Groves of trees in a field

(B) Network landscape

Network of roads in a large plantation	Riparian network of rivers and tributaries in a forest

(C) Interdigitated landscapes

Tributary streams running into a lake	Shifting forest–grassland borders

(D) Checkerboard landscape

Farmland under cultivation for different crops

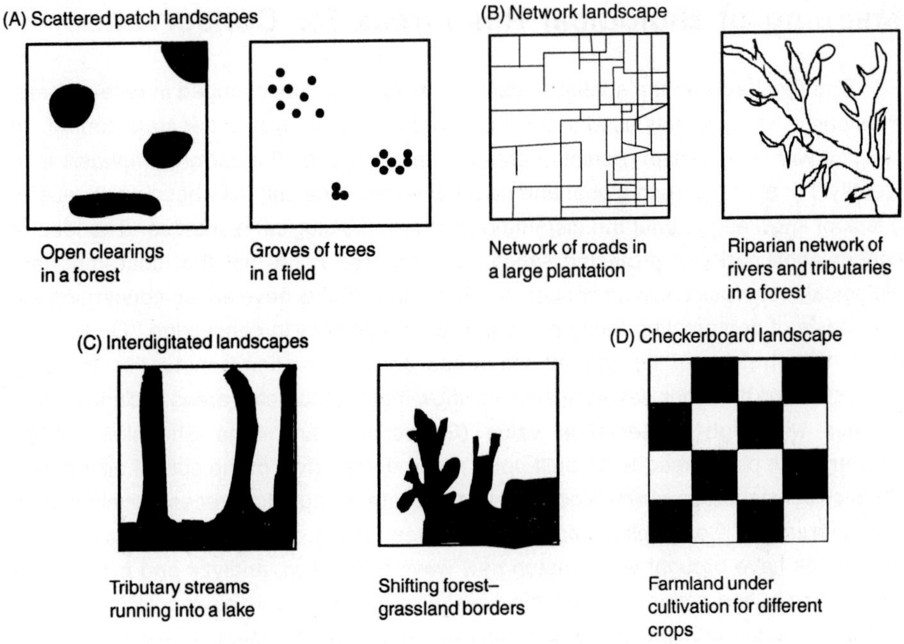

Fig. 8–2. Four landscape types where interacting communities form repetitive patterns.

For species not confined to a single habitat, or those that live on borders where two habitats meet, the patterns of habitat types on a regional scale are of vital importance. The presence and density of many species is influenced by the size of habitat patches and their degree of linkage. For example, the population size of a rare animal species will be quite different in two 100–ha parks, one with an alternating checkerboard of 100 patches of field and forest, each 1 ha in area, the other with a

243

checkerboard of four patches, each 25 ha in area. Different landscape patterns also have different effects on the microclimate, pest outbreaks and animal movement patterns. Different land–uses sometimes produce highly contrasting landscape patterns. Forest areas cleared for shifting agriculture, permanent subsistence agriculture, plantation agriculture, or suburban development have completely different appearances from the air, differing distributions and sizes of remanent forest patches, and different species assemblages.

Mapping of Biological Resources for Conservation

The emphasis on the spatial scales of conservation has changed in recent years. Previously, whole forests used to be conserved and taken over under state control. In keeping with this, certain protected areas were set apart. The current emphasis is to identify 'hot spots' at both global and national levels. The shift has been partly due to a lack of knowledge about the distribution pattern of biological resources. The idea of conservation parks or protected sanctuaries aroused hope that the most important biological resources could be conserved. But today doubts have arisen concerning the very basis of demarcating these parks and their efficiency in conserving. On the one hand, the strategy of fencing off the areas as conservation sanctuaries is being questioned; on the other, several instances show that the protected areas exclude certain patches with high conservation value (Ganeshaiah and Uma Shaanker, 1998). Conservation plans need to be built upon our understanding of the spatial distribution of biological resources, which is generally inadequate. Fortunately, recent developments in the areas of Geographic Information System (GIS) and Remote Sensing (RS) techniques have brought within reach new ways to develop, analyze and monitor the spatial distribution patterns of biological resources. These tools have greatly speeded up the efficiency with which the biological resources can be mapped and managed.

The fact that some countries (including India) do have good data bases on the occurrence and distribution of biological resources (e.g. numerous herbaria), raises the hope that it should be possible to develop initial patterns of spatial distribution of our biological resources. In fact, Mushtak Ali and Ganeshaiah (1998) have already shown the potentiality of these data sets in developing the biodiversity maps of India. Nair and Menon (1998) have mapped the distribution, and estimated the stocks of bamboo resources.

Protected Areas

The global network of international, national and regional protected areas remains an important tool in biodiversity conservation. These areas serve as critical repositories ensuring that at least a minimum of the world's genes, species and ecosystems are conserved (Anonymous, 1994). By 1994, over 8500 protected areas had been designated worldwide, covering about 8 million km^2 (Tables 8–3 and 8–4) (WRI, 1994) which represents only about 6% of the Earth's total land surface. The largest park is in Greenland, covering 972,000 km^2, accounting for about 12% of the global area protected. Yosemite National Park in California was established as the world's first protected area. Since then, about 7000 national parks, reserves, and other protected areas have been established. Additionally, there are over 500 zoos, 1500 botanical gardens, 60 gene banks, and a small number of scientific aquaria, collectively known as *ex–situ*, or off–site conservation facilities that have helped sustain many species, including some at serious risk of extinction. Between 1950 and 1990, the number and extent of protected areas increased more than five times. The average rate of species extinction, though not known precisely, has increased greatly over the same period. So why hasn't custodial management solved the global biodiversity problem? Because protected areas were usually created for purposes other than biodiversity conservation. Park boundaries follow political lines rather than ecological lines (e.g. the limits of a watershed). Many parks are too small to effectively conserve intact ecosystems or provide adequately for their inhabitants. For example, many park animals have to range beyond the boundaries during certain seasons to find enough food to survive.

All too often, protected areas are imposed on a community with no input from and little regard for the local people, thus creating conflict. Conflict also arises when the benefits of the areas go to society at large, or into government or business coffers, while the costs are borne by local people whose use of the area tends to be restricted.

Some activities outside a park's boundaries may have a negative impact inside the park. When land adjacent to a park is altered, there may be changes in breeding and migration of park species, changes in water availability or quality, or air pollution.

Many zoos, botanical gardens and aquaria started long ago as mere menageries of exotic biological curiosities for public display. Some of them still treat plant and animal species strictly as acquisitions. In the past, seed banks collected a limited number of species and storage methods sometimes failed to maintain the viability of the material.

Table 8–3. Protected and managed areas in the world's geographic regions (from : WRI, 1994)

Region	Protected areas (IUCN categories I–V)			Managed areas (IUCN category VI)		
	Number of areas	Size (km²)	Per cent of land area	Number of areas	Size (km²)	Per cent of land area
Africa	704	1,388,930	4.6	1562	746,360	2.5
Asia (incl. former USSR)	2399	1,454,910*	5.5	1150	310,290	1.1
North and Central America	1752	2,632,500	11.7	243	161,470	0.7
South America	667	1,145,960	6.4	679	2,279,350	12.7
Europe	2177	455,330	9.3	143	40,350	0.8
Oceania[a]	920	845,040	9.9	91	50,000	0.6
World	8619	7,922,660	5.9	3868	3,588,480	2.7

* Only 124 countries currently have protected areas.

[a] Australia, New Zealand and the Pacific Islands.

Protected areas cover relatively limited territory and *ex situ* collections hold relatively little genetic material. Indeed, substantial biodiversity exists in areas inhabited by humans.

To respond to today's challenges, many leading zoos, botanical gardens and other facilities have started reorienting their missions through captive breeding and scientific

Table 8–4.   Relative protection of 14 major biomes (after IUCN, 1994)

Biome type	Total area (km²)	Protected areas	Area protected (km²)	Per cent of area protected
Tropical rain forests and moist forests	10,513,210	506	538,334	5.1
Tropical dry forests /woodlands	17,312,538	799	817,551	4.7
Tropical grasslands /savannas	4,264,833	59	235,128	5.5
Subtropical/temperate rain forests/woodlands	3,930,979	899	366,297	9.3
Temperate broadleaved (deciduous) forests	11,216,660	1507	358,240	3.2
Temperate evergreen coniferous forests	3,757,144	776	177,584	4.7
Temperate grasslands	8,976,591	194	99,982	0.8
Warm deserts/semideserts	24,279,842	300	984,007	4.1
Cold deserts	9,250,252	136	364,720	3.9
Boreal forests and woodlands	15,682,817	429	487,227	3.1
Tundra	22,017,390	78	1,645,043	7.5
Islands	3,252,270	530	322,769	9.9
Lake systems	517,694	17	6,635	1.3
Mountain systems	10,633,145	1277	852,494	8.0

research. Leading zoos and botanical gardens seek to breed and propagate rare species. These facilities can maintain viable populations of only a small fraction of the species threatened with extinction. While captive breeding and reintroduction hold some promise, they are expensive and rather limited in scope. These measures cannot control one of the primary threats to endangered species: habitat destruction.

Buffer zones and biosphere reserves have come up. Biosphere reserves have concentric areas zoned for different uses (Fig. 8–3). The 'core zone' is devoted to preserving biodiversity with no human interference. Around the core is a 'buffer zone' in which some settlement and resource use is allowed, surrounded in turn by an indefinite 'transition area' where sustainable development activities are permitted.

As a general rule, the greater the human–caused disturbance, the greater the loss in biodiversity and the narrower the scope of preserving it. The International Union for the Conservation of Nature (IUCN) developed the following system of classification for protected areas that ranges from minimal to intensive allowed use of the habitat by humans (IUCN, 1994):

1. *Strict nature reserves and wilderness areas.* Protect natural organisms and natural processes in an undisturbed state, so as to perpetuate representative samples of biological diversity for scientific study, education, environmental monitoring and maintenance of genetic variation. Included are two subcategories: (Ia) primarily includes nature reserves, for research and monitoring work, and (Ib) primarily includes wilderness areas maintained for recreation, for subsistence economic activities and for protecting natural processes.

2. *National parks.* Large areas of scenic beauty, maintained for scientific, educational and recreational use; usually not used for commercial extraction of resources.

3. *National monuments and landmarks.* Smaller areas designed to preserve unique natural areas of archaeological interest.

4. *Managed wildlife sanctuaries and nature reserves.* Similar to nature reserves, but some human manipulation is encouraged to maintain the community characteristics. Some controlled harvesting is also permitted.

5. *Protected land and seascapes.* These are areas that embody the harmonious interaction of people and the environment through the traditional, non–destructive

248

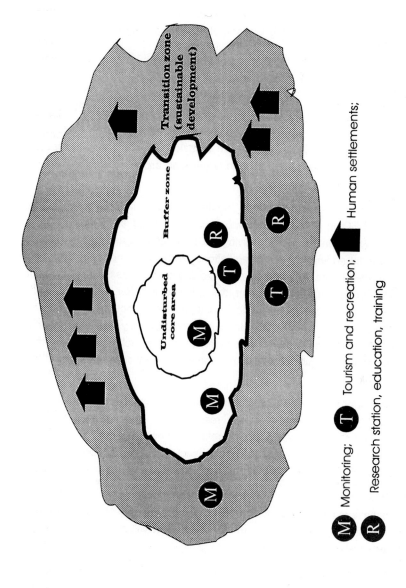

Fig. 8-3. A MAB reserve. A core protected area surrounded by a buffer zone in which human activities are monitored and managed, and a transition zone of sustainable development and experimental research.

(M) Monitoring; (T) Tourism and recreation; ◄ Human settlements;

(R) Research station, education, training

use of natural resources, while concomitantly providing opportunities for tourism and recreation. Include grazing lands, orchards, or fishing villages.

6. *Managed resource protected areas.* These allow sustainable production of natural resources such as water, wildlife, grazing for livestock, timber and fishing. This is done in such a way that the biological diversity is preserved.

The first four or five of the above are protected areas because their habitat is managed primarily for biological diversity. Areas in the last category are not managed principally for biological diversity, though this can occasionally constitute a secondary objective. Managed areas, usually being much larger than protected areas, still may contain many of their original species.

The first 57 biosphere reserves were identified by the Man and Biosphere Programme of UNESCO in 1976. The number has increased since then. Many biosphere reserves were created simply by giving the designation to an existing national park or reserve, without adding new land, regulations, or functions nor have agencies been sufficiently funded to make the complicated zoning system really work. Without local involvement in design and management, the only way a buffer zone might work is if the park agency can effectively enforce the regulations (Anonymous, 1994). A novel conservation technique that addresses the root cause of biodiversity loss is bioregional management, a method that goes beyond the buffer zone approach by involving local people, integrating ecological, economic, cultural and managerial considerations at the regional scale.

The integrative approach centres around the idea of managing whole regions with biodiversity in mind. Dividing government responsibility into isolated forestry, agriculture, parks, and fisheries sectors fails to reflect ecological, social, or economic reality. A 'bioregional' approach requires cross-sectoral and transboundary co-operation and integration, as well as broad participation by all affected constituencies.

Bioregions are areas with high value for biodiversity conservation in which a management regime is established to co-ordinate land-use planning of both public and private landowners and to define development options that will meet human needs without losing biodiversity.

Dinerstein and Wikramanayake (1993) classified tropical Asian countries into four types on the basis of the per cent of their currently protected rain forest and the percent of unprotected forest predicted still to be intact in 10 years (Figure 8–4). Category I countries (Brunei, Indonesia, Bhutan and Malaysia) have protected large amounts of forest and will have remaining unprotected forests in the near future. Category II (Thailand, Sri Lanka, India, Nepal and Pakistan) have many parks, but the remaining unprotected forest is disappearing rapidly. New parks should be created immediately. Category III (e.g. Papua New Guinea, Solomon Islands and Laos) have much forest but no protected areas. Category IV countries (Vietnam, Philippines, China and Tonga) have little protected forest and also little forest left to protect; the remaining unprotected areas are degrading rapidly as a result of human activities. Saving the remaining forest patches in these countries is an urgent conservation priority.

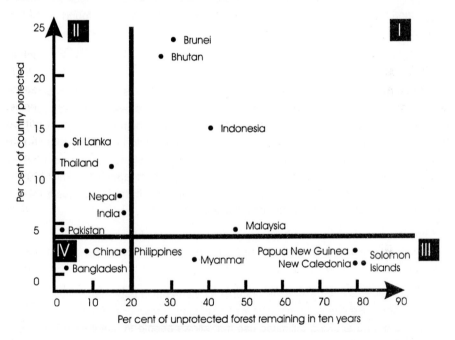

Fig. 8–4. Distribution of some Indo–Pacific countries based on (1) the percentage of their forests that are currently protected and (2) the percentage of unprotected forest predicted to remain intact in 10 years. Figure shows selected countries with at least 20% forest cover but less than 4% of that protected; these are high–priority countries for establishing reserves (after Dinerstein and Wikramanayake, 1993).

251

Although a large number of heritage sites have been set up throughout the world, many of the sites are facing certain problems. These include development (e.g. logging, mining), tourism, external threats, grazing and cultivations, illegal wildlife harvesting, fire, natural threats or calamities, introduced species, and insufficient management etc. The most serious and common problem in Asian sites is that of insufficient or incompetent management and supervision.

A park has to be managed very efficiently to ensure that original habitat types are maintained. Some species only occur in specialized niches and specific successional stages of that habitat. When land is protected the pattern of disturbance and human usage can change so greatly that many species that previously were found on the site vanish. Natural disturbances, including fires and grazing are key factors in the ecosystem required for the presence of certain rare species. Small parks often lack the full range of successional stages, so many species may disappear for this reason.

Protected areas need to be managed competently so as to maintain biological diversity because the original conditions of the area may have been changed by human activities. The best management sometimes involves doing nothing. Effective management begins with a clearly articulated statement of priorities. Parts of protected areas occasionally have to be burned, dug up, or otherwise disturbed by people to create the openings and successional stages needed by some species. This kind of management has proved to be crucial for some endangered butterfly species that need early successional food plants to complete their life cycle.

Keystone resources such as nesting sites and water holes have to be carefully preserved, restored, or even added to protected areas so as to maintain populations of some species.

Local residents and outside visitors are key elements in park management. Quite often a compromise has to be made between banning human use of park resources on the one hand, and allowing unlimited use that allows people to use park resources in a sustainable manner without harming biological diversity, on the other.

Substantial biological diversity exists outside of protected areas, particularly in habitat managed for multiple–use resource extraction. These unprotected habitats are also vital for conservation because protected areas account for only a small percentage of total area. Animal species living in protected areas often forage or migrate on unprotected land where they are exposed to hunting, habitat loss and other threats from humans.

In temperate forests biodiversity can be increased if logging operations minimize fragmentation, and if some late–successional components, including living trees, standing dead trees and fallen trees are left. These trees are important resources for cavity–nesting birds. In Africa, many large animals live predominantly in rangeland outside the parks. Local people and landowners often maintain wildlife on their land for a variety of purposes; further incentives are often given to encourage this practice.

Monitoring

Efforts to monitor, assess and conserve biodiversity have been focused largely on documenting species and habitats and on better understanding the biological functions and values of biodiversity (Wilson, 1988). Increasing attention is now being paid to the links between biodiversity and the human or cultural context, but biodiversity remains essentially a biological concept defined in terms of genes, species and ecosystems that underpin human activities (WRI, 1991). Efforts to conserve biodiversity largely in terms of biological inventory, assessment and monitoring may only document the disappearance of species and the destruction of habitats. To maintain or restore certain types of biodiversity, efforts have to be made to understand the history of human effects on the distribution of species, habitats and ecosystems. Moreover, for effective conservation and restoration of biological diversity and productivity in threatened areas, assessment and monitoring must address the different ways in which people value, use, manage and affect the biodiversity of any given area.

Another response, that of Conservation Biology, argues that conserving biodiversity requires improved understanding of the biological variety of plants and animals through more systematic field research on taxonomy and the functioning of biophysical processes (Soulé, 1986). Wilson (1988) and Ehrlich and Ehrlich (1981) argued that there are sufficient reports of species extinctions and habitat destruction to warrant effective and immediate protection of areas important for biodiversity, such as tropical rain forests.

The conservation biology response has led to the creation of national parks and other types of protected areas, but the view of national parks and related reserves as fortresses is sometime challenged. A more co–ordinated and integrated set of conservation programmes are now being advocated (Nelson and Serafin, 1992).

Adaptive Management

Monitoring is necessary for ascertaining whether or not our management strategies for forests, rangelands or aquatic ecosystems are actually conserving biodiversity. The best way to understanding the impact of our actions is through long–term, systematic monitoring of biodiversity at many levels of organization and spatiotemporal scales. Monitoring should constitute an integral part of management as it can indicate which of our practices are compatible with protecting biodiversity. Conversely, by learning which practices harm biodiversity, such practices can be avoided. The linking of management with monitoring is termed *adaptive management*. It views human activities with some humility and realizes how ignorant we are about biodiversity and how to maintain it. The underlying assumptions of adaptive management as applied to biodiversity have been summarized by Noss and Cooperrider (1994) as follows:

1.   Maintaining optimally functioning ecosystems with all their components (i.e., biodiversity) is an overriding goal.

2.   Ecosystems are extremely complex and human understanding of them is rudimentary.

3.   Human activities may have severe and largely unpredictable effects on ecosystems, and these effects can be irreversible or require centuries for restoration.

4.   Management should therefore be conservative, erring on the side of minimal risk to ecosystems.

5.   Careful, systematic monitoring of ecosystems and how we affect them can help us learn how to avoid causing further harm to them.

Monitoring is the foundation stone of adaptive management because without it one cannot learn to adapt. Adaptive management may be easily applied to a problem of any scale. It is a cyclic process. Table 8–5 lists some indicator variables for monitoring biodiversity.

Range management. It is unfortunate that forestry has changed into a service profession for the timber industry. But foresters are not the only natural resource professionals to have facilitated this change. Range management may be considered a counterpart of forestry for lands without trees. Like forestry, range management has developed in response to the idea that rangelands were deteriorating—from overgrazing. Livestock production has been the primary focus in rangeland management in many advanced countries. Range management involves optimizing the returns from rangelands in those combinations most desired by and suitable to society through the manipulation of range ecosystems. As with forestry, the emphasis is on products and production (returns), on improvement over nature (optimizing) and on technology (Tables 8–6, 8–7).

Wildlife management. This also has a remarkable history parallel to that of forestry and range management. *Wildlife management* includes both fisheries and wildlife management (Noss and Cooperrider, 1994). In some parts of the oceans, humans have virtually annihilated salmon fisheries through dams, logging and other habitat destruction, and then tried to undo this by huge expenditures (but limited success) to raise and release salmon in hatcheries. Like foresters and range managers, wildlife and fisheries managers have also focused on raising a single species or only a few species such as deer, ducks and pheasants for hunting, and bass and trout for fishing. Table 8–8 lists common wildlife management practices and highlights similar purposes and effects on biodiversity as those for forestry and range management.

According to Noss and Cooperrider, because biodiversity conservation is largely an issue of how we treat the land, any national strategy for biodiversity must be land-based; the real threats are logging, grazing, road building, mining, dam building, agriculture, housing development and off-road vehicles. It is necessary to interact with nature gently and more sustainably. Any rational strategy must duly recognize the linkages between proximal threats to biodiversity and the ultimate causes: human population growth, poverty, misperception, anthropocentrism, cultural transitions and economics. It must give incentives for controlling population and resource consumption.

Land management can have good, bad or neutral effects on biodiversity. Good management serves to protect biodiversity from harm or restores an ecosystem previously damaged. It is neutral if it mimics or substitutes for natural disturbance-recovery processes. Negative management is one that leads to biotic impoverishment.

Biodiversity Assessment for Conservation

Identification of prospective conservation areas is usually based on such surrogate information as richness of indicator taxa, taxa restricted to a given area, or higher taxon richness (that is, genus or family richness). It is generally agreed that conservation areas should strive to sample regional features, using sets of grids (Florey *et al.*, 1994; ICBP, 1992) that contain all species in a taxon at least once; the complementarity principle ensures that conservation areas represent all species efficiently and that rare species

255

Table 8-5.   Indicator variables for monitoring of biodiversity at four levels (after Noss and Cooperrider, 1994)

Level	Composition	Indicators — Structure	Function	Monitoring tools
Genetic	Allelic diversity; presence of rare alleles, deleterious recessives, or karyotypic variants	Effective population size; heterozygosity; polymorphism	Inbreeding depression; genetic drift; gene flow; mutation; selection intensity	Electrophoresis; karyotypic analysis; DNA sequencing; morphological analysis
Population/ species	Abundance; frequency; importance or cover value; biomass; density	Dispersion; range; population structure; habitat variables; within–individual morphological variability	Demographic processes and fluctuations; physiology; life history; phenology; growth rate (of individuals); adaptation	Censuses; remote sensing; species–habitat modelling; population viability analysis
Community/ ecosystem	Identity, relative abundance, frequency, richness, evenness, and diversity of species and guilds; endemic, exotic, threatened and endangered species; C_4:C_3 plant species ratios	Substrate and hydrologic variables; slope stream gradient; vegetation biomass and physiognomy; foliage density and layering; horizontal patchiness; canopy openness and gap proportions; abundance, density and distribution of key physical features and structural elements; water and resource availability and quality	Biomass and resource productivity; biotic functions; colonization and local extinction rates; patch dynamics; nutrient cycling and human intrusion rates and intensities	Aerial photography and other remote sensing data; ground–level photography; physical habitat measures and resource inventories; hydrologic measurements; indices of diversity, heterogeneity, layering dispersion, biotic integrity etc.

256

Table 8–5 contd.

Regional landscape	Identity, distribution, richness and proportions of patch (habitat) and landscape types; richness and endemism of species distributions	Heterogeneity; connectivity; spatial linkage; patchiness; porosity; contrast; grain size; fragmentation; perimeter–area ratio; habitat layer distribution	Disturbance processes; nutrient cycling and energy flow rates; patch persistence and turnover rates; rates of erosion and energy flow rates; patch rates of erosion and geomorphic and hydrologic processes; human land–use trends	Aerial photography and other remote sensing data; Geographic Information System (GIS) technology; mathematical indices of pattern, heterogeneity, connectivity, layering, diversity, edge, morphology autocorrelation etc.

Table 8–6. Some forestry practices and their effects on biodiversity (after Noss and Cooperrider, 1994)

Practice	Purpose	Effect on biodiversity
Planting of exotics or genetically 'improved' tree species	Improved yield of commercial trees	Replacement of native species; loss of genetic purity or genotypes of native stock
Pesticide spraying	Protection of commercial trees	Reduction of secondary effects on non–target insect species and vertebrates; ecosystem disruption
Clear–cutting and reforestation	Maximum utilization of existing tree biomass and speeding up new forest growth	Artificial disturbance cycle truncated succession; loss of species richness; loss of structural and functional diversity
Clear–cutting and even–aged management	Efficient forest regulation, maximum profit from growing trees	Truncated succession; loss of structural diversity
Swidden	Site preparation for new forest	Loss of structure, biomass and nutrients from forest ecosystem
Tree thinning	Increased growth of commercial trees	Reduced structural diversity in forest
Maximum production of commercial timber and pulpwood	Maximum forest output; highest profit	Reduced structural and species diversity of forest; deterioration of forest ecosystem

are included (Jaarsveld *et al.*, 1998). The outcome of such a complementarity analysis is not only a good basis for the efficient conservation of the focal taxon, but may also be more widely applicable to other taxa.

Table 8–7. Some common range management practices and their impact on biodiversity (after Noss and Cooperrider, 1994)

Practice	Purpose	Effect on biodiversity
Reseeding with exotic species	Increased forage production for livestock	Displacement of native species
Brush or tree removal	same	Replacement of woody species with grasses or other herbaceous species; loss of structural and species diversity
Water development	Increased water for livestock; better livestock distribution	Usurpation of water required by wildlife species; extension of livestock impacts into weakly grazed landscape
Fencing	Control of livestock movement	Impairment of movement of some wildlife species
Predator control	Livestock protection from native predatory animals	Extirpation of predators; reduction or elimination of non–target species
Salting (leaving salt on range)	Better livestock distribution	Spreading of livestock impacts into previously ungrazed or lightly grazed landscape
Pesticide/herbicide spraying	Control of harmful insects or noxious weeds	Reduction in non–target organisms and plant species diversity; disruption of ecosystem
Maximizing livestock utilization of forage	Maximum livestock production; high profit	Decreased forage availability for wildlife species; reduction of species diversity; ecosystem degradation

It has been commonly observed that richness 'hot spots' (highly species–rich areas) and 'cold spots' (areas poor in species) rarely coincide; nor do hot spots and rare (restricted range) taxa generally coincide. Jaarsveld et al. (1998) analyzed species and higher taxon data for over 9000 South African plants and animals, including vascular plants, mammals, birds, butterflies, and also less well–known taxa, such as termites, antlions (Myrmeleontidae), buprestid beetles (Buprestidae), and scarabaeoid beetles (Scarabaeoidea) (Florey et al., 1994; ICBP, 1992). These workers found that complementary species sets did not coincide and overlapped little with higher taxon sets. Survey extent and taxonomic knowledge did not affect this overlap. Thus the assumptions of surrogacy, on which so much conservation planning is based, are not supported.

Five basic principles of reserve design that have influenced conservation efforts are listed below (see Wilcove et al., 1993).

1.   Well–distributed species are less prone to extinction than those confined to small portions of their ranges.

2.   Large habitat areas containing many individuals of a given species are more likely to sustain that species than are smaller habitats with only a few individuals.

3.   Blocks of habitat in close proximity are preferable to those that are widely dispersed.

4.   Contiguous, unfragmented blocks of habitat are better than fragmented blocks.

5.   Habitat between protected areas is more easily traversed by dispersing individuals the more closely it resembles suitable habitat for the concerned species.

Conservation Targets

About one–half of the world's species may already have been lost (Soulé and Sanjayan, 1998). This has prompted the near–term protection of at least 10% of the total land area in each country or in each ecosystem, so as to double or triple the land area now designated as national parks or biosphere reserves. However, protection of only 10% of the Earth's ecosystems could still make at least one–half of all terrestrial species vulnerable to anthropogenic extinction sooner or later. The situation is particularly serious in the tropics, which contain some two–thirds of the world's terrestrial plant and animal species. The relatively undisturbed tropical forest (area

Table 8–8. Some common wildlife and fisheries management practices and their effects on biodiversity (after Noss and Cooperrider, 1994)

Practice	Purpose	Effect on biodiversity
Artificial stocking	Increased harvest or recreation	Displacement and genetic deterioration of native species
Artificial feeding	Maximum productivity of existing game species	Disease and other problems in native species; dependence upon artificial feeding
Predator control	same	Reduced abundance or extirpation of predators and non–target species
Introduction of exotics	Recreational hunting and fishing	Displacement of native species; disruption of ecosystem function
Vegetation mani-pulation (herbicide spraying, planting)	Better habitat for target wildlife species	Reduction in plant species diversity
Harvest regulation to maximize yield	Maximum harvest of game species	Reduced within–population diversity (sex and age class diversity)
Use of nest boxes, 'guzzlers' etc.	Maximum production of target species	Greater dependence on unnatural habitats
Water development	same	Disruption of hydrologic cycle; draining of small aquifers
Maximizing yield of game species	Increasing recreational opportunities; maximum profit and income to fish and game agencies from licensing	Ecosystem deterioration from focusing on a few species to the detriment of others

already reduced by about half during the past five decades of this century) is currently shrinking at a rate of about 0.8% annually. Only 5% of the tropical rain-forest biome is protected. The increasing global demand for tropical goods is accelerating rates of habitat conversion in developing nations.

It appears that lands outside strictly protected reserves everywhere will be greatly diminished in their capacity to sustain native species and ecosystems by 2050, by which time human populations may have more than doubled (Soulé and Sanjayan, 1998). Therefore to deal with this problem a much larger area than 10% (perhaps as much as over 40%), may need to be set aside—a formidable task indeed in light of the fact that even achieving the 10% target in many countries today would be a herculean venture.

Some general desirable attributes of conservation measures are outlined below:

1.   They must be firmly grounded in the natural sciences, but should also involve the social sciences, humanities, law, education and economics.

2.   They should be implemented at several scales of time and space.

3.   They should aim to harmonize species–oriented and ecosystem–oriented approaches.

4.   They should take into account biological attributes and processes at all levels of the biological hierarchy.

5.   They should work across national, cultural and ecological boundaries.

6.   They should strive to address local community development and conservation needs in an integrated manner.

The diminishing biodiversity has been known to scientists since long, so why the sudden worldwide interest in tackling the problem? Biotechnology has spurred today's new-found urgency. Advances in biotechnology raise the monetary stakes because any species can potentially be 'raw material' for genetic engineering. Pharmaceutical companies are once again interested in natural products research, after slacking off in the late 1970s when chemical synthesis and 'rational drug design' emerged as the techniques of choice. Biotechnology has made screening of natural products a low-cost, potentially lucrative activity. Moreover, when a promising chemical is found, large quantities of it can be produced by transferring the proper genes to bacterial 'hosts'. Pharmaceutical companies now realize that even their most creative chemists may be no match for nature. Two of the most promising drugs in clinical trials have come from plants: the anticancer drug taxol derived from the yew and an antimalarial drug derived from a Chinese herb known as Qunghaosu.

Biotechnology has increased biodiversity's value to agriculture. Genes for pesticide resistance may be transferred from bacteria to plants. The distant relatives of modern crops—once considered useless for breeding purposes—contain unique traits that can now be bred into elite varieties. Biotechnology makes it possible to quickly tailor crop varieties to local soil, climate, or rainfall conditions so they can meet the needs of marginal farmers. Customized crops could also be critical to protecting the world's food supply.

Genetic resources have traditionally been treated as though they were a common heritage of mankind—free to all who could use them. The growing importance of biotechnology has forced a reassessment of the ownership issue. Nations should assert national sovereignty over genetic resources, regulate collection, and decide whether to adopt intellectual property rights protection for knowledge about these resources (Reid, 1992).

Grassroots action in the developing world has driven biodiversity conservation onto national and international agendas. In many of these countries, biodiversity is being conserved *in spite* of government policies, not because of them. Two decades ago, biodiversity conservation would have been limited to saving genes, species and habitats. But now a new conservation framework has emerged, based on saving biodiversity, studying it, and using it sustainably and equitably (Reid, 1992). The steps needed go beyond maintaining protected areas and seed banks to include reforming agricultural, forestry and technological policies (see Fig. 8–5).

Biodiversity conservation is gaining ground precisely because the issue is so broad that it can encompass the interests of many different countries. Although developed countries may have sought an international accord on biodiversity simply to slow the rate of species extinctions, developing countries immediately saw the chance to strengthen their biotechnical capacities by adding technology co-operation provisions to such an agreement. Similarly, while some countries restricted the definition of biodiversity to wild species, others considered conserving the genetic diversity of domesticated species at least as important and added it to the agenda (Reid, 1992).

Species-focused conservation efforts are essential but they must be complemented by efforts to conserve habitats and ecosystems in natural or seminatural states.

263

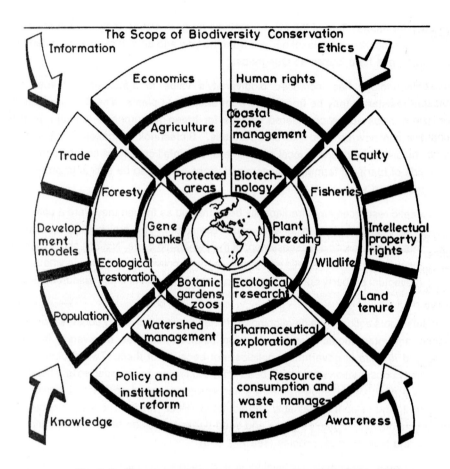

Fig. 8–5. The scope of biodiversity conservation (after Reid, 1992).

Conserving biodiversity over the long run requires an understanding of past and present human land–use and its effects in a holistic way. Biodiversity in an area is the product of the history of interaction between human use and the environment. This legacy includes not only changes in climate, hydrology, geology and other biophysical factors, but also changes in human activities, culture, perceptions, attitudes and values, technology and institutions. Broader inventory, assessment and monitoring systems are needed to collect the range of biophysical and human information that is necessary for planning and managing biodiversity and related matters (Nelson and Serafin, 1992).

Conservation Strategies

The following actions can be taken to promote the conservation and sustainable use of biological diversity: (a) measures to protect particular habitats as National Parks, Biosphere Reserves or other protected areas; (b) measures to protect particular species or groups of species from overexploitation; (c) measures to promote *ex-situ* conservation of species in botanical gardens or in gene banks; and (d) measures to curb the contamination of the biosphere with pollutants.

Protected areas provide a mechanism for conserving wild biodiversity and most countries today have established at least some protected areas.

There are three global objectives of living resource conservation: (a) to maintain essential ecological processes and life–support systems; (b) to preserve genetic diversity; and (c) to ensure the sustainable utilization of species and ecosystems. Biodiversity needs to be conserved as a matter of principle, as a matter of survival and as a matter of economic benefit. The objectives can be achieved by taking action at several different levels (Fig. 8–6). In view of the growing threats to biological diversity, the time has come to appreciate the Earth's biological resources as assets to be conserved and managed for the benefit of all humanity.

Levels for action

BIODIVERSITY CONSERVATION

Fig. 8–6. Various levels for action to achieve biodiversity conservation (after Reid, 1992).

265

Identifying the Specifics

According to Scott *et al.* (1995), biodiversity management may start by (1) compiling a list of plant and animal species, their numbers, distribution patterns and habitats; (2) identifying and mapping for each biological community, existing and potential successional stages; and (3) judging the extent and severity of human disturbances. By comparing these parameters with historical conditions, managers may be able to quantitatively assess biological diversity. There is no doubt that biodiversity concerns are intimately linked to the effect of human disturbances and associated species losses. Lautenschlager (1997) has devised the following system to identify and prioritize major specific concerns (resources, management practices, ecosystems) from local (district or smaller) through larger (region, province, country) scales.

1.   Resource (natural asset, usually biotic) and specific concern. The specific concern can include some ecological process, or a more general concern.

2.   The human activity associated with the specific resource of concern, e.g. fire suppression, a silvicultural system, or environmental changes caused by development activities.

3.   The ecosystem(s) in which this human activity is commonly affects this resource; may range from small ecosystems (a wetland type in a certain forest type or region) to extensive and widely distributed ecosystems.

When the above components are combined, a concern matrix (Table) results.

When agreement among experts about prioritizing concerns, at all scales, cannot be reached, there may be a consensus. Local and regional biological priority lists constitute the first task in identifying larger scale priorities.

In the face of expanding human populations there is an urgent need for increasing both the area and intensity of natural–resource management worldwide. Growing concern about the intensity of natural–resource management in several developed countries has led to increasing natural–resource extraction from tropical or subtropical countries (Kimmins 1992). However, biotas adapted to these more stable ecosystems are commonly less adapted to disturbance than those in northern ecosytems where natural fluctuations are widespread and severe. Both species diversity and threats to diversity decrease with increasing distance from the equator (Pimm *et al.*, 1995). Forest harvesting and slash–and–burn agriculture in tropical and subtropical moist forests are usually rich in endemics and contribute significantly to reductions in global species.

Identified and prioritized specifics can go a long way in achieving realistic goals. They can facilitate implementation of practices ranging from active management to complete protection in an ecosystem context.

For the past two centuries, one of the central themes of biology has been the diversity of life which has now acquired a new urgency for its own sake: as the life–forms are important for human welfare, the extinction of wild species and ecosystems has been accelerating through human action. The dilemma has stimulated renewed biodiversity studies: systematic examination of the full array of organisms and the origin of this diversity, together with the methods by which diversity can be maintained and used for the benefit of humanity. Biodiversity studies combine elements of evolutionary biology, taxonomy, ecology and applied biology. They include the discipline of conservation biology and have potential practical applications in medicine, forestry and agriculture.

Species have long been known to originate by reproductive isolation. Polyploidy involves the multiplication of entire chromosome numbers within individual species or within hybrids of species. It isolates the new breed from its ancestor in one step. This instantaneous mode has generated some 40% of the present–day plant species and a much smaller number of animal species. Equally important is geographic (or allopatric) speciation, the origin of intrinsic isolating mechanisms in two or more daughter populations while they become isolated by a geographic barrier, such as desert basin or mountain range. Yet another mode of speciation is non–polyploid sympatric speciation, in which new species emerge from the midst of parental species even when individuals of both populations are close enough to intermingle during part of their life cycles (Enrlich and Wilson, 1991). Members of the parental species feed upon and mate in the vicinity of one kind of plant; they give rise to an alternate host race that shifts to a second species of host plant growing nearby; the two races, which have become isolated by their microhabitat differences, diverge further in other traits that reinforce reproductive isolation. Sympatric speciation has probably had a key role in the origin of large numbers of insects and other invertebrates.

Certain forms of speciation can occur rapidly, within one to a few generations. And when species meet, they can displace one another genetically within a few generations, reducing competition and the likelihood of hybridization.

267

The Precautionary Principle

We are all painfully aware of a woeful paucity of knowledge. But the problem of continuing loss in biodiversity is so urgent that we must act according to the precautionary principle—i.e., we must not delay a decision to act simply because science cannot at present answer all the questions. Enough is known about how and where biodiversity is being lost to start setting priorities for its protection and to develop practical mechanisms right now.

There is a strong need for a List of Recorded Species, computerized and readily available. Such a list should indicate not only formal aspects of taxonomy, but also ecological information about the species (estimated geographical range; life history and habitat; physical size of the organism, abundance/rarity; etc). Such a list could serve as an indispensable tool for making judicious decisions or choices. Such choices would also increasingly require that we assign some relative measure of 'taxonomic value or distinctness' to species and, as such indices are developed, they should, where appropriate, be included in the list.

Fortunately, India is a land of diversities, having very varied topography and soils. Climate both West to East and South to North varies significantly. We have many harsh or extreme habitats, some of which harbour species at the limit of their viability. Onto this pattern of variation has been imposed the consequent regional differences in rural land–use and the pressures of a fairly long history of natural resource extraction. Such a high degree of variability warrants a much more scientific and systematic approach to conservation and its management than adopted hitherto.

It needs to be emphasized that, unlike other scientific endeavours, the task of understanding the magnitude, causes and consequences of biological diversity has a time limit: half the remaining tropical rain forests are doomed to vanish within the next half a century and, as they vanish, no one knows how many species will be lost forever.

The differing applications of biodiversity data at the local, national and international levels necessitate different scales and resolution of data collection. A clear distinction should be made between surveillance and sustained, repeated monitoring. Because of the lack of standards for data collection, very little systematic monitoring is actually being undertaken, even of such essential criteria as the rates of forest loss. An agreed methodology and a clear definition of what constitutes a rain forest is urgently needed to produce a global overview.

There is a serious lack of reliable survey data in many developing countries. Remote sensing is partially filling the gap but the data are inappropriate for species-level monitoring, and further, there is also the serious problem of 'ground truthing'. Faced with the dearth of comparable data on biological resources in the developing world, a World Conservation Monitoring Centre (WCMC) was established in Britain in 1988. WCMC's role is to support programmes for the conservation and sustainable utilization of biological resources by providing quantitative data in a format that is directly applicable for improved land–use management. As the development pressures upon the world's biological resources inexorably grow, so the need for reliable, up–to–date information correspondingly increases. Using the latest advances in information technology and computer mapping, the WMCM aims to provide information on threatened plant and animal species; habitats of conservation concern, particularly tropical forests, coral reefs, and wetlands; critical sites within these habitats for the conservation of biodiversity; threats to the global network of national parks and protected areas; and the international trade in endangered species. Another project at the global level in which WCMC is currently engaged is the monitoring of the world's tropical forests (Anonymous, 1991).

Loss of forest does not just mean loss of area, but also some loss of condition of the forest through unsustainable use. WCMC is developing the methodology to classify and map forest conditions, which can then be linked to forest auditing against preset management targets. By overlaying such forest maps with species distribution maps covering a wide cross–section of taxa, such as forest primates, endemic birds, snakes and lizards, and swallowtail butterflies, it should be possible to identify 'hot spot' areas of high species diversity. Such information could then be relayed to various agencies to ensure that such sites are adequately surveyed and their ecological integrity maintained through appropriate forest management programmes. For too long conservation has been a fire–fighting operation aimed at preserving the remains of already perturbed ecosystems. What is really warranted is to identify sites of high biological richness and bring them under some form of management which conserves their ecological processes, before they are disturbed by logging, road building, or shifting agriculture.

Restoration Ecology

Conservation biologists can effectively help restore original species and communities in damaged and degraded ecosystems. Restoration is the process of intentionally altering a site to establish a defined, indigenous, historic ecosystem with the objective of emulating the structure, function, diversity and dynamics of the specified ecosystem (Society of Ecological Restoration, 1990). In many cases, business houses are legally required to restore habitats degraded by such activities as strip mining or water pollution. Dumping of sewage into rivers and estuaries by municipalities and chemical pollution on military bases are two examples of governmental activity that damage biological communities. Restoration efforts sometimes constitute a part of the mitigation process in which a new site is created or rehabilitated as a substitute for a site damaged by development (Zedler, 1993).

Sometimes entirely novel environments such as reservoirs, canals, landfills and industrial sites are created by human activity. Neglect of these sites often results in their becoming dominated by exotic and weedy species, which are of no value from a conservation perspective. But if in these sites the native species are reintroduced, native communities can sometimes be restored.

Restoration ecology provides theory and techniques to restore these various types of degraded ecosystems. The following four approaches (Fig. 8–7) can be adopted for restoring biological communities and ecosystems (Cairns and Heckman, 1996).

1. *No action,* if restoration is too expensive, if the ecosystem can recover on its own, or if previous attempts at restoration were not successful.

2. *Replacement* of a degraded ecosystem with another productive type. This is sometimes termed 'habitat creation'.

3. *Rehabilitation* of at least some of the ecosystem functions and some of the original species (e.g. replacing a degraded forest with a tree plantation or replanting a degraded grassland with a few species that can survive). The focus is on dominant species critical to ecosystem function.

4. *Restoration* of the area to its original species composition and structure by means of site modification and reintroduction of the original species.

Establishment of new communities such as wetlands, forests, prairies and lakes enables ecologists to enhance biological diversity in habitats that have no other value. Restoration ecology also provides insight into community ecology by reassembling a community from its original species. The first task in any restoration project is to eliminate or neutralize the factors that prevent the system from recovering. Some combination of site preparation, habitat management and introduction of the original species then allows the community to regain the species and ecosystem characteristics of designated reference sites. Many attempts to restore strongly degraded habitats fail to restore the original species composition. Mitigation involves creating a new habitat in one place to compensate for the destruction of a similar habitat elsewhere; mitigation is not a good conservation strategy. The best strategy is to protect populations and communities where they currently occur.

Ecological restoration simply means restoring an ecological system to its original state. Restoration can be viewed as a distinct form of conservation management, differing from 'preservation', 'conservation' or even 'management' itself. These various forms of manipulation all involve attempts to compensate in a specific, ecologically effective way for alterations typically caused by human activities.

Rehabilitation is a broad term that refers to any attempt to restore structure or function of an ecological system, without necessarily attempting complete restoration to any specified prior condition; for example, replanting of sites to prevent erosion.

The term reclamation denotes rehabilitative work carried out on the most severely degraded sites, such as sites disturbed by open–cast mining or large–scale construction. Though reclamation work often falls short of restoration in the fullest sense (a copy of a native ecosystem is not achieved), it is a necessary first step in the process of restoration under such conditions.

Recreation: Recreation attempts to reconstruct an ecosystem, wholesale, on a site so badly disturbed that virtually nothing is left to restore. The new system may be modelled on a system located outside the range of the historical system, or may be established under conditions different from those under which it occurred naturally. These efforts do not amount to restoration *sensu strictu* but can yield insights into the systems involved and the conditions that support them that can be invaluable in restoration efforts.

Ecological recovery: This involves letting the system alone, hoping that it will regain desirable attributes through natural succession. Such a zero order appoach to restoration may or may not work and is best regarded as a key component of restoration—the contribution of the system itself. In such cases the restorationist seeks to complement and reinforce natural processes.

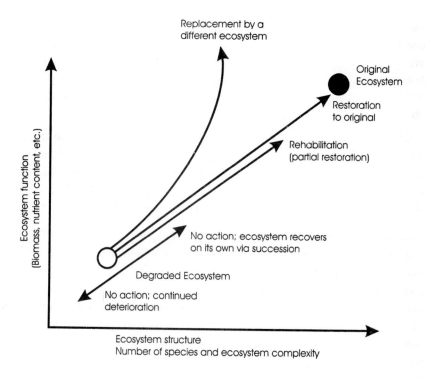

Fig. 8–7. Approaches for restoration of degraded ecosystems (after Bradshaw, 1995).

Perspective in Community and Ecosystem Restoration Ecology

It is not easy to measure restoration at the community level because of the variability found in most natural communities. This needs special attention to restoration of community function (e.g., trophic structure) rather than merely restoration of particular species. Much debate is underway concerning the possible benefits and limitations of using species composition or biodiversity measures as end–points in restoration ecology (Palmer *et al.,* 1997). Since re-establishment of all native species is usually impossible, there is need for research on the relationship between species richness and community stability of restored sites and functional redundancy among species. Efforts targeted at restoring system function must take into account the role of individual (keystone) species, particularly if some species play a disproportionate role in processing material or are strong interactors. Some attempts are being made to understand the relationship between physical habitat structure and restoration ecology. In those cases wherein community development is highly predictable, it may be feasible to manipulate a speed–up in natural succession processes.

Species diversity is the central pillar of community ecology, in particular the creation and maintenance of local and regional biodiversity (e.g. Huston, 1994). It is generally agreed that restoring biodiversity is desirable for ecological, applied and aesthetic reasons. It is desirable to know the minimum numbers and types of species necessary for proper community functioning. Is it possible to increase community or ecosystem stability by adding more species (enhancing diversity) or particular species in the restoration process? If the answer to this is affirmative, it implies that restoration success may depend on careful consideration of community level attributes, not just a focus on single species or clusters of 'desirable' (e.g., endangered) species (Palmer *et al.*, 1997). According to May (1973), diverse systems are less stable than simpler ones: the more diverse a community, the more complex the web of species interactions and thus the larger the effect disturbances would have on the system. Diversity can make individual species more vulnerable to extinction, but total community or ecosystem properties (e.g. energy transformation, biomass) usually tend to stabilize, since some species compensate functionally for others (Naeem *et al.*, 1994; Tilman, 1996).

It now appears that some communities or ecosystems are more stable if their diversity is increased but individual species may or may not be persistent. If the restoration goals are related to management of endangered species, then a restorationist's concern with biodiversity need not be to maximize the number of species, but simply to understand how biodiversity affects the establishment and persistence of the focal species. If the goal is to restore a community to a proper functional state, then we may ignore individual species and focus instead on restoring functional groups or suites of species (Palmer *et al.*, 1997).

Restoration efforts also need to take into account a proper ecosystem perspective which provides a framework within which other aspects of the ecology of restoration may be incorporated. The restorationist must consider the placement of the project in the landscape—its boundaries, its connections or lack thereof to adjoining ecosystems, and its receipts and losses of materials and energy from its physical surroundings (Ehrenfeld and Toth, 1997). These characteristics delimit types of biological communities that can be established on the site. The ecosystem perspective also provides restorationists with conceptual tools for structuring and evaluating restorations. These include the mass balance approach to nutrient, pollutant, and energy budgets; subsidy/stress effects of inputs; food web architecture; feedback among ecosystem components; nutrient efficiency transfers, primary productivity and decomposition; and disturbance regimes. The large spatial scale of most restorations and the ability to manipulate species, soil, water, and even the landscape could allow ecosystem–level experiments to be conducted that could not be performed otherwise (Ehrenfeld and Toth, 1997).

Table 8–9 lists some ecosystem parameters and their relevance to restoration ecology.

Dynamic Conservation by Fisherfolk

In situ conservation of aquatic biodiversity is central to the strategies of *nurture fisheries* adopted by artisanal fishing communities and differs markedly from the modern industrial approach to fishing, using *capture fishery* strategies. *Nurture fishery* technologies are necessarily selective, passive, low-energy and ecologically efficient. They do not bring in the biggest catch in the short term, but do ensure the sustainability of the fishery through their harmonious interaction with the dynamics of the ecosystem, on which depends the aquatic biodiversity (Mulvany, 1996).

Some agricultural production comes from traditional methods which conserve fish stocks *in situ*. Aquaculture contributes to genetic diversity by the development of domestic breeds, and shares with agriculture the need to conserve this man-made diversity along with wild aquatic diversity. Combination of diverse fish species of different food habits and ecological niches allows optimum use of available food in the fish pond. Multispecies aquaculture (polyculture) is based on the harmonious stocking of different varieties of fish species at different levels of population. Planktonic feeders (at the pond surface and in mid-water) feed directly off the 'phytoplankton' and 'zooplankton' produced by the natural productivity of the pond. Their faeces enhance the productivity of the pond, as does pond manuring. Fish species which feed on larger organisms in mid-water (small fish, insects etc.) and the pond bottom (snails, worms etc.) are also stocked. Consequently, energy flow and transformation are extremely efficient. Sustainability of this method of conservation *in situ* can be promoted by decentralized production, using diverse, environmentally sensitive techniques. Protection from introduced species and diseases is also required.

Table 8–9. Some useful ecosystem descriptors for designing ecological restorations (after Ehrenfeld and Toth, 1997)

Parameter	Characteristics
Boundaries	Physical, biological, or artificial? Relationship of restoration boundaries and ecosystem boundaries. Permeability of boundaries to resource fluxes.
Energy Inputs/ Outputs	Forms of energy. Ability to manipulate or manage inputs. Energy inputs as subsidies or stressors.
Material Inputs/ Outputs	Magnitude of inputs and outputs on existing site. Expected magnitudes for restored ecosystem. Local conditions that may produce extreme, and hence limiting, rates of input or output.
Material Retention and Loss	Extent of retention of important nutrients and/or pollutants on the existing site. Anticipated retention/loss characteristics of target ecosystem. Mechanism of retention available on site. Probability that retention mechanisms can be restored.
Ecosystem Components Intrasystem Cycling:	Definition of components (e.g., herbivores, fungivores, primary consumers). Food web structure. Feedback loops among components.
Decomposition	Rates for different types of plant material, different microhabitats; effects of soil-food web on rates.
Nutrient Uptake	Rates for different nutrients and plant species.
Deposition in Litter	Rates for different nutrients, plant species, plant tissues.
Turnover; Mean Residence Times	Relative importance of soil organic matter, litter, coarse woody debris as long-term storage pools.
Efficiency of Transfer among Components	Resorption or retention of nutrients.
Net Primary Productivity	Rates. Target level and its relation to species diversity. Appropriate species to achieve target level. Change of NPP rate over time. Balance between above- and below-ground production. Apportionment of production among stems, leaves, reproductive structures.
Standing Crop Biomass Dynamics	Size. Seasonal changes. Distribution among plant tissues.
Disturbance Regime	Disturbance types, frequency, intensity, duration, spatial extent.
Resilience	Temporal and spatial response to disturbances, rate of recovery.
Resistance Trajectories	Temporal changes in other ecosystem descriptors during succession.

Safeguarding of Aquatic Biodiversity by Fisherfolk

The management systems of *capture fisheries* are technically based whereas those of *nurture fisheries* are socially and spiritually inspired (Baines, 1995). Community-based management is vital to sustaining the fishery as it is geared towards sustaining the aquatic ecosystem and the fishery resource base. It advocates harvesting rather than hunting approaches in the exploitation of aquatic resources.

Over the last two decades several attempts have been made to create management systems that recognize traditional rights. Both the Territorial User Rights in Fisheries (TURFs), which confer rights to fish in particular waters, and Customary Marine Tenure (CMT) systems, which define the ownership of a particular fishery, have promise if developed in a manner that ensures that rights are conferred on local communities rather than individuals (Fairlie *et al.*, 1995). Any strategy that entrusts responsibility to individuals is destined to fail in achieving long-term security: it is the community as a whole that is crucial to ensuring sustainability and equity (Mulvany, 1996).

Chapter 9

GERMPLASM CONSERVATION AND SEED BANKS

Introduction

Biodiversity can be conceived from different angles: for some the central issue may be the conservation of biodiversity as such; the threat to rich genetic resources is invoked as an argument to stop destructive new developments such as the construction of roads and dams, or the introduction of uniform agricultural varieties replacing landraces. Others view biodiversity in a more dynamic way, in the context of developments more in tune with the needs of local inhabitants and the environment. Biodiversity should enable many poor people to reduce risks, insecurity and dependence not by simplifying or standardizing but by complicating and diversifying their livelihoods and social relations. Diversity is not a static quality to be preserved through capture and protection, but a function of the permanence of change.

Can the replacement of landraces by more uniform varieties, accelerated by certain biotechnologies, form an argument to exclude particular biotechnologies or varieties from patenting? Assessment of the impact on the environment cannot be made by lawyers or economists; expertise from other sources too will be needed. One flaw in patent considerations relates to the ambiguity inherent in the definition and concept of the term *gene*, and the equivocal relationship between genes and characteristics encoded by them. Similar genes often behave differently in different organisms, while also the effect of genes in one organism may change in a different environment. Individual genes could be important for the expression of a concrete characteristic of an organism but can never fully control its expression. If genes are not acting independently, this should question the legitimacy of patenting gene structures or gene functions. If genes indeed behave differently in different species and/or environments, what are the implications for biosafety aspects of genetically modified organisms?

Until 1992 when the *Convention on Biological Diversity* came into force, the world's genetic resources were considered to be the common heritage of humankind and open to free access even though several developing countries were opposed to the principle of common heritage of genetic resources. They felt that developed countries had no right to obtain genetic resources from developing countries, protect the products through patents and plant breeders rights, and then sell these protected products at high prices

277

even to the same country from which the material had been collected. Developing countries favoured the idea of national sovereignty over their genetic resources. Successful and forceful negotiations by developing countries resulted in the convention accepting their demands: the convention affirmed that nations have the sovereign right to exploit their own resources in tune with their own environmental policies. The Convention also stated that the authority to determine access to genetic resources rests within the national governments and is subject to national legislation. This was elaborated as follows:

1. States shall facilitate *access to genetic resources* for environmentally sound use.

2. Access will be subject to *prior informed consent* and based on mutually agreed terms.

3. There should be provision for the *sharing of benefits* derived from genetic resources with the country of origin, or the country providing such resources if acquired in accordance with the Convention.

The Convention made it possible for developing countries to reap benefits from biological diversity but it is up to these countries to frame regulatory and legislative measures to achieve these benefits. Countries need to develop registers of biological resources, harmonize and match their national laws in tune with the provisions of the Convention and establish appropriate institutions to enforce the regulations. Indigenous knowledge, innovations and practices must be encouraged and protected.

Sharing the benefits of biological resources with indigenous and local communities becomes especially important because these groups have historically and traditionally played an important role in the selection and propagation of current genetic resources. But established institutions that safeguard the rights of indigenous and local communities do not exist. Most national laws pertaining to biodiversity and intellectual property protection are silent about the rights of indigenous and local communities (Mugabe and Ouko, 1994). Hence they are unable to derive benefits from the conservation of biological diversity and cannot assert their rights over genetic resources, knowledge and innovations (Khalil *et al.*, 1992).

Developing countries can derive actual economic gains from their biological resources; restrict free access to their genetic resources by public and private individuals from the industrialized countries; and govern access to genetic resources. But since prior informed consent is necessary, the countries must develop policies and legislation which include the creation of appropriate national agencies concerned with defining the scope of prior informed consent. The countries providing genetic resources also have to improve the existing protection measures so as to prevent unlawful harvesting of genetic resources. They need to improve record–keeping, link collections with patents, and regulate transfer of collected materials to third parties. This can lead to more beneficial relationships between the owners of the genetic resources and the recipients. During the Convention, developing countries argued that access to genetic resources by industrialized countries should facilitate access for the South to products arising from the genetic resources, as well as technologies (Juma and Mugabe, 1994) pertaining to the conservation and use of the resources (Mugabe and Ouko, 1994). The Convention has recognized the links between access to genetic resource and transfer of technology, and has offered developing countries new opportunities for building up their capabilities to conserve and sustainably utilize biodiversity.

Many of the existing patent laws in developing countries are quite ambiguous and ignore the rights of the suppliers of genetic material. The laws need revision and these rights should be recognized and protected. A protocol covering cultural property rights of indigenous peoples ought to strengthen the provision on indigenous knowledge within the Convention. The value of genetic raw materials increases if the material is properly identified, collected and screened by the owners of the biological resources, before presenting it to a potential recipient.

Seeds of crop plants once travelled fortuitously from country to country and continent to continent along ancient caravan routes, in the ballast of ships and the packing of merchandise, in the bedding of slaves, the equipment of armies, and the simple bundles carried by pilgrims. Migrants from the Old World to the Americas or to the various parts of the British Empire, took along some seeds and plant material from their native crops. Maize varieties were imported to Europe in the wake of the discoveries of Columbus.

During the last few decades Western scientific principles and techniques have greatly influenced the development of crop plants. N.I. Vavilov greatly increased our knowledge of the major centres of plant diversity and of the wild relatives of the cultivated varieties. His efforts in collecting a large number of plants on the basis of their genetic content are of great value. The findings and views of Vavilov were integrated into conservation strategies in industrialized countries and modern gene banks were created in the 1960s and 1970s. These developments prompted many scientists to organize the conservation and use of genetic resources at the global level. Attempts were made to halt or minimize genetic erosion while assembling genetic resources for breeding purposes, especially by the FAO (see Pistorius, 1997). Programmes were started to collect and conserve threatened gene pools. These laid the foundation for the scientific premises behind current international *ex–situ* conservation. In the late 1960s, *ex–situ* conservation was considered preferable to *in–situ* conservation (Pistorius, 1997). Public support for gene banks emerged following the general criticism of the agricultural policies of the green revolution.

Some political pressure to modify conservation strategies in the 1980s developed into a new rich–poor issue leading to increased public awareness of the economic and strategic value of genetic resources. But *ex-situ* conservation still continues to be closely associated with the mainstream breeding programmes which gave rise to the green revolution, even though greater attention is now paid to the needs of small farmers. With the recent upsurge of interest and concern with environmental problems, *in-situ* conservation is now receiving greater focus though not primarily for utilitarian reasons. The crucial question is: Will the biodiversity issue overrule the genetic resources issue? It seems safe to assume that conservation and related breeding practices will continue to influence farmers' practices in the coming decades.

Until the 1960s, the general trend was to develop germplasm collections for availability to prospective users rather than for conservation. Conservation started attracting focus from the early 1970s onwards. In Europe, at first several ecoregional gene banks were set up but this approach gradually gave way to a crop–specific approach. The FAO concentrated on the conservation of genetic resources and several World Catalogues of Genetic Stocks (wheat, rice, maize, barley) were created.

The interest and commitment of breeders in early conservation work in the 1960s had a dual impact; firstly conservation and use were closely linked, and secondly, storage in the first instance took place in industrialized countries mostly in plant breeding institutes. This resulted in a preference for *ex-situ* conservation instead of *in-situ* conservation (Pistorius, 1997). *Ex-situ* preservation of landraces using low–temperature storage soon became standard practice in gene banks. However, alternative strategies were suggested by some experts who were worried that if *ex-situ* conservation became dominant, crop development and conservation might become too separated, thereby reducing genes to 'stocks' for breeding purposes and consequently the locally improved crops (landraces) would lose their adaptive complexes, becoming more vulnerable to pests and pathogens (Bennett, 1968, 1970).

Uses of Genetic Information in Conservation

There are two principal uses of genetic data in the conservation of populations and species in the wild. The quantity and geographic distribution of genetic variation in species can be described by means of hierarchical gene diversity analysis. This approach can be useful in estimating historical levels of gene flow among populations — information that could determine whether artificial gene flow is necessary to retain natural geographic patterns of genetic diversity. Electrophoretic or other genetic data may be used to identify unique gene pools attracting special protection. This is particularly true for identification of unique alleles present in one population but absent in others. Some qualitative guidelines for genetically based conservation strategies are listed below.

1. Large genetically effective population sizes are better than small ones because they lose genetic variation more slowly.

2. Since the adverse effects of genetic drift and inbreeding are inversely proportional to population size, management of unnaturally small populations should be avoided.

3. Management of wild populations should be in keeping with the history of their genetic patterns and processes.

4. Low genetic diversity per se is no cause for alarm, but any sudden and abnormally high losses of diversity in natural or captive populations are always cause for concern.

5. Artificial selection in captivity should be avoided by keeping breeding populations in captivity for as few generations as possible, and also by simulating wild conditions as nearly as possible.

6. After a population has crashed, rapid population growth needs to be encouraged.

7. Possible outbreeding depression caused by breeding distantly related populations should be avoided, if other options are available.

8. Introduction of exotic alleles into wild or captive populations should be prevented.

9. Harvesting of wild stocks (hunting, fishing) can select for genetic changes that affect the future evolution of the population or species. Selection in harvesting wild stocks is to be avoided.

10. Maintenance of genetic diversity in captive stocks cannot be a substitute for genetic diversity in the wild.

According to Jackson *et al.* (1995), successful ecological restoration is determined by four overall factors: the specific ecological circumstances under which restoration proceeds, the various judgments made about the process, the values that are brought to the project or under which it must work, and the social commitment to the project and its goals (Fig. 9–1).

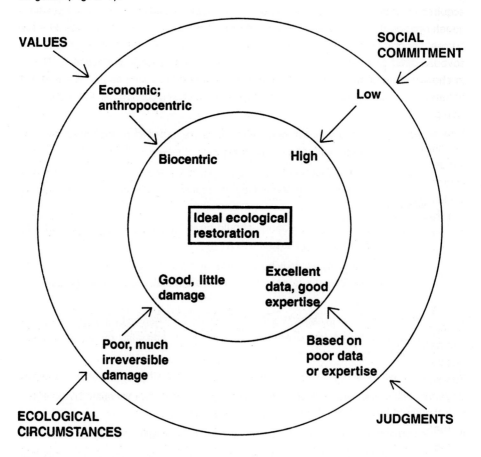

Fig. 9–1. Four factors that determine the success of restoration projects. The closer one can come to the ideal state (towards the centre), the more successful the restoration will be (after Jackson *et al.*, 1995).

An American biotechnology company, Agracetus (Middleton, Wisconsin), currently holds wide-ranging patents on transgenic soybean and cotton. Agracetus specializes in gene delivery and in molecular and cellular biology. Its main business operations include (1) use of plants as bioreactors, i.e., the production of biopharmaceuticals in green plants; (2) *Accell-FE* gene therapy, i.e., gene-based treatment of genetic and acquired illness; and (3) specialty fibres, i.e., high-performance cotton fibres made by genetic engineering. Both biopharmaceuticals and gene therapy are developed for the human health market. Most of its research has, however, focused on cotton and soybean. With the use of its Accell-FE technique, Agracetus was, in 1990, the first to show that soybean could be genetically engineered. The chosen agronomic traits of transgenic cotton and soybean include pest resistance and herbicide tolerance. The Company has genetically engineered cotton with the idea of developing and marketing special quality fibres having the preferred appearance and texture of cotton and meeting the cherished needs of the textile industry. These fibres will have greater strength, enhanced dyeability, improved dimensional stability and better absorbency. They may also contain enzymes that would biodegrade environmental contaminants. These fibres could be fitted into filters for clearing contaminated water as it flows through them. There is a tremendous demand for a natural blue cotton fibre, of interest to makers of jeans. Attempts are being made to insert into cotton plants the genes responsible for the production of the blue colour in the indigo plant.

Genetic Erosion

We do not have much hard data on the pace and extent of genetic erosion in world agriculture. Obviously, clearing forests, building dams and constructing roads or airports has had, and continues to have, devastating effects on biological diversity. Over the last several decades India has probably grown over 30,000 different landraces of rice. The situation has altered drastically over the past 30 years, however, and in another 20 years this enormous rice diversity is likely to be reduced to no more than 50 varieties, with the top ten accounting for over three-quarters of the subcontinent's rice acreage. In 1983, high-yielding varieties covered 54% of India's ricelands. In 1987, at least 65% of India's harvested rice area was planted with the uniform high-yielding varieties (HYVs). It is doubtful whether the displaced varieties were collected or conserved. The National Gene Bank in Delhi has the capacity to hold 600,000 accessions but currently less than 7000 rices are in long-term storage there. In Sri Lanka, farmers used to grow 2000 traditional varieties of rice in 1959. Today they grow essentially five.

There is no reason to believe that genetic erosion is not equally advancing in other cereals, fruits, vegetables and root crops throughout the world. Most of South America's sorghum landraces have been replaced by Texas hybrids, while the enormous diversity of traditional tall wheats in such countries as Portugal, Greece and Pakistan has disappeared from farmers' fields, where mainly uniform semidwarfs are now grown. In Latin America, home of maize, nearly half of the region's crop is sown with modern or hybrid varieties. Clearly, the process of genetic erosion has not declined over the past few decades.

A comparison (see Fig. 9–2) of estimates from the beginning of the 1980s with more recent ones shows that the bulk of the world's collected genetic resources continue to be stored under the control of the North. The total numbers of seeds stored in the banks have increased and a lot more gene banks have been built in the South. But some two-thirds of the genes in the banks are still under control of the North, either directly through their national gene banks or indirectly through the seed stores of the International Agricultural Research Centres (IARCs), which are largely funded and managed by the industrialized countries.

World's gene bank (seed) holdings

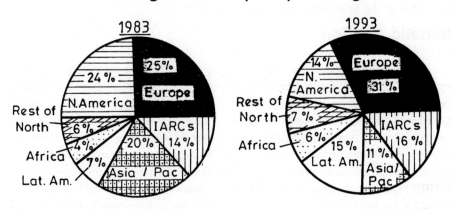

Fig. 9–2. World's gene bank holdings in 1983 and 1993.

There have been alarming reports on seeds dying in gene banks. It appears that the exclusive focus on gene banks as a way to conserve genetic diversity may be quite wrong and also technically risky. A parallel, on-farm, seed-saving system is desperately needed.

Numerically, participation in the plant breeding effort to supply farmers with quantity seed has grown more concentrated and is increasingly driven by the private, rather than the public sector. Most important though is the issue of whether the new seedmen are offering farmers more or less diversity in their crops? In view of the concentration of breeding programmes, the little use breeders make of gene bank collections, and the current focus on single supergenes rather than broad genetic complexes, the answer to that question seems obviously negative.

Biology of the Species/Accession

Genetic variation within species includes variation in the characteristics that influence optimal regeneration procedures. The following factors should be considered at the accession level, not just at the species level.

1.   Adaptation to abiotic environmental conditions (climate, soil, photoperiod).

2.   Seed physiology (storage conditions, dormancy, germination etc.)

3.   Growth morphology.

4.   Biotic environments (e.g. symbiosis, stresses, diseases etc.).

5.   Genetic structure (breeding system, fecundity, dispersal systems, effective population size of populations in-situ).

6.   Farmer management (for cultivated taxa).

7.   Risk assessment (weediness, toxic and allergenic phytochemicals in relation to humans handling seed and plants).

Maintaining Genetic Integrity

Maintenance of genetic integrity involves maintaining the joint frequency distribution of all alleles at all loci. The ideal but usually unachievable plan is to maintain the joint frequency distribution constant, which depends on the various processes and mechanisms of change and their consequences for genetic integrity.

Apart from human errors which can lead to incorrect placement or labelling at any step, resulting in a seed sample being incorrectly ascribed to the wrong accession, alien genes can be accidentally introduced as plants, seed or pollen, at several stages, such as during seed preparation, during or after sowing, and during or after harvesting. In some cases, the regeneration plot is contaminated with alien seed from previous crops or weeds.

Even with no contamination by alien genes, accessions sometime change in their genotypic composition by any of the following processes: differential loss of viability during storage, mutation, genetic composition of the seed subsample used for regeneration differing from that of the original accession, e.g. by inadequate mixing; some plants of an accession in a regeneration plot may die or may not mature before harvest; surviving plants may contribute unequal numbers of female and/or male gametes to the next generation of seed; genetic composition of the pollen population contributed by each parent plant may differ from that of the parent; genetic composition of the ovule population contributed by each parent plant may differ from that of the parent; and the pollen source for each zygote may result in loss of certain genotypes and/or production of novel recombinant genotypes and/or inappropriate (high or low) levels of heterozygosity (Sackville Hamilton and Chorlton, 1997). All eight processes except the first, i.e., differential loss of viability during storage, occur during regeneration. All except mutation apply only to genetically variable accessions and not to inbred pure lines.

The changes can be of two types : drift and selection. All eight processes listed above are subject to drift. All except mutation are subject also to selection.

Drift involves random changes such as sampling error and the effects of uncontrolled microenvironmental variation on growth, survival and reproduction. In contrast, selection refers to non–random changes that can occur by unconscious selection, rogueing or differential reactions of plants to the regeneration environment.

Random changes (drift) in allelic frequency may result in complete extinction or fixation of an allele from an accession, or smaller changes without extinction. Whereas losses of alleles by drift tend to accumulate over successive cycles of regeneration, smaller changes in allele frequency by drift, being random, are not necessarily cumulative.

The probability of losing an allele is highest for rare alleles but can be reduced by using more parents for regeneration. Likewise, the expected magnitude of all random changes, whether or not they involve allele extinction, can be decreased by using more parents (Sackville Hamilton and Chorlton, 1997).

In contrast to its adverse effect on genetic diversity within accessions, drift usually has no such effect on diversity among accessions, for the following reasons.

1. The risk of allelic loss from the entire collection increases only for those alleles that are rare at both accession level and collection level, i.e., that are present at low frequency in very few accessions and absent from most accessions.

2. Drift increases the expected genetic variance among accessions.

3. Inbreeding further increases the expressed genetic variance among accessions by expressing the effects of recessive alleles. It also increases the genetic distances and the statistical significance of differences among accessions, by reducing genetic variance within accessions thereby increasing the ratio of genetic variance among accessions to that within accessions (Sackville Hamilton and Chorlton, 1997).

Whereas drift affects all polymorphic loci, selection affects only traits for which there is genetic variation associated with differential survival or reproduction in the environments used for storage and regeneration — traits of much interest for breeding work. Natural selection will change: (1) allele frequency at a locus if the phenotypic effects of those alleles have differential consequences for survival or reproduction; (2) allele frequency at a locus that is genetically linked to the locus in 1; and (3) expression of characters that are pleiotropic expressions of loci controlling the characters that directly affect survival or reproduction.

It needs to be borne in mind that regeneration is done in an environment that is usually quite different from the environment from which the original population sample was taken. Further, while the environments occupied by natural populations and primitive landraces are highly variable, the regeneration environment is quite uniform. This results in uniform, directional selection pressure that: favours genotypes, which may not be predominant in the original population; progressively eliminates other genotypes; reduces genetic variance within accessions; and progressively changes mean phenotype away from the original population (Sackville Hamilton and Chorlton, 1997).

Such selective changes can accumulate over successive cycles of regeneration. Adaptation to spatial and temporal variation of the environment is only one of the classes

287

of evolutionary mechanisms that maintain genetic diversity within populations. Other mechanisms include neutral genes, heterozygote advantage and frequency–dependent selection. This means that environmental uniformity does not totally eliminate genetic diversity. Further, most regeneration plots do not completely eliminate environmental diversity or climate variability and so do not eliminate genetic diversity associated with such.

Regenerating accessions in a common environment tends to impose convergent selection pressure. In the uniform environment there is likely to be a single group of genotypes with higher fitness than all others in that environment and therefore a tendency for all accessions to change their genetic composition by natural selection towards that group. They naturally converge towards a common end–point, reducing genetic diversity among accessions. Such convergence depends on genetic variance within and among populations, the potential for transgressive segregation through recombination and new mutation, and the number of regeneration cycles (Sackville Hamilton and Chorlton, 1997).

Introgression between accessions during seed multiplication occurs if the accessions are not fully isolated, enabling gene flow to occur by pollen transfer which reduces genetic variance between accessions by increasing the sharing of genes. The combination of introgression with convergent selection is worse than either alone; introgression both increases the rate of convergence and removes any limit to the extent of convergence.

Compared with the effects of drift, selection essentially affects fewer loci, affects only non–neutral loci, which are more likely than neutral loci to be of agronomic significance, and potentially has more adverse effects on conservation of diversity both within and among accessions.

In regeneration work, highest priority should be given to preventing the loss of rare alleles and to minimizing non–random changes by selection, since these are more detrimental than drift in terms of losing agronomically significant diversity from the entire collection.

Considerable background knowledge is a must for making sound regeneration decisions. An outline is given above (Biology of species/accession).

Technology

Recent developments in biotechnology have stimulated some restructuring of the seed industry; the new technologies allow for a much more deterministic approach to modifying crops and animals and ultimately the food we eat. Rather than messing around with complicated crossing and backcrossing breeding programmes, hopes within the industry were set high to develop a technology that isolates and inserts specific genes into crops and microbes. Before anything of such a nature was even technically (let alone commercially) possible, company officials went around promising a chemical-free agriculture and a world without hungry people. Still, apart from the initial hype about its possibilities and promises, the new biotechnologies are profoundly restructuring the industry as well as the agriculture. They basically allow scientists to look for solutions at the molecular/cellular level, rather than at the level of plants in their environment. Early concerns were limited to the environmental implications of the release of genetically modified organisms, but quickly the concern broadened to the socioeconomic impact of the new biotechnologies on food, farming and health. In the past few years, there has been some corporate quest for engineering crops that provide for tolerance against herbicides, or crops that rely for their resistance against pests and diseases on one or very few genes. Campaigns have been organized against the use of biotech–manufactured growth hormones in cattle. Largely, the new biotechnologies still have to find their way to the farmers' fields, but the decisions on what they will bring and whom they will benefit are being taken right now.

Rights

The attempts to patent life go back several decades when plant breeders began calling out for a means to get a return on their investment in crop improvement. The European lobby started among fruit tree breeders in the 1920s, and the US breeders got a limited 'Plant Patent Act' in 1930. After long debates, it was seen that the patent system was not adequate to cover biological 'inventions'. Plants reproduce themselves, they are part of nature, they are the basis of the food supply. For these reasons and others, a specialized system of protection for new plant varieties was set up in 1961 at the signing of the UPOV Convention (Union for the Protection of New Varieties of Plants). 'Plant Breeders' Rights' (PBR) were itended to be a soft form of intellectual property right. The monopoly was limited to the commercial use of the variety without covering the germplasm of the plant itself. Thus, plant breeders could freely use protected varieties as sources of initial variation for new varieties; farmers could reuse seed from their harvest grown from PBR–covered varieties.

Much recent debate on PBR has been eclipsed by growing public concern over a much stronger form of intellectual property rights: the industrial patent system. Some organizations are fighting against its extension to plants and animals. In the 1980s, the patenting of life-forms sounded like nightmarish science fiction. Today, there are heated policy discussions, aggressive lobby activities and vigorous legal battles to prevent this from becoming reality. The push for patents on life initially focused entirely on the OECD countries, with the US patent office granting its first plant patent in 1985 and its first animal patent in 1988, and the EC commission proposing a biotech patent 'directive' in 1988. But soon the patent question showed its North–South dimensions when Third World countries pushed the debate into FAO and onto the negotiations for the Biodiversity Convention. At the same time, the North is determined to see that the South accepts some form of intellectual property rights on life-forms.

Indian farmers have begun a massive action to save their inalienable rights as breeders and users of seeds. Protesting against the entry of large multinationals in India's seed sector and denouncing the GATT proposals on intellectual property, some one thousand farmers stormed the office of Cargill Seeds in southern India in December 1992. Cargill is the world's top grain trader and sixth largest seed company in the world. It entered India to import and sell seeds in 1988, when the government opened the market to foreign companies. Farmers belonging to the Karnataka Rajya Raitha Sangha (KRRS) thronged the Cargill building, destroyed many files and seeds that they found. The farmer–activists on the street voiced their protest and handed out leaflets stating that their action is to protect the rights of farmers to produce, modify and sell seeds. Their appeal urged that genetic resources are national property and farmers have the right to produce, reproduce and innovate on seeds—a right the multinational seeds companies want to restrict through intellectual property rights (IPR).

Dynamic Diversity (*In-Situ* Conservation)

Farmers have an important role in safeguarding biodiversity through their crop husbandry, and livestock keepers and fisherfolk likewise help safeguard biodiversity for food security.

The biodiversity of food species is also referred to as *agricultural biodiversity (agrobiodiversity) or the genetic resources for food and agriculture.* Being the basis of food security, it has been developed by small farmers, herders and artisanal fishermen in a wide range of ecosystems over millennia in order to produce food of desired qualities and taste, for local nutritional, social and economic needs (Mulvany, 1996). Food producers developed locally diverse production systems, increasing the reliability of production and minimizing risk. Within these production systems the biodiversity of their crops and livestock was developed for varied environments such as drought or floods, poor or rich soils, pests and diseases. Fishermen have traditionally nurtured a rich aquatic biodiversity which has sustained local fish populations.

Even today, some conservation and development of biodiversity is continuing on the farms and rangelands, and in the coastal waters, used by these food producers. It is called *in–situ* conservation; it is dynamic in the sense that the genetic resources develop through utilization and selection. The production systems supporting this biodiversity ensure food and livelihood security, provide food for some one-third of the world's population and generate livelihoods for most of the world's poor, including the majority of farmers and herders and all those dependent on artisanal fisheries.

For some time, however, these locally diverse food production systems have been subjected to threat and, with them, the local knowledge and skills of the food producers are also threatened. Consequently, the biodiversity of all food species is disappearing extensively. More than 75% of crop varieties have disappeared and about a half of the breeds of several domestic animals have been lost. In fisheries, all the world's 17 main fishing grounds are now being fished at or above their sustainable limits, with many fish populations becoming extinct.

The genetic erosion of the biodiversity of food species occurs by the loss of forest cover, coastal wetlands and other 'wild' uncultivated areas, and the destruction of the aquatic environment, leading to losses of 'wild' relatives important for the development of biodiversity, and losses of 'wild' foods essential for food provision in times of famine (Mulvany, 1996).

The two broad approaches to effective conservation are *in–situ* and *ex–situ* conservation. *In–situ* conservation can be achieved through maintaining and developing biodiversity in farmers' fields and gardens, on rangelands and in coastal waters where the genetic resources develop through utilization and selection.

Ex-situ Conservation

Ex-situ conservation is the conservation of species and varieties outside their habitats, for instance in zoos and gene banks. It involves species-by-species conservation rather than conservation of ecosystems. It is essential for ensuring the long-term safety and continued availability of plant genetic resources and for achieving global food security. The storage of dry seed at low temperature is the most widely practised method of *ex situ* conservation.

Ex situ techniques are complementary to *in situ* conservation, and *in situ* methods need not necessarily always be the best.

Conserving plant genetic resources is a kind of insurance. Modern agricultural systems rely on a small number of high–yielding varieties; they have little genetic variation with which to withstand onslaughts of diseases and pests. A broad base of genetic resources is needed to be able to develop new plant varieties which can resist pests, diseases or other environmental stresses. Conservation is urgent, since as land is converted to agriculture, the wild relatives of crop plants disappear. *In situ* conservation is an ideal which may not be practical for many of today's crop plants. Over 80,000 samples (in the form of seed) of rice and over 125,000 of wheat are stored in the world's gene banks. It is totally impractical to conserve such large numbers *in situ*, especially given the pressing needs of many countries for land and food, and the large number of sites which would be required to cover the ecogeographical range of each crop. However, *ex situ* conservation has some drawbacks. Technical and human error can lead to loss of varieties; not all seeds are suited to storage in seed banks; not all pollen is easily preserved; not all plants can be held in botanical gardens; *ex situ* collections are at risk from directional (artificial) selection and are relatively expensive to maintain.

One interesting example of the strategic value of gene banks is the discovery of almost complete resistance to carrot root fly in an old European variety of carrot held at the Vegetable Gene Bank, Wellesbourne.

Ex situ conservation of genetic resources can be achieved in gene banks or in living collections located away from the production systems that developed the resources. This strategy can only preserve material taken from farms and the local environment: it cannot develop diversity. It provides collateral support to *in situ* conservation and development rather than vice versa.

A third strategy is the formation of Genetic Reserves, usually in remote environments, in which communities are discouraged from developing their crop varieties and animal breeds. From some Marine Genetic Reserves, artisanal fisherfolk are excluded so their expert management of the ecosystem, which has developed aquatic biodiversity for human use, suffers.

292

To achieve better conservation of agricultural biodiversity, policies and programmes, at all levels, need to promote the conservation, development and legal use of a wide range of biodiversity of food species, increase consumption of locally produced foods, emphasize *in-situ* conservation and utilization, maintaining dynamic diversity rather than freezing (and losing) diversity in gene banks. *Ex-situ* gene banks may only be used as a backup to the living, dynamic and evolving collections used and nurtured by food providers. Special priority needs to be accorded to local development of genetic resources for food and agriculture.

Potential of Botanical Gardens

The great potential of botanical gardens as resource centres for conservation, education and development is often not appreciated. The world's 1500 botanical gardens and arboreta maintain the largest array of plant diversity outside nature—estimated at about 80,000 species in cultivation. With proper infrastructure and facilities, the gardens and arboreta can help conserve *ex-situ* stocks of most of the currently endangered plant species of the world. It has been estimated that about 300–400 of the world's total number of botanical gardens will be capable of holding major conservation collections on a long–term basis. Likewise, about 250 gardens may be able to establish and maintain seed banks at an accepted scientific and technical level. On this basis, up to 20,000 rare or endangered plant species could be effectively conserved in the botanic garden system either as seed in long-term storage or as growing plants or tissue cultures (Anonymous, 1991).

A potential role of botanical gardens is in conservation of medicinal plants. In developing countries in particular, medicinal plants are used by a large proportion of the people to supply the bulk of the raw materials used in their traditional medicines. Due to population growth and loss of habitats many of the medicinal plants used in medicines are becoming rare and losing much of their genetic variation. Many of these species are threatened with local extinction through overexploitation and it is necessary to culture them to ensure their availability. In order to grow them, their cultural requirements need to be studied. Several botanical gardens around the world are engaged in such work and in providing seed sources, especially in China, India, Sri Lanka and Indonesia.

293

Connections Between Conservation Strategies and Breeding Strategies

For crop species, conservation strategies are intimately connected to breeding strategies because the latter largely determine the use and need for genetic resources. The need for supporting both *in-situ* and *ex-situ* conservation of landraces and wild relatives cannot be overemphasized. Nevertheless, in the 1970s *ex-situ* conservation was the dominant conservation strategy. Only in the late 1980s and early 1990s did *in-situ* conservation again come into the limelight as a necessary and additional means of storing genetic resources. In general, the prevailing breeding practices have greatly influenced the current worldwide emphasis on *ex-situ* conservation, especially the breeding strategies for crop resistance employed by pathologists and/or geneticists. The subordinate status of *in-situ* conservation may have been partly a consequence of the domination of resistance–breeding, which was geared toward exploiting single–gene resistance, which benefits from relatively easy access to genetic resources that could be conveniently stored in *ex-situ* storage, except for certain seeds which could not be stored as, for example, many tropical perennials, where *ex-situ* field collections were established.

In-situ conservation in the 1970s and 1980s by and large did not interface with agricultural practices, particularly in respect of conservation of landraces in farmers' fields and orchards.

Landraces and wild relatives of cultivated plants are of undoubted scientific interest, being a reservoir of genes and gene combinations of potential value in plant breeding. Regrettably, some of the wild relatives of cultivated species have been viewed as weeds and accordingly are threatened by civilization (Worthington, 1975).

Not only do many genetic resources need to be collected and conserved, but also the conservation of landraces and wild relatives is instrumental in acquiring a better understanding of coevolutionary and adaptational mechanisms between plants and their environments.

Genetics and Conservation Strategies

The dominance of the *ex-situ* approach to conservation strategies until the early 1970s also stemmed from the inability of ecologists to design alternative strategies based on the stability-diversity concept (see Oldfield, 1984). Geneticists went a step further

294

by assuming that when the genetic mechanisms behind coevolutionary processes (supporting stability) became better known, they could facilitate crop improvement, particularly where they could add to durable resistance. Harlan (1975) stated that landraces, unlike advanced cultivars in high–input cultivations, are usually better adapted to the specific local environments in which they evolve, resulting in a wider diversity between them. Landraces have a certain 'genetic integrity' and are recognizable morphologically. Different landraces differ in adaptation to soil type, time of seeding, date of maturity, height, nutritive value, use and other properties. They are genetically diverse, balanced populations—variable in equilibrium with both environment and pathogens, and genetically dynamic (Harlan, 1975). Harlan's research prompted many breeders and geneticists to argue against the rapidly increasing reliance on 'pure-line' and often susceptible high-yielding varieties.

It was the 'imbalance' between crop and environment that became one of the most fundamental criticisms of the green revolution as it emphasized the view that crops in modern agriculture have been developed in spite of, rather than in harmony with their natural environment, and that consequently the crop's ability to counter pathogen races has diminished. The criticism was mainly on crop breeding programmes in which modern pure-line varieties only contained short-term resistance against changing pathogen races.

Genecological Approach

Genecology is defined as the study of population genetics in relation to habitats. In 1956 J.W. Gregor described his findings when plant populations were transferred from their native habitats to an experimental garden: these samples possessed much higher genetic variability than in the original habitats (Bennett, 1965; Gregor, 1956).

Genecologists have usually assumed that the genetic basis of an organism's (phenotypic) adaptation to a new environment may be attributed not to single genes, but to the joint action of several genes. This assumption was based on the observation that although changes in yield and resistance have been attributed to single gene changes, most crop improvement work was based, historically, on selection of complex polygenic variability (Dempsey, 1990). This meant that crop improvement could best be achieved through a combination of genes and not through concentrating on one or a few. In the genecological approach, variability in a plant relying on several non–allelic genes all affecting the same character (or 'polygenes') was much more significant for plant breeding than single genes as entire groups of characters affecting the phenotype at many levels and in many ways may be responsible for adaptive fitness. This view was similar to the opinion of Van der Planck and others that exposure of populations to pathogens could best be countered by polygenic resistance. Genecological information could therefore be instrumental in tracing adaptive disease resistance, also referred to as 'field resistance', depending on polygenic variation.

These views shifted the focus of conservation strategies from single genes to genotypes. It was further realized that in order to maintain the dynamic interaction between gene complexes and the environment, the isolation of genetic material in seed storage *ex-situ* would stop this process, thereby rendering it undesirable from a genecological perspective. However, the genecological approach did have some limitations. Although it was agreed that variation within populations could be useful for further breeding purposes, there was almost no practical experience in making selections of plants that contained the required polygenic variation. No one knew how to sample when not only the distinct traits of a plant, but also the relation of these traits to different environments had to be reflected in future collections. How to fix selection criteria during sampling was the question. To be effective, sampling not only needed to include collecting samples, but also to be accompanied by a careful survey of climate and its local variations, soil types, topography, distribution of crops and knowledge of local crop varieties. Regions of less–advanced agricultural crop varieties were especially interesting because of the close adaption of the varieties to local environments.

From the viewpoint of plant breeders, *ex–situ* conservation may be the best way to find the easiest genes to work with. Ideally, it should be possible to take out genetically simple traits from storage and transfer them to elite lines without disturbing other desirable characters. Agronomy tames the environment and through breeding, one can tailor the crop to this environment. Consequently, the adaptive complexes of crop populations, built up over millennia, may occasionally be interpreted merely as weediness or other constraints on yield improvement (Dempsey, 1990).

The support for the *in-situ* option in the genecological tradition came principally from the idea that resistance did not necessarily have to be built up from (single) extractable genes, but was rather a matter of polygenic inheritance (Pistorius, 1997). *In-situ* conservation, because of the practical difficulties associated with it, was considered more useful as a 'safety valve' against continuing genetic erosion than in terms of its direct

296

usefulness in crop improvement. One of the strongest critics of *ex situ* conservation was Erna Bennett who felt that the purpose of conservation is not to catch today's evolutionary time, but to conserve material so that it will continue to evolve. She felt that such 'continued evolution' could only be possible in *in situ* collections (Bennett, 1968).

Harrington (1970), in contrast, favoured *ex situ* conservation and believed that the best way of preserving plant gene resources is seed storage because under proper conditions the seeds of many species remain viable for up to many years, but proper conditions include both optimum techniques of seed preparation and optimum storage environment (Harrington, 1970).

In the 1970s the general consensus was that the most practical solution was that the FAO should co-ordinate national and international efforts concerned with the exploration, conservation and utilization of plant genetic resources in the areas of agriculture and forestry, including those of existing institutes of germplasm storage and conservation.

An *ex situ* conservation strategy under the co-ordination of FAO was felt to be the best option for preservation of landraces but this did not immediately solve the issue of how to lay down criteria so as to prevent the accumulation of unco-ordinated, unstructured and oversized collections.

Socioeconomic Implications of Single-gene Resistance

Interestingly, only farmers in temperate climates, who largely depend on monocropping, have opted for disease-free crops. This is particularly true for intensive agriculture in industrialized countries. By and large, farmers in developing countries have been relying on locally selected landraces which contain polygenic resistance. This type of resistance tends to have commercial limits with regard to intensive agricultural crops (e.g. potatoes) in industrialized countries and in some horticultural crops that are easy to breed (e.g. onions, tomatoes) (Robinson, 1976).

The preference of single-gene over polygenic resistance has been based mostly on the criteria of agricultural practices of farmers working in temperate climates. In these climates pathogens are usually less active than in warmer climates and the farmers can afford to buy the costlier new varieties. The question is whether the use of polygenic resistance, in spite of fixed losses due to direct host-pathogen reactions, would ultimately prove more beneficial to farmers in developing countries than the use of high-yielding varieties with less durable single-gene resistance? The application of single-gene resistance in short-term boom-and-bust cycles on less intensive and less uniform local farming in tropical areas has generated grave socioeconomic problems (Dempsey, 1990). Breeding techniques developed for temperate climates and based on single-gene resistances are not usually appropriate for many tropical farmers, who lack access to agrochemicals to control losses when single-gene resistance breaks down. An unplanned spillover of high-yielding varieties to marginal environments damages farmers' interest, as these varieties have not been bred for such environments. However, there are some exceptions and high-yielding varieties have occasionally been gainfully used in low-input systems. Also, even in developed countries, problems can occur with high yielding varieties grown under marginal conditions, or within appropriate levels of inputs. It has sometimes been noted for instance that, compared with the high-yield stability of green revolution varieties in Asia, the poor stability of American cereal yields is a result of both a periodic expansion of production to more marginal conditions, and a very high application of fertilizer (which increases yield instability).

Frankel (1954) elegantly illustrated the ability of agriculture to modify the environment versus the ability of breeders to adapt new releases (Fig. 9–3). Figure 9–3 shows the strong connection between agriculture and plant breeding versus the weak connection between natural selection and agriculture, thereby indicating that mainstream crop improvement (in those times) involved very little natural selection mechanisms. This Figure was drawn on the basis of data then available on the relation between the level of modification of the environment versus the adaptation of the crop, before the green revolution. If one were to redraw the same figure in the 1970s (after the advent of the green revolution), a tremendous increase in the ability of agriculture to modify the environment would be discernible. Further, if designed in the light of genecological principles, the same Figure would look very different. The links between the different crop categories with natural selection would be much more pronounced whereas those between different crops and plants and environmental modifications of the environment would be much less.

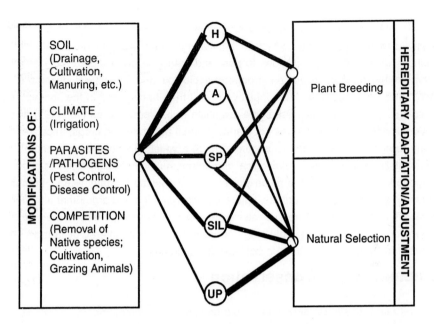

Fig. 9–3. Establishment of crop plants into new environments and the roles played by modification of environment and adaptation of heredity in the main crops. The relative intensities of adaptive influences are indicated by the thickness of connecting lines. The thickness of each line roughly denotes the extent to which different crops and plants (central part in the Figure) either require a modification of the environment (far left) or a modification of their own heredity (far right). Horticulturists, for example, equipped with glasshouses, can best manipulate the environmental conditions in favour of production. Open air agriculture is less able to do so and generally depends much more on plant breeding. H = horticultural crops; A = agricultural crops; SP = pasture plants in sown pastures; UP = pasture plants invading natural pastures; SIL = silvicultural crops (after Frankel, 1954).

Agriculture, biology and ecology should all be strongly concerned with conservation. Sadly, whereas in the agricultural world conservation of plant genetic resources started attracting serious attention in the 1960s, ecological and biological initiatives lagged far behind. This was largely due to lack of an interdisciplinary merger of ecological, biological and agricultural ideas on the conservation and use of genetic resources.

However, in the decade of the 1960s, ecologists and biologists did start discussing the 'stability–diversity hypothesis', which in agricultural terms focused on adaptational responses of host plant populations to pest and pathogen populations. One happy outcome of this interaction was a marriage of ecological and agricultural ideas on the genetic interaction between plant populations and their habitat, within the concept of genecology. Of course there are some scientists (e.g. Wood and Lenné, 1993) who believe that local adaptation does not lead to optimal adaptation in crops, because of farmers' access to a restricted local gene pool of a widely distributed crop; and also farmers' ability to select for morphological characters that could rapidly restrict the on–farm genepool and counter the much slower natural selection. Many NGOs, both in developing and developed countries, ignore this view and instead argue that although breeders have access to a more extensive gene pool than farmers, breeders are unable to select for adaptation to the great range of environments encountered by farmers. It appears that there is some truth in both these statements.

Complementary Conservation

In situ and ex situ conservation should be viewed as complementary strategies. Ex situ conservation can never take over the function of in situ conservation as a means of storing the world's genetic diversity of crop plants or their wild relatives with a potential use and vice versa. Nevertheless, the following questions crop up from time to time: to what extent should wild relatives and landraces of important plants be conserved ex situ rather than in situ? To what extent should farmers' efforts be supported to maintain landraces in situ? To what extent should nature parks or reserves conserve both landraces and wild relatives? Historically, the ex situ approach has been the primary tool for the conservation of crop plants. There exist over 4 million accessions in some 500 ex situ collections throughout the world (see, for example, FAO, 1996). According to Frankel (1985), ex situ preservation using low–temperature storage and sound management is to be preferred over in situ conservation of primitive cultivars as the latter approach is impracticable in view of the large numbers involved and the technical and social problems to be met. For short-lived plants, ex situ germplasm collections are the only practicable solution for the long-term preservation of large numbers of accessions. Indeed, breeding for high-yielding crops would have been a far more arduous task had ex situ gene banks not existed. During the creation of an ex situ network, gene banks were thought to be the best way of preventing the rapid rate of genetic erosion. But in the 1980s the centralization of ex situ conservation strategy began to be questioned and so did the claim of its superiority as an option for conserving genetic resources. Decentralization of responsibility and control over *ex situ* collections may be a good objective but is difficult to achieve.

Merits and Demerits of *Ex Situ* Conservation

Some arguments in favour of *ex situ* conservation of storable, non–recalcitrant seeds refer to the following:

(a)   it is most suitable for long–term conservation;

(b)   its storage facilities can store greater diversity and quantity of accessions of seeds;

(c)   its evaluation is easier than in *in situ* circumstances, and

(d)   it offers wider availability to breeders than do *in situ* collections.

Some potential drawbacks of long–term *ex situ* conservation are:

(a)   differential survival of genotypes in storage: long–term storage causes a loss in germination rate;

(b)   selection during rejuvenation: after several cycles of rejuvenation, accessions show little resemblance to the original parent(s) collected in nature;

(c)   outcrossing with other species: it is difficult to provide adequate isolation to prevent outcrossing between different entries during regeneration;

(d)   it is impossible to store recalcitrant seeds *ex situ*;

(e)   *ex situ* conservation 'freezes evolution' (or leads to evolutionary stasis), and

(f)   *in vitro* storage *ex situ* may cause loss of diversity (Hawkes, 1991).

Farmers as Saviours of Biodiversity

Over the millennia, from thousands of species of edible plants around the world, farmers and food providers could develop and nurture hundreds of species. From these, they created countless varieties of useful plants. Domestication of the world's major food crops catalyzed the greatest transformation in human civilization: the development of a diverse, complex and location–specific settled agriculture.

This type of early agriculture can still be seen in less fertile areas such as uplands, savannas, swamps, near–deserts and forests, predominately in the South. It is this

301

Table 9–1. Two approaches to the conservation of agricultural biodiversity (after Mulvany, 1996)

	Static diversity	Dynamic diversity
Biodiversity explanation	'Frozen' in time. Seeds conserved outside their natural environment (*ex situ*)	Dynamically changing and increasing over time with new production challenges. Conservation *in situ*
Biodiversity perception	In terms of numbers of accessions	As a web of relationships that ensure balance and sustainability
Location	Gene banks, databases	Fields, forests, rangelands, farmers' knowledge
Actors	Scientists, administrators	Farmers, indigenous people
Conservation	Through collection, annotation and storage	Through use: seeds develop through farmers' selection in current growing conditions; farmers' knowledge increases
Focus	Main crop staples and high commercial potential	Wide variety of crops and plants that ensure local food and livelihood security
Disadvantages	Only succeeds when set up with the help of farmers and indigenous people	Varieties may be lost if they are not useful to communities, but genes may survive through crossing into new varieties
	Seeds saved may not be farmers' choice	Seed stores and associated knowledge are decentralized and difficult to access

Table 9–1 contd.

	Seeds cannot adapt to changing environmental conditions	Conservation strategies are complex and diverse, hence difficult to manage
	Seeds may die in storage	Conflict, natural disasters and economic pressures can cause heavy losses
Advantages	Easy access; well–documented collections	High incentive for conservation: livelihoods depend on it
	Saves seeds with no immediate apparent use or value	Seeds adapt to changing environmental conditions and needs
	Acts as essential back–up when all *in-situ* seeds have been lost	Seed supplies safeguarded by communities through diverse production systems

agriculture that provides food for nearly 35% of the world's population and most of its poorest. It relies on the farmers' crop varieties that are well adapted to the growing conditions in these areas and still provides a livelihood for over half of the world's farmers. Farmers are the world's Seed Keepers and continue to develop agricultural biodiversity in these diverse food production systems (see Table 9–1). These farmers not only plant crops, but also perform several other complementary activities to sustain their livelihoods such as tending their livestock; hunting, collecting wild plants and animals to eat and sell; and making various things for sale, such as pots, baskets and jewellery. Their food production strategies integrate farmland and wildland resources which diversifies their livelihood systems and enables them to survive in adverse environments in order to ensure a year–round balanced diet and augment their income.

Genetic Erosion of Agricultural Biodiversity

More than 75% of global agricultural biodiversity has disappeared during the past several decades and the decline is continuing (Pretty, 1995). A few examples of genetic erosion in the South are given below:

1. In China, of 10,000 rice varieties used in production in 1949, 80% of which were farmers' varieties, only 1000 remained in use in the 1970s, 5% of which were farmers' varieties (FAO, 1996).

2. In India, more than 30,000 rice varieties were once grown but only 10 rice varieties now cover 75% of the rice-growing area (Pretty, 1995).

Genetic erosion appears to be equally acute in the North:

1. 97% of the varieties of 75 vegetables on the US Department of Agriculture's old lists of varieties in use between 1804 and 1904, had become extinct by 1983.

2. Over 1500 vegetable varieties have vanished in Europe since 1974 (HDRA, 1995). In the Netherlands, in the late 1980s a single potato variety provided 80% of the crop and 90% of wheat lands were planted to only three varieties.

Some of the causes of genetic erosion in agricultural biodiversity include variety replacement, economic processes, deforestation and land clearance, environmental effects (e.g. desertification, flooding and pollution), introduction of new pests and diseases, and increasing urbanization.

Farmers' strategies for conservation *in situ* are dynamic and help in securing their food supply and sustaining livelihoods. In contrast, the formal sector has generally tended to regard conservation as a static process of collecting and preserving genetic material *ex situ*. In some cases, enlightened and progressive farmers concerned about the disappearance of traditional varieties have themselves set up new mechanisms to conserve and utilize their varieties *in situ* in their farms and communities (see Mulvany, 1996).

Sometimes, farmers' varieties have been found to fare better than modern varieties. For example, in Nepal, in the 1980s, a local wheat variety known as 'Balankha Local', which grows on poor, rainfed *bari* land, was found to yield twice as much as an exotic, semidwarf variety which could only be grown on the more fertile, irrigated *khet* land in the same area (Ashley and Khatiwada, 1992).

Local, informal seed-saving initiatives are conserving valuable resources in some advanced countries as well, through a combination of *in–situ* conservation in gardens and smallholdings supported by *ex-situ* collections held by NGOs. In fact, The Henry Doubleday Research Association shares 1000 vegetable varieties, kept alive by 'Seed Guardians' among its amateur gardener members (Chertas and Fanton, 1996). Most of these varieties have been deleted from official European seed lists, which makes their trade illegal.

The Seed Savers Exchange in the USA conserves 5000 vegetable varieties built up gradually from collections brought by immigrant families to North America, through its network of 630 farmers and gardeners. Of about 1800 heirloom varieties of beans conserved by Seed Savers, only 147 could be found in government collections (see Mulvany, 1996).

Seed Banks and Biodiversity

Seed banks are important for the preservation of biological diversity. These banks and clonal repositories store and preserve plant genetic material offsite, i.e,, away from the places it is found in nature. The technologies used in seed banks are designed to preserve an adequate amount of germplasm, sustain its viability and preserve its original genetic constitution. The status of seed bank initiatives in various countries generally may be summarized as follows:

1. Seed storage techniques are being used to conserve the genetic diversity of cereals, legumes and many other crop species. Priorities for collecting and maintaining the germplasm of major crop plants are internationally co-ordinated, but are not well organized for minor crops or for wild plants which are endangered or which have economic potential (OECD, 1991).

2. New technologies can increase the success of maintaining diversity offsite, but there is a lack of fundamental research. Pending major breakthroughs in biotechnologies which might eventually lead to fundamental changes in how biological diversity is maintained in seed banks, existing technologies, such as cryogenic storage of germplasm, should be improved.

Internationally, there are roughly 2 million accessions of plant germplasm in seed banks. The International Board for Plant Genetic Resources co–ordinates a global network of gene banks to provide plant breeders with the genetic resources necessary to develop better crops. Begun in 1974, it now involves 106 countries and gene banks now number more than 100, 40 of which have agreed to long-term maintenance of genetic resources (OECD, 1991).

It may indeed be a surprise to some to learn that we are dependent on very few crops for our survival, most of which originated in the Third World (see Fig. 9–4). Despite millennia of crop breeding by farmers and gardeners throughout the world, the precious resource base of food security has been shrinking dramatically under the blanket of high-yielding varieties and is being monopolized by a few. The green revolution, the biases in corporate breeding strategies and the spread of plant breeders' rights in the industrialized countries, which control most of the world's gene banks, may be responsible for this.

Regeneration

Seed gene banks worldwide have at least two common objectives, viz., ensuring long-term conservation of the genetic diversity represented in the seed collections they hold, and maintaining a sufficient stock of seed for distribution to users. It is necessary to periodically regenerate the seed accessions so as to maintain optimal seed viability over the long term as well as to replenish the seed stock.

For effective regeneration practices, it is necessary to know about the reproductive biology and the extent and distribution of the genetic diversity of the material to be conserved. Also, genetic drift and genetic shift which might occur during the regeneration process have to be minimized. The effect of seedborne pathogens on the maintenance of genetic integrity of accessions has also to be kept in view. It is particularly difficult to regenerate cross–pollinated species because the most effective isolation techniques, pollination control procedures and mating methods for them are not well understood.

Regeneration is a costly procedure requiring such resources as land and labour. A good protocol for regeneration depends on the breeding system and seed storage traits of the species concerned, the physiological condition and genetic composition of the original sample, its expected usage and its perceived value within the collection, and operational constraints on gene bank activities, such as funds, personnel, infrastructure and equipment. In developing countries, power supply and quality can be a serious constraint. Regeneration procedures must, therefore, be flexible enough to meet the needs of gene banks and accessions located in different places.

Timely regeneration must be a priority activity of gene banks everywhere. Effective regeneration programmes are essential for maintaining the viability and genetic

306

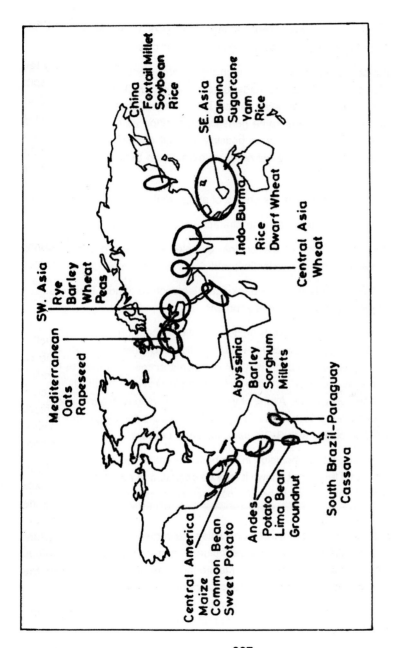

Fig. 9–4. Map of the Centres of Genetic Diversity based on those identified by N.I. Vavilov showing the principal origins and centres of diversity of twenty major crops. These account for about 90% of the world's food supply.

integrity of *ex-situ* seed collections. Sadly, many gene banks are experiencing a large backlog and continuing difficulties with regenerating their collections (FAO, 1996).

The principal objectives of a regeneration programme should be to : (1) ensure timely identification of accessions with inadequate quality or quantity of seed; (2) at the earliest opportunity, produce a new seed sample that, as far as possible, has maximum quality, optimum quantity, and the same genetic composition as the original; and (3) achieve the above as cost effectively as possible without compromising the quality, quantity and genetic integrity or the utilization of germplasm (Sackville Hamilton and Chorlton, 1997).

The following factors influence the choice of an optimal protocol for regeneration:

1. breeding system and seed storage characteristics of the species concerned;

2. the genetic composition of the original sample, its expected usage, and its perceived value within the collection; and

3. operational constraints on gene bank activities such as funds, labour, electric supply, other infrastructure and equipment.

The need for regeneration depends on how and why accessions are stored. Three main conceptual categories of collection — base, active and safety duplicate — serve different purposes. A base collection is a set of distinct accessions that, in terms of genetic integrity, are as close as possible to the sample provided originally, which is preserved for the long–term future. As the emphasis here is on conservation, accessions in the base collection need to be held in optimal conditions for long–term storage, preferably at −18⁰C or cooler with 3–7% seed moisture content.

As a rule, to be eligible for inclusion in the base collection, an accession must be genetically unique, but if this is not known it may be desirable to adopt the second best approach and accept uniqueness based on passport data as a sufficient criterion for distinctness.

An active collection is a set of accessions which are immediately available for use. Here the focus is on utilization, not conservation; these accessions can have an important role in breeding and/or research. Maintenance needs are therefore defined in terms of the immediate user base of the collection rather than in terms of conservation (Sackville Hamilton and Chorlton, 1997). Storage conditions for an active collection should be such that accession viability remains above at least 65% for 10 to 20 years.

Regrettably, this condition (FAO/IPGRI, 1994) is not really satisfied by the majority of gene banks which maintain an active collection under less stringent conditions than the base: various gene banks maintain the active collection under conditions ranging from -10^0 C to 5^0 C and 15–50% relative humidity (ICRISAT, 1995).

A safety duplicate collection means a duplicate copy of accessions held at a distant site or series of sites and preserved for the long–term future, as an insurance against accidental loss of germplasm through natural disaster, chronic electricity failures or other calamities. This type of collection should contain all accessions in the base collection and should likewise be held in optimal conditions for long–term storage, as applicable to a base collection. Quite often, safety duplicates are held by some different gene bank.

The choice of the overall site is determined by adaptation of the crop to the regeneration environment and the need for maintaining its genetic integrity. The types of location at a site include field, glasshouse or other facilities for better control of the environment.

Selection of accessions for regeneration requires the definition of threshold levels for seed quality and quantity, below which regeneration is required; a protocol for monitoring seed quality and quantity, and a protocol for prioritizing accessions when the number warranting regeneration is beyond the gene bank capacity. Highest priority is given to regenerating accessions that have seed of low quality in the base collection.

Selection of seed to be used to provide parental plants depends on the source of seed, the number of seeds to be used and their identity. Special focus should be on using seed held in the base collection to replenish seed stocks in the active collection so as to avoid cumulative degradation of genetic integrity. The number of seeds to be used is also critical and is determined by the number required for the satisfactory maintenance of genetic integrity and the number of offspring seeds to be produced (Sackville Hamilton and Chorlton, 1997). Seed for use as parents is usually selected at random from the available seed.

The rest of the regeneration procedure depends strongly on the agronomy and biology of the species concerned. Throughout the regeneration process, it is crucial to ensure accuracy and avoid contamination by alien plants, seed or pollen. These precautions need to be taken right from preparation of regeneration plots to storing the harvested seed. Complete isolation from all alien pollen is strongly advisable for all species except obligate inbreeders and obligate apomicts. Another important issue is maximizing uniformity among plants in their contribution of male and female gametes to the offspring generation. Pruning and manual pollination are some of the more labour-intensive measures to be considered to increase uniformity where variation between plants is high (Sackville Hamilton and Chorlton, 1997). From anthesis onwards, the highest possible health and viability of offspring seed should be ensured; these depend on proper disease control, harvesting and rapid post–harvest processing, particularly for seed–drying and threshing.

Chapter 10
SUSTAINABLE DEVELOPMENT

Introduction

Three chief trends that have contributed substantially to excessive pressure on the earth's natural systems in the past few decades have been the doubling of the world's population, quintupling of global economic output and widening gap between the rich and the poor (Oyen *et al.*, 1996). The environmental impact of the earth's population of over 5.5 billion has been greatly multiplied by economic and social systems which strongly favour growth over equity and poverty alleviation; that turn a blind eye to wasteful consumption; that do not discriminate between environment–friendly means of production and those that are not environment–friendly; and that pay scant attention to unplanned burgeoning urbanization.

One plausible approach to removing some of the above anomalies might be a strong shift from population control and family planning services to proper appreciation of the importance of women's social and economic status, and of sufficiently educating and enabling women to participate fully in the process of development. This may more effectively tackle the problem of population explosion than contraceptives for family planning. All over the world, the basic resources on which future generations will depend for their survival and welfare are being depleted now, and environmental pollution is becoming more and more serious, driven by explosive growth in human numbers (Lutz, 1994; Lassonde, 1997), widespread and persistent poverty (Regnell, 1995), social and economic inequality, and much wasteful consumption. Improving the status of women, especially in the underdeveloped countries, would increase their decision–making capacity in many spheres of life, and is essential for long–term success of population control programmes (see Oyen *et al.*, 1996).

There exists a strong nexus between the complex environment, development, population and urbanization. Some elements of the principal driving forces influencing our earth and our lives are the following (see Tolba, 1995)

1. The growing inequity in income between rich and poor. In 1960, about 20% of the world's people absorbed 70% of the global income; by 1990, the wealthy's share had increased to over 80% (Tolba, 1995). Meanwhile, the poorest 20% had their share of global income fall from an already low of 2.3% to a miniscule

1.4%. The ratio of the richest fifth's share to the poorest's thus increased from 30:1 in 1960 to 60:1 in 1990.

2. Before *Homo sapiens* began exerting significant impact, the world's forests, grasslands and other ecosystems could potentially produce a net total of some 150 billion tons of organic matter annually. Mankind has destroyed outright about 12% of this terrestrial net primary productivity (NPP) and now uses or co–opts an additional 27%. Man has appropriated some 40% of the terrestrial food supply leaving only 60% to be shared by the millions of other species.

3. The earth's supporting capacity for humans does not depend only on our basic food requirements; it is also determined by our consumption levels of many resources (Redclift, 1996), by the amount of waste we generate and by the technologies adopted for our diverse activities (Tolba, 1995). The global problems of ozone depletion and climate change clearly highlight the danger of crossing the earth's ability threshold to absorb our waste products.

4. The consequences of overstepping the sustainable supply of essential resources are somewhat less well recognized. The earth's environmental assets are quite insufficient to sustain the current levels of economic activity. If current trends in resource consumption continue, by the year 2010 per capita availability of rangeland could drop by 20% and the fish catch by 10%, seriously jeopardizing the world's supply of animal protein. The per capita area of irrigated land, which at present yields about a third of the global food harvest, will decline by over 10% and cropland area and forest land per person will drop by 20 and 30% respectively. Urgent action is warranted to reduce overconsumption throughout the world, especially by the rich. Any move away from wasteful environment–degrading production and consumption in no way decreases living standards. The rich must stop squandering the resources (Regnell, 1995; Redclift, 1996).

4. Internalizing of environmental costs is critical for reducing the kinds of economic growth that harm the environment. Since the environment itself is not exchanged, it eludes a market price and an assigned value. Economists confine value only to exchange at the expense of non–market values such as biological diversity or clean water. Natural climate and port access used to be crucial to production specialization and comparative advantage in classical economic theory, while resource scarcity or pollution-sink capacity used to be mostly irrelevant. In the industrialized world, once a resource was depleted a new source was found. Thus, while industrial plants, materials, machinery and buildings are routinely

312

treated as productive capital whose value undergoes depreciation in the course of time, nature's bounty is not so valued. Further, there is a widespread tendency to overestimate the natural regenerative ability of most natural resources, leading to a corresponding undervaluation of these resources (Tolba, 1995). It is indeed high time that depreciation values were assigned to soils, water, air, forests and fisheries.

There is growing concern over the state of world food security and its prospects. Over 800 million people today are suffering from chronic malnutrition. With further growth in world population, it seems certain that pressure to intensify agricultural production will increase and make even greater demands on natural resources. Global food security has improved greatly since the early 1960s and current trends suggest that world aggregate food production will be sufficient to meet demand in the coming few decades. Of course, food production will not increase at the same high rates as in the past but neither will population — demographic growth is expected to decline from the present annual rate of 1.5% to 1% by the year 2020. Unfortunatley, in sub-Saharan Africa, per capita food production continues to stagnate and by 2010 over a third of its population may be chronically malnourished.

In many low-income countries, birth rates continue to be high and the majority of the population survive on persistently low levels of income and food consumption. Should these trends continue, by 2010 one–tenth of humankind may live in societies experiencing widespread hunger but little 'market demand' for food. This is because food security is not just a matter of how much food the world's agriculture can produce; an even more important issue is that the food be physically available and within the purchasing power of the world's people.

What is needed is a new, people-centred, sustainable development with a focus on broad rural development which can prove to be the most effective way of tackling poverty. Most of the world's poor people live in villages. Rural/urban links should be strengthened through improved rural service centres and small towns, infrastructure and transportation. Initiatives for small industrial enterprises should be incorporated into an integrated rural development framework. These efforts should be so designed as to benefit the rural poor. Since environmental degradation has resulted partly due to defective policies, lack of resources and current production/consumption patterns, the need for democratic institutions, people-based development and proper implementation cannot be overemphasized.

Sustainability

Sustainability deals with concrete and immediate problems, for instance, the plight of a billion people struggling to survive on less than a dollar a day. Over 100 million children of primary school age cannot attend school and so are denied access to the knowledge and skills that could enable them to sustain themselves better. Sustainability poses a choice between a culture of war and a culture of peace, a choice between living within the limits required to preserve natural environments and reaping the riches of the earth without regard to the needs of future generations. Above all, sustainability poses a choice between policies of development aimed at meeting the basic needs of all and those directed towards careless growth regardless of its cost in environmental degradation.

Most current educational systems cannot meet the great challenge posed by unsustainable life styles. New educational approaches are required if people are to act upon awareness, if they are to achieve the necessary changes of life styles, in mobilizing support for public and private initiatives, developing a new ecological vision and promoting a sense of global solidarity. Education for sustainability is a new vision for education. Education is just as important to arrive at sustainability as the economy, legislation, science and technology and, furthermore, is a prerequisite for all of the aforesaid.

Wild species and their genetic variability can contribute substantially to the development of agriculture, medicine and industry. For future generations, biological diversity holds great potential in terms of feeding an alarmingly growing population. Only four decades from now we will have to produce three times as much food as we do today. This strengthens the need to maintain the richest possible pool of genes.

Ninety-eight per cent of all livestock production worldwide stems from only ten wild animal and bird species. Wild species are still being used to improve the characteristics of domesticated animals.

The plant kingdom is estimated to include some 75,000 edible species. Just 20 or so of these account for 90% of the world's food base. There are probably thousands of wild species and strains that could be used to improve these crops.

Had it not been for the genes of a few wild species found in Ecuador and Peru, tomatoes simply could not have been grown for profit today. A special type of tomato from the Galapagos Islands has been used to make the world's cultivated tomatoes machine-harvestable.

Biodiversity aids waste management and environmental clean-up efforts through bioremediation in which micro–organisms possessing unusual metabolisms and nutritional requirements are employed. A bacterium found in the sediments of the Potomac river can break down the ozone destroying chemicals, chlorofluorocarbons (CFCs) (Lovley and Woodward, 1992). Certain microbes which degrade organic molecules in oil spills are already in commercial use (Lovejoy, 1994).

A new bioflocculant is derived from the tree *Strychnos potatorum* found in Andhra Pradesh; it apparently is able to clean up uranium and nuclear wastes, and to remove heavy metals such as cadmium and mercury from effluents.

Without the genes from wild Indonesian sugar–cane, cane sugar production would probably not be commercially viable anywhere in the world. It is believed that the genetic material of a wild strain in Hawaii could be used to develop a sugar–cane that is resistant to rodent attack (Hanneberg, 1992).

The cultivated cocoa plant has benefited most from crossing with its wild relatives, followed by tobacco, which has been made resistant to a number of serious diseases.

Ninety per cent of all grain production is accounted for by wheat, rice, maize and barley. These four cereals have been greatly improved with the help of genes from closely related wild species. Many viral diseases, rusts and other fungal diseases have been combated and grain yields increased.

In India, advances have been made in cassava harvests as well as green vegetables, timber trees, fodder crops, fruits and oilseeds.

In the animal kingdom, improved varieties of meat and egg producers, fish and insects such as the honeybee and the silkworm have been developed.

These examples attest to the great potential of the species found in the unspoilt natural environment. The input of genetic material from nature not only increases the growth and net output of important food crops and animals, but can also make crops better able to withstand pathogens; contrarily, spraying with chemicals often engenders greater resistance in the parasites and other agents of plant disease, thereby necessitating application of ever larger doses.

In medicine, too, there is an immense potential for development, thanks to the genetic variation of wild species. Many medicines come from a wild plant or animal species. As mentioned earlier, today a child suffering from leukaemia has four chances in five of survival, thanks to treatment with drugs containing active substances discovered in the rosy periwinkle, a tropical forest plant found in Madagascar. Three decades ago, the same child would have had only one chance in five. In the tropical rain forests and other ecosystems, there may occur thousands of medicinal plant species that could be of great value to humanity, but are still undiscovered.

Substituting for Ecosystem Services

Living organisms in natural and agricultural ecosystems play enormous and critical roles in making Earth a suitable habitat for *Homo sapiens.*

Virtually all human attempts at complete or large-scale substitution for ecosystem services are ultimately unsuccessful, whether it be substitution of synthetic pesticides for natural pest control, inorganic fertilizers for natural ones, or chlorination for natural water purification (Ehrlich and Ehrlich, 1992). Substitutes generally require a large energy subsidy, which adds to humanity's general impact on the environment. Most substitutes are not completely satisfactory even in the short run. There is little to suggest that humanity will be able to substitute adequately for the ecosystem services that will be lost as the epidemic of extinctions now under way escalates. Biologists know these rates are far too high and are rising.

Many current approaches to protecting biodiversity are focused on areas or species of special interest and natural beauty or areas rich in endemic species. The highest value is usually placed on unique and unusual biota, with scant regard to the nature and quality of general biodiversity. What is needed is designation of priorities using the geological past, the nature of the ecosystem and the characteristics of the region. For marine areas, the following strategies are notable.

1. Surveys and inventories of biodiversity in areas of high scientific or conservation value as determined by a rigorous selection process.

2. Biological monitoring programmes using selected groups of bioindicator organisms of high quality.

3. Cataloguing existing historical collections from reef systems deposited in natural history museums.

4. Publication of primary taxonomic monographs, identification guides, keys and manuals, especially computerized, graphically based manuals for non–specialists and resource managers.

5. Parataxonomic training programmes for specific taxa and geographic regions.

Sustainable development is related indirectly to biodiversity through the need to

316

maintain overall environmental values. As its aim is to sustain both man and nature, it is directly related to conservation and the wise use of resources, including biodiversity. In the tropics, the major focus of conservation has been on controlling the deforestation process (Table 10–1). While all the strategies listed in Table 10–1 may be viewed as forms of sustainable development, the extraction of products and values from existing forest may be the approach that most directly links biodiversity to sustainable development. This so-called 'use it or lose it' approach has recently received considerable attention (Bawa, 1992; Janzen, 1992). Here the idea is that forests or other habitats can be maintained if they provide direct value to people who coexist with the forests.

Table 10–1. Techniques for mitigating deforestation and maintaining tropical forest habitat (after Kangas, 1997)

Strategy	Mechanism	Examples
Preservation	Deforestation eliminated as a land–use option	National parks, Community sanctuaries, Biosphere reserve
Conversion from extensive to intensive agriculture	Less land used to produce same amount of yield, freeing other land for forest preservation	Polycropping, Intercropping, Fertilization, Agroforestry, Intensive pasture
Extraction of products and values from existing forest	Forest maintenance because of demonstrated market values	Selective logging, Ecotourism, Harvest of non-timber products
Reforestation	Restored forest directly replaces deforested land	Managed succession, Tree planting

McKelvey Box Classification of Biodiversity

If extraction is considered a form of sustainable development, then biodiversity is a resource to be utilized by people. In fact, each species is a potential resource. To clarify the role of species in sustainable development, Kangas (1997) pointed to the analogy of classification used for mineral deposits (McKelvey, 1972). The McKelvey box separates mineral deposits based on the knowledge of their existence and their economic concentration (Fig. 10–1). The term 'reserves' means identified deposits of sufficiently high concentrations to be mined economically. All other deposits are termed 'resources'. A hypothetical example of biodiversity (higher plants) is given in Fig. 10–2.

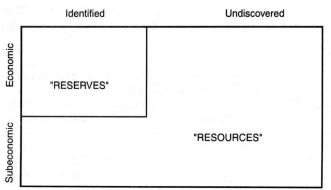

Fig. 10–1. The McKelvey box classification of geological mineral deposits (McKelvey, 1972).

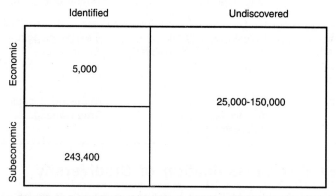

Fig. 10–2. A hypothetical McKelvey box classification of biodiversity of species of higher plants (numbers are tentative) (after Kangas, 1997).

The McKelvey box represents a single time frame. Over time, the numbers inside the box would change and the number of undiscovered species would go down. With continuing technological advances, the number of economically useful species would increase.

Obstacles to Sustainable Development

While the concept of sustainable development is attractive, there are serious and practical problems in its implementation. Some impediments to sustainable development include overharvesting of renewable resources; lack of markets for products from sustainably developed operations; short–sighted political economies that fail to properly value sustainability or the contributions of nature to economies; land–tenure problems and the uneven distribution of landholdings; Government subsidization of counter–productive land–use programs; political backlash caused by the influence of developed countries on land–use and on conservation decisions of lesser developed countries; and violent conflicts, especially over natural resources (Kangas, 1997).

Biodiversity and Sustainable Forestry

Many large forest mammals and birds, in particular top predators and forest specialists, have disappeared from large parts of Europe, and many other species of forest specialists are now endangered.

In northern Europe the principal forest types extend longitudinally and there are distinct differences between East and West. The industrial revolution intensified habitat alteration, which spread from West to East. Habitat alteration and greater control of hunting increased the population of large game herbivores and beavers (*Castor fiber*). Management of these animals generated conflict between forest and game managers. Only in remote parts of eastern Europe have forests remained relatively undisturbed and retained viable populations of many bird and insect species that are endangered in the West (Viksne, 1989; Angelstam *et al.*, 1997).

Even though compulsions of development require intensification of forest production to help local and national economies, in some cases low operational efficiency has benefited to some extent the preservation of biodiversity. But now biodiversity is being threatened by the rapid implementation of traditional non–sustainable forest management for short-term gains. There is a great need to balance forest production and environmental concerns. The focus of intensive production is in new secondary plantation forests as this can allow a reduction in the intensity of management of semi–natural forests (Colchester and Lohmann, 1993).

The challenge is to preserve biodiversity of forests while allowing for the use of a valuable natural resource, by imitating the natural spatial and temporal patterns of forest regeneration and development (Angelstam, 1996).

In 1994, Phillips and colleagues published two papers on worldwide patterns in forest turnover in the tropics. Phillips and Gentry (1994) showed a trend for increasing rates of turnover through time and Phillips *et al.* (1994) stated that high turnover was a predictor of high tree diversity. The trend for increasing turnover is most probably due to gradually increasing CO_2 concentration. High CO_2 increases plant growth, so it may be assumed that overall forest growth increases and if trees grow faster, recruitment and mortality rates (the metrics of turnover) will increase as high diversity tends to correlate with high or intermediate productivity. Even small increases in forest productivity can increase diversity. However, some criticisms of the work of Phillips *et al.* have been voiced on statistical, artefactual and theoretical grounds (see Condit, 1997). It is also doubtful whether higher turnover is due to higher forest productivity, as Phillips *et al.* claim. Possibly, high–turnover sites are not more productive, but simply more disturbed (Condit *et al.*, 1996) and these disturbances promote diversity. Likewise, moist sites may be more productive but not more dynamic (Condit, 1997). Although increased turnover may correlate with slightly higher local diversity, it is unlikely to be a driver of broad diversity patterns. Most tree species in a forest are in a small (shade–tolerant) demographic space and the added diversity in highly diverse forests is in this group. The converse may be more likely: major diversity differences may drive slight changes in forest turnover. Low-diversity forests have more uniform canopies where neighbouring trees better protect each other from wind-throw (Condit, 1997).

The idea of forest sustainability has been around in one form or another for several centuries, though its meaning has undergone changes. Broadly speaking, in the 18th century it chiefly referred to the rate of wood production, in the 19th century it meant profitability of wood production, while in the 20th century the concept has covered the whole range of effects and output of forests (Tzschupke, 1998).

Goals of forest management may be quite divergent and yet be in harmony with sustainability. For instance, maximizing financial revenue may be fully within the meaning of the modern, more comprehensive definition of sustainability, even if this involves clear-cutting and the planting of exotic trees — only there should be no infringement of the main option of pursuing any other goal of forest management after a reorientation phase, that is, to the extent such options are feasible under the prevailing local conditions. Conversely, at the opposite extreme, the complete cessation of forest management in a national park does not violate the sustainability principle because forest land in a national park can at any time be converted to other uses in case of need.

One may distinguish two categories of forest sustainability, viz. static and dynamic. Ultimately, the permanent use of a forest's effects and performance presupposes its dynamic sustainability which should be the immediate goal of any forest management. Static sustainability, by contrast, denotes the continuance of a state that permits the sustained productivity of a forest and so is an indispensable precondition for the former. It primarily requires the preservation of forest land and the stability and sustained productivity of forest soils (see Fig. 10–3).

In the forest resolution adopted at the Second Ministerial Conference on the Protection of Forests in Europe held in Helsinki in June, 1993, sustainable management was defined as 'the management and utilisation of forest areas in a manner which preserves their biological diversity, productivity, regenerative vigour, vitality, and their capability to fulfil important ecological, economic, and social functions at the local, national, and international level now and in the future and does not harm other ecosystems' (BMELF, 1994, cited in Tzschupke, 1998).

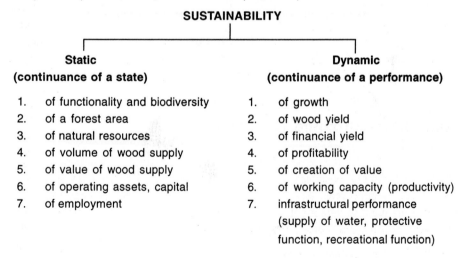

SUSTAINABILITY

Static	**Dynamic**
(continuance of a state)	**(continuance of a performance)**
1. of functionality and biodiversity	1. of growth
2. of a forest area	2. of wood yield
3. of natural resources	3. of financial yield
4. of volume of wood supply	4. of profitability
5. of value of wood supply	5. of creation of value
6. of operating assets, capital	6. of working capacity (productivity)
7. of employment	7. infrastructural performance (supply of water, protective function, recreational function)

Fig. 10–3. Two kinds of forest sustainability (after Speidel, 1972).

321

At the same conference, sustainability criteria were defined as follows:

1) Preservation and appropriate improvement of forest resources and their contribution to the global carbon cycle; 2) Preservation of the health and vitality of forest ecosystems; 3) Preservation and promotion of the productive functions of forests (wood and non-wood products); 4) Preservation and improvement of the biodiversity of forest ecosystems and of protective functions concerning forest management (in particular, soil and water); and 5) Preservation of other socioeconomic functions and aspects.

Fig. 10–4 illustrates the goals of sustainable development.

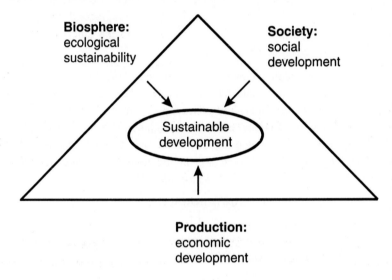

Fig. 10–4. The goals of sustainable development.

Natural Disturbance Regimes

The variety of biotopes in nature is chiefly determined by differences in soil, topography, nutrient availability and disturbance patterns. Disturbances vary along continuums — large-scale (fire, hurricanes) to small-scale, localized (gap formation, flooding); frequent to infrequent; low-intensity stand alteration to high-intensity stand replacement (Angelstam *et al.*, 1997).

Many temperate-lowland forests and boreal forests have suffered from two important stresses, viz. (1) loss and fragmentation of forests from agriculture and urbanization and (2) habitat changes in forested areas from reductions in structural complexity and malfunction of important ecological processes. Sometimes forest fragmentation per se may not increase; forest cover may be extensive and increasing, while many biotopes and complex structures suffer decreases within the forest. Over long periods of time, these two changes are reversible unless basic ecosystem attributes have been disturbed, e.g. by accumulation of toxic compounds or soil degradation and erosion. Many ecosystem characteristics and processes can thus be restored or recreated by active management (Angelstam et al., 1997).

The northern boreal forest (taiga) is the world's largest biome. Both open areas and closed–canopy areas with large trees are natural attributes of boreal forests (Kuusela, 1990). In some of these forests, intense management has contributed to marked decreases in diversity of plants and animals that are forest specialists (Angelstam, 1996). However, some remote areas in the Russian taiga are still in a near-natural state.

Effective restoration of important forest components depends on site-specific conditions influencing local disturbance regimes. Natural habitats in taiga forests have been fragmented by fire disturbance which affects three major factors; 1) Relationships between soil types, soil moisture and flammability of vegetation affect the probability of fire whose frequency tends to increase along a soil–moisture gradient from wet to dry. Parallel gradients occur from fine to coarse soils and from herbaceous vegetation to dwarf–shrubs and lichens. 2) Fire frequencies vary, depending on geomorphology and topography. Convex areas burn more frequently than concave and south slopes more frequently than north slopes. 3) Increased relative humidity over increasing longitude and altitude usually decreases fire frequency (Johnson, 1992). There usually exists an inverse relationship between fire frequency and intensity.

The pristine temperate-lowland zone typically has deciduous trees, such as beech (Fagus sylvatica), oaks (Quercus petraea and Q. robur), lime (Tilia cordata), elms (Ulmus spp.) and ash (Fraxinus excelsior). In these forests, natural secondary successions have only rarely been affected by stand–replacing perturbations such as crown and surface fires. Instead, temperate–lowland deciduous forests have suffered local and small–scale disturbances that triggered gap dynamics—wind, drought, snow and disease. Another disturbance has sometimes been caused by the impact of large herbivores (May, 1993). Semiopen woodlands are disappearing as modern forestry takes over and agriculture is intensified.

Cultivation has strongly impacted forests since time immemorial and as of today virtually all natural temperate-lowland forests have disappeared. As farmland increased, some species of non-forest vascular plants colonized the agricultural landscape. Biodiversity in forests decreased through losses and changes in forests; biodiversity in the ancient agricultural landscapes declined through intensified farming.

Riparian forests make up a fairly minor portion of any landscape but they are nevertheless important for biodiversity because they provide a corridor of vegetation in a productive environment and have properties that vary according to the hydrology of the area. Variations in flooding frequency, length and speed of inundation, and sedimentation create complex niches that make riparian forests a dynamic, species-rich system (Angelstam et al., 1997).

The chief disturbance in riparian forests is undoubtedly seasonal flooding. Unlike boreal and temperate-lowland forests, in which secondary succession predominates, riparian forests are a mixture of primary and secondary succession. In places where new islands and banks form, poplars (Populus spp.) and willows (Salix spp.) rapidly colonize the new substrate. Generally riparian communities show a vertical zonation (from forest affected only at the high-water level to shrub and herbaceous communities close to the river bed). Beavers cause flooding in some areas; extensive open drainage systems in farmland have allowed beavers to flourish, causing serious impacts on local forests.

Sustainable Forestry

Diverse disturbances have altered forests, particularly in Europe (Table 10–2). According to Angelstam et al., (1997), the following properties, important to preserve biodiversity, are now absent or uncommon in most managed forests.

1) old-growth forests and large, old trees;
2) diversified tree species composition;
3) wide range of forest structure components;
4) dead, standing, and downed trees;
5) untrained forests;
6) unregulated rivers;
7) balanced natural processes (browsing, predation, nutrient supply).

Further deterioration of forest environmental quality may be halted by the following measures:

Table 10–2. Relative importance of major natural disturbance types in three main forest types in central and northern Europe: 3 = very important; 1= less important; X = not important.

	Forest type		
Disturbance	Boreal	Temperate lowland	Riparian
Fire	3	1	x
Flooding	x	x	3
Gap phase	1	3	1
Browsing	1	1	x
Grazing	x	1	1
Wind	1	1	1
Beaver	x	x	1

1) reducing pollution levels;
2) avoiding fragmentation and isolation of forest complexes;
3) re-establishing of functional corridors and networks that allow dispersal and recolonization of species;
4) connecting fragments of wet forests along water;
5) mimicking natural disturbance in management;
6) restoring multispecies, multilayered and uneven-aged forests;
7) letting very old trees and dead wood to remain on the ground (Angelstam *et al.*, 1997).

Alternatives for Sustainable Management of Dipterocarp Residual Forests

A residual forest silvicultural system (RFSS) with no silvicultural treatment can give a potential sustained yield at 60-year felling cycle with 15% increase in harvest cut and 20% increase in growing stock. With timber stand improvement (TSI) and supplemental planting of dipterocarp species, RFSS can attain a potential sustained yield at 60–year felling cycle with 59% increase in harvest cut and 35% increase in growing stock. RFSS with TSI and supplemental planting of fast-growing species can potentially give sustained yield at 30–40 year felling cycle with 18% increase in harvest cut and 158% increase in growing stock (see Virtucio, 1997).

In some countries, e.g. the Philippines, logging has shifted from the old–growth forests to plantations and second-growth production forests. These latter generally constitute residuals of the virgin stands that have been logged under a system in which only the mature and overmature and defective trees are cut while adequate healthy residuals are left behind for the succeeding felling cycle, generally set at 35 years. Generally, under this practice trees over 60-cm diameter breast height (dbh) are cut and loggers have to leave 60% of the healthy residuals to constitute the stands for the next felling cycle (Virtucio, 1997).

A recent study was conducted on second-growth stands of about 20 years and older logged under the RFSS in the Philippines with the objective of developing suitable sustainable management regimes for the third-growth dipterocarp production forests. The effect of TSI and supplemental planting was seen with the general increase in volume per dbh class compared with no TSI and supplemental planting. Faster recruitments per dbh class due to TSI caused faster volume development in each felling cycle but was most pronounced in the 60–year felling cycle. It was observed that growing stock may not be depleted.

It was estimated that two decades after relogging, the remaining or initial growing stock would build up to about 140 cu m, from which only 46 cu m could be harvested, which is very much lower than the initial cut of 108 cu m. Extending the cutting cycle to 30 years would increase the growing stock of 180 cu m with harvestable volume of only 61 cu m, a yield still lower than the initial harvest. At 40–year felling cycle, the growing stock would reach 209 cu m with harvestable third–growth volume of 76 cu m, which is 32 cu m less than the initial second-growth harvest of 108 cu m (Virtucio, 1997).

A felling cycle of 60 years would build up the growing stock to 294 cu m and yield a harvestable volume of 123 cu m, higher than the initial harvest cut. Thus it appears that after RFSS application on the second-growth forest, the resultant third–growth stands could attain yield sustainability without silvicultural treatments at 60–year felling cycle.

Fast-growing species need to be used for supplemental planting in log landings

326

as second priority when dipterocarp species are not available. Supplemental planting with fast-growing species may be used in at most two rotations subject to research as to their possible adverse effects on the conservation of biological diversity of the natural forests (Virtucio, 1997).

Sustainable Farming

Achieving and maintaining sustainable agriculture is a major concern in several countries today. Hitherto, agricultural policies were driven chiefly by the narrow focus on maximizing short–term profits rather than long–term sustainable management of local resources by farmers. Doubtless, this is understandable from the point of view of those concerned with food security, employment, foreign exchange and population growth; however, it does not sufficiently take into account the interests of individual farmers and rural communities and does not contribute to their betterment and welfare.

The need of the hour is to reorient production and growth in harmony with sustainable resource management and to give due weightage to long-term perspectives. Sustainable agriculture can be realized well through the individual and collective activities of farmers and communities pursuing their own strategies to secure their livelihood.

There are millions of small farmers in the tropics who grow their crops under rainfed conditions in diverse and risky environments. In their struggle for survival, these people have developed countless ways of obtaining food, fibre and other useful products from plants and animals. Many different farming systems have evolved and adapted to the local ecological conditions, being intimately entwined with the local culture. These 'traditional' farming systems are not static; they have changed over the generations but most rapidly over the last few decades.

Conventional extension practices in the tropics have relied on 'modern' agriculture with high levels of external inputs, e.g. agrochemicals, hybrid seed and fuel–based mechanization, with a view to increasing production of such commodities as rice, maize and wheat. These activities have led to an overall increase in world food production but have brought little benefit to most small farmers. Indeed they have sometimes even worsened their lot by forcing them onto more marginal land while capital-intensive cropping and ranching expands over the better land.

In recent times, the adverse environmental and social impacts of high external input agriculture (HEIA) have become manifest, and new approaches are being sought for

327

agricultural development that will benefit small holders, halt degradation of natural resources and possibly improve these resources. The call for sustainable agriculture has been increasing in volume and there is a need for developing agricultural systems that focus as much attention on people as they do on technology, as much on resources as on production, as much on long-term as on short–term well-being. Only such systems may be able to meet the challenge of the next few decades.

Agriculture may be deemed to be sustainable if it is ecologically sound, economically viable, socially just, humane and adaptable. The quality of natural resources should be maintained and the vitality of the entire agroecosystem—from humans, crops and animals to soil organisms— is enhanced, by ensuring that the soil is managed and the health of crops, animals and people is maintained through biological processes (self–regulation). Local resources should be used in such a way that losses of nutrients, biomass and energy are minimal and pollution is avoided. The chief emphasis is on the use of renewable resources. Farmers should be able to produce enough for self–sufficiency and/or income, and gain sufficient returns to recover their labour and other costs involved. Resources and power should be distributed in such a way that the basic needs of all members of society are met and their rights to land–use, capital, technology and market opportunities are assured. All forms of life need to be duly respected. Rural communities should be capable of adjusting to the constantly changing conditions for farming: population growth, policies and market demand (Reijntjes *et al.*, 1992). These criteria of sustainability may occasionally conflict and can be seen from different viewpoints: those of the farmer, the community, the country and the world. A judicious balance needs to be achieved for each particular situation.

Production and consumption should be balanced on an ecologically sustainable level. Sustainability is a dynamic concept which allows for the changing needs of an increasing global population but basic ecological principles warrant that agricultural productivity has finite limits.

It is necessary to realize that many of the environmental problems of developing countries stem from overexploitation of land, extension of cropping and deforestation. Large irrigated areas are often seriously affected by salinization. Increased use of pesticides and synthetic fertilizers has caused environmental problems. Degradation of soil fertility and scarcity of fuelwood point to the gravity of the situation. Some estimates by FAO reveal that 42 developing countries lack sufficient fuelwood and can meet fuelwood needs only by depleting tree stocks; 27 countries face such acute scarcity that even overcutting would not supply their needs. In 1980 more than a billion

328

people had a deficit supply of fuelwood and over 110 million suffered an acute scarcity (Alexandratos, 1988).

Most traditional farming systems were sustainable for centuries in terms of their ability to maintain a continuing, stable level of production. These systems were exposed to strong changes during and since the colonial period: introduction of foreign education and technology in agriculture and health care; increased population pressure; and changes in sociopolitical relations. Originally subsistence-oriented systems have become increasingly market oriented and improved communication has increased the demand for consumer goods.

Farming systems in the tropics tend to change towards one of two extremes: (1) excessive use of external inputs, i.e. high external input agriculture (HEIA) and (2) intensified use of local resources with few or no external inputs, to the extent that the natural resources are degraded, i.e., low external input agriculture (LEIA). Low external input agriculture, also called resource-poor or undervalued-resource agriculture is practised in diverse highly complex risk-prone areas where the properties of the physical environment and/or the weak infrastructure do not allow widespread use of purchased inputs. Often, only small quantities of chemical fertilizers and pesticides are sporadically used and then only for a few cash crops and by a small elite group of farmers. Over one billion people depend for their livelihood on this form of agriculture. It is found in the rainfed, undulating hinterlands of developing countries—the drylands, highlands and forest lands with fragile or problematic soils. In many LEIA areas, production growth lags behind population growth. As new technologies for good sustainable land-use are not available to the farmers, they are forced to exploit their land beyond its carrying capacity. Many tropical land-use systems are in the midst of such a downward spiral of nutrient depletion, loss of vegetative cover, soil erosion, and economic, social and cultural disintegration.

In well-adapted LEIA systems, crops, trees, shrubs, herbs and animals have not only productive but also ecological functions, such as producing organic matter, creating a nutrient reservoir in the soil, natural crop protection and controlling erosion. These functions are important for the continuity and stability of farming and are involved in producing internal inputs. These systems are comparable to mature natural ecosystems, in which nearly all biomass produced is reinvested to maintain fertility and biotic stability of the system. However, reinvestment in the LEIA system is more limited since humans take out some part of the production from an agroecosystem. By replacing natural internal inputs such as manure and compost by external inputs such

329

as artificial fertilizers, more products can be extracted from the agroecosystem. Also, by replacing natural processes by human-controlled processes, such as irrigation, variability in production can be reduced.

In HEIA systems, this replacement of ecological functions by man has gone much further than in LEIA systems. Diversity is replaced by uniformity for technology efficiency and market considerations. In the short term, use of external inputs yields great increases in land-use intensity, but over a long term these increases cannot be sustained.

Traditional agriculture with its bias towards high-potential areas, export crops and affluent farmers has produced results which are out of the reach of most farmers and inappropriate for LEIA areas. This has been, *inter alia,* because of its focus on single commodities, mainly market orientation and associated nutrient leakage, disregard of environmental effects, serious neglect of rainfed areas, local resources, and indigenous knowledge, and extension of incomplete products (Reijntjes *et al.*, 1992).

External Inputs and LEIA Farmers

A few important reasons why LEIA farmers have been unwilling or unable to use various external inputs are:

1)   their non–availability or unreliable (untimely) availability because of poor commercial infrastructure and services;

2)   their high costs;

3)   they are risky and often inefficient under variable and vulnerable ecological conditions;

4)   their low profitability.

Some dangers involved in promoting the introduction of such inputs into LEIA areas include loss of diversity in the farming system, making them unstable and more vulnerable to ecological and economic risks; irretrievable loss of local genetic resources and traditional knowledge about ecologically oriented husbandry and local alternatives to purchased inputs; sociocultural breakdown and marginalization of poor farmers, and environmental damage resulting from excessive use of agrochemicals.

Other Options for LEIA

Some optional alternatives to 'green revolution' that may enable LEIA farmers to

330

develop productive and sustainable forms of agriculture are outlined below.

1. Agroecology. This is the holistic study of agroecosystems, including all environmental and human elements and focuses on their interrelationships and the processes in which they are involved. Any agricultural field is a complex system in which ecological processes such as nutrient cycling, predator/prey interactions, competition, symbiosis and successional changes occur. A good understanding of these ecological relationships and processes can allow manipulation of agroecosystems to improve production and to produce more sustainably, with fewer negative environmental or social impacts and fewer external inputs (Altieri, 1987). The sustainability of many local practices lies in the ecological models they follow. By designing farming systems that mimic nature, optimal use of sunlight, soil nutrients and rainfall is possible.

2. Indigenous Knowledge and Farming Practices. Most indigenous agricultural practices that were non–sustainable have failed to survive (e.g. shifting cultivation) as conditions changed. Nevertheless, there are several land–use systems developed by traditional farming communities that exemplify careful management of soil, water and nutrients. These are just the type of methods needed to make farming sustainable. Many traditional farmers know how to improve soil structure, water–holding capacity and nutrient and water availability without the use of artificial inputs.

The strength of indigenous farming systems arises from their effective integration of different resources and farming techniques. By integrating land–use functions (producing food, wood, conserving soil and water; protecting crops; maintaining soil fertility) and the use of a variety of biological components, food crops, fodder crops, natural pasture plants, trees, herbs, green manures etc., the stability and productivity of the farm system as a whole is greatly increased and the natural resource base is well conserved.

Low External Input and Sustainable Agriculture (LEISA)

Most farmers in developing countries have only limited access to artificial external inputs and these inputs have only a limited utility under LEIA conditions. The socio-ecological threats of 'green revolution' technology and the dangers of basing production on non–renewable energy sources as well as the strong emphasis on HEIA in agricultural development are questionable. However, it is also questionable whether we can increase global food production sufficiently without the use of such external inputs. Furthermore, even natural (as opposed to artificial) inputs can have some detrimental environmental effects (Reijntjes *et al.*, 1992).

The LEISA option is accessible to a large number of farmers and can nicely complement other forms of agricultural production. Here the emphasis is on technologies based on efficient use of local resources. LEISA refers to those forms of agriculture that optimize the use of locally available resources by combining the different components of the farm system (plants, microbes, animals, soil, water, climate and people) so that they complement each other and have the greatest possible synergistic effects; they use external inputs only to the extent really needed to provide elements that are deficient in the ecosystem and to enhance available biological, physical and human resources. In using external inputs, the focus is primarily on maximum recycling and minimum detrimental impact on the environment. The crucial aim of LEISA is not to achieve maximum production of short duration but rather to strive for a stable and adequate production level over the long term. It seeks to maintain and possibly enhance the natural resources and make maximum use of natural processes. It implies the need for effectively monitoring and managing flows of nutrients, water and energy so as to achieve a balance at a high level of production. Its management principles at different spatial levels include harvesting water and nutrients from the watershed, recycling nutrients within the farm, managing nutrient flow from farm to consumers and back again, using aquifer water judiciously, and using renewable sources of energy. It incorporates the best components of indigenous farmers' knowledge and practices, ecologically sound agriculture, conventional science and modern systems approach, agroecology and biotechnology.

While LEISA is not a panacea for the world's pressing agricultural and environmental problems, it is certainly helpful in solving some of them. It is particularly suitable for application in the hitherto neglected areas of rainfed agriculture (Reijntjes *et al.*, 1992).

The Farm As a System

Whereas scientists have traditionally divided farming into disciplines such as agronomy, pathology and economics, farmers regard farming as a whole (holistic) system that is more than the sum of the parts seen by the specialists. Farming is not merely a collection of crops and animals to which one can apply this input or that and expect immediate results. Rather, it is a complicated network of soils, plants, animals, implements, workers, other inputs and environmental influences with the strands held

332

and manipulated by the farmer who produces output from the inputs and technology available.

The term **'farming system'** means a particular arrangement of farming enterprises (e.g. cropping, livestock–keeping, processing farm products) that are managed in response to the physical, biological and socioeconomic environment, and in accordance with the farmers' aims and resources.

A variety of farming systems have developed throughout the world: e.g. nomadism, shifting cultivation, irrigated cropping, ley farming, horticulture and various combinations of these. The orientation of these systems ranges from subsistence to commercial. Several farming systems sometimes exist simultaneously in the same area. Within a farm system (Fig. 10–5), physical resources interact to create unique conditions of temperature, wind and rainfall. These conditions affect the functioning of the crops, livestock, birds, insects, weeds and micro–organisms. These living organisms interact with each other through processes such as competition, succession, symbiosis and allelopathy. These physical and biological resources and processes are consciously manipulated by the human resources within the system—the farm family with its knowledge and skills (Reijntjes *et al.*, 1992).

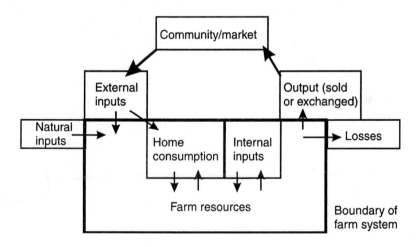

Fig. 10–5. A simple farm system (after Reijntjes *et al.*, 1992).

To be sustainable, any farm system has to achieve a certain level of production that satisfies the material (productivity) and social (identity) needs of the farm household, within certain margins of security and without much long–term resource depletion.

Farm systems are dynamic. Farm households that survive are successful because they constantly adjust themselves to change. In many places farming communities have successfully survived for generations by using only locally available resources and by relying on genetic and physical diversity.

A wide variety of crops, livestock and trees is used, primarily in ways that suit the ecological conditions. Crop mixtures enhance growth and total yield. Advantage is taken of complementarity between crops, e.g. by combining legumes and cereals in order to improve nutrient availability and control diseases. Animals are also used in a complementary way: they are fed on wastes and by-products, provide manure and protein-rich food, and serve as a buffer in case of crop failure.

Maintaining Diversity and Flexibility

The sustainability of any farm system critically depends on its flexibility under changing circumstances. The availability of a broad diversity of genetic resources at the farm level enhances this flexibility.

Biological diversity can be ensured by using mixtures of different species, mixtures of different varieties of the same species, or varieties whose genetic composition is itself variable (Jiggins, 1990). Species contribute to harvest security under unfavourable controls. Variety mixtures provide diversity in the timing of germination, flowering, growth, seed–filling and harvest.

Growing two or more crops in the same field at the same time or immediately after each other is called 'multiple cropping'. The term 'crops' generally refers to annual or biennial plants, but scientists are increasingly recognizing that perennials (trees, shrubs, grasses, herbs) can be combined advantageously with these crops and may also be considered crops themselves. Combining arable crops with woody species is termed agroforestry, agrosilviculture or multistorey cropping (a term emphasizing the design of the vegetation canopy).

In human history, the first forms of agriculture were multiple cropping systems. During the past century, technologies were developed (e.g. use of chemical fertilizers, pesticides, hybrid seed) to maximize the productive functions of cropping systems by externalizing the reproductive and protective functions. This led to specialization (sole cropping), which favoured mechanization.

Some advantages of multiple cropping for small holders are listed below.

1. Productivity of harvestable products per unit area is higher than under single cropping with the same level of management.

2. As several crops are grown, failure of one crop to produce enough can be compensated by other crops. This decreases farming risks.

3. Multiple cropping systems with perennial grasses and trees are less prone to soil erosion.

Sustainable Governance of the Oceans

The world's oceans are vital not only for sound development and sustainability of humankind but also for the health of the biosphere. But humans are exerting so much pressure on the world's resources that even the vast oceans are affected and a new paradigm for governance of ocean resources in the face of growing uncertainty has become necessary.

Five major problems that face the oceans are overfishing, ocean disposal and spills, the destruction of coastal ecosystems, land–based contamination and climate change (Costanza et al., 1998). Overfishing is the simplest of these five problems. Of the 200 major fish stocks accounting for 77% of world marine landings, 35% are currently classified as overfished. Overfishing has been decreasing the production of fish as food, limiting the economic productivity of fisheries, and diminishing genetic diversity and ecological resilience.

Principles of Sustainable Governance

Adaptive management is the key to achieving sustainable governance of the oceans. This management is integrated (across disciplines, stakeholder groups and generations). Six core principles cover the essential criteria for sustainable governance. In fact, the six principles collectively form a related group of basic guidelines governing the use of all environmental resources, including marine and coastal resources.

Principle 1 : Responsibility. Access to environmental resources carries responsibilities to use them in an ecologically sustainable, economically efficient and socially fair manner.

Principle 2 : Scale–matching. Ecological problems are seldom confined to a single scale. Decision–making on environmental resources should internalize costs and benefits. Appropriate scales of governance will be those that can integrate across scale boundaries.

Principle 3 : Precaution. There is uncertainty about some potentially irreversible environmental impacts, so decisions concerning their use should err on the side of caution. The burden of proof should shift to those whose activities potentially damage the environment.

Principle 4 : Adaptive management. Given that some level of uncertainty always exists in environmental resource management, decision–makers should collect and integrate appropriate ecological, social and economic information with the aim of adaptive improvement.

Principle 5 : Full–cost allocation. All of the internal and external costs and benefits (including social and ecological) of alternative deicsions concerning the use of environmental resources should be identified and allocated. Markets should reflect full costs.

Principle 6 : Participation. All stakeholders should be engaged in the formulation and implementation of decisions concerning environmental resources, as this contributes to sound rules and responsibilities (Costanza *et al.*, 1998).

Adhering to the above six principles can help ensure that governance of oceans is inclusive, fair, scale–sensitive, adaptive and sustainable (Costanza *et al.*, 1998).

Adverse Effects of Toxic Algal Blooms on Sustainable Management of Marine Fisheries

Throughout the world there have recently been increases in the frequency and extent of blooms of harmful marine microalgae and heterotrophic dinoflagellates. Some of these algal species are exerting significant direct and indirect influences on marine fisheries. Algal blooms produce acute lethal as well as chronic sublethal effects on fishes, including long–term changes in behaviour, increased susceptibility to diseases, depressed feeding and impaired reproduction. For some harmful algal species, indirect impacts that promote critical habitat loss or disrupt the microbial food web balance have also been documented (Burkholder, 1998). Certain 'red tide' dinoflagellates often increase independent of human influences other than physical transport. But some newly discovered toxic algal species have been correlated with cultural eutrophication in poorly flushed fish nursery grounds such as estuaries and coastal waters (Burkholder, 1998). Outbreaks of certain warm–optimal species have coincided with El Niño events, suggesting that warming trends in global climate change probably stimulate their growth and broaden or shift their range.

In the last few decades the ocean's fishing grounds with harvest efforts have been increasing and several wild stocks have been declining (Holmes, 1994). Also, more subtle but significant influences on fish populations have tended to be ignored in policy considerations (Beddington, 1995).

During the last few years there has been a global increase in marine microalgae that are not only harmful to finfish and shellfish, but also to their human consumers (Shumway, 1995) Over 55 species of toxic dinoflagellates (Pyrrhophyta, Desmophyceae and Dinophyceae) have been recorded so far. The most widespread form of shellfish contamination by harmful marine phytoplankton is paralytic shellfish poisoning (PSP; from saxitoxin and derivatives), caused by certain dinoflagellates. Other human diseases linked to toxic marine algae include diarrhoeal, neurotoxic and amnesic shellfish poisoning (DSP, from okadaic acid and other toxins; NSP, from brevetoxins; and ASP, from domoic acid respectively. Most of these are caused by dinoflagellates, except for ASP, which has been tracked to certain benthic diatoms (Bacillariophyceae) that formerly were considered benign (*Pseudonitzschia* spp; Table 10–3; Wright *et al.*, 1989; Maranda *et al.*, 1990; Fritz *et al.*, 1992; Lundholm *et al.*, 1994). Another group of dinoflagellate toxins (the ciguatoxins or ciguateratoxins of benthic species, e.g., *Gambierdiscus toxicus* and *Prorocentrum micans*) causes various physiological impacts on humans ranging from mild diarrhoea to neurological dysfunction and death. Ciguatera finfish poisoning (CFP) is a very common harmful microalgae-related intoxication to humans from finfish. The marine blue-green alga *Trichodesmium erythraeum* also has toxins with ciguatera-like properties.

Most of these algae produce endotoxins that become troublesome to humans who consume shellfish (in PSP, DSP, NSP and ASP) that have accumulated the toxins by filter-feeding and concentrating the algae. Carnivorous gastropods, crustaceans and finfish (e.g., barracuda, grouper and mackerel whose consumption causes CFP) bioaccumulate the toxins as well from feeding on lower order consumers (Shumway, 1995). Acute effects of most of these toxins on finfish and shellfish are well known especially for the brevetoxins responsible for massive fish kills in low densities (≥ 300

337

Table 10–3. Some connections between harmful marine algae and anthropogenic nutrient loading to coastal waters. ('harmful' includes non–toxic as well as toxic species) (condensed from Burkholder, 1998)

Alga	Link to cultural eutrophication
Chattonella antiqua, Gymnodinium mikimotor, Gonyaulax polygramma, Noctiluca scintillans	Blooming under cumulative loading of poorly treated sewage and other wastes, coinciding with human population growth.
Pfiesteria piscicida	Most kills occur in P– and N–enriched estuaries (e.g., near phosphate mining, sewage inputs, or animal waste operations). Preys upon flagellated algae that are stimulated by inorganic nutrients.
Prorocentrum minimum	Blooms coincide with cumulative high loading of N from sewage, agricultural runoff and atmospheric loading.
Prymnesium parvum	Toxic outbreaks occur under eutrophic conditions.
Pseudonitzschia spp.	Linked with sewage and other wastes, associated with hypereutrophic conditions, anthropogenic nutrient loading and drought.

cells/mL) and for some saxitoxin–producing species that are lethal to larvae and juveniles of commercially important finfish. The toxic predatory dinoflagellate *Pfiesteria piscicida* directly attacks live fish and their fresh tissues (Steidinger *et al.*, 1996). It produces certain lipophilic exotoxin(s) that kill finfish and shellfish. Ciguatoxins seem to have a chronic role in causing disease and reducing long–term survival of reef finfishes. They are neurotoxic, haemolytic, and/or haemoagglutinating. They can be lipid– or water–soluble and are regarded as the most widespread and least understood of the dinoflagellate toxins.

Direct parasitism by non–toxic marine dinoflagellates is another common mechanism of fish death, mass mortalities in finfish and shellfish (Burkholder, 1998). Not only directly toxic and sublethal chronic effects, but also more insidious effects of toxic dinoflagellates and chrysophytes, harmful brown–tide organisms, estuarine/marine blue–green algae, and parasitic dinoflagellates have been documented on fish prey fish recruitment, reproduction, and immune system function, and possibly even to higher trophic levels such as mammals (Table 10–4), which would directly or indirectly affect fish diversity through trophic interactions.

Designing sustainable management approaches to mitigating impacts from harmful marine microalgae and heterotrophic dinoflagellates on marine fisheries would not only require proper identification and knowledge of the life cycles of the causal organisms and their toxins, but also better understanding of climatic influences, nutritional controls and potential biocontrol feedbacks.

Table 10–4. Selected examples of chronic or sublethal, direct and indirect impacts of harmful estuarine/marine phytoplankton on finfish and shellfish and their associated food webs (after Burkholder, 1998)

Impact	Causative agent	Affected species
NATIVE FINFISH		
Lethargy	*Pfiesteria piscicida*	Atlantic croaker, Atlantic menhaden, red drum, southern flounder, striped bass
Impaired swimming behaviour, loss of balance and appetite; increased vulner– ability to predators	*Gymnodinium breve, Alexandrium* spp., *Gonyaulax polyedra, P. piscicida, Gambierdiscus toxicus*	Various species
Mucus production, suffocation	*Chaetoceros concavicornis*	Chinook salmon
Loss of selective cell permeability in gills	*Prymnesium parvum, Chrysochromulina polylepis*	Various finfish and shellfish
Edema and degenerative change of the epithelium	*Heterosigma akashiwo*	Chinook salmon
Pathological changes in gills, liver, and intestines; blanching of skin	*Gambierdiscus toxicus*	Several species
Hepatic disease	Blue–green algae (microcystin from feed)	Cultured Atlantic salmon
Ulcerative diseases	*Pfiesteria* species	Atlantic menhaden, American eel, Atlantic croaker, pinfish, red drum, river herring, southern flounder, striped bass, white perch
NATIVE SHELLFISH		
Altered feeding	*Alexandrium* spp., *Pfiesteria piscicida, Gyrodinium aureolum*	Various molluscs, Pacific oyster, Shellfish spp., Scallops, mussels
Increased mucus production	*Alexandrium* spp.	Mollusca
Poor shell growth	*Prorocentrum minimum, Chrysochromulina polylepis*	Eastern oyster mussels

Table 10–4 cont'd.

Poor growth	*Gyrodinium aureolum*	Mussels
Shell disease	*Pfiesteria piscicida*	Blue crab
Inhibition of feeding	*Prorocentrum minimum*	Bay scallop, eastern oyster
Neoplasia	*Prorocentrum minimum*	Oysters
Mantle and gill lesions	*Gyrodinium aureolum*	Eastern oyster
Blood, gastrointestinal, and reproductive diseases	Parasitic dinoflagellate spp.	Various decapod crustaceans
Improper settling	*Pfiesteria piscicida*	Eastern oyster
Recruitment failure	*Gymnodinium breve*	Bay scallop

FOOD RESOURCES AND HABITAT

Reduced fecundity of zooplankton	*Chrysochromulina polylepis; Pfiesteria piscicida Pseudonitzschia pungens, Aureococcus anophagefferens*	Microcrustaceans, rotifers
Castration and feminization	Parasitic dinoflagellate spp.	Microcrustaceans, ciliates
Mortality of zooplankton and other microfauna	*Chattonella marina*	Microcrustaceans tintinnids
Phytoplankton mortality	*Chrysochromulina polylepis*	Dinoflagellate (*Heterocapsa*)
Reduced growth of microflora and microfauna	*C. polylepis*	Diatoms, ciliates, heliozoans
Gill clogging, breathing impairment	*Trichodesmium erythraeum*	Sharks

References

Abramovitz, J.N. Investing in biological diversity: U.S. Research and Conservation Efforts in Developing countries. WRI, Washington, DC (1991).

Adams, P.W., Hairston, A.B. Calling all experts–using science to direct policy. *J. For.* 94: 27–39 (1996).

Agardy, T.S. *Marine Protected Areas and Ocean Conservation.* Acad. Press, NY (1997).

Aksornkoae, S., Thailand. In: Umali, R.M. (ed). *Mangroves of Asia and the Pacific. Status and Management,* pp. 131–150. Technical Report of the UNDP/UNESCO Research and Training Pilot Programme on Mangrove Ecosystems in Asia and the Pacific. Quezon City, Metro Manila (1987).

Alexandratos, N. *World Agriculture Toward 2000: An FAO Study.* FAO/Belhaven Press, Rome/London (1988).

Alpert, P. Applying ecological research at integrated conservation and development projects. *Ecol. Appl.* 5: 857–860 (1995).

Altieri, M.A. *Agroecology: The Scientific Basis of Alternative Agriculture.* Westview Press, Boulder, CO (1987).

Altieri, M.A., Anderson, M.K. Peasant farming systems, agricultural modernization and the conservation of crop genetic resources in Latin America. In : Fiedler, P.L., Jain, S.K. (eds.) *Conservation Biology: The Theory and Practice of Nature Conservation, Preservation and Management,* pp. 49–64. Chapman & Hall, NY (1992).

Andersen, T. *Pelagic Nutrient Cycles.* Springer, Berlin (1997).

Angel, M.V. Biodiversity of the pelagic ocean. *Conserv. Biol.* 7: 760–72 (1993).

Angelstam, P. Ghost of forest past–natural disturbance regimes as a basis for reconstruction of biologically diverse forests in Europe. In : DeGraaf, R., Miller, R.I. (eds.) *Conservation of Faunal Diversity in Forested Landscapes,* pp. 287–336. Chapman & Hall, London (1996).

Angelstam, P.K., Anufriev, V.M., Balciauskas, L., Blagovidov, K.A., Borgegård, Hodge, S.J., Majewski, P., Ponomarenko, S.V., Shvarts, E.A., Tishkov, A.A., Tamialojc, L., Wesolowski, T. Biodiversity and sustainable forestry in European forests: how East and West can learn from each other. *Wildlife Soc. Bull.* 25: 38–48 (1997).

Anonymous. Conserving the World's Biological Diversity: How can Britain Contribute? Proc. of Seminar, Dept. Environment and Natural History Museum, London, 13–14 June, 1991. Deptt. Environment, London (1991).

Anonymous. Animal alarm. *Seedling Newsletter.* Genetic Resources Action International (GRAIN). Barcelona, pp. 3–10 (March 1994).

Arnold, M.L. *Natural Hybridization and Evolution.* Oxford Univ. Press, Oxford (1997).

Arora, R.K., Nair, E.R. *Wild Relatives of Crop Plants in India.* NBPGR Sci. Monogr. No. 7. National Bureau of Plant Genetic Resources, New Delhi, p. 90 (1984).

Ashley, J., Khatiwada, B. Local wheat makes the grade in Nepal. *Appropriate Tech. J.,* Vol. 18, No. 4, IT Pub., London (1992).

Atherton, P. First aid plant. *Chem. in Britain,* pp. 33–36 (May 1998).

Baines, G. Lessons for modern management from the South Pacific. *Appropriate Tech. J.* Vol. 22, No. 2, IT. Pub., London (1995).

Balmford, A., Long, A. Avian endemism and forest loss. *Nature* 372: 623–624 (1994).

Balmford, A., Green, M.J.B., Murray, M.G. Using higher–taxon richness as a surrogate for species richness: I. Regional tests. *Proc. R. Soc. London Ser. B.* 263: 1267–1274 (1996a).

Balmford, A., Jayasuriya, A.H.M., Green, M.J.B. Using higher–taxon richness as a surrogate for species richness: II. Local application. *Proc. R. Soc. London Ser. B* 263: 1571–1575 (1996b).

Barbier, E.B., Burgess, J.C., Folke, C. *Paradise Lost? The Ecological Economics of Biodiversity.* Earthscan, London (1994).

Barraclough, T.G., Vogler, A.P., Harvey, P.H. Revealing the factors that promote speciation. *Phil. Trans. R. Soc. Lond.* 353: 241–249 (1998).

Baskin, Y. Ecosystem function of biodiversity. *BioScience* 44: 657–660 (1995).

Batisse, M. A challenge for biodiversity conservation and regional development. *Environment* 39: 7–33 (1997).

Bawa, K.S. The riches of tropical forests: Non–timber products. *Trends Ecol. Evol. (TREE)* 7: 361–363 (1992).

Beddington, J. The primary requirements. *Nature* 374: 213–214 (1995).

Begon, M., Harper, J.L., Townsend, C.R. *Ecology: Individuals, Populations and Communities.* Blackwell, Oxford (1986).

Bengtsson, J., Jones, H., Setälä, H. The value of biodiversity. *TREE* 12: 334–337 (1997).

Bennett, E. Plant introduction and genetic conservation: genecological aspects of an urgent world problem. In : *Scottish Plant Breeding Station Records*, pp. 27–113. UK (1965).

Bennett, E. FAO/IBP. Technical Conference on the Exploration, Utilization and Conservation of Plant Genetic Resources. FAO, Rome (1968).

Bennett, E. Adaptation in wild and cultivated plant populations. In: Frankel, O.H., Bennett, E. (eds.) *Genetic Resources in Plants: Their Exploration and Conservation,* pp. 115–129. IBP Handbook No. 11. Blackwell Sci. Pub., Oxford (1970).

Berger, L., Speare, R., Daszak, P. and 11 others. Chytridiomycosis causes amphibian mortality associated with population declines in the rain forests of Australia and Central America. *Proc. Natl. Acad. Sci.* USA 95: 9031–9036 (1998).

Bibby, C.J., Collar, N.J., Crosby, M.J., Heath, M.F., Imboden, C., Johnson, T.H., Long, A.J., Stattersfied, A.J., Thirgood, S.J. Putting biodiversity on the map: Priority areas for global conservation. ICBP Cambridge (1992).

Blockstein, D.E., Tordoff, H.B. Gone forever: a contemporary look at the extinction of the passenger pigeon. *Amer. Birds* 39: 845–851 (1985).

BMELF. *Nationaler Waldbericht der Bundesrepublik.* Bonn (1994).

Boo, E. *Ecotourism: The Potentials and Pitfalls,* Vols. 1–2. WWF, Washington (1990).

Bradshaw, A.D. The reclamation of derelict land and the ecology of ecosystems. In: Jordan, W.R., Gilpin , M.E., Aber, J.D. (eds.) *Restoration Ecology. A Synthetic Approach to Ecological Research,* pp. 53–74. Camb. Univ. Press, Cambridge (1990).

Bradshaw, A.D. Alternative endpoints for reclamation. In : Cairns, J. (ed.) *Rehabilitating Damaged Ecosystems* (2 ed.) pp. 165–185. CRC Press, Boca Raton, FLA (1995).

Briggs, J.C. Species diversity: land and sea compared. *Syst. Biol.* 43: 130–135 (1994).

Brooks, J.L. Speciation in ancient lakes. *Q. Rev. Biol.* 25: 30–60, 131–176 (1950).

Brown, K., Pearce, D., Perrings, C., Swanson, T. *Economics and the Conservation of Global Biological Diversity.* Global Environment Facility. The World Bank, Washington, DC (1993).

Brown, M., Wyckoff-Baird, B. Designing Integrated Conservation and Development Projects, The Biodiversity Support Program. WWF, Baltimore, MD (1992).

Brown, S., Lugo, A.E. The storage and production of organic matter in tropical forests and their role in the global carbon cycle. *Biotropica* 14: 161–187 (1982).

Brune, A. Termite guts: the world's smallest bioreactors. *TIBTECH* 16: 16–21 (1998).

Brunner, R.I., Bott, T.L. Reduction of mercury to the elemental state by a yeast. *Appl. Microbiol.* 27: 870–73 (1974).

Buchalo, A.S., Nevo, E., Wasser, S.P., Oren, A., Molitoris, H.P. Fungal life in the extremely hypersaline water of the Dead Sea: first records. *Proc. R. Soc. Lond.* B 265: 1461–1465 (1998).

Burkholder, J.M. Implications of harmful microalgae and heterotrophic dinoflagellates in management of sustainable marine fisheries. *Ecol. Appl.* 8 (1): Suppl. S37–S62 (1998).

Burton, J.A. A bibliography of red data books. *Oryx* 18: 61–64 (1984).

Cairns, J., Heckman, J.R. Restoration ecology: The state of an emerging field. *Ann. Rev. Energy Environ.* 21: 167–189 (1996).

Caldecott, J. *Designing Conservation Projects.* Camb. Univ. Press, Cambridge (1996).

Caley, M.J., Schluter, D. The relationship between local and regional diversity. *Ecology* 78: 70–80 (1997).

Caley, M.J., Schluter, D. The relationship between local and regional diversity: reply. *Ecology* 79: 1827–1829 (1998).

Callicott, J.B. A review of some problems with the concept of ecosystem health. *Ecosystem Health* 1: 101–112 (1995).

Champion, H.G., Seth, S.K. *A Revised Survey of Forest Types in India and Burma.* Manager Pub., New Delhi (1968).

Chapin, F.S., Schulze, E.D., Mooney, H.A. Biodiversity and ecosystem processes. *TREE* 7: 107–108 (1992).

Chapman, V.J. Mangrove phytosociology. *Trop. Ecol.* 2: 1–19 (1970).

Charan, A.K. Phytogeography of Western Rajasthan, Ph.D. thesis, Univ. Jodhpur (1978).

Charan, A.K., Sen, D.N. The distribution of *Calligonum polygonoides* L. in Western Rajasthan, India–A phytogeographical appraisal. *J. Arid Environ.* 8: 121–131 (1985).

Chertas, J., Fanton, M. *The Seed Savers Handbook.* Grover Books, London (1996).

Chivian, E., McCally, M., Hu, H., Haines, A. *Critical Condition, Human Health and the Environment.* MIT Press, Cambridge, MA (1994).

Claridge, M.F., Boddy, L. Species recognition systems in insects and fungi. In: Hawksworth, D.L. (ed.). *The Identification and Characterization of Pest Organisms,* pp. 261–74. CAB Intl., Wallingford (1994).

Colchester, M., Lohmann, L. (eds.). *The Struggle for Land and the Fate of the Forests.* World Rainforest Movement, Penang (1993).

Colwell, R.K. Towards a unified approach to the study of species diversity. In: Grassle, J.F., Patil, G.P., Smith, W., Taillie, C. (eds.) *Ecological Diversity in Theory and Practice,* pp. 75–91. Intl. Coop. Pub. House, Fairland (1984).

Colwell, R.K., Coddington, J.A. Estimating terrestrial biodiversity through extrapolation. *Phil. Trans. R. Soc. Lond.* B 345: 101–118 (1994).

Colwell, R.R. Microbial biodiversity and biotechnology. In : Reaka–Kudla, M.L. *et al.* (eds.) *Biodiversity, II,* pp. 279–298. J. Henry Press, Washington, DC (1997).

Condit, R. Forest turnover, diversity, and CO_2. *TREE* 12: 249–250 (1997).

Condit, R., Hubbell, S.P., Foster, R.B. Assessing the response of plant functional types in tropical forests to climatic change. *J. Veg. Sci.* 7: 403–416 (1996).

Connell, J.H. Some mechanisms producing structure in natural communities: A model and evidence from field experiments. In: Cody, M.L., Diamond, J. (eds.) *Ecology and Evolution of Communities,* pp. 460–490. Harvard Univ. Press, Cambridge, MA (1975).

Connell, J.H. Diversity in tropical rain forests and coral reefs. *Science* 199: 1302–1310 (1978).

Cook, R.J. Challenges and rewards of sustainable agriculture research and education. In : *Sustainable Agriculture Research and Education in the Field,* pp. 32–76. Natl. Acad. Press, Washington, DC (1991).

Cook, S. A diversity of approaches to the study of species richness. *TREE* 13: 340–341 (1998).

Costanza, R. *et al.* The value of the world's ecosystem services and natural capital. *Nature* 387: 253–260 (1997).

Costanza, R., Andrade, F., Antunes, P., van den Belt, M., Boersma, D., Boesch, D.F., Catarino, F., Hanna, S., Limburg, K., Low, B., Molitor, M., Pereira, J.G., Rayner, S., Santos, R., Wilson, J., Young, M. Principles for sustainable governance of the oceans. *Science* 281: 198–199 (1998).

Cousins, S.H. *TREE* 6: 190–192 (1991).

Cropper, A. Small is vulnerable. *Our Planet* 6 (1): 9–12. UNEP, Nairobi (1994).

Crozier, R.H. Preserving the information content of species: Genetic diversity, phylogeny, and conservation worth. *Ann. Rev. Ecol. Syst.* 28: 243–268 (1997).

CSE. *The State of India's Environment.* 1984–85. Centre for Science and Environment, New Delhi (1985).

Dallmeier, F. (ed.). Long-term Monitoring of Biological Diversity in Tropical Forest Areas. MAB Digest No. 11. UNESCO, Paris (1992).

Daniels, R.J.R. A landscape approach to conservation of birds. *J. Biosci.* 19: 503–509 (1994).

DeAngelis, D.L. *Dynamics of Nutrient Cycling and Food Webs.* Chapman & Hall, London (1992).

DeAngelis, D.L. Nutrients, algae and grazers. *TREE* 13: 127 (1997).

Delong, E.F., Wu, K.Y., Prezelin, B.B., Jovine, R.V.M. High abundance of Archaea in Antarctic marine picoplankton. *Nature* 371: 695–697 (1994).

Dempsey, G.J. *Genetic Diversity and Disease Resistance in Crops: Two Debates over the Conservation and Use of Plant Genetic Resources.* Univ. Sussex Press, Sussex (1990).

Dhindsa, M.S., Saini, H.K. Agricultural ornithology: an Indian perspective. *J. Biosci.* 19: 391–402 (1994).

Diamond, J.M. Factors controlling species diversity: overview and synthesis. *Annals Missouri Botanical Garden* 75: 117–29 (1988).

Diamond, J.M. The present, past and future of human–caused extinction. *Phil. Trans. R. Soc. London* B. 25: 469–478 (1989).

Dietz, J.M. Conservation of biodiversity in neotrpical primates. In: Reaka–Kudla, M.L. *et al.* (eds.). *Biodiversity II,* pp. 341–356. J. Henry Press, Washington, DC (1997).

Dinerstein, E., Wikramanayake, E.D. Beyond hot spots: How to prioritize investments to conserve biodiversity in the Indo–Pacific region? *Conserv. Biol.* 7: 53–65 (1993).

Dobson, A. Biodiversity and human health. *TREE* 10: 390–391 (1995).

Dobson, A., Absher, R. How to pay for tropical rain forests. *TREE* 6: 348–351 (1991).

Dominey, W.J. Effects of sexual selection and life history on speciation: Species flocks in African cichlids and Hawaiian *Drosophila*. In: Echelle, A.A., Kornfield, I. (eds.) *Evolution of Fish Species Flocks,* pp. 231–249. Univ. Maine Press, Orono, ME (1984).

Dunlap, W.C., Yamamoto, Y. Small–molecule antioxidants in marine organisms: antioxidant activity of mycosporine–glycine. *Comp. Biochem. Physiol.* 112B: 105–114 (1995).

Dworkin, R. *Life's Dominion.* Vintage Press, NY (1994).

Ehrenfeld, D.W. Why put a value on biodiversity? In : Wilson, E.O., Peter, F.M. (eds.) *Biodiversity,* pp. 212–216. Nat. Acad. Press, Washington, DC (1988).

Ehrenfeld, J.G., Toth, L.A. Restoration ecology and the ecosystem perspective. *Restoration Ecology* 5: 307–317 (1997).

Ehrlich, P. *The Machinery of Nature.* Simon and Schuster, NY (1986).

Ehrlich, P.R., Ehrlich, A.H. *Extinction: The Causes and Consequences of the Disappearance of Species.* Random House, NY (1981).

Ehrlich, P.R., Ehrlich, A.H. *The Population Explosion.* Simon and Schuster, NY (1990).

Ehrlich, P.R., Ehrlich, A.H. The value of biodiversity. *Ambio* 21: 219–226 (1992).

Ehrlich, P.R., Ehrlich, A.H., Daily, G.C. *The Stork and the Plow: The Equity Answer to the Human Dilemma.* Putnam, NY (1995).

Ehrlich, P.R., Wilson, E.O. Biodiversity studies: Science and policy. *Science* 253: 758–762 (1991).

Elliott, N.G., Ward, R.D. Enzyme variation in orange roughy, *Hoplostethus atlanticus* (Teleostei: Trachichthyidae), from southern Australian and New Zealand waters. *Aust. J. Mar. Freshwat. Res.* 43: 1561–1571 (1992).

Elton, C. *The Ecology of Animals.* Methuen, London (1933).

Embley, T.M., Hirt, R.P., Williams, D.M. Biodiversity at the molecular level: the domains, kingdoms and phyla of life. *Phil. Trans. R. Soc. Lond.* B. 345: 21–33 (1994).

Erwin, R.L. An evolutionary basis for conservation strategies. *Science* 253: 750–752 (1991).

Erwin, T.L. Tropical forests. Their richness in Coleoptera and other arthropod species. *Coleopt. Bull.* 36: 74–75 (1982).

Erwin, T.L. Biodiversity at its utmost: Tropical forest beetles. In : Reaka–Kudla, M.L., Wilson, D.E., Wilson, E.O. (eds.) *Biodiversity II.* pp. 27–40. J. Henry Press, Washington, DC (1997).

Estes, J.A., Palmisano, J.F. Sea otters: Their role in structuring nearshore communities. *Science* 185: 1058–1060 (1974).

Etter, R.J., Grassle, J.F. Patterns of species diversity in the deep sea as a function of sediment particle size diversity. *Nature* 360: 576–578 (1992).

Ewel, J.J. Differences between wet and dry successional tropical ecosystems. *Geo–Eco–Trop.* 1: 103–177 (1977).

Ewel, J.J. Succession, In: F.B. Golley (ed.) *Tropical Rain Forest Ecosystems: Structure and Function,* pp. 217–223. Elsevier, Amsterdam (1983).

Fairlie, S., Hagler, M., O'Riordan, N.J. The politics of overfishing. *The Ecologist* 25: 5 (June, 1995).

Faith, D.P. Systematics and conservation: on predicting the feature diversity of subsets of taxa. *Cladistics* 8: 361–373 (1993).

Faith, D.P. Phylogenetic pattern and the quantification of organismal biodivesity. *Phil. Trans. R. Soc. Lond.* B 345: 45–58 (1994).

FAO. *Harvesting Nature's Diversity.* FAO, Rome (1993).

FAO. *Global Plan of Action for the Conservation and Sustainable Utilization of Plant Genetic Resources for Food and Agriculture.* FAO, Rome (1996).

FAO. *The State of the World's Plant Genetic Resources for Food and Agriculture.* Background Documentation prepared for the International Technical Conference on Plant Genetic Resources, 17–23 June 1996. FAO UN, Rome (1996).

FAO/IPGRI. *Genebank Standards.* FAO UN, Rome/IPGRI, Rome (1994).

Farnsworth, N.R. Screening plants for new medicines. In : Wilson, E.O., Peter, F.M. (eds.). *Biodiversity,* pp. 83–97. Natl. Acad. Press, Washington, DC (1988).

Farrell, B.D., Dussourd, D.E., Mitter, C. Escalation of plant defense: do latex and resin canals spur plant diversification? *Amer. Nat.* 138: 881–900 (1991).

Feder, H.M. Cleaning symbiosis in the marine environment. In Henry, S.M. (ed.) *Symbiosis,* pp. 327–380. Acad. Press, NY (1966).

Fenical, W. Marine bacteria: developing a new chemical resource. *Chem. Rev.* 93: 1673–1683 (1993).

Fitter, A. Black box or Pandora's box? *TREE* 10: 88–89 (1995).

Fitter, R., Fitter, M. *The Road to Extinction.* IUCN, Gland, Switzerland (1987).

Flessa, K.A. Causes and consequence of extinction. In : Raup, D.M., Jablonski, D. (eds.) *Patterns and Processes in the History of Life,* pp. 235–257. Springer-Verlag, Berlin (1986).

Florey, P.L., Humphreys, C.J., Vane-Wright, R.I. (eds.). *Systematics and Conservation Evaluation,* pp. 327–350: Clarendon, Oxford (1994).

Folke, C., Holling, C.S., Perrings, C. Biological diversity, ecosystems and the human scale. *Ecol. Appl.* 6: 1018–1024 (1996).

Fong, F.W. Nipa swamps — a neglected mangrove resource. Asian Sympos. Mangrove Environment. Res. Management, Kuala Lumpur (1980).

Freeman, S., Rodriguez, R.J. Genetic conversion of a fungal plant pathogen to a non-pathogenic, endophytic mutualist. *Science* 260: 75–78 (1993).

Frankel, O.H. Invasion and evolution of plants in Australia and New Zealand. *Caryologia* 6: 600–619 (1954).

Frankel, O.H. Genetic resources: the founding years. *Diversity,* No. 7. Washington, DC (1985).

Fritz, L., Quilliam, M.A., Wright, J.L.C., Beale, A.M., Work, T.M. An outbreak of domoic acid poisoning attributed to the pennate diatom *Pseudonitzchia australis. J. Phycol.* 28: 439–442 (1992).

Fuhrman, J.A., McCallum, K., Davis, A.A. Phylogenetic diversity of subsurface marine microbial communities from the Atlantic and Pacific oceans. *Appl. Environ. Microbiol.* 59: 1294–1302 (1993).

Funch, P., Kristensen, R.M. Cycliophora is a new phylum with affinities to Entoprocta and Ectoprocta. *Nature* 378: 711–714 (1995).

Gadgil, M. Social restraints on resource utilization: the Indian experience. In : McNeely, J.A., Pitt, D. (eds.) *Culture and Conservation: The Human Dimension in Environmental Planning,* pp. 135–154. Croom Helm, London (1985).

Gadgil, M. Conserving India's biodiversity: the societal context. *Evolutionary Trends in Plants* 5: 3–8 (1991).

349

Gadgil, M. Conserving biodiversity as if people matter: a case study from India. *Ambio* 21: 266–270 (1992).

Gadgil, M. Deploying student power to monitor India's lifescape. *Current Sci.* 71: 688–697 (1996).

Gadgil, M., Meher-Homji, V.M. Localities of great significance to conservation of India's biological diversity. *Proc. Ind. Acad. Sci.* (Anim. Sci./Plant Sci.) Suppl., pp. 165–180 (1986).

Gadgil, M., Devasia, P., Seshagiri Rao, P.R. Following up on the Convention on Biological Diversity: An Indian agenda. Centre for Ecol Sci., Ind. Inst. Sci., Bangalore (1995).

Gajadhar, A.A., Marquardt, W.C., Hall, R., Gunderson, J., Carmona, E.V.A., Sogin, M.L. Ribosomal RNA sequences of *Sarcocystis murin, Theileria annulata,* and *Crypthecodinium cohnil* — renal evolutionary relationship among apicocomplexans, dinoflagellates, and ciliates. *Mol. Biochem. Parasitol.* 45: 47–154 (1991).

Ganeshaiah, K.N., Chandrashekara, K., Kumar, A.R.V. Avalanche Index : A new measure of biodiversity based on biological heterogeneity of the communities. *Current Sci.* 73: 128–133 (1997).

Ganeshaiah, K.N., Uma Shaankar, R. Sensing and mapping of biological resources for conservation. *Current Sci.* 75: 176 (1998).

Garcia, N. Current situation, trends and prospects in world capture fisheries. Paper presented Conf. Fisheries Management, Seattle, Wash., USA, June 1994. FAO Fisheries Dept. Rome (1994).

Garcia-Brokhausen, S. Genetic resources. *GATE Newsletter* (Eschborn) 2/97: 18–22 (June, 1997).

Gaston, K.J. The magnitude of global insect species richness. *Conserv. Biol.* 5: 283–296 (1991).

Gaston, K.J. Regional numbers of insect and plant species. *Funct. Ecol.* 6: 243–247 (1992).

Gaston, K.J. What is biodiversity? In : Gaston, K.J., (ed.) *Biodiversity,* pp. 1–9. Blackwell, Oxford (1996).

Gaston, K.G. Spatial patterns of species description: How is our knowledge of the global insect fauna growing? *Biol. Conserv.* 67: 37–40 (1994).

Gaston, K.G., Mound, L.A. Taxonomy, hypothesis testing and the biodiversity crisis. *Phil. Trans. R. Soc. London* 251 B: 139–142 (1993).

Gaussen, H. Theories et classification des climats et des microclimat. *Proc. 8th Internat. Bot. Congr.* (Paris) Sec. 7, pp. 125–130 (1954).

Gaussen, H., Legris, P., Gupta, R.K., Meher-Homji, V.M. International map of vegetation and environmental conditions. Sheet Rajputana. ICAR, New Delhi, Institute Francais, Pondicherry, *Trav. Sec. Sci. Tech. Hors. Serie.* No. 17 (1971).

Gentry, A.H. Tree species richness of upper Amazonian forests. *PNAS* (USA) 85: 156–159 (1988).

Gess, F.W., Gess, S.K. Effects of increasing land utilization on species representation and diversity of aculeate wasps and bees in the semi–arid areas of southern Africa. In : LaSalle, S.J., Gould, I.D. (eds.) *Hymenoptera and Biodiversity,* pp. 83–113. CAB Intl., Wallingford (1991).

Gilpin, M. Community–level competition: asymmetrical dominance. *PNAS* (USA) 91: 3252–3254 (1994).

Gleason, H. The individualistic concept of the plant association. *Bull. Torrey Bot. Club* 53: 1–20 (1926).

Goodman, S.M., Patterson, B.D. (eds.). *Natural Change and Human Impact in Madagascar.* Smithsonian Inst. Press, Washington, DC (1997).

Gorham, E. Shoot height, weight and standing crop in relation to density of monospecific plant stands. *Nature* 279: 148–150 (1979).

Grassle, J.F., Lasserre, P., MacIntyre, A.D., Ray, G.C. Marine biodiversity and ecosystem function: A proposal for an international research program. *Biol. Int.* Special Issue No. 23, IUBS, Paris (1991).

Gray, J.S. *Marine biodiversity: patterns, threats and conservation needs.* GESAMP Studies 6: 1–24. Intl. Maritime Org. London (1997).

Greenwood, P.H. Cichlid fishes of Lake Victoria, East Africa: The biology and evolution of a species flock. *Bull. Brit. Mus. Nat. Hist.* (Zool.) Suppl. 6: 1–134 (1974).

Greenwood, P.H. *The Haplochromine Fishes of the East African Lakes.* Kraus Internat. Publ., Munich (1981).

Gregor, J.W. Genotypic environmental interaction and its bearing on a practical problem of international interest. In : Proc. VII Intl. Grasslands Congress. Palmerston North, 5, pp. 3–11 (1956).

Grizzle, R.E. Environmentalism should include human ecological needs. *BioScience* 44: 263–268 (1994).

Groombridge, B. (ed.) *Global Biodiversity Status of the Earth's Living Resources.* Chapman & Hall, London (1992).

Guimaraes, R.P. *Ecopolitics of Development in the Third World.* L. Rienner, Boulder, CO (1991).

Häder, D.P., Worrest, R.C., Kumar, H.D., Smith, R.C. Effects of increased solar ultraviolet radiation on aquatic ecosystems. *Ambio* 24: 174–180 (1995).

Hajra, P.K., Mudgal, V. *Plant Diversity Hot Spots in India — An Overview.* Botanical Survey of India, Calcutta (1997).

Hairston, N.G., Smith, F.E., Slobodkin, L.B. Community structure, population control and competition. *Amer. Nat.* 94: 421–425 (1960).

Halliday, T. A declining amphibian conundrum. *Nature* 394: 418–419 (1998).

Hammond, P.M. Species inventory. In : Groombridge, B. (ed.) *Global Biodiversity. Status of the Earth's Living Resources,* pp. 17–39. Chapman & Hall, London (1992).

Hammond, P.M. Described and estimated species numbers: an objective assessment of current knowledge. In: Allsopp, D., Hawksworth, D.L., Colwell, R.R. (eds.) *Microbial Biodiversity and Ecosystem Function,* pp. 11–25. CAB Intl., Wallingford (1994).

Hammond, P.M. Practical approaches to the estimation of the extent of biodiversity in species groups. *Phil. Trans. R. Soc. Lond.* B. 345: 119–136 (1994).

Hanneberg, P. Biodiversity—a key resource for development. *Enviro* 14: 7–9 (Dec. 1992).

Hanneberg, P. Sustainable development must be defined locally. *Enviro* 14: 18–21 (1992).

Harlan, J.R. Our vanishing genetic resources. *Science* 188: 618–621 (1975).

Harms, R.R. Biological diversity: from conceptual framework to practical application. *The Wildlifer* 263: 34 (1994).

Harper, J.L. *Population Biology of Plants.* Acad. Press, London (1977).

Harper, J.L., Hawksworth, D.L. Biodiversity: measurement and estimation. Preface. *Phil. Trans. R. Soc. Lond.* B 345: 5–12 (1994).

Harrington, J.F. Seed and pollen storage for conservation of plant gene resources. *In* : Frankel, O.H., Bennett, E. (eds.) *Genetic Resources in Plants: Their Exploration and Conservation.* IBP Handbook No. 11. Blackwell Sci. Publ., Oxford (1970).

Harvey, P.H. The state of systematics. *TREE* 6: 345–346 (1991).

Harwood, C.R. Plasmids, transposons and gene flux. In : Goodfellow, M., O'Donnell, A.G. (eds.) *Handbook of New Bacterial Systematics,* pp. 115–150. Acad. Press, London (1993).

Hawkes, J.G. International workshop on Dynamic In-Situ Conservation of Wild Relatives of Major Cultivated Plants: Summary of final discussion and recommendations. *Israel J. Bot.* 40: 529–536 (1991).

Hawksworth, D.L., Colwell, R.R. (eds.) Biodiversity amongst microorganisms and its relevance. *Biodiv. Conserv.* 1: 221–345 (1992).

Hawksworth, D.L., Kalin-Arroyo, M.T. In *Global Biodiversity Assessment.* Cambridge (1995).

Hawksworth, D.L., Kirk, P.M., Sutton, B.C., Pegler, D.N. *Ainsworth and Bisby's Dictionary of Fungi.* (8th ed.) CAB Intl., Wallingford (1995).

HDRA. *About the Heritage Seed Programme.* The Henry Doubleday Research Association, Ryton, Coventry (1995).

Herliczek, J. Where is ecotourism going? *Amicus J.* 18: 31–35 (1996).

Hershkovitz, P. *Living New World Monkeys,* Vol. I. Univ. Chicago Press, Chicago, ILL (1977).

Heywood, V.H. *Global Biodiversity Assessment.* Camb. Univ. Press, Cambridge (1995).

Heywood, V.H. The measurement of biodiversity and the politics of implementation. In : Florey, P.L., Humphries, C.J., Vane-Wright, R.I. (eds.) *Systematics and Conservation Evaluation,* Vol. 50: pp. 15–22. System. Assoc. Sp. Vol. Clarendon Press, Oxford (1994).

Hoffman, A. *Arguments on Evolution.* Oxford Univ. Press, Oxford (1989).

Holdridge, L.R. *Life Zone Ecology.* Tropical Science Center, San Jose, Costa Rica (1967).

Holdridge, L.R., Grenke, W.C., Hatheway, W.H., Liang, T., Tosi J.A. *Forest Environments in Tropical Life Zones, a Pilot Study.* Pergamon, NY (1971).

Holling, C.S. Cross-scale morphology, geometry, and dynamics of ecosystems. *Ecol. Monogr.* 62: 447–502 (1992).

Holling, C.S. What barriers? What bridges? In : Gunderson, L.H., Holling, C.S., Light, S.S. (eds.) *Barriers and Bridges to the Renewal of Ecosystems,* pp. 3–34. Columbia Univ. Press, NY (1995).

Holm-Nielsen, L.B., Nielsen, I.C., Balslev, H. (eds.). *Tropical Forests.* pp. 239–251. Academic, London (1989).

Holmes, B. Biologists sort the lessons of fisheries collapse. *Science* 264: 1252–1253 (1994).

Hubbell, S.P. Tree dispersion, abundance, and diversity in a tropical dry forest. *Science* 203: 1299–1309 (1979).

Huston, M. *Biological Diversity: The Coexistence of Species in Changing Landscapes.* Camb. Univ. Press, Cambridge (1994).

Hvengaard, G.T., Butler, J.R., Krystofiak, D.K. Economic values of bird watching at Point Pelee National Park, Canada. *Wildlife Soc. Bull.* 17: 526–531 (1989).

ICBP. (International Council for Bird Preservation). *Putting Biodiversity on the Map: Priority Areas for Global Conservation.* Birdlife Intl., Cambridge, UK (1992).

ICRISAT. Consultation Meeting on the Regeneration of Seed Crops and Their Wild Relatives. Hyderabad, Dec. 4–7 (1995).

Iltis, H.H. Serendipity in the exploration of biodiversity: What good are weedy tomatoes? In : Wilson, E.O., Peter, F.M. (eds.) *Biodiversity,* pp. 98–105. Natl. Acad. Press, Washington, DC (1988).

Induchoodan, N.C. Ecological studies on the sacred groves of Kerala. Ph.D. thesis, Pondicherry Univ., Pondicherry (1996).

IPGRI. An IPGRI Strategy for *in situ* conservation and agricultural biodiversity. (Unpubl.), IPGRI, Rome (1995).

IUCN. (International Union for Conservation of Nature and Natural Resources) *Guidelines for the Management of Tropical Forests*, Gland, Switzerland (1989).

IUCN. *Guidelines for Protected Area Management Categories.* IUCN, Gland, Switzerland (1994).

Jaarsveld, A.S. van., Freitag, S., Chown, S.L., Muller, C., Koch, S., Hull, H., Bellamy, C., Krüger, M., Endrödy-Younga, S., Mansell, M.W., Scholtz, C.H. Biodiversity assessment and conservation strategies. *Science* 279: 2106–2108 (1998).

Jablonski, D. Heritability at the species level: analysis of geographic ranges of Cretaceous molluscs. *Science* 238: 360–363 (1987).

Jackson, L.L., Lopoukhine, N., Hillyard, D. Ecological restoration: A definition and comments. *Restor. Ecol.* 3: 71–75 (1995).

Jain, S.K. *A Manual of Ethnobotany.* Sci. Publ., Jodhpur (1987).

Janzen, D.H. Insect diversity of a Costa Rican dry forest: why keep it and how? *Biol. J. Linn. Soc.* 30: 343–356 (1987).

Janzen, D.H. A south–north perspective on science in the management, use, and economic development of biodiversity. In : Sandlund, O.T., Hindar, K., Brown, A.H.D. (eds.) *Conservation of Biodiversity for Sustainable Development,* pp. 27–52. Scandinavian Univ. Press, Oslo (1992).

Jha, P.K. Environment and biodiversity in South Asia : An overview. In : Jha, P.K., Ghimire, G.P.S., Karmacharya, S.B., Baral, S.R., Lacoul, P. (eds.) *Environment and Biodiversity. In the Context of South Asia,* pp. 12–25. Ecol. Soc. (ECOS), Kathmandu (1996).

Jiggins, J. *Crop Variety Mixtures in Marginal Environments.* Gatekeeper Series 19: IIED, London (1990).

Johnson, E.A. *Fire and Vegetation Dynamics: Studies from the North American Boreal Forest.* Camb. Univ. Press, Cambridge (1992).

Johnson, K.H., Vogt, K.A., Clark, H.J., Schmitz, O.J., Vogt, D.J. Biodiversity and the productivity and stability of ecosystems. *TREE* 11: 372–377 (1996).

Jones, B. Do fungi occur in the sea? *The Mycologist* 2: 150–157 (1988).

Jones, C.G., Lawton, J.H., Shachak, M. Organisms as ecosystem engineers. *Oikos* 69: 373–386 (1994).

Juma, C., Mugabe, J. *Technological Development and the Convention on Biodiversity: Emerging Policy Issues.* ACTS, Nairobi (1994).

Kamarck, A.M. *The Tropics and Economic Development.* World Bank, Washington, DC (1976).

Kangas, P. Tropical sustainable development and biodiversity. In : Reaka-Kudla, M.L., Wilson, D.E., Wilson, E.O. (eds.) *Biodiversity II,* pp. 389–409. J. Henry Press, Washington, DC (1997).

Kareiva, P. Biodiversity: No shortcuts in new maps. *Nature* 365: 2992–2993 (1993).

Kareiva, P., Wennergren, U. Connecting landscape patterns to ecosystem and population processes. *Nature* 373: 299–302 (1995).

Kaushik, J.P. Changing patterns of plant diversity in central India. In : Jha, P.K. *et al.* (eds.). *Environment and Biodiversity: In the Context of South Asia,* pp. 220–225. Ecol. Soc. (ECOS), Kathmandu (1996).

Kelleher, G., Bleakley, C., Wells, S. *A Global Representative System of Marine Protected Areas.* World Bank, Washington, DC (1995).

Kerr, J.T., Packer, L. Habitat heterogeneity as a determinant of mammal species richness in high-energy regions. *Nature* 385: 252–254 (1997).

Khalil, H.K., Reid, W.V., Juma, C. *Property Rights, Biotechnology and Genetic Resources.* ACTS Biopolicy International Series no. 7. ACTS, Nairobi (1992).

Kihara, H. *Fauna and Flora of Nepal Himalaya.* Fauna and Flora Res. Soc. Kyoto Univ., Kyoto, Japan (1955).

Kimmins, J.P. *Balancing Act – Environmental Issues in Forestry.* Univ. British Columbia Press, Vancouver, BC (1992).

Klug, M.J., Tiedje, J.M. Response of microbial communities to changing environmental conditions: chemical and physiological approaches. In Guerrero, R., Pedros-Alio, C. (eds.) pp. 371–378. Spanish Soc. Microbiol., Barcelona (1994).

Knight, R., Gutzweiler, K. (eds.). *Wildlife and Recreationists.* Island Press. Washington, DC (1995).

Kohlmeyer, J., Kohlmeyer, E. *Marine Mycology. The Higher Fungi.* Acad. Press, NY (1979).

Kozhov, M. Lake Baikal and its life. *Monographs in Biology* 11: 1–344 (1963).

Kremen, C. Assessing the indicator properties of species assemblages for natural areas monitoring. *Ecol. Appl.* 2: 203–17 (1992).

Kristensen, R.M. Loricifera, a new phylum with Aschelminthes characters from the meiobenthos. *Z. Zool. Syst.* 21: 163–180 (1983).

Kumar, H.D. *General Ecology.* Vikas, New Delhi (1995).

Kumar, H.D., Kumar, S. *Modern Concepts of Microbiology.* Vikas, New Delhi (1998).

Kurtzman, C.P., Robnett, C.J. Orders and families of ascosporogenous yeasts and yeast-like taxa compared from ribosomal RNA sequence similarities. In : Hawksworth, D.L. (ed.) *Ascomycete Systematics: Problems and Prospects in the Nineties.* Plenum Press, NY (1994).

Kuusela, K. *The Dynamics of Boreal Coniferous Forest.* Finnish Natl. Fund for Res. and Dev., Helsinki (1990).

Lande, R. Models of speciation by sexual selection on polygenic characters. *PNAS (USA)* 78: 3721–3725 (1981).

Landres, P.B., Verner, J., Thomas, J.W. Ecological uses of vertebrate indicator species: a critique. *Conserv. Biol.* 2: 316–28 (1988).

Lanly, J.P. Tropical Forest Resources. FAO Forestry Paper 30. FAO, Rome (1982).

LaSalle, J., Gould, I.D. Hymenoptera: their diversity, and their impact on the diversity of other organisms. In LaSalle, J., Gould, I.D. (eds.) *Hymnoptera and Biodiversity,* pp. 1–26. CAB Intl., Wallingford (1993).

Lassonde, L. *Coping with Population Challenges.* Earthscan, London (1997).

Lautenschlager, R.A. Biodiversity studies: science and policy. *Science* 253: 758–762 (1997).

Lawton, J.H., Brown, V.K. Redundancy in ecosystem. In : Schulze, E.D., Mooney, H.A. (eds.). *Biodiversity and Ecosystem Function,* pp. 255–270. Springer, Berlin (1993).

Lawton, J.H., May, R.M. (eds.). *Extinction Rates.* Oxford Univ. Press, Oxford (1995).

Lee, K.E. The diversity of soil organisms. In : Hawksworth, D.L. (ed.). *The Biodiversity of Microorganisms and Invertebrates: Its Role in Sustainable Agriculture,* pp. 73–87. CAB Intl., Wallingford (1991).

Leipe, D.D., Gunderson, J.H., Nerad, T.A., Sogin, M.L. Small subunit ribosomal RNA of *Hexamita inflata* and the quest for the first branch in the eukaryotic tree. *Mol. Biochem. Parasitol.* 59: 41–48 (1993).

Lesser, W. *Sustainable Use of Genetic Resources under the Convention on Biological Diversity: Exploring Access and Benefit Sharing Issues.* CAB Intl., Wallingford (1998).

Li, Y., Engle, M., Weis, N., Mandelco, L., Wiegel, J. *Clostridium thermoalcaliphilum* sp. nov., an anaerobic and thermotolerant facultative alkaliphile. *Int. J. Syst. Bacteriol.* 44: 111–18 (1994).

Lodge, D.M. Species invasions and deletions: community effects and responses to climate and habitat change. In : Kareiva, P.M., Kingsolver, J.G., Huey, R.M. (eds.) *Biotic Interactions and Global Change,* pp. 367–387. Sinauer Assoc. Sunderland, MA (1993).

Lokesha, R., Vasudeva, R. Patterns of life history traits among rare/endangered flora of South India. *Current Sci.* 73: 171–172 (1997).

Lovejoy, T.E. The quantification of biodiversity: an esoteric quest or a vital component of sustainable development? *Phil. Trans. R. Soc. Lond. B.* 345: 81–87 (1994).

Lovejoy, T.E. Opportunities for creative conservation. In Meffe, G.K. *et al. Principles of Conservation Biology,* pp. 653–654. Sinauer Assoc., Sunderland, MA (1997).

Lovley, D.R., Woodward, J.C. Consumption of freons CFC11 and CFC12 by anaerobic sediments and soils. *Environ. Sci. Technol.* 26: 925–929 (1992).

Lugo, A.E. Estimating reductions in the diversity of tropical forest species. In: Wilson, E.O., Peter, F.M. (eds.) *Biodiversity,* pp. 58–70 Natl. Acad. Press, Washington, DC (1988).

Lugo, A.E., Brown, S. Tropical lands: Popular misconceptions. *Mazingira* 5 (2): 10–19 (1981).

Lugo, A.E., Schmidt, R., Brown, S. Tropical forests in the Caribbean. *Ambio* 10: 318–324 (1981).

Lundholm, N., Skov, J., Pockligton, R., Moestrup A.E. Domoic acid, the toxic amino acid responsible for amnesic shellfish poisoning, now in *Pseudonitzschia serrata* (Bacillariophyceae) in Europe. *Phycologia* 33: 475–478 (1994).

Lutz, W. (Ed.). *The Future Population of the World: What Can We Assume Today?* Earthscan, London (1994).

MacArthur, R.H., Wilson, E.O. *The Theory of Island Biogeography.* Princeton Univ. Press, Princeton, NJ (1967).

MacArthur, R.H. *Geographical Ecology: Patterns in the Distribution of Species.* Harper and Row, NY (1972).

Mace, G.M. Classifying threatened species: means and ends. *Phil. Trans. R. Soc. Lond. B.* 344: 91–97 (1994).

Mace, G.M., Balmford, A., Ginsberg, J.K. *Changing World.* Camb. Univ. Press, Cambridge (1998).

Mackie, R.I., White, B.A. (eds). *Gastrointestinal Microbiology.* Chapman & Hall, London (1997).

Maclean, R.H., Jones, R.W. *Aquatic Biodiversity Conservation: A Review of Current Issues and Efforts.* Strategy Intl. Fisheries Res., Ottawa (1995).

Maranda, L., Wang, R., Masuda, K., Shimizu, Y. Investigation of the source of domoic acid in mussels. In : Granéli, E., Sundstrom, B., Edler, L., Anderson, D.M. (eds.) *Toxic Marine Phytoplankton,* pp. 300–304. Elsevier NY, (1990).

Martin, M.O. Biological conservation strategies: optimizing *in situ* and *ex situ* approaches. *TREE* 10: 227–228 (1995).

Maser, C. *Sustainable Community Development: Principles and Practices.* St. Lucie Press, Delray Beach, Florida (1997).

May, R.M. *Stability and Complexity in Model Ecosystems.* Princeton Univ. Press, Princeton, NJ (1973).

May R.M. *Exploitation of Marine Communities.* Springer, Berlin (1984).

May, R.M. Biological diversity: Differences between land and sea. *Phil. Trans. R. Soc. Lond.* 343B: 105–111 (1994).

May, R.M. Conceptual aspects of the quantification of the extent of biological diversity. *Phil. Trans. R. Soc. Lond. B* 345: 13–20 (1994).

May, T. Beeinflussten Grossäuger die Waldvegetation der Pleistozänen Warmzeiten Mitteleuropas? *Natur und Museum* 123: 157–170 (1993).

Maynard Smith, J., Dowson, C.C., Spratt, B.C. Localized sex in bacteria. *Nature* 349: 29–31 (1991).

McKelvey, V.E. Mineral resource estimates and public policy. *Amer. Sci.* 60: 32–40 (1972).

Meffe, G.K., Carroll, C.R. *et al. Principles of Conservation Biology,* (2nd ed.). Sinauer Assoc., Sunderland, MA (1997).

Menon, S., Bawa, K.S. Applications of geographic information systems, remote-sensing, and a landscape ecology approach to biodiversity conservation in the Western Ghats. *Current Sci.* 73: 134–145 (1997).

Mercer, E.D., Hamilton, L.S. Mangrove ecosystems: Some economic and natural benefits. *Nature and Resources* 20 (1): 14–19 (1984).

Meyer, A., Kocher, T.D., Basasibwaki, P., Wilson, A.C. Monophyletic origin of Lake Victoria cichlid fishes suggested by mitochondrial DNA sequences. *Nature* 347: 550–569 (1990).

Miller, D.R., Rossman, A–Y. Biodiversity and systematics: Their application to agriculture. In : Reaka-Kudla, M.L., Wilson, D.E., Wilson, E.O. (eds.) *Biodiversity II*, pp. 217–229. Joseph Henry Press, Washington, DC (1997).

Miller, K., Cole, R., Battershill, C. The spread of the introduced Asian alga, *Undaria*, in New Zealand waters. *Water and Atmosphere* (NIWA) 5: 8–9 (1997).

Mitra, S., Landel, H., Pruett-Jones, S. Species richness covaries with mating system in birds. *Auk* 113: 544–551 (1996).

Mooers, A.O., Heard, S.B. Evolutionary processes from tree shape. *Q. Rev. Biol.* 72: 31–54 (1997).

Mooney, P.R. *Seeds of the Earth: A Private or a Public Resource?* Intl. Coalition for Development Action, London (1979).

Mooney, P.R. The law of the seed. *Development Dialogue,* Dag Hammarskjold Foundation, Uppsala (1983).

Moore, K.S., Wehrli, S., Roder, H., Rogers, M., Forrest, J.N., McCrimmon, D., Zasloff, M. Squalamine: an aminosterol antibiotic from the shark. *Proc. Natl. Acad. Sci. USA* 90: 1354–1358 (1993).

Moran, E.F. (ed.). *The Ecosystem Approach in Anthropology: From Concept to Practice.* Univ. Michigan Press, Ann Arbor, MI (1990).

Morell, V. Earth's unbounded beetlemania explained. *Science* 281: 501–503 (1998).

Mueller-Dombois, D., Ellenberg, H. *Aims and Methods of Vegetation Ecology.* John Wiley and Sons, NY (1974).

Mugabe, J., Ouko, E. Control over genetic resources. *Biotech. Devel. Monitor* 21: 6–7 (1994).

Mugabe, J., Wandera, P. Structural adjustment and wildlife management in Kenya: institutional reforms. In: Juma, C., Monteith, H., Krugmann, H., Angura, T., Acquay, H.M., Akinlo Anthony, E., Wandera, P., Mugabe, J. (eds.) *Economic Policy Reforms and the Environment: African Experience,* pp. 181–211. UNEP, Geneva (1995).

Mulvany, P. (ed.). Dynamic diversity: Farmers safeguarding agricultural diversity through their crop husbandry. Intermediate Technology, Rugby, England (1996).

Mulvany, P. (ed.) Dynamic diversity: Fisherfolk safeguarding aquatic diversity through their fishing techniques. IT, Rugby (1996).

Mushtak Ali, T.M., Ganeshaiah, K.N. Mapping diversity of ants and root grubs. *Current Sci.* 75: 176 (1998).

Myers, N. *The Sinking Ark. A New Look at the Problem of Disappearing Species.* Pergamon, NY (1979).

Myers, N. Threatened biotas: "Hotspots" in tropical forests. *Environmentalist* 8: 1–20 (1988).

Myers, N. Mass extinctions: what can the past tell us about the present and the future? *Glob. Planet. Change* 82: 175–85 (1990a).

Myers, N. The biodivesity challenge: expanded hotspots analysis. *The Environmentalist* 10: 243–256 (1990b).

Myers, N. Tropical deforestation: The latest situation. *BioScience* 41: 282–283 (1991).

Myers, N. Environmental services of biodiversity. *PNAS* (USA) 93: 2764–2769 (1996).

Myers, N. The rich diversity of biodiversity issues. In : Reaka-Kudla M.L. *et al.* (eds.) *Biodiversity II*, pp. 125–138. J. Henry Press, Washington, DC (1997).

Naeem, S., Thompson, L.J., Lawler, S.P., Lawton, J.H., Woodfin, R.M. Declining biodiversity can alter the performance of ecosystems. *Nature* 368: 734–737 (1994).

Naiman, R.J., Decamps, H. The ecology of interfaces: Riparian zones. *Ann. Rev. Ecol. Syst.* 28: 621–658 (1997).

Nair, P.V., Menon, A.R.R. Estimation of bamboo resources in Kerala by remote sensing techniques. *Current Sci.* 75: 176 (1998).

NAP. *Conserving Biodiversity*. Natl. Acad. Press, Washington, DC (1992).

Nayar, M.P. *Hot Spots of Endemic Plants of India, Nepal and Bhutan. Trop. Bot. Garden and Res. Inst.*, Thiruvananthapuram (1997).

Negi, H.R., Gadgil, M. Genus level diversity in lichens of Nanda Devi Biosphere Reserve, India. In : Jha, P.K. *et al.* (eds.) *Environment and Biodiversity: In the Context of South Asia*, pp. 192–202. Ecol. Soc. (ECOS), Kathmandu (1996).

Nelson, J.G., Serafin, R. Assessing biodiversity: a human ecological approach. *Ambio* 21: 212–218 (1992).

Ngoile, M. The Oceans: diminishing resources, degraded environment and loss of biodiversity. *Connect* (UNESCO newsletter) 22: 1–2 (1997).

Nicol, D. Species, class, and phylum diversity of animals. *Q. J. Fla. Acad. Sci.* 34: 191–194 (1971).

Niklas, K.J., Tiffney, B.H. The quantification of plant biodiversity through time. *Phil. Trans. R. Soc. Lond. B.* 345: 35–44 (1994).

Norse, E.A. *Ancient Forests of the Pacific Northwest*. Island Press, Washington, DC (1990).

Norse, E.A. (Ed.). *Global Marine Biological Diversity: A Strategy for Building Conservation into Decision Making*. Island Press, Washington, DC (1993).

Noss, R.F. Indicators for monitoring biodiversity: a hierachical approach. *Conserv. Biol.* 4: 355–364 (1990).

Noss, R.F. Maintaining ecological integrity in representative reserve Networks. A World Wildlife Fund Canada/World Wildlife Fund–United States Discussion Paper. World Wildlife Fund Canada. Toronto, Ontario (1994).

Noss, R.F., Cooperrider, A.Y. *Saving Nature's Legacy.* Island Press, Washington, DC (1994).

O'Donnell, A.G., Goodfellow, M., Hawksworth, D.L. Theoretical and practical aspects of the quantification of biodiversity among micro–organisms. *Phil. Trans. R. Soc. Lond.* B345: 65–73 (1994).

OECD. *The State of the Environment.* Organization for Economic Cooperation and Development, Paris (1991).

Oldfield, M.L. *The Value of Conserving Genetic Resources.* U.S. Dept. Interior, Natl. Park Service, Washington, DC (1984).

Oren, A. The Dead Sea–alive again. *Experientia* 49: 518–522 (1993).

Orr, H.A. The population genetics of speciation: the evolution of hybrid incompatabilities. *Genetics* 139: 1805–1813 (1995).

Owen-Smith, N. *Megaherbivores: The Influence of Very Large Body Size on Ecology.* Camb. Univ. Press, Cambridge (1988).

Oyen, E., Miller, S.M., Samad, S.A. *Poverty — A Global Review: Handbook on International Poverty Research.* Scandinavian Univ. Press, Oslo (1996).

Palmer, M.A., Ambrose, R.F., Poff, N.L. Ecological theory and community restoration ecology. *Rest. Ecol.* 5: 291–300 (1997).

Pascal, J.P. *Wet Evergreen Forests of the Western Ghats of India.* Institut Francais, Pondicherry (1988).

Patrick, R. Biodiversity: Why is it important? In : Reaka–Kudla, M.L. Wilson, D.E., Wilson, E.O. (eds.). *Biodiversity II,* pp. 15–24. J. Henry Press, Washington, DC (1997).

Pearson, D.L. Selecting indicator taxa for the quantitative assessment of biodiversity. *Phil. Trans. R. Soc. Lond.* B. 345: 75–79 (1994).

Pearson, D.L., Cassola, F. World-wide species richness patterns of tiger beetles (Coleoptera: Cicindelidae): indicator taxon for biodiversity and conservation studies. *Conserv. Biol.* 6: 376–391 (1992).

Pei, S. Indigenous knowledge and conservation of biodiversity in the mountain ecosystems. Jha, P.K *et al.* (eds.) *Environment and Biodiversity: In the Context of South Asia,* pp. 51–58. Ecol. Soc. (ECOS), Kathmandu, Nepal (1996).

Perrings, C. *Economy and Environment : A Theoretical Essay on the Interdependence of Economic and Environmental Systems.* Camb. Univ. Press, Cambridge (1987).

Perrings, C., Folke, C., Maler, K.G. The ecology and economics of biodiversity loss. *Ambio* 21: 201–211 (1992).

Perrings, C., Maler, K.G., Folke, C., Holling, C.S., Jansson, B.O. (eds.). *Biodiversity Loss: Ecological and Economic Issues.* Camb. Univ. Press, Cambridge (1995).

Peters, R.L. Effects of global warming on forests. *Forest Ecology and Management* 35: 13–33 (1990).

Peters, R.L., Myers, J.P. Preserving biodiversity in a changing climate. *Issues in Science and Technology,* pp. 66–72 (1992).

Phillips, O.L., Gentry, A.H. Increasing turnover through time in tropical forests. *Science* 263: 954–958 (1994).

Phillips, O.L., Hall, P., Gentry, A.H., Sawyer, S.A., Vasquez, R. Dynamics and species richness of tropical rain forests. *Proc. Natl. Acad. Sci. (PNAS)* USA 91: 2805–2809 (1994).

Pianka, E.R. On *r–* and *K–*selection. *American Naturalist* 104: 592–597 (1970).

Pimm, S.L. *The Balance of Nature.* Univ. of Chicago Press, Chicago (1991).

Pimm, S.L., Gittleman, J.L. Biological diversity: where is it? *Science* 255: 940 (1992).

Pimm, S.L., Russel, G.J., Gittleman, J.L., Brooks, T.M. The future of biodiversity. *Science* 269: 347–350 (1995).

Pistorius, R. *Scientists, Plants and Politics.* Intl. Plant Gen. Res. Inst., Rome (1997).

Pistorius, R., Van Wijk, J. Biodiversity prospecting: Commercializing genetic resources for export. *Biotechnol. Develop. Monitor* 15: 12–15 (1993).

Plucknett, D.L. *Gene Banks and the World's Food.* Princeton Univ. Press, Princeton, NJ (1987).

Power, M.E., Mills, L.S. The keystone cops meet in Hilo. *TREE* 10: 182–184 (1995).

Pramod, P., Joshi, N.V., Ghate, U., Gadgil, M. On the hospitality of Western Ghats habitats for bird communities. *Current Sci.* 73: 122–127 (1997).

Prendergast, J.R. Rare species, the coincidence of diversity hot spots and conservation strategies. *Nature* 365: 335–337 (1993).

Pressey, R.L., Humphries, C.J., Margules, C.R., Vane Wright, R.I., Williams, P.H. Beyond opportunism: key principles for systematic reserve selection. *TREE* 8: 124–128 (1993).

Pretty, J.N. *Regenerating Agriculture: Policies and Practice for Sustainability and Self-reliance.* Earthscan, London (1995).

Price, P.W. *Biological Evolution.* Saunders, Fort Worth, TA (1996).

Puri, G.S., Meher-Homji, V.M., Gupta, R.K., Puri, S. *Forest Ecology,* Vol. 1, *Phytogeography and Forest Conservation.* Oxford & IBH, New Delhi (1983).

Purvis, A. Using interspecies phylogenies to test macroevolutionary hypotheses. In : Harvey, P.H., Leigh Brown, A.J., Maynard Smith, J., Nee, S. (eds.) *New Uses for New Phylogenies,* pp. 153–168. Oxford Univ. Press, Oxford (1996).

Quammen, D. *The Song of the Dodo: Island Biogeography in an Age of Extinctions.* Simon and Schuster, NY (1997).

Rainey, F.A., Janssen, P.H., Morgan, H.W., Stackebrandt, E. A biphasic approach to the determination of the phenotypic and genotypic diversity of some anaerobic cellulolytic, thermophilic, rod-shaped bacteria. *Antonie van Leeuwenhoek* 64: 341–354 (1994).

Ramakrishnan, P.S., Purohit, A.H., Saxena, K.G., Rao, K.S., Maikhuri, R.K. (eds.). *Conservation and Management of Biological Resources in Himalaya.* G.B. Pant Inst. of Himalayan Environment and Development, Kosi-Katarmal and Oxford & IBH, New Delhi (1997).

Rao, A.N.: Mangrove ecosystems of Asia and the Pacific. In: Umali, R.M. (ed.) *Mangroves of Asia and the Pacific: Status and Management,* pp. 1–48. Technical Report of the UNDP/UNESCO Research and Training Pilot Programme on Mangrove Ecosystems in Asia and the Pacific, Quezon City, Metro Manila (1987).

Raup, D.M. Mathematical models of cladogenesis. *Paleobiology* 11: 42–52 (1985).

Raven, P. Why it matters? *Our Planet* 6 (4): 5–8 (1994).

Reaka-Kudla, M.L. The global biodiversity of coral reefs: A comparison with rain forests. In Reaka-Kudla, M.L., Wilson, D.E., Wilson, E.O. (eds.) *Biodiversity II,* pp. 83–108. J. Henry Press, Washington, DC (1997).

Redclift, M. *Wasted: Counting the Costs of Global Consumption.* Earthscan, London (1996).

Regnell, H. (Ed.). *The Challenge of World Poverty: Essays on International Development Issues.* Lund Univ. Press, Lund (1995).

Rehner, S.A., Samuels, G.J. Taxonomy and phylogeny of *Gliocladium* analysed from nuclear large subunit DNA sequences. *Mycol. Res.* 98: 625–634 (1994).

Reid, W.V. Conserving life's diversity. *Environ. Sci. Technol.* 26: 1090–1095 (1992).

Reid, W.V. Biodiversity hot spots. *TREE* 13: 275–279 (1998).

Reid, W.V., Miller, K.R. *Keeping Options Alive: the Scientific Basis for Conserving Biodiversity.* WRI, Washington, DC (1989).

Reijntjes, C., Haverkort, B., Waters-Bayer, A. *Farming For the Future.* Macmillan, London (1992).

Remsen, J.V. Jr. The importance of continued collecting of bird specimens to ornithology and bird conservation. *Bird Conserv. Internat.* 5: 145–180 (1995).

Renner, S.S., Ricklefs, R.E. Systematics and biodiversity. *TREE* 9: 78 (1994).

Rennie, J. A census of stranglers. *Sci. Amer.* p. 25 (Apr. 1992).

Rex, M.A. An oblique slant on deep-sea biodiversity. *Nature* 385: 577–578 (1997).

Ricklefs, R.E. Schluter, D. (eds.) *Species Diversity in Ecological Communities.* Univ. Chicago Press, Chicago, ILL (1993).

Ricklefs, R.E. Schluter, D. Species diversity: Regional and historical influences. In: Ricklefs, R.E., Schluter, D. (eds.). *Species Diversity in Ecological Communities,* pp. 350–363. Univ. Chicago Press, Chicago, ILL (1993).

Ritchie, M. Shocking hybrids. *TREE* 13: 123–124 (1998).

Ritz, K., Dighton, J., Giller, K.E. (eds.). *Beyond the Biomass: Compositional and Functional Analysis of Soil Microbial Communities.* Wiley, NY (1994).

Robbins, R.K., Opler, P.A. Butterfly diversity and a preliminary comparison with bird and mammal diversity. In: Reaka-Kudla, M.L. *et al.* (eds.). *Biodiversity. II,* pp. 69–82. J. Henry Press, Washington, DC (1997).

Robinson, R.A. *Plant Pathosystems.* Springer-Verlag, Berlin (1976).

Rodgers, W.A., Panwar, H.S. *Planning a Wildlife Protected Area Network in India,* Vols. 1–2, Wildlife Inst. India, Dehra Dun (1988).

Rosen, D. The importance of cryptic species and specific identifications as related to biological control. In : Romberger, J.A. *Biosystematics in Agriculture,* pp. 23–35. Beltsville Symp. Agric. Res. Allanhead, Osmun and Co., Montclair, NJ (1977).

Rosenthal, J., Grifo, F. (eds.). *Biodiversity and Human Health.* Island Press, Washington, DC (1995).

Rosenzweig, M.L. *Species Diversity in Space and Time.* Camb. Univ. Press, Cambridge (1995).

Rosenzweig, M.L., Abramsky, Z. How are diversity and productivity related? In: Ricklefs, R.E., Schluter, D. (eds.) *Species Diversity in Ecological Communities,* pp. 52–65. Chicago Univ. Press, Chicago, ILL (1993).

SAARC. Regional study on the causes and consequences of natural disasters and the protection and preservation of the environment. South Asia Assoc. Reg. Coop., Kathmandu (1992).

Sackville Hamilton, N.R., Chorlton, K.H. *Regeneration of Accessions in Seed Collections: A Decision Guide.* Handbook for Genebanks No. 5. IPGRI, Rome (1997).

Sale, P. A promise not yet fulfilled. *TREE* 13: 125 (1997).

Sample, V.A. *Remote Sensing and GIS in Ecosystem Management.* Island Press, Washington, DC (1994).

Samways, M.J. Insect conservation ethics. *Environ. Conserv.* 17: 7–8 (1990).

Schluter, D., Ricklefs, R.E. Species diversity, an introduction to the problem. In : Ricklefs, R.E., Schluter, D. (eds.) *Species Diversity in Ecological Communities,* Univ. Chicago Press, Chicago, ILL (1993).

Schmidt, H. Facing one world: A report by an independent group on financial flows to developing countries (Excerpt). *International Environmental Affairs* 2: 174–181 (1990).

Schonewald-Cox, C.M. Conclusions. Guidelines in management: A beginning attempt. In : Schonewald Cox, C.M., Chambers, S.M., MacBryde, B., Thomas, L. (eds.) *Genetics and Conservation: A Reference for Managing Wild Animals and Plant Populations,* pp. 414–445. Benjamin/Cummings, Menlo Park (1983).

Schulze, E.D., Mooney, H.A. (eds.). *Biodiversity and Ecosystem Function.* Springer, NY (1994).

Scott, J.M., Ables, E.D., Edwards, T.C. Jr., Eng, R.L., Gavin, T.A., Harris, L.D., Haufler, J.B., Healy, W.M., Knopf, F.L., Torgerson, O., Weeks, H.P., Jr. Conservation of biological diversity: perspectives and the future for the wildlife profession. *Wildlife Soc. Bull.* 23: 646–657 (1995).

Scriber, J.M. Latitudinal gradients in larval feeding specialization of the world Papilionidae. *Psyche* 80: 355–373 (1973).

Sebens, K.P. Biodiversity of coral reefs: What are we losing and why? *Amer. Zool.* 34: 115–133 (1994).

Sen, D.N. Biodiversity and conservation of vegetation in Indian desert. In : Jha, P.K. *et al.* (eds.) *Environment and Biodiversity: In the Context of South Asia,* pp. 34–41. Ecol. Soc. (ECOS) Kathmandu (1996).

Shafer, C.L. *Nature Reserves: Island Theory and Conservation Practice.* Smithsonian Inst. Press, Washington, DC (1991).

Shah, N.C. Endangered medicinal and aromatic herbs of the Indian Himalayas. *Proc. 2nd Internatl. Cong. Ethnobiology.* October 22–26, 1990 Kunming, China (1990).

Shands, H.L., Kirkbride, J.H. Systematic botany in support of agriculture. *Symbolae Botanicae Uppsaliensis* 28: 48–54 (1989).

365

Sheldon, S. The effects of feeding by a North American weevil, *Euhrychiopsis lecontei*, on the Eurasian water milfoil, *Myriophyllum spicatum. Aquat. Bot.* 45: 245–256 (1993).

Shrestha, G.L., Shrestha, B. New frontiers of knowledge on Nepalese plants. In : Jha, P.K. *et al.* (eds.) *Environment and Biodiversity: In the Context of South Asia,* pp. 161–171. ECOS, Kathmandu (1996).

Shumway, S.E. Phycotoxin-related shellfish poisoning: bivalve molluscs are not the only vectors. *Rev. Fishery Sci.* 3: 1–31 (1995).

Siemann, E., Tilman, D., Haarstad, J. Insect species diversity, abundance and body size relationships. *Nature* 380: 704–706 (1996).

Signor, P.W. The geological history of diversity. *Ann. Rev. Ecol. System.* 21: 509–39 (1990).

Silva, P.C. Geographic patterns of diversity in benthic marine algae. *Pacific Sci.* 46: 429–437 (1992).

Singh, J.S., Raghubanshi, A.S., Varshney, C.K. Integrated biodiversity research for India. *Current Sci.* 66: 109–122 (1994).

Slatkin, M. In defense of founder-flush theories of speciation. *Amer. Nat.* 147: 493–505 (1996).

Smith, F.D.M., May, R.M., Pellew, R., Johnson, T.H., Walter, K. How much do we know about the current extinction rate ? *TREE* 8: 375–378 (1993).

Smith, T.M., Shugart, H.H., Woodward, F.I. (eds.). *Plant Functional Types: Their Relevance to Ecosystem Properties and Global Change.* Camb. Univ. Press, NY (1997).

Society of Ecological Restoration: Program and Abstracts. 3rd Annual Conf. Orlando, Florida, 18–23 May, 1991.

Sogin, M.L., Hinkle, G. Common measures for studies of biodiversity: Molecular phylogeny in the eukaryotic microbial world. In : Reaka-Kudla, M.L. *et al.* (eds.) *Biodiversity II,* pp. 109–122. J. Henry Press, Washington, DC (1997).

Solbrig, O.T. *Biodiversity.* MAB Digest 9, UNESCO, Paris (1991).

Solbrig, O.T., Nicolis, G. Biology and complexity. In: Solbrig, O.T., Nicolis, G. (eds.). *Perspectives in Biological Complexity,* pp. 1–6. IUBS, Paris (1991).

Solis, M.A. Snout moths: unravelling the taxonomic diversity of a speciose group in the neotropics. In: Reaka-Kudla, M.L. *et al.* (eds.). *Biodiversity II,* pp. 231–242. J. Henry Press, Washington, DC (1997).

Somasundaram, T.R. *A Handbook on the Identification and Description of Trees, Shrubs and Some Important Herbs of the Forests of the Southern States.* Southern Forests Ranges College, Coimbatore and Manager Publ., New Delhi (1967).

Soulé, M. (Ed.). *Conservation Biology: Science of Scarcity and Diversity.* Sinauer Assoc., Sunderland, MA (1986).

Soulé, M.E., Kohm, K. *Research Priorities for Conservation Biology.* Island Press, Washington, DC (1989).

Soulé, M.E., Sanjayan, M.A. Conservation targets: do they help? *Science* 279: 2060–2061 (1998).

Sournia, A., Chretiennot-Dinet, G. Marine phytoplankton: How many species in the world ocean? *J. Plankton Res.* 13: 1093–1099 (1991).

Southwood, T.R.E. Habitat, the templet for ecological strategies? *J. Anim. Ecol.* 30: 1–8 (1977).

Spande, T.F., Garraffo, H.M., Edwards, M.W., Yeh, H.J.C., Pannell, L., Daly, J.W. Epibatidine: a novel (chlorophyridyl) Azabicycloheptane with potent analgesic activity from an Ecuadorean poison frog. *J. Amer. Chem. Soc.* 114: 3476–3478 (1992).

Speidel, G. *Planung im Forstbetrich.* Berlin (1972).

Stattersfield, A.J., Crosby, M.J., Long, A.J., Wege, D.C. *Endemic Bird Areas of the World: Priorities for Biodiversity Conservation.* Birdlife Internatl, Cambridge (1998).

Steadman, D.W. Human–caused extinction of birds. In Reaka-Kudla, M.L. *et al* (eds.) *Biodiversity II,* pp. 139–161. J. Henry Press, Washington, DC (1997).

Stehli, F.G., Wells, J.W. Diversity and age patterns in hermatypic corals. *Syst. Zool.* 20: 115–126 (1971).

Steidinger, K.A., Burkholder, J.M., Glasgow, H.B., Truby, E.W., Garrett, J.K., Noga, E.J., Smith, S.A. *Pfiesteria piscicida* gen. et sp. nov. (Pfiesteriaceae, fam. nov.) a new toxic dinoflagellate genus and species with a complex life cycle and behavior. *J. Phycol.* 32: 157–164 (1996).

Steinberg, C.E.W., Geller, W. Biodiversity and interactions within pelagic nutrient cycling and productivity. In : Schulze, E.D., Mooney, H.A. (eds.) *Biodiversity and Ecosystem Function,* pp. 43–64. Springer, NY (1993).

Stix, G. Back to roots: drug companies forage for new treatments. *Scient. Amer.* 268: 142–143 (1993).

Stork, N.E. Insect diversity. Facts, fiction and speculation. *Biol. J. Linn. Soc.* 35: 321–337 (1988).

Stork, N.E. How many species are there? *Biodiv. Conserv.* 2: 215–232 (1993).

367

Strauss, R.E. Allometry and functional feeding morphology in haplochromine cichlids. In: Echelle, A.A., Kornfield, I. (eds.) *Evolution of Fish Species Flocks,* pp. 217–230. Univ. Maine Press, Orono, ME (1984).

Stuart, P.L., Lawton, J.H. Planning for biodiversity. *Science* 279: 2068–2069 (1998).

Subash Chandran, M.D. On the ecological history of the Western Ghats. *Current Sci.* 73: 146–155 (1997).

Subramanya, S. Non–random foraging in certain bird pests of field crops. *J. Biosci.* 369–380 (1994).

Tawnenga; Uma Shankar; Tripathi, R.S. Evaluating second year cropping on jhum fallows in Mizoram, north-eastern India. Phytomass dynamics and primary productivity. *J. Biosci.* 21: 563–575 (1996).

Tawnenga; Uma Shankar; Tripathi, R.S. Evaluating second year cropping on jhum fallows in Mizoram, north-eastern India. Energy and economic efficiencies. *J. Biosci.* 23: 605–613 (1997a).

Tawnenga; Uma Shankar; Tripathi, R.S. Evaluating second year cropping on jhum fallows in Mizoram, north-eastern India. Soil fertility. *J. Biosci.* 23: 615–625 (1997b).

Terborgh, J. Keystone plant resources in the tropical forest. In: Soulé, M.E. (Ed). *Conservation Biology: The Science of Scarcity and Diversity,* pp. 330–344. Sinauer Assoc., Sunderland, MA (1986).

Terborgh, J. On the notion of favorableness in plant ecology. *Amer. Nat.* 107: 481–501 (1973).

Terborgh, J., Robinson, S.K., Parker, T.A., Munn, C.A., Pierpont, N. Structure and organization of an Amazonian forest bird community. *Ecol. Monogr.* 60: 213–238 (1990).

Thorne-Miller, B., Cantena, J. *The Living Ocean: Understanding and Protecting Marine Biodiversity.* Island Press, Washington, DC (1991).

Tilman, D. Biodiversity: Population versus ecosystem stability. *Ecology* 77: 350–363 (1996).

Tilman, D., Pacala, S. The maintenance of species richness in plant communities. In : Ricklefs, R.E., Schluter, D. (eds.) *Species Diversity in Ecological Communities,* pp. 13–25. Univ. Chicago Press, Chicago, ILL (1993).

Tilman, D., Downing, J.A. Biodiversity and stability in grasslands. *Nature* 367: 363–365 (1994).

Tolba, M.K. Towards a sustainable development. *Ambio* 24: 66–67 (1995).

Tuomisto, H., Ruokolainen, K., Kalliola, R., Liina, A., Danjoy, W., Rodriguez, Z. Dissecting Amazonian biodiversity. *Science* 269: 63–66 (1995).

Turner, I.M. Species loss in fragments of tropical rain forest: a review of the evidence. *J. Appl. Ecol.* 33: 200–209 (1996).

Tzschupke, W. Forest sustainability — A contribution to conserving the basis of our existence? *Pl. Res. Develop.* 47/48: 14–28 (1998).

Udvardy, M.D.F. *A Classification of the Biogeographical Provinces of the World.* IUCN Occasional Paper No. 18. Morges, Switzerland (1975).

Uma Shankar, Murali, K.S., Uma Shaankar, R., Ganeshaiah, K.N., Bawa, K.S. Extraction of non-timber forest products in the forests of Biligiri Rangan Hills, India 3. Productivity, extraction and prospects of sustainable harvest of amla, *Phyllanthus emblica* (Euphorbiaceae). *Econ. Bot.* 50: 270–279 (1996).

Uma Shankar, Murali, K.S., Uma Shaankar, R., Ganeshaiah, K.N., Bawa, K.S. Extraction of non–timber forest products in the forests of Biligiri Rangan Hills, India. 4. Impact of floristic diversity and population structure in a scrub forest. *Econ. Bot.* 52: 280–293 (1998a).

Uma Shankar, Hegde, R., Bawa, K.S. Extraction of non-timber forest products in the forests of Biligiri Rangan Hills, India 6. Fuelwood pressure and management options. *Econ. Bot.* 52: 298–1314 (1998b).

Uma Shankar, Lama, S.D., Bawa, K.S. Ecosystem reconstruction through taungya plantations following commercial logging of a dry mixed deciduous forest in Darjeeling Himalaya. *Forest Ecol. Management* 102: 131–142 (1998c).

UNESCO. *State of the Environment in Asia and the Pacific. 1990.* UN Economic and Social Commission for Asia and the Pacific, Bangkok (1990).

UNESCO. Biodiversity. Science, conservation and sustainable use. UNESCO Environmental Brief, Paris (1994).

Uthoff, D. From traditional use to total destruction—forms and extent of economic utilization in the southeast Asian mangroves. *Natural Resources and Development* 43/44: 58–94 (1996).

Utkarsh, G., Joshi, N.V., Gadgil M. On the patterns of tree diversity in the Western Ghats of India. *Current Sci.* 75: 594–603 (1998).

Venu, P. A review of floristic diversity inventory and monitoring methodology in India. *Proc. Ind. Natl. Sci. Acad. (PINSA)* 64B: 281-292 (1998).

Veron, J.E.N. *Corals in Time and Space.* Univ. New South Wales Press, NSW (1995).

Viksne, J. (Ed.). *Latvian Breeding Bird Atlas.* Zinatne, Riga, Latvia (1989).

Virtucio, F.D. Silviculture alternatives for sustainable management of dipterocarp residual forests in the Philippines. *Canopy Internatl.* pp. 1–12 (Nov.–Dec. 1997).

Vitousek, P., Ehrlich, P., Ehrlich, A., Matson, P. Human appropriation of the products of photosynthesis. *Bioscience* 36: 368–73 (1986).

Vogel, G. Doubled genes may explain fish diversity. *Science* 281: 1119–1121 (1998).

Wagner, F.H. Principles for the conservation of wild living resources: another perspective. *Ecol. Appl.* 6: 365–367 (1996).

Wali, M.K. A song of sweet and sore. *Ecology* 73: 718–719 (1992).

Walker, B. Biodiversity and ecological redundancy. *Conserv. Biol.* 6: 18–23 (1992).

Ward, D.M. Microbiology in Yellowstone National Park. *ASM News* 64: 141–146 (1998).

Warren, D.M. *Indigenous Knowledge and Development* (Rev.). Background Paper for Seminar Session on Sociology, Natural Resource Management and Agricultural Development. The World Bank, Washington, DC, December 3, 1990.

Wayne, P.M., Bazzaz, F.A. Assessing diversity in plant communities: the importance of within–species variation. *TREE* 6: 400–404 (1991).

WCMC (World Conservation and Monitoring Centre). *Global Biodiversity: State of the Earth's Living Resources.* Chapman & Hall, London (1992).

WRI (World Resources Institute). *World Resources 1990–91.* Oxford Univ. Press, NY (1990).

Weber, P. *Net Loss : Fish, Jobs and the Marine Environment.* WWI, Washington, DC (1994).

West-Eberhard, M.J. Sexual selection, social competition and speciation. *Q. Rev. Biol.* 58: 155–183 (1983).

Westoby, M. The relationship between local and regional diversity: comment. *Ecology* 79: 1825–1827 (1998).

Whittaker, R.H. Evolution and measurement of species diversity. *Taxon* 21: 213–251 (1972).

Wilcove, D.S., McMillan, M., Winston, K.C. What exactly is an endangered species? An analysis of U.S. endangered species list: 1985–1991. *Conserv. Biol.* 7: 87–93 (1993).

Wilcox, B.A. Insular ecology and conservation. In : Soulé, M.E., Wilcox, B.A. (eds.) *Conservation Biology: An Ecological–Evolutionary Perspective,* pp. 95–117. Sinauer Assoc., Sunderland, MA (1980).

Wilcox, B.A., Murphy, D.D. Conservation strategy: the effects of fragmentation on extinction. *Amer. Nat.* 125: 879–887 (1985).

Wilson, D.S. Holism and reductionism in evolutionary ecology. *Oikos* 53: 269–273 (1988).

Wilson, E.O. *Biophilia: the Human Bond with Other Species.* Harvard Univ. Press, Cambridge, MA (1984).

Wilson, E.O. The current state of biological diversity. In : Wilson, E.O., Peter, F.M. (eds.) *BioDiversity,* pp. 3–18. Natl. Acad. Press, Washington, DC (1988).

Wilson, E.O. *The Diversity of Life.* Belknap Press, Harvard University, Cambridge, MA (1992).

Wilson, E.O. Introduction. In Reaka-Kudla, M.L., Wilson, D.E., Wilson, E.O. (eds.) *Biodiversity II,* pp. 1–3. J. Henry Press, Washington, DC (1997).

Wilson, E.O., Peter F.M. (eds.). *BioDiversity.* Natl. Acad. Press, Washington, DC (1988).

Winkler, D. The forests of the eastern part of the Tibetan plateau. *Pl. Res. Develop.* 47/48: 184–210 (1998).

Woese, C.R., Kandler, O., Wheelis, M.L. Towards a natural system of organisms: Proposal for the domains Archaea, Bacteria and Eucarya. *PNAS (USA)* 87: 4576–4579 (1990).

Wood, D., Lenné, J. *Dynamic Management of Domesticated Biodiversity by Farming Communities.* Proc. Norway/UNEP Conf. Biodiversity, Trondheim (1993).

Woodruff, D.S. *Biodiversity: Conservation and Genetics.* Proc. 2nd Princess Chulabhorn Cong. Sci. Tech., Bangkok (1992).

Woodwell, G. (Ed.). *The Earth in Transition: Patterns and Processes of Biotic Impoverishment.* Camb. Univ. Press, NY (1990).

Worthington, E.B. (ed.). *The Evolution of IBP.* Camb. Univ. Press, Cambridge (1975).

WRI. *World Resources Report 1991–1992. A Guide to the Global Environment.* Oxford Univ. Press, NY (1991).

WRI. *World Resources 1992–93.* Oxford Univ. Press, Oxford (1992).

WRI. *World Resources 1994.* Oxford Univ. Press, NY (1994).

Wright, D.H. Species-energy theory: An extension of species-area theory. *Oikos* 41: 496–506 (1983).

Wright, J.L., Boyd, R.K., De Freitas, A.S.W., Falk, M., Foxall, R.A., Jamieson, W.D., Laylack, M.V., McCulloch, A.W., McInnes, A.G., Odense, P., Pathak, V., Quillam, M.A., Ragan, M.A., Sim, P.G., Thibault, P., Walter, J.A., Gilgan, M., Richard, D.J.A., Dewar, D. Identification of domoic acid, a neuroexcitatory amino acid, in toxic mussels from eastern Prince Edward Island. *Can. J. Chem.* 67: 481–490 (1989).

Wuketits, F.M. The status of biology and the meaning of biodiversity. *Naturwissenschaften* 84: 473–479 (1997).

Yang, A. Review on the derivation of Xizang (Tibetan) drugs and the advance of its research. In: *Acta Bot. Yunnanie. Adit.* 1, China 1988. Bhotahity, Kathmandu (1988).

Yoda, K., Kira, T., Ogawa, H., Hozumi, H. Self-thinning in overcrowded pure stands under cultivated and natural conditions. *J. Inst. Polytech.* (Osaka City Univ.), ser. D 14: 107–129 (1963).

Yoon, C.K. Counting creatures great and small. *Science* 260: 620–22 (1993).

Zedan, H. The economic value of microbial diversity. *Biotech. Appl. Microbiol.* 43: 178–185 (1993).

Zedler, J.B. Ecological issues in wetland mitigation: An introduction to the forum. *Ecol. Appl.* 6: 33–37 (1996).

Zeh, D.W., Zeh, J.A., Smith, R.L. Ovipositors, amnions and eggshell architecture in the diversification of terrestrial arthropods. *Q. Rev. Biol.* 64: 147–168 (1989).

Zentilli, B. Forests, trees and people. *Environ. Sci. Technol.* 26: 1096–1099 (1992).

(N.B. *PNAS* = *Proceedings of the National Academy of Sciences,* USA.
TREE = *Trends in Ecology and Evolution*)

GLOSSARY

Accession. Plant sample, strain or population held in a gene bank or breeding programme for conservation or use.

Adaptation. The process of change in an organism's structure(s) and/or function(s) that makes it better suited to survive in an environment. Adaptations refer to favourable combinations of genes which are tried, accumulated and preserved by natural selection.

Agroecology. The holistic study of agroecosystems, including all environmental and human elements, their interrelationships and the processes in which they are involved, e.g. symbiosis, competition, successional change.

Agroecosystem. An ecological system modified by people to produce food, fibre, fuel and other products desired for human use.

Agroforestry. 1. The deliberate use of woody perennials (trees, shrubs, palms, bamboo) on the same land-management unit as arable crops, pastures and/or animals, either in a mixed spatial arrangement in the same place at the same time, or in a sequence over time. 2. The integration of trees and shrubs into agricultural systems.

Agropastoralism. Land-use system in which arable cropping and the keeping of grazing livestock are combined.

Agropisciculture. Combining cropping and the controlled breeding, hatching and rearing of fish within a farm.

Agrosilviculture. Land-use system in which herbaceous crops and trees or shrubs are combined.

Allele. One of a pair of genes at a particular genetic locus.

Allelopathy. The release by a plant of a chemical that influences the growth of other plants.

Allopatric. Two or more populations or species that occur in geographically separate areas.

Allozyme. One of several possible forms of an enzyme that is the product of a particular allele at a given gene locus.

Alpha (α)–richness. The number of species occurring within a given habitat.

Anthropocentrism. Any human–oriented perspective of the environment, but usually used to emphasize a distinction between humans and non–humans.

Apomixis. A type of asexual reproduction in which seeds are produced without fertilization and hence descendant lines are genetically identical to the parent plant.

Asexual reproduction. Any reproductive process which does not involve the union of gametes (or haploid germ cells).

Backcross. The cross of a hybrid to either of its parents (or a genetically equivalent individual).

Backcross breeding. A plant breeding system in which recurrent backcrosses are made to one of the parents of a hybrid, accompanied by specific selection for a particular character or set of characters.

Background extinction rate. Historical rates of extinction due to environmental causes not influenced by human activities, such as the rate of species going extinct because of long–term climate change.

Balanced/unbalanced (seed) bulk. An unbalanced bulk is formed by bulking all the seed produced by a population of plants, thereby creating a single seed sample. Each plant in the parental generation is then represented in the offspring generation in proportion to the number of seeds it produces. A balanced bulk is formed by taking an aliquot of seed from each mother plant and combining them into a single seed lot. Each plant in the parental generation is then equally represented in the offspring generation, at least in terms of seed production (not necessarily in terms of pollen contribution).

Beta (β)–richness. The change or turnover of species from one habitat to another.

Biocentrism. A perception of the world that values the existence and diversity of all biological species, as opposed to a human–centred perspective (anthropocentrism).

Biodiversity. An umbrella term for the variability among living organisms from all sources including terrestrial, marine and other aquatic ecosystems and the ecological complexes of which they are part. Biodiversity includes diversity within species, between species and of ecosystems. Biodiversity is a function of both time (evolution) and space (biogeographic distribution).

Biodynamic farming. A holistic system of agriculture devised by Rudolph Steiner that seeks to connect nature with cosmic creative forces. An attempt is made to create a whole–farm organism in harmony with its habitat. Compost and special preparations (e.g. plant–derived sprays) are used. Synthetic fertilisers and pesticides are avoided.

Biological control. The use of natural enemies to control pests, including both control with imported natural enemies and augmentation and conservation of natural enemies through manipulation of the pest host, the environment and/or the enemies themselves.

Biological species concept (BSC). A species concept based on reproductive isolation, which defines a species as groups of actually or potentialy interbreeding populations, which are reproductively isolated from other such groups.

Biomass. The weight of material produced by a living organism or collection of organisms, plant or animal.

Biome. A large, regional ecological unit, usually defined by some dominant vegetative pattern, such as the coniferous forest biome.

Biophilia. A term coined by E.O. Wilson to describe humans' seemingly innate, positive attitudes about, and love for nature and natural diversity.

Biosphere Reserve. A reserve design in which a large tract of natural area is set aside, containing an inviolate core area for ecosystem protection, a surrounding buffer zone in which non–destructive human activities are permitted, and a transition zone in whcih human activities of greater impact are permitted. Three goals of a biosphere reserve are conservation, training (education) and sustainable human development compatible with conservation.

Biotechnology. Any technique that uses living organisms (or parts of organisms) to make or modify products, to improve plants or animals, or to develop micro–organisms for specific uses.

Botanical pesticide. A plant–derived pesticide.

Centre of diversity. The geographic region in which the greatest variability of a crop occurs. A primary centre of diversity is the region of presumed origin and secondary centres of diversity are regions of high diversity which have developed as a result of the subsequent spread of a crop.

CGIAR. The Consultative Group on International Agricultural Research, an association of private and public donor agencies which support the work of 16 international agricultural research centres.

Characterization. Determination of the structural or functional attributes of a plant in order to distinguish between lines.

Cladistics. A system of classification based on historical (chronological) sequences of divergence from a common ancestor.

Cladogram. A diagram of cladistic relationships. An estimate or hypothesis of true genealogical relationships among species or other groupings.

Classification. The arrangement of organisms into a hierarchical order or system to identify them and to express their interrelationships.

Community. A naturally occurring group of various organisms that inhabit a common environment, interact with each other and are independent of other groups.

Complementarity. A state in which one element, in combination with one or more other elements, completes the whole.

Complementary conservation. Combining *ex situ* and *in situ* technologies as appropriate to ensure an integrated conservation strategy.

Conservation. The active management of biological resources so that they yield the greatest benefit to present generations while maintaining their potential to meet the needs of future generations. Unlike preservation, conservation provides for the long–term retention of natural communities under conditions (e.g. in nature reserves) that provide the potential for continuing evolution. A basic tenet of the Convention on Biological Diversity is that ways must be found to enable people to use biodiversity sustainably in order for conservation to be successful (the 'use it or lose it' philosophy). For this reason, the Convention refers to the 'conservation and sustainable use of biodiversity'.

Conservation (genetic). The collection, maintenance and preservation of intra– and intergenetic variation, e.g. a representative sample of the genetic variation of a particular species.

Conservation biology. An integrative approach to the protection and management of biodiversity that uses appropriate principles and experiences from basic biological fields such as genetics and ecology; from natural resource management fields such as fisheries and wildlife; and from social sciences such as anthropology, sociology, philosophy and economics.

Convergent selection pressures. Selection pressures acting to decrease differences between two or more populations that are initially distinct. Occurs when there is a single optimal (i.e. with highest evolutionary fitness) genotype, so that all populations evolve towards that genotype as a common end–point regardless of their initial genotypic composition. Usually used in the context of natural selection, the concept is equally applicable to artificial selection.

Core collection. A limited set of accessions derived from an existing germplasm collection, chosen to represent the genetic spectrum in the whole collection.

Cover crop. Annual crop sown to create a favourable soil microclimate, decrease evaporation and protect soil from erosion. Cover crops also produce biomass which can be used for soil fertility management.

Crop. Annual or perennial plants cultivated to yield products desired for human consumption or processing, e.g. grain, vegetables (edible roots, stems or leaves), flowers, fruit, fibre, fuel.

Crop evolution. The adaptation of a crop over generations of association with man, to forms more advantageous to man and brought about by generally unconscious selection, provision of nutrients and protection from pests and diseases. It may occur to the extent that the domesticated form loses the ability to survive in nature.

Cryopreservation. Storage of living materials at very low temperatures, usually in liquid nitrogen.

Cultivar. A variety of a plant produced by selective breeding.

Cultural diversity. Cultural differences reflecting life styles and human strategies for survival in different environments, and sometimes considered a component of biodiversity. The diversity of human perceptions of the environment and natural resource management practices can provide potential options for using biodiversity sustainably.

Deforestation. The removal of a forest tree or trees, usually by human action, but it can also be caused by environmental change.

Demand. The aggregate desire for economic goods and services. The quantity of a good or service that consumers are willing to purchase at various prices. Demand involves the relationship between quantity and price.

Deme. A randomly interbreeding (panmictic) local population.

Density–dependent factors. Life history or population parameters that are a function of population density.

Density–independent factors. Life history or population parameters that are independent of population density.

377

Desertification. Process of continued decline in the biological productivity of arid/ semiarid land resulting in skeletal soil that is difficult to revitalize; refers also to land degradation, i.e. reduction in the capability of land to satisfy a particular use.

Disease. A deleterious alteration in the dynamic interaction between an individual and the environment, caused by a biotic or an abiotic factor.

Diversity. The existence of alternate forms (genetic or otherwise) (also: variability).

Drift. Random changes in the genetic composition of a population caused by chance factors, such as sampling error and the effects of uncontrolled microenvironmental variation on growth, survival and reproduction.

Duplicate accession. Accessions held by one or more gene banks that are derived from the same original seed sample without deliberate selection and so are in some sense duplicates of each other.

Ecological species concept (ESC). A species concept based on adaptive zones used by organisms.

Ecology. The study of organisms consisting of one or more ecotypes, capable of interbreeding in relation to their environment.

Ecosystem. The complex of an ecological community, together with the non–living components of the environment, which function together as a stable system and in which exchange of materials follows a circular path.

Ecosystem diversity. The number and relative abundance of habitats, biotic communities and ecological processes on the Earth. Ecosystem diversity is difficult to measure, because ecosystems (particularly marine ecosystems) change continuously and do not have clear temporal or geographic boundaries.

Ecosystem management. An approach to maintaining or restoring the composition, structure, and function of natural and modified ecosystems for the goal of long–term sustainability. It is based on a collaboratively developed vision of desired future conditions that integrates ecological, socioeconomic and institutional perspectives, applied within a geographic framework defined primarily by natural ecological boundaries.

Ecotype. The product of a genotypic response of a species (or a part thereof) to a particular habitat or environment, as a result of natural selection.

Edge effect. 1. The negative influence of a habitat edge on interior conditions of a habitat, or on species that use an interior habitat. 2. The effect of adjoining habitat types on populations in the edge ecotone, often resulting in more species in the edge than in either habitat alone.

Elite germplasm. Germplasm that has been manipulated for use in a breeding programme.

Endangered species. A species in imminent danger of extinction throughout all or a significant portion of its range.

Endemic. Any localized process or pattern, but usually applied to a highly localized or restrictive geographic distribution of a species.

Environment. The sum of the non–genetic factors which surround and influence an organism.

Equilibrium. A state reached when a population's birth and immigration rates are equal to its mortality and emigration rates.

Erosion. The gradual displacement or disappearance of parts of a system under the influence of external factors, e.g. erosion of soil by water or wind, erosion of indigenous knowledge, genetic erosion.

Ethnoveterinary medicine. The indigenous knowledge, skills, methods and practices pertaining to the health care of animals.

Evaluation. Determination of the characteristics of a plant that are important for adaptation and production, such as yield potential, stress tolerance and pest and disease resistance.

Evolution. The transformation of the form and mode of existence of an organism in such a way that the descendants differ from their predecessors.

Evolutionary dynamics. The process, force and rate of change in a population.

Ex-situ conservation. Conservation of a plant outside its original or natural habitat, e.g. in a gene bank.

Externality. A cost, usually in terms of environmental degradation, that results from an economic transaction, but which is not included as a debit against economic returns.

Fallow. Land left uncultivated for one or more growing seasons; it is often colonised by natural vegetation and may be grazed.

Farmers' rights. Rights arising from the past, present and future contributions of farmers in conserving, improving and making available plant genetic resources, especially those in the centres of origin/diversity.

Feedback. A system whose output modifies input to the system. Prices play this role in market systems.

Fencerow scale. The connection of habitat patches by narrow rows of habitat to create corridors that are usually effective only for small, edge–tolerant species.

Formal sector. Government–supported national, international and regional organizations involved in genetic resources activities.

Founder effect. The idea that the founders of a new population carry only a random fraction of the genetic diversity found in the larger, parent population.

Fragmentation. 1) The disruption of extensive habitats into isolated and small patches. Has two negative components for biota: loss of total habitat area and creation of smaller, more isolated, remaining habitat patches. 2) The process by which an area of continuous habitat is broken into smaller pieces or fragments.

Functional diversity. The quantity of different organisms, species or cultivars hat contribute to increasing the stability, productivity or continuity of an agroecosystem.

Fungi. Plural of fungus; any of a large group of plants (including moulds, mildews, mushrooms, rusts and smuts) which are parasites on living organisms or feed on dead organic material, lack chlorophyll, roots, stem and leaves, and reproduce by means of spores.

Gaia hypothesis. A model of planetary dynamics postulating a tight interrelationship between life processes and the conditions on earth that support life. Feedback mechanisms are proposed whereby biological processes modify the physical and chemical conditions appropriate for the biological processes. In the extreme viewpoint, the Gaia hypothesis holds that the earth is a superorganism. Now usually refers to the belief that biotic processes are the major regulators of physical processes.

Gamma (γ)–richness. The number of species found within a large region, which typically includes several habitats.

Gap analysis. The use of various remote–sensing data sets to build overlaid sets of maps of various parameters (e.g., vegetation, soils, protected areas, species distributions) to identify spatial gaps in species protection and management programmes.

Gender analysis. The systematic effort to understand and document the differential roles, resources and constraints of women and men within a given context.

Gene. The basic unit of active transmission of the genetic information that determines patterns of inheritance.

Gene bank. Facility where germplasm is stored in the form of seed, pollen in *in–vitro* culture, or in the case of a field gene bank, as plants growing in the field.

Genecology. The study of population genetics in relation to habitats. All the genetic information encoded in the total gene composition of a population of sexually reproducing organisms at a given time.

Genetic diversity. The diversity of the genes in the individual plants, animals and micro-organisms that inhabit the Earth. Species are made up of individuals with different inherited (genetic) characteristics. According to current theories of evolution, the variety of characteristics allows species to evolve gradually and survive changing environmental conditions. Genetic diversity is the ultimate source of diversity at the species and ecosystem levels of the biological hierarchy. Genetic diversity within a species includes variation both among distinct populations of the same species (e.g. the thousands of traditional rice varieties in India) and within a population (e.g. the relative lack of genetic variability in wild cheetah populations in Africa).

Genetic drift. Random gene frequency changes in a small population due to chance alone.

Genetic erosion. Loss of genetic diversity between and within populations of the same species over time or reduction of the genetic base of a species due to human intervention, environmental changes etc.

Genetic resources. Genetic material of plants, animals and other organisms which is of value as a resource for present and future generations of people.

Genetic stock. A variety or strain known to carry(a) specific gene(s).

Genetic variation. An inheritable variation brought about by a change in (a) gene(s), as distinct from differences due to environmental factors.

Genotype. 1) The genetic constitution of an organism. 2) A group of organisms with similar genetic constitutions.

Geographic information system (GIS). A computerized system of organizing and analyzing any spatial array of data and information.

Geographic variation. Change in a species' trait over distance or among different distinct populations. Measurable character divergence among geographically distinct populations that are often, though not necessarily, the result of local selection.

Germplasm. 1) The genetic material which forms the physical basis of heredity and which is transmitted from one generation to the next by means of germ cells. 2) A set of genotypes that may be conserved or used.

Germplasm collection. Collection of genotypes, gene libraries or alleles of one or more species.

Green manure. Green plant biomass used as fertiliser.

Green revolution. The use of a package of inputs, including modern varieties, pesticides, fertilizers and frequently also irrigation, in an attempt to increase farm yields in developing countries.

Habitat. A specific place occupied by an organism or community, where interactions with other organisms and the environment occur.

Herbicide. A class of pesticides that destroys or reduces the negative effects of weeds.

Hot spot. A geographic location characterized by unusually high species richness, often of endemic species.

Identity. The collective aspect of a set of characteristics by which something is recognizable or known, referring here to the characteristics of a farm system which are recognized by its users as being in harmony with their culture, their social relations and their relations to crops, animals and nature in general.

***In situ* conservation.** Conservation of plants or animals in the areas where they developed their distinctive properties, i.e., in the wild or in farmers' fields.

In vitro. 'In glass'. The term is generally applied to biological procsses made to occur in isolation from whole organisms. Or collections of parts of whole organisms in the laboratory. (The opposite is *in vivo*.)

Inbreeder/Outbreeder. Obligate inbreeders are always self-pollinated. Obligate outbreeders cannot naturally self–pollinate and can be fertilized only by pollen from other plants. These are two extremes of a continuum: most species are intermediate, showing a greater or lesser tendency to self- or cross-pollinate.

Inbreeding depression. A reduction in fitness and vigour of individuals as a result of increased homozygosity through inbreeding in a normally outbreeding population.

Indicator species. A species used as a gauge for the condition of a particular habitat, community, or ecosystem. A characteristic, or surrogate species for a community or ecosystem.

Indigenous/local knowledge. Knowledge that develops in a particular area and accumulates over time through being handed down from generation to generation.

Informal sector. Grassroots–level, non–governmental and farmers' organizations.

Integrated pest management (IPM). A strategy which, in the context of the farm's environment and the population dynamics of the pest species, uses all suitable measures (biological, genetic, mechanical and chemical) in the most compatible manner possible so as to maintain pest populations at levels below those causing economic injury.

Integrated plant nutrition. Strategy to maintain and possibly increase soil fertility for sustaining crop productivity through optimizing all possible sources, organic and inorganic, of plant nutrients needed for crop growth and quality in an integrated way, appropriate to each crop system and specific ecological and socioeconomic situation.

Intellectual property protection (IPP). Protection of an invention through use of legal instruments, e.g. patents, copyrights, plant breeders' rights.

Intercropping. Growing two or more crops simultaneously in the same field.

Introgression. The repeated pollination of plants in one population with pollen from another population. Usually applied when the two populations are genetically distinct.

Keystone species. A species whose impacts on its community or ecosystem are large, and much larger than would be expected from its abundance.

Landraces. Farmer-developed cultivars or varieties of crop plants which are adapted to local environmental conditions.

Litter. Uppermost layer of organic material on the soil surface, including leaves, twigs and flowers, freshly fallen or slightly decomposed.

Livelihood system. A combination of people, resources and environment in which the stocks and flows of food and cash are used to meet the basic needs of the people. The livelihood system of a rural household may include cropping, tree-growing, animal-keeping, fishing, hunting, gathering, processing, trading, paid employment and a wide variety of other non-farm activities.

Manuring. Application of animal dung, compost or other organic material used to fertilize the soil.

Mass extinction. The extinction of large numbers of taxa during a relatively brief geologic time frame, such as the extinction of dinosaurs at the end of the Cretaceous Period.

Maximum sustained yield (MSY). The largest harvestable level of a renewable resource that can be sustained over several generations. Harvest of a natural population at the population size representing the maximum rate of recruitment into the population, based on a logistic growth curve.

Metapopulation. A network of semi-isolated populations with some migration and gene flow among them, in which individual populations can become extinct but are then recolonized from other populations.

Minimum tillage. Soil management practices which seek to minimize labour inputs and soil erosion, to maintain soil moisture and to reduce soil disturbance and exposure. Crop stubble is left or mulch is applied to protect the soil. Also known as conservation tillage or reduced tillage. In its most extreme form (zero- or no-tillage), seeds are drilled directly into the otherwise undisturbed soil.

Mobile link species. Mobile keystone species which influence the survival or reproductive success of other species through their movement over a geographic area; e.g., highly specific pollinators.

Molecular marker. A gene or gene product of known chromosomal location or function that marks another gene or selected character.

Monetizing. Attaching monetary value on typically non-monetary goods and processes such as biological material or ecological processes. The process of converting values to economic units.

Monoculture. The growing of a single plant species in one area, usually the same type of crop grown year after year.

Mulch. Protective covering of the soil surface by various substances such as green or dry organic matter, sand or stones applied to prevent evaporation of moisture, regulate temperature and control weeds.

Mutualism. An interspecific relationship in which both organisms benefit; frequently a relationship of complete dependence.

Mycorrhiza. Symbiotic associations of the filaments of a fungus with the roots of higher plants, which can increase the plant's capacity to absorb nutrients from the soil.

Natural catastrophe. A major environmental cause of mortality, such as a volcanic eruption, that can affect the probability of survival for a population.

Natural farming. A system of agriculture devised by Masanobu Fukuoka that seeks to follow Nature by minimizing human interference: no mechanical cultivation, no synthetic fertilizers or prepared compost, no weeding by tillage or herbicides, no dependence on chemicals.

Network. A reserve system connecting multiple nodes and corridors into a landscape that allows material and energy flow among the various components.

Networking. Establishing and strengthenning links between individuals, groups and organizations with similar interests and objectives.

Niche. A space in the ecosystem which, because of the specific local ecological, physical and/or social characteristics, is suited to a particular plant or animal species or a particular activity.

Non–renewable resource. Resources such as oil, coal and mineral ores which cannot be naturally regenerated on a time scale relevant to human exploitation.

Nutrient cycling. The recurrent flow of nutrients through a farm or larger agroecosystem such that the major part of the mobile nutrients are kept within the system and reused.

Nutrient harvesting. Deliberate activities to capture nutrients from outside the farm system or from other parts within the farm system and to concentrate them in particular areas in the farm.

Option value. Assigning a value to some resource whose consumption is deferred to the future.

Panmictic. Random breeding among individuals of a population.

Parasite. An organism that lives in or on a living organism (host) of another species from which it derives all of its nutrients while conferring no benefit in return.

Participatory Technology Development (PTD). The process of combining the indigenous knowledge and research capacities of the local farming communities with that of research and development institutions in an interactive way, in order to identify, generate, test and apply new techniques and practices and to strengthen the existing experimental and technology management capacities of the farmers. Also referred to as People–centred Technology Development.

Passport data. Information about a sample or specimen and the site of collection, the time and any other data, recorded at the time of collection.

Pastoralism. The rearing of livestock which graze primarily natural pasture. Nomadic pastoralism refers to a more or less constantly wandering mode of livestock–keeping. In nomadic pastoralism, the herds are moved seasonally or periodically between two regions of differing climate regimes (e.g. mountain/valley); the pastoralists occupy a permanent residence in at least one of these regions. In sedentary pastoralism, the animals are kept year–round near a permanent residence.

Patch dynamics. A conceptual approach to ecosystem and habitat analysis that emphasizes dynamics of heterogeneity within a system. Diverse patches of habitat created by natural disturbance regimes are critical to maintenance of diversity.

Patent. A legal instrument granting an inventor the exclusive right, for a limited time, to exploit the invention in exchange for disclosure.

Pathogen. An organism capable of causing a disease in another organism (a host).

Perennial. A plant that lives for more than two years, often for a number of years; many flower annually.

Pest. Any form of plant or animal life or any agent pathogenic (harmful) to plants or plant products.

Phenetic. Pertaining to phenotypic similarities; a classification system based on phenotypic traits. Based on numerical measurements of individuals and mathematical analyses of morphological discontinuities.

Phenotype. The observable characters of an organism. Used to designate a group of individuals with similar appearance but not necessarily identical genotypes.

Phylogenetic species concept (PSC). A species concept based on branching, or cladistic relationships among species or higher taxa. The PSC hypothesizes the true genealogical relationship among species, based on the concept of shared, derived characteristics (synapomorphies).

Plant breeders rights. A legal instrument granting the developer of a plant variety the exclusive right to market it for a limited time. Varieties protected by such legislation may be used by others in the development of new varieties after the time limit has expired.

Plasticity. The condition of genetically based, environmentally induced variation in characteristics of an organism.

Plesiomorphic. An evolutionarily primitive character shared by two or more taxa.

Pluralism. The view that species concepts should vary with the taxon under consideration. Many different species definitions would be employed.

Polyploidy. Possessing more than two complete sets of chromosomes.

Preservation. Policies and programmes that provide for the maintenance of individuals or groups but not for their evolutionary change (e.g. zoos and botanical gardens).

Productivity. The relationship between the quantity of goods or services produced and the factors used to produce them; farm productivity can be expressed as output per unit of land, capital, labour time, energy, water, nutrients etc.

Protection. The control of human activities in natural areas to maintain biological diversity.

Pyramiding. Backcrossing of several genes into a certain background.

Recalcitrant seed. Seed that cannot be dried and so cannot be stored at low temperatures without damage.

Regeneration. Growing a sample from an accession to replenish the viability of the original accession.

Remote sensing. Any technique for analyzing landscape patterns and trends using low–altitude aerial photography or satellite imagery. Any environmental measurement done at a distance.

Rescue effect. The recolonization of a habitat when a subpopulation of a metapopulation has gone locally extinct.

Residuals. In restoration ecology, the remnants of natural systems that can provide the building blocks for system restoration or rehabilitation.

Resource conservation ethic. The perception of nature as a collection of natural resources to be used for the greatest good of the greatest number for the longest time.

Restoration ecology. Use of ecological principles and experience to return a degraded ecological system to its former or original state.

Rogueing. Manually removing atypical plants from a stand.

Sample. A small number of observations or individuals taken from, and intended to represent, a larger population.

Scale. The magnitude of a region or process.

Secondary extinction. Loss of a species as a result of the loss of another species.

Selection. The process that results in non-random changes in the genetic composition of a population (compare Drift). These occur whenever genetic variation within a population is expressed as phenotypic variation among plants for any component of evolutionary fitness; that is, the offspring generation systematically contains more of certain selected gene combinations and less of others. Artificial selection is selection deliberately imposed by man. Natural selection is the process resulting in directed evolutionary change. It occurs not only in natural populations, but also in artificial situations such as regeneration plots, for example by differential reactions of plants to the regeneration environment. It may include inadvertent selection.

Shattering. The opening or distintegration of the seed, coat, fruit or husk before harvesting, with the consequent loss of seed.

Shifting cultivation. A form of agriculture in which soil fertility is maintained by rotating fields rather than crops. A piece of land is cropped until the soil shows signs of exhaustion or is overrun by weeds; the land is than left to regenerate naturally while cultivation is done elsewhere. New sites are usually cleared by firing (slash–and–burn). Also known as swidden or 'jhum' agriculture.

SLOSS. An acronym for 'single large or several small', reflecting a debate about whether, all else being equal, it is better to have one large reserve or several small reserves of the same total size.

Source and sink dynamics. Spatial linkage of population dynamics such that high-quality habitat (sources) provide excess individuals that maintain population density, through migration, in low-quality habitats (sinks).

Speciation. The processes by which new species form.

Species. A group of actually or potentially interbreeding natural populations which normally are reproductively isolated from other such groups and/or show common characteristics.

Species diversity. The number and variety of species found in a given area in a region, where a 'species' is generally a group of organisms that can interbreed or a group of organisms whose members have the greatest mutual resemblance. One useful study approach is to divide the species of an ecosystem into two categories on the basis of function: (1) different functional types (e.g. feeding guilds, plant growth froms); and (2) functionally similar taxa, referred to as 'functional

388

analogues' (Solbrig, 1991). Although the 'species' is the taxonomic category used most frequently in discussions about biodiversity, the standard definition cannot be applied to organisms that reproduce by non–sexual means (e.g. viruses). These organisms represent a significant portion of the Earth's biodiversity.

Stochastic. Random; any random process, such as mortality due to weather extremes.

Strain. A group of individuals from a common origin; generally a more narrowly defined group than a variety.

Strip corridor. A broad corridor consisting of some interior habitat and intact and functioning communities.

Subsistence agriculture. Farming systems in which a large part of the final yield is consumed by the producer. Most subsistence systems involve production of some crops or animals for sale, but the ratio of subsistence to cash production may vary greatly from year to year.

Succession. 1) An orderly process of change in a community (of plants, animals, soil microbes etc.) that resutls from modification of the environment by organisms and culminates in a system attaining a steady state, or climax. 2) The natural, sequential change of species composition of a community in a given area.

Supply. The aggregate amount of goods or services available to satisfy economic needs or wants. The quantity of a good or service which producers are willing to sell at different prices. Supply involves the relationship between quantity and price.

Susceptibility. The inability of a host plant to suppress or retard invasion by a pathogen or pest or to withstand adverse environmental conditions.

Sustainable agriculture. Management of resources for agriculture to satisfy changing human needs, while maintaining or enhancing the quality of the environment and conserving the natural resources.

Sustainable development. Attempts to meet economic objectives in ways that do not degrade the underlying environmental support system. Also defined as human activities that respect the intrinsic value of the natural world, the role of the natural world in human well–being, and the need for humans to live to the income from nature's capital rather than the capital itself.

Symbiosis. The relationship of two or more different organisms in close association, which is beneficial to each organism.

Sympatric. Two or more populations or species that occur in the same geographic area.

Synergy. The action of two or more substances, organs or organisms to achieve an effect which each individually cannot produce.

Systems approach. An approach for studying a system as an entity made up of all its components and their interrelationships, together with relationships between the system and its environment.

Taxonomy. The study and naming of the diversity of life on Earth. The ability to correctly identify and name organisms is essential to all fields of natural biological science.

Technology. The combination of knowledge, inputs and management practices which are deployed together with productive resources to produce a desired output.

Threatened species. A species likely to become endangered in the near future.

Thresholds for regeneration. Minimum standards of a sample, below which it must be regenerated to produce a new seed sample of higher standard. Two thresholds must be defined: quality threshold, defining the minimum standard for seed quality, and quantity threshold, defining the minimum standard for seed quantity.

Tragedy of the commons. The idea that unregulated use of a common, public resource for private, personal gain will result in overexploitation and destruction of the resource.

Transgenic plant. Genetically engineered plant or progeny of genetically engineered plants. The transgenic plant usually contains genetic material ('transgenes') from at least one unrelated organism, such as from a virus, animal or other plant.

Transgressive segregation. A form of inheritance of continuous variation under polygenic control wherein, by recombination and segregation of genes at different loci affecting the same continuously variable character, the offspring generation may contain genotypes that are more extreme than the most extreme parental genotype.

UNCED (The Earth Summit). United Nations Conference on Environment and Development, which took place in Rio de Janeiro, Brazil in June 1992.

Usufruct. The right to use and enjoy the yield of resources (land, vegetation, livestock etc.) which belong to someone else.

Utilitarian view. A philosophical term applied to any activity that produces a product useful to humans, typically in some economic sense. Also used to describe a system of values which is measured by its contribution to human well–being, usually in terms of health and economic standard of living.

Utility. The 'want–satisfying' power of goods; personal satisfaction received through an economic gain.

Variability. The state of being variable, i.e., being able to change characteristics, form or nature.

Variety. A subdivision of a species below subspecies.

VIR. N.I. Vavilov All–Union Scientific Research Institute of Plant Industry, St. Petersberg, Russia.

Water harvesting. Collection and storage (in a tank or in the soil) of water, either runoff or stream flow, for securing and improving water availability for crop growth and/ or animal and human consumption.

Weed. A plant in a place where it is not wanted by humans.

Wild relative. 1) A non–cultivated species which is more or less closely related to a crop species (usually in the same genus). It is not normally used for agriculture but can occur in agroecosystems (e.g. as a weed or a component of pasture or grazing lands). 2) Uncultivated relative of a crop species.

Zoning. A reserve design that controls human activities within and near conservation reserves, so that the reserve function may be protected while some human activities, including those supplying some economic benefit, may take place.

INDEX

ABER, J.D. **344**

ABLES, E.D. **365**

ABRAMOVITZ, J.N. 135, **342**

ABRAMSKY, Z. 164, 165, 166, **364**

ABSHER, R. 145, 148, **347**

Acacia 187, 201

Acanthus 175

Acid deposition/rain 143, 215

ADAMS, P.W. 83, **342**

Adaptive management 204–206, 253
    255, 335, 336

Adonis 125

Aeluropus 201

Aerva 201

Aesculus 125

AGARDY, T.S. 155, **342**

Aglaia 198

Agrobiodiversity 290, 291

Agroecology 331, 332

Agroecosystems 27, 32, 49, 102, 330

Agroindustry 13, 14, 16

Agropyron 194

Aitreococcus 341

AKSORNKOAE, S. 171–173, **342**

Albizia 185, 187

ALEXANDRATOS, N. 329, **342**

Alexandrium 340

Algal blooms 336–341 ˙

Algal toxins 154

ALLSOPP, D. **352**

Alnus 120

Aloe 124

ALPERT, P. 54, **342**

Alpha diversity 54, 200

Alpha taxonomy 88

Alternanthera 180

ALTIERI, M.A. 27, 331, **342**

Alveolates 62, 63

Amaranthus 180, 195

AMBROSE, R.F. **361**

Ammi 126

Amphibian populations, declines in 220

Anabasis 125

Ancistrocladus 118, 121, 222

Andean tomato 94

ANDERSEN, T. 148, 149, **342**

ANDRADE, F. **346**

Andrographis 125

ANGEL, M.V. 152, **348**

ANGELSTAM, P. 319–325, **342**

Anogeissus 187

Anthelminthic compounds 123

Anthraquinones 128

Anthropogenic eutrophication 148

ANTUNES, P. **346**

ANUFRIEV, V.M. **342**

Aphids 181, 182

Apomicts 309

Aquaculture 158, 170, 274

Arboreta 234, 293

Archaea 50, 62, 105

Areca 125

Argemone 180

Aristida 201

ARNOLD, M.L. 235, **343**

ARORA, R.K. 196, **343**

Artemisia 222

Artemisin 221

Artisanal fisherfolk 147, 274, 290, 291,
    292

Artocarpus 198

ASHLEY, J. 304, **343**

Asparagus 195

Asterias 157

Ateles 168

Athene 204

ATHERTON, P. 124, 128, **343**

393

395

405

Notes: (i) Generic names printed in italics, (ii) For multi-author works, up to first three authors only are indexed. (iii) Page numbers in bold refer to entries in reference list.